GUN CONTROL

INTERNATIONAL VIEWS, PERSPECTIVES AND COMPARISONS

RICHARD SKIBA

AFTER MIDNIGHT PUBLISHING

Skiba, Richard (author)

Shadows of Catastrophe

ISBN 978-0-9756446-2-1 (paperback) 978-0-9756446-3-8 (eBook)

Non-fiction

CONTENTS

INTRODUCTION

This book provides an in-depth exploration of gun control policies, firearm-related subjects, and sociological aspects of sports shooting. The aim of this book is not to provide legal advice with regard to firearm laws but rather firstly to profile the range of approaches to gun control around the world and secondly to compare and contrast the many worldviews related to gun control from an international perspective. If you are seeking legal advice concerning firearms, it is advisable to engage with an attorney specializing in firearms law or criminal defence. Various options are available, such as local attorneys who possess knowledge of state and federal gun laws. Online legal directories like Avvo, FindLaw, or Martindale-Hubbell facilitate searches based on practice areas and location. State bar association websites often provide directories for locating attorneys with expertise in firearms law within your region. Firearms advocacy organizations may offer legal resources or referrals to specialized attorneys. Seeking referrals from friends, family, or colleagues who have faced similar legal issues is another effective approach. The public defender's office can be contacted if facing criminal charges related to firearms and unable to afford private representation.

It is important to note that laws and regulations pertaining to gun control are subject to change. Therefore, individuals seeking the most up-to-date information are advised to refer to the latest legal documents or consult with local authorities to ensure compliance with current regulations and requirements.

Firearms laws vary widely around the world, reflecting the diverse cultural, historical, and political contexts of different countries. The regulations and restrictions on firearm ownership and purchase are influenced by a variety of factors, including constitutional rights, federal and state laws, and historical events. For instance, in the United States, the Second Amendment of the U.S. Constitution protects the right to bear arms, leading to a mix of permissive and restrictive laws across different states (Sarchiapone et al., 2011). Similarly, in Canada, firearms are generally regulated by the federal government, and there are restrictions on certain types of firearms, with a relatively strict approach to handgun ownership (Zeoli et al., 2017). In contrast, the United Kingdom has strict firearm control laws, heavily restricting handguns and prohibiting automatic weapons, with ownership requiring a valid reason, where self-defence is not typically considered a valid reason (Chapman et al., 2015). Australia also has highly regulated firearms, with strict licensing requirements, and a significant buyback program in 1996 led to the confiscation of many semi-automatic firearms after a mass shooting in Port Arthur (Saunders et al., 2017).

The effectiveness of gun control measures in preventing crime and ensuring public safety is a complex and debated issue. Research has shown that restrictions on access to common means of suicide, including firearms, have led to lower overall suicide rates in many countries (Burrows et al., 2013). Additionally, the intersection of firearms and intimate partner homicide has been studied in 15 nations, highlighting the variations in laws regarding domestic violence as a factor in firearm ownership (Toigo et al., 2023). Furthermore, the impact of regulatory reforms on firearm-related deaths has been examined, with studies showing significant declines in firearm deaths following legislative changes (Antonio R. Andrés & Katherine Hempstead, 2011; Cheung & Dewa, 2005; Ozanne-Smith et al., 2004).

It is also important to consider the cultural, historical, and social factors that influence each country's approach to firearm regulation. For example, in Japan, extremely strict gun control laws have resulted in low rates of gun ownership and gun-related crime (McPhedran, 2017). On the other hand, South Africa has both strict regulations and high rates of gun ownership, indicating the influence of historical and social factors on firearm laws (Fleming et al., 2018).

Firearm regulations vary significantly across different countries, reflecting a complex interplay of cultural, historical, and social factors. The impact of these regulations on public safety and crime prevention is a subject of ongoing research and debate, with studies highlighting the effectiveness of certain measures in reducing firearm-related deaths and suicides, many of which are considered in this book.

Gun control encompasses the realm of politics, legislation, and the enforcement of measures aimed at limiting access to, possession of, and usage of firearms, particularly in the context of individual liberties (Charles, 2024). The topic of gun control stands as one of the most contentious and emotionally charged issues in various countries, often revolving around debates on whether regulations infringe upon an individual's right to bear arms and whether a correlation exists between firearms and crime. Advocates for gun-control legislation argue that stringent enforcement of such laws preserves lives and diminishes criminal activity. Conversely, opponents of gun control contend that minimal restrictions on firearms ensure individuals have sufficient means for self-defence, contributing to safer communities through broader firearm ownership (Charles, 2024).

The book draws on a wide range of references to support its comprehensive exploration, providing a valuable resource for academics, policymakers, and anyone interested in understanding the complex and multifaceted issues surrounding gun control, firearms, and sports shooting. The main chapters cover a wide range of topics, including gun control policies, firearms, the United States gun ownership landscape, the impact of gun control policies in the USA, gun ownership and control in various countries, varying perspectives on gun ownership, effective gun control policies, and sociological aspects of sports shooting.

Chapter 1 serves as an introduction, setting the stage for the subsequent discussions. Chapter 2 delves into various gun control policies, emphasizing their roles in preventing crime and violence, enhancing public safety, reducing mass shootings, addressing mental health concerns, preventing domestic violence, and minimizing illegal firearm trafficking. Chapter 3 focuses on firearms, covering their definition, civilian firearm use and ownership, the quantity of guns owned, and the argument asserting that responsible gun owners don't commit crimes. Chapter 4 explores the laws, ownership, and use of firearms in the United States, discussing key aspects such as the Second Amendment, federal regulations, state laws, concealed carry laws, background checks, open carry, castle doctrine, stand your ground, gun ownership statistics, and gun-related crime in the United States. Chapter 5 analyses the impact of gun control policies in the United States, assessing their effectiveness in either reducing or increasing violent crime and mass shootings.

Chapters 6 through 12 delve into the gun control landscapes of several countries, including Canada, the United Kingdom, Australia, Germany, Switzerland, Japan, Brazil, South Africa, and Russia. These chapters explore firearm ownership, policies, and their effects on gun-related crime in each respective country. Chapter 13 broadens the discussion to encompass global perspectives on gun ownership, examining factors that influence approaches to gun control and the intricacies involved in the process of purchasing a firearm. Chapter 14 introduces a rating system for evaluating effective gun control policies and explores the global spectrum of firearm policies. The final chapter, Chapter 15, investigates the historical development of sports shooting and explores cultural, social, economic, and political factors influencing the emergence and evolution of shooting sports. It also delves into community dynamics, inclusivity, and the role of shooting clubs in fostering a sense of belonging, as well as controversies, deviance, and the impact of sports shooting on health and well-being.

GUN CONTROL POLICIES

G un control policies are implemented for various reasons, with the primary goal being to enhance public safety and reduce the risks associated with firearm ownership and use. Gun control policies are implemented for various reasons, with the primary goal being to enhance public safety and reduce the risks associated with firearm ownership and use. One of the key reasons for gun control is to reduce the incidence of firearm-related crimes and violence. By regulating the purchase, possession, and use of firearms, authorities aim to prevent criminals and individuals with violent tendencies from easily accessing and using weapons. This is crucial in preventing crime and violence, as it reduces the likelihood of firearms being used in criminal activities and acts of violence. Additionally, gun control measures are implemented to protect the safety of the general public. Regulating the availability and use of firearms helps minimize the potential for accidents, suicides, and domestic violence incidents involving guns. This is essential in ensuring public safety and reducing the risks associated with firearm ownership.

Gun control policies may target the prevention of mass shootings by restricting access to high-capacity magazines and certain types of firearms. The intention is to limit the lethality of such incidents and enhance public safety. This is a critical aspect of gun control as it directly addresses the threat posed by mass shootings and aims to mitigate their impact on society. In addition, some gun control measures are designed to address mental health issues by preventing individuals with serious mental illnesses or a history of violence from obtaining firearms. This aims to reduce the risk of individuals using guns to harm themselves or others. By addressing mental health concerns, gun control policies contribute to the overall reduction of firearm-related incidents.

Gun control laws may include provisions to protect victims of domestic violence by restricting firearm access for individuals subject to restraining orders or with a history of domestic violence. This is an important aspect of gun control as it directly addresses the intersection of firearms and domestic violence, aiming to protect vulnerable individuals from further harm. Regulations may also be put in place to ensure responsible gun ownership and storage, reducing the likelihood of accidental shootings, especially involving children who might have access to firearms. This aspect of gun control is crucial in preventing unintentional harm caused by firearms and promoting safe storage practices among gun owners.

Governments may implement gun control measures to maintain national security and prevent the unauthorized acquisition of weapons by individuals or groups with malicious intent. This is essential in safeguarding the nation from potential threats posed by the misuse of firearms. Additionally, gun control policies often target the illegal trafficking of firearms across borders. By regulating the legal market and imposing strict penalties for illegal possession and trade, authorities seek to curb the flow of weapons to criminals. This is crucial in addressing the global issue of illegal firearm trafficking and its impact on crime and violence.

Furthermore, governments implement gun control to maintain public order and prevent the escalation of conflicts. This includes regulating the carrying of firearms in public spaces to avoid the potential for confrontations. By maintaining public order, gun control policies contribute to the overall stability and safety of communities. It is important to note that the reasons for gun control can vary based on the cultural, historical, and political context of each country. The balance between individual rights and public safety is often a central theme in debates surrounding gun control. Different countries may adopt different approaches based on their unique circumstances and values. Therefore, it is essential to consider the specific socio-political context when analysing the reasons for implementing gun control measures.

It is important to note that the reasons for gun control can vary based on the cultural, historical, and political context of each country. The balance between individual rights and public safety is often a central theme in debates surrounding gun control. Different countries may adopt different approaches based on their unique circumstances and values. Likewise, there are arguments against gun control. As an example, National Rifle Association of America (2024) argues against the effectiveness of gun control measures in the USA, asserting that they fail to achieve their intended purpose and may infringe upon the Second Amendment rights of law-abiding citizens. National Rifle Association of America (2024) contends that criminals, by nature, do not adhere to the law, rendering gun control laws ineffective as they primarily impact law-abiding citizens. The inadequacy of background checks is highlighted, emphasizing that they often do not prevent individuals with criminal intent or mental health issues from acquiring firearms (National Rifle Association of America, 2024).

Contrary to the belief that making firearms more accessible would lead to increased crime, National Rifle Association of America (2024) suggests that allowing law-abiding citizens easier access to guns can help reduce violent crime. National Rifle Association of America (2024) cites instances where armed citizens have deterred or stopped mass murderers and argues that cities with strict gun control laws, such as Chicago and New York, often experience high crime rates. The proposed solution advocates for crime control instead, focusing on enforcing existing laws against criminals who misuse firearms (National Rifle Association of America, 2024). The success of programs like "Project Exile" is presented as evidence that targeting gun criminals, rather than imposing restrictions on law-abiding citizens, is more effective in curbing violent crime (National Rifle Association of America, 2024).

On an international scale, gun control is a widespread concern, and each country holds the sovereign authority to govern firearms within its borders (Charles, 2024). The majority of developed nations maintain strict gun-control regulations. For instance, Japan imposes limitations on the possession and use of all firearms, allowing exceptions only for specific purposes such as hunting, athletic events, and research. Canada allows firearms possession for competitions and target practice but prohibits handguns unless an individual demonstrates a genuine need for self-defence (Charles, 2024). The United Kingdom has implemented a complete ban on handguns, permitting firearm possession only for activities like hunting, target shooting, pest control, and slaughtering. In Germany, ownership of certain firearms is permissible, contingent upon meeting requirements for a firearms ownership license, which includes being 18 years or older, possessing expert knowledge in firearm handling, and demonstrating a legitimate necessity for firearm possession (Charles, 2024).

The historical roots of gun control can be traced back to ancient Rome if defined as the imposition of legal restrictions on arms to safeguard civil society (Charles, 2024). In Rome, the perception of arms as a means to maintain standing armies prompted the implementation of laws prohibiting military arms from crossing the Rubicon. This regulation aimed to prevent standing armies from undermining civil authority, a principle that endured until Julius Caesar violated it, marking a significant turning point in the decline of the Roman Empire.

In England, the control of arms by Parliament and the crown was intricately tied to socioeconomic status. John Sadler, an English reformer and Member of Parliament, emphasized in 1649 that Parliament defined who was entitled to "provide and bear arms, how, and when, and where," highlighting the strict regulation of arms for the common defence of the realm (Charles, 2024). During the reign of Henry VIII, gun-control laws were enacted, restricting the presence of "weapons" and "defensive armour" in specific locations, with further regulations on the length of guns, qualifications for gun possession, and when and where they could be fired (Charles, 2024).

While gun restrictions in England were rarely debated in Parliament, occasional proposals arose from the mid-17th to the late 18th century seeking to lift restrictions and allow English householders to maintain guns for defence (Charles, 2024). However, these proposals faced opposition, with concerns that arming the public would lead to potential mob violence, deemed unsafe for any government.

Gun-control measures in England were multifaceted, serving purposes beyond government safety. Restrictions supported game hunting and access to game preserves, crime prevention, and murder reduction. Arguments against restrictions, such as those put forth by Adam Ferguson and Soame Jenyns in the 18th century, advocating for the establishment of a national militia, did not alter the well-established gun-control landscape (Charles, 2024). Even as militia reform occurred in the mid-18th century, arms were kept under the control of local officials and distributed only during militia muster and training, maintaining a practice dating back to the 1550s.

Gun control encompasses the laws and regulations governing the manufacture, sale, transfer, possession, and use of firearms (World Population Review, 2024). While most nations, including the United States, have some form of gun control, the approach to these regulations varies significantly worldwide. The debate over gun control is particularly intense in the United States, where the right to bear arms is constitutionally protected, contributing to the country's high gun ownership rates, which account for a disproportionate percentage of the world's civilian-owned guns (World Population Review, 2024).

Permissive gun control laws, characterized by a "shall-issue" basis for gun licenses, are observed in countries like Albania, Austria, Honduras, and the United States. On the other hand, nations with restrictive gun control laws, following a "may-issue" approach, include Argentina, Canada, and Germany, where individuals seeking permits must demonstrate a specific need for firearm ownership. In countries with the strictest gun control laws, often labelled as "no-issue" nations, the legal possession of guns by ordinary citizens is extremely challenging or virtually impossible. In these countries, such as China, Greece, and North Korea, exclusive gun ownership is typically limited to the police and military. The global diversity in gun control laws underscores the complex and contentious nature of the issue, with varying perspectives on the balance between individual rights and public safety.

Permissive and restrictive gun control laws represent distinct approaches to regulating firearms, with implications for public safety and individual rights. Permissive laws, often implemented on a "shall-issue" basis, emphasize broader access to firearms for law-abiding citizens, provided they meet predetermined legal requirements (Loftin et al., 1991). These laws are associated with the issuance of gun licenses or permits to individuals who meet specific criteria, such as age restrictions, passing background checks, and possibly completing safety courses (Loftin et al., 1991). Research has examined the impact of "shall-issue" concealed handgun laws on violent crime rates, shedding light on the implications of permissive gun control laws on public safety (Tomislav Victor Kovandzic et al., 2005).

On the other hand, restrictive gun control laws, operating on a "may-issue" basis, focus on more controlled access to firearms, with authorities having discretion in issuing gun licenses based on demonstrated need or justification for owning a firearm (Loftin et al., 1991). Evidence from the District of Columbia suggests that restrictive licensing of handguns was associated with a prompt decline in homicides and suicides by firearms (Loftin et al., 1991). Additionally, discussions on moderate gun control laws provide insights into the balance between individual rights and public safety, contributing to the broader debate on the regulation of firearm ownership and use (DeGrazia, 2014).

Furthermore, comparative studies on firearm access and ownership in different countries, such as Israel and Switzerland, offer valuable perspectives on the implications of varying gun control laws on public safety and individual rights (Rosenbaum, 2011). These insights contribute to the understanding of the diverse approaches to regulating the ownership, possession, and use of firearms, reflecting the broader discussion on the balance between individual rights and public safety.

Preventing Crime and Violence

The implementation of gun control measures is fundamentally driven by the goal of preventing crime and violence. This objective is achieved through a combination of strategies aimed at regulating legal firearm transactions, restricting access for high-risk individuals, and addressing illegal activities related to firearms (Filindra & Kaplan, 2017). Gun control policies often involve comprehensive background checks for individuals seeking to purchase firearms, aiming to identify those with criminal records, a history of violence, or mental health issues, thereby preventing them from obtaining firearms legally (Filindra & Kaplan, 2017). Waiting periods between the initiation of a firearm purchase and the actual acquisition allow authorities additional time to conduct thorough background checks, reducing the risk of impulsive or hasty firearm acquisitions by potentially dangerous individuals (Filindra & Kaplan, 2017). Additionally, stricter regulation of sales and monitoring of gun shows and private sales are implemented to minimize the likelihood of weapons ending up in the hands of criminals (Filindra & Kaplan, 2017).

Gun control laws often include provisions prohibiting specific categories of individuals from owning firearms, such as those with felony convictions, individuals subject to restraining orders, and those with a history of domestic violence, aiming to prevent potential violence (Filindra & Kaplan, 2017).

A felony conviction is a formal judgment by a court of law, signifying that an individual has been found guilty of committing a serious criminal offense known as a felony. Felonies are more severe than misdemeanours and often entail harsher penalties, including imprisonment for more than a year, fines, and other legal consequences.

Felony offenses encompass a range of serious crimes, each with its distinctive characteristics. Murder involves unlawfully causing the death of another person with malice aforethought, while robbery entails using force or the threat of force to take property from someone else. Burglary consists of illegally entering a building with the intent to commit a crime, often theft, and kidnapping involves unlawfully taking and holding a person against their will. Drug trafficking encompasses illegally selling, transporting, or distributing controlled substances, and fraud entails engaging in deceptive practices to gain an unfair advantage or cause financial harm to others. Sexual assault comprises committing non-consensual sexual acts against another person, and grand theft involves stealing property or money valued above a certain threshold. Each of these offenses represents a serious violation of the law, and convictions for such crimes can lead to significant legal consequences.

The classification of felonies and the associated penalties can vary between jurisdictions. In the United States, for instance, felony classifications may include different degrees (e.g., first-degree felony, second-degree felony) based on the severity of the offense. A felony conviction has repercussions beyond imprisonment and fines; it can impact various aspects of a person's life, affecting employment opportunities, housing, and the restoration of certain civil rights.

It is important to note that the legal definitions and classifications of felonies can differ by jurisdiction. Therefore, the specifics may vary depending on the laws of the particular state or country in question.

Laws addressing the safe storage of firearms in households with minors are also in place to reduce the risk of unauthorized access to firearms by children or teenagers, preventing accidents or intentional harm (Filindra & Kaplan, 2017). Secure storage requirements for firearms are mandated to prevent gun theft, aiming to reduce the likelihood of firearms falling into the hands of criminals (Filindra & Kaplan, 2017).

Public Safety

Gun control measures play a crucial role in enhancing public safety by addressing various aspects of firearm-related risks. One critical aspect is the prevention of accidents, which can occur due to mishandling, improper storage, or unintended use of firearms (Beidas et al., 2020). Regulatory measures such as mandatory safety training, secure storage requirements, and waiting periods for firearm purchases aim to mitigate the risk of unintentional injuries and fatalities caused by firearms (Beidas et al., 2020). Additionally, gun control measures are instrumental in addressing the complex issue of suicides involving firearms. Studies consistently highlight the correlation between the availability of firearms and an increased risk of successful suicide attempts (Raissian, 2015).

By implementing regulations that restrict access to firearms, especially during periods of mental health crises, authorities aim to reduce the lethality of suicide attempts (Raissian, 2015). Furthermore, gun control's role in public safety extends to addressing incidents of domestic violence where firearms are involved. Research indicates a higher risk of lethal outcomes in domestic violence situations when firearms are present (Frattaroli

& Vernick, 2006). Through regulations targeting individuals with a history of domestic violence or those subject to restraining orders, authorities seek to create protective mechanisms that minimize the potential for firearms to escalate domestic disputes into fatal confrontations (Frattaroli & Vernick, 2006).

Reducing Mass Shootings

Gun control policies targeting mass shootings aim to address the specific and alarming facet of public safety posed by these incidents. These policies primarily focus on restricting access to high-capacity magazines and certain types of firearms to limit the lethality of mass shootings and enhance overall public safety (D. Webster et al., 2020). High-capacity magazines enable shooters to fire a large number of rounds without reloading, significantly increasing the potential for casualties in a short amount of time. By imposing restrictions on the size of magazines that can be legally owned or sold, authorities aim to disrupt the ability of individuals to carry out prolonged and devastating attacks, providing crucial moments for intervention by law enforcement or civilians, potentially saving lives (D. Webster et al., 2020).

In addition to magazine capacity restrictions, gun control policies may also focus on certain types of firearms associated with a high rate of fire or designed for military-style rapid shooting. By identifying and regulating these specific firearms, authorities aim to address the unique challenges posed by weapons that can cause significant harm in a short period. This approach recognizes that certain firearm features contribute to the increased lethality of mass shootings, and restrictions on these features can act as a preventive measure (D. Webster et al., 2020).

The intention behind these measures is not only to hinder the effectiveness of potential mass shooters but also to create a safer environment for the general public. By limiting the firepower available to individuals who may pose a threat, gun control policies seek to reduce the potential magnitude of mass shootings and, consequently, minimize the harm inflicted on innocent lives (D. Webster et al., 2020).

It's important to note that while these measures aim to reduce the lethality of mass shootings, addressing the complex issue of mass violence requires a multifaceted approach that may also involve mental health interventions, community support, and comprehensive law enforcement strategies (D. Webster et al., 2020). Gun control policies focusing on mass shootings represent a proactive step toward enhancing public safety and preventing large-scale tragedies (D. Webster et al., 2020)

Addressing Mental Health Concerns

Gun control measures that address mental health concerns aim to recognize the intricate relationship between firearms and mental well-being, with the primary goal of preventing potential harm to individuals and the broader community. These measures involve implementing restrictions on individuals with serious mental illnesses from obtaining firearms and incorporating mental health criteria into background checks for gun purchases. By doing so, authorities seek to identify and prevent those with severe mental health issues from accessing potentially lethal weapons, aligning with the broader public health goal of mitigating the risk of impulsive or harmful actions by individuals experiencing significant mental distress (Swanson et al., 2015). Additionally, these policies may address individuals with a history of violence or those deemed a threat to themselves or others due to mental health considerations, aiming to create a protective barrier that minimizes the risk of gun-related incidents (Swanson et al., 2015).

The implementation of mental health-focused gun control measures also reflects a broader societal commitment to destigmatizing mental health issues and encouraging responsible firearm ownership. Education and awareness campaigns may accompany these policies, emphasizing the importance of recognizing and addressing mental health concerns for the well-being of individuals and the safety of the community. It is crucial to note that the goal of these measures is not to stigmatize individuals with mental health challenges but to strike a balance between individual rights and public safety, aiming to prevent instances where firearms might be used impulsively or dangerously due to an individual's mental state (Swanson et al., 2015).

While addressing mental health concerns through gun control is a valuable preventive strategy, it is essential to complement these measures with comprehensive mental health support, community resources, and destigmatization efforts. An integrated approach acknowledges the complex interplay of factors contributing to gun-related incidents involving mental health and strives to create a safer and more supportive environment for all individuals (Swanson et al., 2015).

Domestic Violence Prevention

Gun control laws addressing domestic violence prevention play a crucial role in safe-guarding individuals at risk within their homes by restricting firearm access for individuals subject to restraining orders or those with a documented history of domestic violence. Restraining orders, also known as protective orders, are court-issued legal directives designed to protect victims of domestic violence by prohibiting the alleged abuser from approaching or contacting the victim (Lynch et al., 2021). Gun control laws may extend these protections by explicitly restricting the subject's access to firearms during the duration of the restraining order (Wallin & Durfee, 2020). This is significant as firearms play a critical role in the murder of intimate partner violence (IPV) victims, and laws prohibiting protective order respondents from possessing a firearm reduce IPV fatalities (Lynch et al., 2021).

Furthermore, gun control measures may address individuals with a history of domestic violence by incorporating domestic violence convictions or incidents into background checks for firearm purchases. Research has shown that when a firearm is used in a violent encounter, the risk of homicide is greatly increased when other weapons are used, regardless of the intent to kill (Zeoli et al., 2017). Therefore, integrating domestic violence convictions or incidents into background checks for firearm purchases is crucial in identifying and preventing individuals with a documented history of domestic violence from obtaining firearms, thus interrupting the potential cycle of violence and protecting survivors from further harm.

The presence of a firearm can significantly increase the risk of lethality in abusive relationships, and by temporarily removing or restricting access to firearms for individuals involved in domestic violence situations, authorities seek to create a safer environment and empower survivors to seek help without the added threat of lethal force (Wallin & Durfee, 2020). Women's risk of intimate partner homicide (IPH) victimization increases fivefold when an intimate has access to firearms, highlighting the importance of firearm restriction in domestic violence situations (Wallin & Durfee, 2020).

These gun control measures complement the overall legal framework aimed at providing comprehensive protection for victims of domestic violence and contribute to a holistic approach that combines legal interventions, support services, and community awareness to create an environment where survivors feel safer and empowered to break free from abusive relationships (Bonomi et al., 2021). It is important to note that the effectiveness of these measures is enhanced when combined with broader initiatives addressing domestic violence prevention, including support services, education, and awareness campaigns (Bonomi et al., 2021).

Preventing Accidental Shootings

The aspect of gun control dedicated to preventing accidental shootings underscores the importance of responsible firearm ownership and storage. Accidental shootings, particularly those involving children who might gain access to firearms, present a significant risk to public safety. Regulations are implemented to establish guidelines for responsible gun ownership, emphasizing safe storage practices to minimize the likelihood of unintended firearm use. One key component of these regulations involves promoting safe storage practices for firearms, such as in locked cabinets, safes, or with the use of trigger locks. Authorities may require gun owners to store their firearms securely to prevent unauthorized individuals, particularly children, from accessing firearms without the knowledge and supervision of responsible adults. This preventive measure acknowledges the inherent curiosity of children and the potential for tragic consequences when firearms are left unsecured.

The importance of safe firearm storage is highlighted in various studies. Levine and McKnight (2017) provide evidence indicating that the spike in gun exposure following the Sandy Hook school shooting increased the incidence of accidental firearm deaths, particularly among children. Similarly, Azad et al. (2020) emphasize the significance of firearm-related fatalities among children and the need for preventive measures. Furthermore, Stroebe et al. (2017) note that mass public shootings are typically followed by a spike in gun sales as well as calls for stricter gun control laws, indicating the impact of such incidents on public perception and policy.

Research by Prickett et al. (2014) sheds light on the relationship between state firearm laws, firearm ownership, and safety practices among families with preschool-aged children, emphasizing the complexity of disentangling the effects of state-level firearm laws. Additionally, King et al. (2020) highlight the association between safe firearm storage and lower risk of unintentional and intentionally self-inflicted firearm injuries among children and adolescents, further underscoring the importance of responsible storage practices.

Regulations may include requirements for the use of gun safes or lockboxes, especially in households with children, to add an extra layer of protection, ensuring that firearms are not easily accessible to unauthorized individuals. Emphasizing responsible storage aligns with the broader goal of minimizing the risk of accidental shootings and creating a safer environment within homes. In addition to safe storage practices, gun control measures aimed at preventing accidental shootings may also include educational components. Education campaigns can raise awareness about the importance of storing firearms securely and highlight the potential dangers associated with leaving guns accessible to children. These initiatives contribute to a culture of responsible firearm ownership, where gun owners are not only aware of the legal requirements but also understand the critical role they play in preventing unintentional firearm-related incidents.

The implementation of regulations for preventing accidental shootings recognizes that a substantial number of such incidents result from firearms being left unsecured, leading to tragic consequences. By emphasizing responsible ownership and storage practices, authorities seek to reduce the incidence of accidental shootings, protect vulnerable populations, and foster an environment where firearm ownership is accompanied by a strong commitment to safety. It is crucial to note that these measures are not designed to infringe upon the rights of responsible gun owners but rather to strike a balance between individual rights and public safety. Responsible storage practices contribute to the overall goal of preventing unintended firearm use, particularly in households with children, and play a vital role in creating a safer and more secure community.

National Security

Gun control measures implemented for national security purposes are crucial for safeguarding a nation against potential threats posed by the unauthorized acquisition and possession of firearms by individuals or groups with malicious intent. These measures are designed to strike a balance between individual rights and the collective well-being of society, aiming to prevent acts of violence and protect the general population from harm (Lee et al., 2017).

One key objective of gun control measures for national security is to prevent the unauthorized acquisition of firearms by individuals with malicious intent, such as terrorists or those involved in organized crime. By establishing stringent regulations, background checks, and monitoring mechanisms, governments seek to identify and block access to firearms for individuals who may pose a threat to the security of the nation. This proactive approach aligns with the broader national security strategy, aiming to prevent acts of violence and protect the general population from harm (Lee et al., 2017).

Additionally, these measures may involve restricting the availability of certain types of firearms or imposing limitations on the quantity of ammunition an individual can purchase. By doing so, authorities aim to curb the potential for large-scale violence orchestrated by individuals or groups with malicious intent. The intention is to create barriers that impede the ability of those with harmful intentions to acquire the firepower necessary for acts of terrorism, insurgency, or other forms of violence against the state or its citizens (Krüsselmann et al., 2021).

Furthermore, gun control measures for national security often include efforts to address the illegal trafficking of firearms across borders. Governments may collaborate on international initiatives to regulate and monitor the movement of firearms, preventing the flow of weapons to individuals or groups with hostile intentions. This approach recognizes that porous borders and the international trafficking of firearms can pose significant challenges to national security, requiring coordinated efforts to curb the illicit trade of weapons (Krüsselmann et al., 2021).

It is important to note that the implementation of gun control measures for national security is part of a broader strategy that may include intelligence gathering, counterterrorism efforts, and international cooperation. By regulating access to firearms, governments seek to create a more secure environment, minimizing the potential for internal and external threats that could compromise the safety and stability of the nation (Lee et al., 2017). While addressing national security concerns through gun control measures, governments must navigate the delicate balance between protecting the public and respecting individual rights. Striking this balance requires careful consideration of legal frameworks, effective enforcement, and ongoing evaluation of the evolving nature of security threats in the domestic and global contexts (Lee et al., 2017).

Minimizing Illegal Firearm Trafficking

Gun control policies aimed at minimizing illegal firearm trafficking are used in addressing organized crime, violence, and the proliferation of weapons in illicit markets. Regulating the legal market through comprehensive background checks, waiting periods, and documentation requirements for legal firearm transactions is essential to create a controlled and traceable environment, preventing the diversion of legally purchased firearms into the illicit market (Webster et al., 2009). Imposing strict penalties for illegal possession and trade acts as a deterrent and disrupts criminal networks engaged in trafficking operations (Hureau & Braga, 2018). International cooperation is vital in enhancing information-sharing, joint investigations, and coordinated efforts to intercept and disrupt illicit arms shipments (Ak & Fidelia, 2018). Additionally, tracing technologies and databases enable authorities to track the origins and movement of firearms, providing valuable insights into the patterns of illicit arms trade and helping dismantle trafficking networks (Hureau & Braga, 2018).

The goal of minimizing illegal firearm trafficking is not only to prevent criminal organizations from accessing weapons but also to enhance overall public safety. By disrupting the supply chain of illicit firearms, authorities aim to reduce the incidence of violent crimes committed with illegally obtained weapons, protecting communities from the detrimental impact of armed criminal activities (Braga & Pierce, 2005). However, it is essential for governments to strike a balance between addressing the illicit trade of firearms and respecting the legal rights of law-abiding citizens (Braga & Pierce, 2005). Effective gun control policies against illegal trafficking require a comprehensive and coordinated approach, involving legislation, law enforcement efforts, international collaboration, and technological advancements to address the multifaceted challenges posed by illicit arms trade (Braga & Pierce, 2005).

Maintaining Public Order

The implementation of gun control measures to maintain public order reflects a commitment by governments to strike a delicate balance between individual rights and the broader safety and harmony of society (Lee et al., 2017). By regulating the possession and carrying of firearms, authorities aim to prevent the escalation of conflicts and reduce the potential for confrontations in public spaces (Lee et al., 2017). One key aspect of maintaining public order through gun control involves regulating the carrying of firearms in public spaces. This may include the imposition of restrictions on openly carrying firearms or requiring individuals to obtain permits for concealed carry (Lee et al., 2017). Such regulations are designed to ensure that the presence of firearms in public settings does not create an atmosphere of heightened tension or fear, mitigating the risk of confrontations that could lead to violence (Lee et al., 2017).

By establishing clear guidelines for carrying firearms in public, governments seek to provide law enforcement with the tools necessary to maintain order and respond effectively to potential threats (Lee et al., 2017). This regulatory framework helps prevent misunderstandings or disputes that may arise when individuals openly carry firearms, contributing to a safer and more predictable environment in public spaces (Lee et al., 2017). Additionally, gun control measures for maintaining public order may involve the designation of specific areas where carrying firearms is prohibited (Lee et al., 2017). These restricted zones may include places with high population density, such as schools, government buildings, or public events, where the presence of firearms could pose an increased risk to public safety (Lee et al., 2017). Restricting the carrying of firearms in such areas aims to create secure environments and prevent potential conflicts that may arise in sensitive or crowded settings (Lee et al., 2017).

The goal of maintaining public order through gun control also extends to addressing instances where the open display or use of firearms may incite fear or panic among the public (Lee et al., 2017). Regulations may prohibit the brandishing of firearms in a manner that is likely to create alarm or disturb the peace (Lee et al., 2017). This proactive approach seeks to prevent situations where the mere presence of a firearm contributes to a sense of insecurity or unease within the community (Lee et al., 2017). It is essential to recognize that maintaining public order through gun control is not about infringing upon the rights of responsible gun owners but rather about establishing reasonable regulations that prioritize the overall safety and well-being of the community (Lee et al., 2017). Striking a balance between individual freedoms and collective security requires a nuanced approach, and these measures contribute to creating an environment where citizens can coexist peacefully without the heightened threat of firearm-related conflicts (Lee et al., 2017).

FIREARMS

Guns Defined

A gun is a firearm designed to launch projectiles, such as bullets, shells, or other ammunition, through the force of rapidly expanding high-pressure gases produced by a chemical reaction within a confined space. Guns come in various forms, commonly classified into two main types: handguns and long guns.

The terms "firearm" and "gun" are often used interchangeably, but there are subtle distinctions between the two. In a broader and more formal context, a firearm is an encompassing term for any portable weapon designed to expel projectiles through gunpowder, gas, or other explosive force, including handguns, rifles, and shotguns (Azrael et al., 2018). On the other hand, "gun" is a more colloquial and generic expression commonly used to describe handheld firearms, particularly smaller firearms like handguns and specific types of portable long guns (Azrael et al., 2018). While "gun" can be a general term for firearms, it is often associated with smaller firearms and specific types of portable long guns. Essentially, all guns fall under the category of firearms, but not all firearms are casually labelled as guns (Azrael et al., 2018). "Firearm" is a comprehensive and formal term used in legal and technical contexts, while "gun" is a familiar and informal expression frequently utilized in everyday conversations (Azrael et al., 2018).

The distinction between "firearm" and "gun" is important in various contexts, including legal and technical discussions. For instance, in the context of firearm storage in gun-owning households with children, it is crucial to understand the differences between firearms and guns to ensure safe storage practices. A study found that approximately 7% of US children live in homes where at least one firearm is stored loaded and unlocked, highlighting the importance of firearm safety and storage (Azrael et al., 2018). Additionally, the National Instant Criminal Background Check System Improvement Amendments Act of 2007, in the USA is expected to impact the identification of individuals belonging to the prohibited class, emphasizing the legal implications associated with firearms (Price & Norris, 2010).

Furthermore, the effects of state-level firearm seller accountability policies in the US on firearm trafficking demonstrate the relevance of understanding the distinctions between firearms and guns in the context of gun control and commerce. Research has shown that criminals' reliance on out-of-state sources for guns was negatively correlated with measures of gun availability to criminals, indicating the potential impact of firearm policies on firearm trafficking (Webster et al., 2009). Similarly, US state firearm laws have been associated with the incidence and severity of mass public shootings, highlighting the importance of firearm regulations in addressing public safety concerns (Siegel et al., 2020).

Guns exhibit a diverse array of shapes and sizes, housing various firing mechanisms. To comprehend their functioning, it is informative to delve into the operation of bullets—the small, pointed metal components responsible for penetrating targets (Roza, 2024). Bullets operate akin to fireworks, relying on a smaller fuse to ignite a larger explosion, propelling them out of the gun's barrel. Four essential components—primer, propellant, bullet case, and bullet—are contained within a cartridge, also known as a round or shell (Roza, 2024).

Handguns consist of pistols, where the chamber is an integral part of the barrel, and ammunition is loaded through a magazine, and revolvers, which have a rotating cylinder containing multiple chambers, each holding a cartridge (Zhang et al., 2023). The cylinder rotates to align a chamber with the barrel for firing. Refer to Figure 1 for examples.

Figure 1: Examples of a handguns - Clockwise from top left: Glock G22, Glock G21, Kimber Custom Raptor, Dan Wesson Commander, Smith & Wesson .357, Ruger Blackhawk .357, Ruger SP101, Sig Sauer P220 Combat. Joshuashearn, CC BY-SA 3.0 <https://creativecom mons.org/licenses/by-sa/3.0>, via Wikimedia Commons.

Long guns, as shown in Figure 2, include rifles, featuring rifling (spiral grooves) inside the barrel to impart a spin for increased accuracy, typically fired from the shoulder, and shotguns designed to fire a shell containing pellets or a slug. Shotguns may have a smooth bore or rifled barrel, serving various purposes like hunting and sport shooting.

Figure 2: Assortment of .22 LR and .30-06 rifles. Left to right: Ruger 10/22, .22 Long Rifle. M1903 Springfield, .30-'06. M1 Garand, .30-'06. Mossberg M1944 trainer, .22 Long Rifle. Henry Golden Boy, .22 Long Rifle. Ruger 10/22, .22 Long Rifle. Mitch Barrie, CC BY-SA 2.0 <https://creativecommons.org/licenses/by-sa/2.0>, via Wikimedia Commons.

Moving into firing modes—semi-automatic, automatic, burst, and single shot—provides a nuanced understanding. The term "gun" encompasses a broad category, spanning from handheld firearms to massive howitzers firing artillery shells. This discussion, however, focuses on firearms, particularly those more accessible to the public than heavy machine guns or rocket launchers. Modern firearms predominantly fall into four firing modes: semi-automatic, automatic, burst, and single shot.

Semi-automatic firearms discharge one shot per trigger pull, while automatic firearms continuously fire until the trigger is released, and burst firearms release multiple shots with each trigger pull.

Diverse types of guns include pistols, characterized as small firearms held in one hand. Revolvers, a subset of pistols, feature revolving chambers, firing cartridges in rotation.

Semi-automatic pistols utilize magazines to feed bullets, relying on recoil to cycle the firearm and load a new cartridge. This design yields larger magazine capacities, but misfires may occur.

Rifles, larger than pistols, operate similarly to semi-automatic pistols but with larger bullets and longer barrels. Rifles, featuring rifled barrels, offer enhanced accuracy and power over longer distances, requiring two-handed use.

The term "assault weapon" lacks specificity, but assault rifles refer to firearms capable of semi-automatic, automatic, or burst firing. Confusion often arises between semi-automatic-only rifles, such as the AR-15, and assault rifles due to their visual similarities.

The term "assault rifle" is commonly used to refer to a specific type of firearm that combines characteristics of both rifles and automatic weapons. Assault rifles are designed to be capable of selective fire, meaning the shooter can choose between firing in semi-automatic (one shot per trigger pull) or fully automatic (continuous automatic fire as long as the trigger is held) modes. Some may also have a burst mode, allowing a fixed number of rounds to be fired with a single trigger pull.

Assault rifles typically use an intermediate cartridge, which is smaller and less powerful than the full-sized cartridges used in traditional battle rifles. This design allows for more controllable automatic fire. These firearms use detachable magazines that can be quickly replaced, enabling the shooter to reload rapidly. The effective range of assault rifles is designed for engagement at intermediate ranges, typically up to a few hundred meters. The combination of selective fire and intermediate cartridges aims to provide a balance between the range of a rifle and the rapid-fire capability of a submachine gun.

In terms of ergonomics, assault rifles often incorporate features such as pistol grips, adjustable stocks, and handguards to enhance ease of handling. It's crucial to note that the term "assault rifle" is sometimes used inaccurately or interchangeably with other terms like "assault weapon." Additionally, specific definitions and classifications may vary by country and legal jurisdiction.

The use of assault rifles has been a subject of debate, particularly concerning civilian ownership and their role in military or law enforcement. Some countries have implemented strict regulations or bans on civilian ownership of firearms with assault rifle characteristics. The term has also been integral to broader discussions about gun control and firearm legislation.

Machine guns, see Figure 3 as an example, larger than rifles, exclusively operate on automatic, designed for sustained firing and typically mounted for stability. Submachine guns, akin to automatic pistols, rapidly fire bullets at close range.

Figure 3: Danish Machine gun M60E6. Flemming Diehl, CC BY-SA 4.0 <https://creati vecommons.org/licenses/by-sa/4.0>, via Wikimedia Commons.

Shotguns operate similarly to other firearms but differ in their ammunition. Rather than firing a single bullet, shotguns discharge a cluster of tiny pellets known as shot. Alternatively, some shotguns may propel a single large metal bullet called a slug. The preference for shot arises among hunters due to its short-range effectiveness, providing a safety advantage in areas with numerous people. The scattering pellets prove advantageous for capturing small, agile targets, such as mid-flight pheasants. Certain shotguns are favoured by police and military personnel for their formidable power at close range (Roza, 2024). While automatic shotguns exist, the more dependable ones are typically single-shot variants. Users either engage in a pump-action mechanism, requiring them to pump a new round into the chamber after each shot, or they employ a break-open method to manually slide new rounds into the chamber, reminiscent of a revolver (Roza, 2024).

Figure 4: A Remington 870 Wingmaster 12-gauge shotgun, two Remington 1100 12-gauge shotguns, boxes of shells and clay targets are laid out on the fantail of the battleship USS MISSOURI (BB-63) in preparation for skeet shooting practice. DoD photo by: PHAN MILNE/PHAN DILLON, Public domain, via Wikimedia Commons.

Distinguishing between these firearm types can be challenging, and misperceptions often arise, particularly concerning assault rifles, machine guns, and submachine guns (Roza, 2024). Practice in discerning these distinctions becomes essential, enhancing the ability to identify different firearms accurately.

Key components of a gun encompass the barrel (the tube through which the projectile travels), action (the mechanism for loading, firing, and unloading), stock (the part held by the shooter), trigger (initiating the firing sequence), and magazine (a container for cartridges, not applicable to all guns) (Zhang et al., 2023).

The cartridge's primer, akin to a firework fuse, ignites the propellant—a highly explosive gunpowder—upon pulling the trigger. This ignition results in a powerful explosion that propels the bullet out of the cartridge at high speed. Simultaneously, the bullet case, or shell casing, is ejected from the gun's side (Roza, 2024). This entire process transpires instantaneously upon triggering. While certain military-grade guns can fire up to 100 rounds per second, not all guns share this capability (Roza, 2024).

Guns serve diverse purposes, including self-defence, hunting, sport shooting, law enforcement, and military applications. The ongoing debate over gun control often centres around individual rights, public safety, and regulating firearms to prevent misuse.

The term "firearm" generally refers to a portable gun designed to expel one or more projectiles through the action of gunpowder or another explosive force (Jussila & Normia, 2004). In the context of firearms, they are designed as weapons and are commonly used for self-defence, hunting, sport shooting, law enforcement, and military applications. While the primary purpose of firearms is often related to their use as weapons, there are instances where firearms are adapted for non-lethal purposes. For example, certain types of firearms can be modified to fire less-lethal projectiles, such as rubber bullets or bean bags, for crowd control or riot situations.

The adaptability of firearms allows for applications beyond traditional lethal use in certain situations. For instance, non-legislative prevention measures have been found to be more effective in reducing suicide by firearms in the United States, particularly by respectfully engaging firearm owners (Garverich et al., 2023). Additionally, there are instances where firearms are adapted for non-lethal purposes, such as the use of less-lethal projectiles for crowd control or riot situations.

It is important to note that the use of firearms, whether for lethal or non-lethal purposes, carries significant implications. For instance, an abuser's gun ownership or access to guns creates a sense of fear and unpredictability, particularly in cases of intimate partner violence (Kafonek et al., 2021). Furthermore, the illegitimate or unauthorized application of non-lethal firearms, such as electroshock weapons, can lead to public outcry and censure (Talapins & Agafonovs, 2020).

In summary, while firearms are primarily designed as weapons, their adaptability allows for applications beyond traditional lethal use in certain situations. However, the use of firearms, whether for lethal or non-lethal purposes, must be carefully considered due to the significant implications associated with their use.

To understand the concept of weapons, it is essential to recognize that they are tools or devices designed and used to cause harm, damage, or injury to living beings, structures, or systems (Moczek & Nijhout, 2004). Weapons serve military, self-defence, or offensive purposes and are employed for protection, intimidation, or combat (Moczek & Nijhout, 2004). They can take various forms, including firearms, melee weapons, explosives, chemical devices, and more (Moczek & Nijhout, 2004). The use and possession of weapons are often subject to legal regulations, and their development and deployment are influenced by cultural, historical, and technological factors (Moczek & Nijhout, 2004).

Firearm preferences vary significantly among countries due to a combination of cultural norms, legal frameworks, and military practices (König et al., 2018). These pref-

erences are subject to change over time, influenced by evolving laws and societal attitudes (Kapusta et al., 2007). The attitudes of firearm owners towards their weapons are
complex and diverse, extending beyond mere ownership to encompass motivations and
understandings of firearms (Steidley & Yamane, 2021). Additionally, the accessibility and
storage practices of firearms have been linked to increased suicide risk, particularly among
military personnel (Dempsey et al., 2019).

It is evident that firearm preferences are deeply intertwined with cultural, legal, and
societal factors, and understanding these dynamics is essential for addressing public health
and safety concerns related to firearms. The multifaceted nature of firearm ownership
and its implications for suicide risk highlight the need for comprehensive strategies that
consider not only legislative measures but also cultural competence and clinical approaches to firearm safety and prevention (Pallin & Barnhorst, 2021; Pirelli & Witt,
2017). The impact of firearm legislation reforms on firearm availability and mortality rates
underscores the potential of policy interventions in shaping firearm preferences and their
associated risks (Kapusta et al., 2007).

Civilian Firearm Use and Ownership

The following provides examples of common and popular firearms employed in various
countries.

The civilian firearm choices in the United States encompass a variety of weapons,
including the AR-15/M16 (See Figure 5), civilian versions of military rifles, Glock pistols
(see Figure 6), and the Remington 870 pump-action shotgun. These firearms are widely
utilized for sport shooting, home defence, and by law enforcement. The widespread
ownership of firearms in the United States is evident, with an estimated 270 million
civilian-owned firearms, including handguns, rifles, and shotguns (Yamane, 2017). This
prevalence of firearms has been linked to various societal implications, including an increased likelihood of firearm-related suicides and overall suicides (Richardson & Hemenway, 2011) Additionally, high public gun ownership has been identified as a risk factor for
occupational mortality for law enforcement officers in the United States (Swedler et al.,
2015).

Figure 5: American Tactical OMNI AR15. Picanox, CC BY-SA 4.0 <https://creativecom mons.org/licenses/by-sa/4.0>, via Wikimedia Commons.

Figure 6: An early "third generation" Glock 17 (full-size pistol chambered for 9x19mm Parabellum). Ken Lunde, http://lundestudio.com, CC BY-SA 3.0 <https://creativecomm ons.org/licenses/by-sa/3.0>, via Wikimedia Commons.

These examples represent only a fraction of the diverse landscape of firearm preferences in the United States. The popularity of specific gun models can vary regionally and may be influenced by factors such as state regulations, individual preferences, and cultural considerations. Additionally, the dynamic nature of the firearm market and evolving trends contribute to the ongoing diversity of popular gun models among American civilians.

The firearms landscape in Russia is characterized by the widespread use and export of weapons, high-quality military equipment, and historical developments in the thinking and production of firearms. The prominent firearms in Russia include the AK-47/AKM (see Figure 7), the Makarov PM (See Figure 8), and the Saiga-12, which have gained global recognition and are widely used by the military and police forces (Nawrotek, 2020).

Figure 7: Russian Type III Izhevsk 1956 AK47 with Russian bayonet attached. Gunrunner123, Public domain, via Wikimedia Commons.

Russia has been a major producer and exporter of arms and military equipment for many years (Баурина et al., 2019). The quality of Russian-made weapons and military equipment, including communication equipment and avionics, has been demonstrated in the Russian military campaign in Syria (Domagała, 2018). Additionally, Russia has provided economic and military support to various governments, including delivering weapons, technical assistance, and military support in combat (Tsvetkov, 2021).

Figure 8: Makarov PM airsoft. Алексей Трефилов, CC BY-SA 4.0 <https://creativecomm ons.org/licenses/by-sa/4.0>, via Wikimedia Commons.

It's important to note that civilian firearm ownership in Russia is regulated, and access to certain models may be influenced by government policies. The popularity of specific gun models among civilians can be shaped by factors such as legal considerations, intended use, and cultural preferences within the country.

Germany showcases firearms like the HK MP5, a submachine gun used by military and law enforcement units, the Walther PPK, a compact pistol often utilized by the police, and the HK G36, an assault rifle adopted by the German military.

In Germany, civilian firearm ownership is subject to strict regulations designed to ensure public safety. Firearms for civilian use are primarily intended for sports shooting and hunting. Here are some examples of firearms that are popular for civilian use in Germany:

- Bolt-Action Rifles: These are commonly used for hunting purposes. Bolt-action rifles are manually operated, and each shot requires the shooter to manually manipulate the bolt to load a new cartridge.

- Semi-Automatic Rifles: While subject to stringent regulations, some semi-automatic rifles are allowed for civilian use, particularly for sports shooting. These rifles automatically eject the spent cartridge and load a new one with each shot.

- Shotguns: Shotguns are widely used for hunting and sports shooting. They are versatile firearms, with applications ranging from bird hunting to clay target shooting.

- Handguns: Handguns for civilian use are typically limited to revolvers and semi-automatic pistols. These are often used in sports shooting competitions, and ownership is subject to strict regulations.

It's crucial to understand that German gun laws are comprehensive and prioritize public safety. Individuals seeking to own firearms must undergo background checks, complete safety courses, and obtain a license from the local authorities. Additionally, the types of firearms civilians can own are specified, and automatic weapons are generally prohibited for civilian use. The regulatory framework is stringent, and German gun laws aim to strike a balance between the rights of individuals and public safety considerations.

Switzerland's firearm choices include the SIG SG 550, the standard issue rifle for the Swiss Armed Forces, the SIG P210, a semi-automatic pistol known for its accuracy, and the Strumgewehr 57, an older battle rifle that has been phased out but is still present.

In Switzerland, civilian firearm ownership is deeply ingrained in the country's culture, with a significant focus on the role of firearms in the Swiss militia system. The Swiss have a tradition of mandatory military service, and after completing their service, individuals may keep their military-issued firearms or purchase other firearms for civilian use. Popular firearms for civilian use in Switzerland include:

- SIG SG 550: The SIG SG 550 is a standard issue rifle for the Swiss Armed Forces, and civilians may own versions (see Figure 9 for an example) of this rifle. It is a selective-fire rifle known for its accuracy and reliability.

- SIG P210: The SIG P210 is a semi-automatic pistol with a reputation for exceptional accuracy. It is a popular choice among Swiss civilians for sports shooting and other recreational purposes.

- Strumgewehr 57: While phased out from military service, the Strumgewehr 57 is still present among Swiss civilians. It is an older battle rifle and holds historical significance.

Switzerland's firearm regulations are unique, reflecting the country's militia system and the trust placed in its citizens regarding responsible firearm ownership. Swiss gun laws require individuals to obtain a permit to purchase firearms, and there are specific regulations regarding the storage and use of firearms. The approach aims to balance individual freedoms with public safety considerations.

Figure 9: Sig Sauer SG 516. Rizuan, CC BY-SA 3.0 <https://creativecommons.org/license s/by-sa/3.0>, via Wikimedia Commons.

Israel employs firearms like the Tavor X95, a bullpup-style assault rifle used by the Israeli Defence Forces, the Jericho 941, a semi-automatic pistol in various calibres, and the Uzi, a submachine gun with historical significance.

In Canada, civilian firearm ownership is subject to stringent regulations designed to ensure public safety. The types of firearms allowed for civilian use are categorized, and individuals must obtain the necessary licenses and adhere to strict regulations. Popular firearms for civilian use in Canada include:

- Bolt-Action Rifles: Commonly used for hunting purposes, bolt-action rifles are manually operated, requiring the shooter to manipulate the bolt to load a new cartridge after each shot.

- Semi-Automatic Rifles: Some semi-automatic rifles are permitted for civilian use, particularly those used for sports shooting. These rifles automatically eject the spent cartridge and load a new one with each shot.

- Shotguns: Shotguns are widely used for hunting and sports shooting in Canada. They are versatile firearms with applications ranging from bird hunting to clay target shooting.

- Handguns: Handgun ownership is permitted under specific regulations, and individuals must obtain a restricted firearms license. Handguns are commonly used in sports shooting competitions.

Canada's firearm regulations are comprehensive, and individuals wishing to own firearms must go through a thorough licensing process, including background checks and safety training. Automatic firearms are generally prohibited for civilian use. The regulatory framework in Canada seeks to balance the rights of individuals with public safety considerations.

In Canada, the popularity of gun models for civilian use is diverse and contingent upon their intended applications, such as hunting, sports shooting, or self-defence. Among Canadian civilians, certain firearm models are commonly owned and widely favoured.

Bolt-action rifles like the Lee-Enfield are prevalent, particularly in hunting and sport shooting contexts. The Lee-Enfield's design and accuracy make it suitable for these purposes.

The Ruger 10/22, a semi-automatic rimfire rifle, enjoys frequent use among Canadians engaged in plinking, small game hunting, and sports shooting. Its versatility and reliability contribute to its popularity.

For hunting and home defence, the Remington 870, a pump-action shotgun, is widely chosen. Its effectiveness in various scenarios makes it a staple among firearm enthusiasts.

The Ruger Mini-14, a semi-automatic rifle known for its adaptability, finds applications in both hunting and sports shooting, reflecting its popularity among Canadian gun owners.

In sports shooting competitions, the SIG Sauer P226, a popular semi-automatic pistol, is often preferred for its accuracy and reliability.

The Smith & Wesson M&P Series, encompassing models like M&P9 and M&P15, holds popularity among Canadian gun owners engaged in sports shooting and home defence due to their performance and features.

The Benelli M4, a semi-automatic shotgun, is commonly used for diverse purposes, including sports shooting, reflecting its versatility and appeal among civilians.

It's crucial to acknowledge that the popularity of specific gun models may evolve over time, and individual preferences among gun owners can vary. Furthermore, the legal framework and regulations surrounding firearm ownership in Canada play a significant role in determining the types of firearms accessible to civilians.

China's firearm selection includes the Type 56, a local variant of the AK-47 widely used, the Norinco CQ, a copy of the Colt M16 used by Chinese forces, and the QSZ-92, the standard issue pistol for the People's Liberation Army.

In Australia, civilian firearm ownership is subject to strict regulations aimed at ensuring public safety. Firearms intended for civilian use are typically categorized based on their purpose, and ownership is contingent upon obtaining the appropriate licenses. Popular firearms for civilian use in Australia include:

- Bolt-Action Rifles: These rifles are commonly used for hunting purposes. Bolt-action rifles are manually operated, requiring the shooter to manipulate the bolt to load a new cartridge for each shot.

- Shotguns: Shotguns find application in various activities such as sports shooting and hunting. They are versatile firearms with different configurations for different purposes, including bird hunting and clay target shooting.

- Semi-Automatic Rifles (Restricted): Some semi-automatic rifles are permitted for civilian use, albeit under stringent regulations. These rifles automatically eject spent cartridges and load new ones with each shot.

- Handguns: Handguns for civilian use are subject to strict regulations, and ownership is often restricted to specific purposes such as sports shooting competitions. Semi-automatic pistols and revolvers fall into this category.

Australia's firearm regulations are comprehensive and prioritize public safety. Individuals seeking to own firearms must undergo background checks, complete safety courses, and obtain the necessary licenses from local authorities. Automatic and self-loading firearms are generally prohibited for civilian use. The regulatory framework reflects a balance between individual rights and considerations for public safety in Australia.

In the United Kingdom, firearms such as the SA80, a bullpup-style assault rifle used by the British Armed Forces, the Browning Hi-Power, a semi-automatic pistol with a historic connection, and the Benelli M4, a semi-automatic shotgun used by military and police, are prominent.

In the United Kingdom, civilian firearm ownership is heavily regulated, and the types of firearms permitted for civilian use are limited. The most common firearms for civilian use in the UK are shotguns and rifles used for sporting and recreational purposes such as hunting and target shooting. Handguns, semi-automatic, and automatic firearms are subject to stricter regulations, and ownership is generally restricted to specific situations, such as professional sporting events or historical reenactments.

The Firearms Act of 1968 and subsequent amendments regulate civilian firearm ownership in the UK. Firearms owners must obtain a firearm certificate from the police, and the type of firearm allowed is specified on the certificate. Shotguns and rifles used for sporting purposes are more accessible to civilians, but even their ownership is subject to rigorous background checks and safety requirements.

It's important to note that the UK has significantly stricter gun control laws compared to countries with more permissive regulations, such as the United States. The emphasis in the UK is on maintaining public safety and minimizing the risks associated with civilian firearm ownership.

These examples offer insights into firearms commonly associated with different countries. Nevertheless, firearm popularity is subject to various influences, and this list is not exhaustive. Additionally, firearm regulations may affect civilian access to specific types of firearms in different regions.

In terms of production, in 2018, the Small Arms Survey revealed that there are over one billion small arms globally, with 857 million (85 percent) in civilian possession. U.S. civilians alone own 393 million (46 percent) of the worldwide total (Hays & Jenzen-Jones, 2018). The world's armed forces control about 133 million small arms, with significant holdings in Russia (30.3 million) and China (27.5 million). Law enforcement agencies possess about 23 million small arms. Oxfam estimated firearm cartridge production at 12 billion per year in 2012 (Hays & Jenzen-Jones, 2018).

Estimates of Kalashnikov AK-47 production vary, with figures ranging from 35 to 150 million. Other notable firearms include the Mauser Gewehr 98, M16/M4/AR-15, Lee–Enfield, SKS, Mossberg 500, Remington 870, IMI Uzi, Glock, and many others.

Noteworthy among the listed firearms are the Kalashnikov AK-47, with estimates from 40 to 150 million; Mauser Gewehr 98, with 20 to 102 million; Mosin–Nagant, with 37 million; M16/M4/AR-15, with 15 to 20 million; Lee–Enfield, with 16 to 17 million; and SKS, with 5 to 15 million.

Other notable firearms include the Mossberg 500, Remington 870, Marlin Model 60, IMI Uzi, Arisaka Type 30/38/99, Glock, Makarov pistol, M1 Garand, Heckler & Koch G3, Winchester Model 1894, FN FAL, and many more.

The list includes popular handguns like the Smith & Wesson M&P Series, Beretta 92, and Ruger P-series. Rifles such as the Ruger 10/22, Remington 700, and Springfield M1903 are also featured.

The production estimates for various firearms range widely, reflecting the diversity and historical significance of these weapons. The data provides insight into the global distribution and prevalence of small arms, emphasizing their widespread presence across different countries and regions.

Gun ownership rates exhibit significant variation globally, influenced by diverse cultural, legal, and historical factors. The United States holds the highest gun ownership rate globally, boasting 120.5 firearms per 100 people, followed by Yemen with 52.8 firearms per 100 people (Wisevoter, 2024). These figures underscore the prevalence of firearm possession in these nations.

Several European countries, including Switzerland, Finland, Norway, and Austria, also report comparatively high gun ownership rates, attributed to hunting traditions, recreational shooting, and historical factors like citizen militias. Conversely, East Asian countries like Japan, South Korea, and Taiwan maintain extremely low gun ownership rates, often nearing zero per 100 people due to stringent gun control laws and cultural emphasis on public safety through alternative means (Wisevoter, 2024).

The top ten countries with the highest gun ownership rates are the United States, Yemen, New Caledonia, Montenegro, Serbia, Canada, Uruguay, Cyprus, Finland, and Lebanon. Notably, the U.S. stands out as the most armed country globally, with a complex interplay of historical, cultural, and legal factors contributing to its unique position (Wisevoter, 2024). The constitutional Second Amendment, granting the right to bear arms, and the country's vast size and regional diversity further contribute to the intricate landscape of gun ownership in the United States (Wisevoter, 2024).

Considering the Wisevoter (2024) data on gun ownership rates and gun death rates in different countries, in isolation of other factors and considerations, yields several noteworthy observations and inferences. In the United States, there exists the highest gun ownership rate at 120.5 per 100, accompanied by a relatively elevated gun death rate of 4.12 per 100k. This juxtaposition suggests a potential correlation between higher gun ownership and increased gun-related deaths.

In Yemen, a high gun ownership rate of 52.8 per 100 coexists with a relatively low gun death rate of 0.83 per 100k. This scenario implies that factors beyond gun ownership, such as social, economic, or political conditions, may also influence gun-related deaths.

Many European countries, including New Caledonia, Montenegro, Serbia, Finland, Iceland, and Bosnia and Herzegovina, exhibit varying gun ownership rates but generally low gun death rates. This diversity suggests that the relationship between gun ownership and gun deaths can vary significantly across regions.

Canada maintains a moderate gun ownership rate of 34.7 per 100 and a low gun death rate of 0.5 per 100k. This indicates a relatively lower correlation between gun ownership and gun deaths compared to the United States.

Uruguay, with a gun ownership rate similar to Canada, reports a higher gun death rate of 4.02 per 100k. This implies that factors beyond gun ownership contribute to the disparities in gun-related deaths.

In Middle Eastern countries like Lebanon, Iraq, and Kuwait, there are relatively high gun ownership rates, and in some instances, higher gun death rates. The data hints at a more intricate relationship influenced by various socio-political factors.

Several Latin American countries, such as Venezuela, Guatemala, Honduras, and El Salvador, exhibit both high gun ownership rates and high gun death rates, indicating a potential correlation.

Many Asian countries, including Japan and Singapore, maintain low gun ownership rates and low gun death rates, supporting the idea that lower gun ownership is associated with fewer gun-related deaths.

The data for African countries is diverse, with some having low gun ownership rates and low gun death rates, while others report higher rates. Factors such as political stability and socio-economic conditions may play a role in this diversity.

It is crucial to note that while correlations may exist, causation cannot be directly inferred from this data. Other contributing factors, such as gun control policies, socio-economic conditions, and cultural elements, also play pivotal roles in the complex relationship between gun ownership and gun deaths. Additionally, incomplete data for some countries may limit the accuracy of conclusions.

As an example of other relevant and contributing factors, the study "Collateral Crises of Gun Preparation and the COVID-19 Pandemic: Infodemiology Study" by Caputi et al. (2020) aimed to assess the extent to which interest in gun preparation has increased amid the COVID-19 pandemic using data from Google searches related to purchasing and cleaning guns (Caputi et al., 2020). The study focused on the impact of the pandemic on public interest in firearms, particularly in the United States, and utilized infodemiology methods to analyse online search behaviour related to gun acquisition and maintenance.

The findings of the study revealed a significant surge in public interest in gun preparation during the COVID-19 pandemic, as evidenced by increased Google searches for purchasing and cleaning guns. This increase in interest was indicative of a collateral crisis associated with the pandemic, reflecting the concerns and behaviours of the population during this period (Caputi et al., 2020). The study's results shed light on the potential implications of the pandemic on firearm-related activities and the need for further research and public health interventions to address this phenomenon.

Additionally, the study highlighted the importance of infodemiology in understanding societal responses to public health crises such as the COVID-19 pandemic. By leveraging data from online sources, researchers were able to capture and analyse shifts in public interest and behaviour, providing valuable insights into the collateral effects of the pandemic on firearm-related activities (Caputi et al., 2020).

In a related study by Xue et al. (2020), the authors discussed the impact of pandemic-related fear, stigma, and mental health concerns on public trust during subsequent waves or surges of the COVID-19 pandemic. This finding aligns with the collateral crises observed in the study by Caputi et al. (2020), emphasizing the broader societal implications of the pandemic beyond direct health effects.

The motivations for gun ownership are diverse and multifaceted, encompassing various individual beliefs, experiences, and cultural factors. Self-defence is a commonly cited reason for owning guns, with individuals perceiving firearms as a means of personal security and protection (Stroebe et al., 2017). Additionally, engagement in recreational activities, as shown in Figure 10 and Figure 11, such as hunting and sport shooting serves as another prevalent motivation for gun ownership, providing opportunities for skill development and social interaction (Stroebe et al., 2017).

Figure 10: 20 gauge double barrel shotgun shooting. Valerie Hinojosa, CC BY-SA 2.0 <htt ps://creativecommons.org/licenses/by-sa/2.0>, via Wikimedia Commons.

Furthermore, the collection of firearms as a hobby is driven by an appreciation for the historical, mechanical, or aesthetic aspects of guns, contributing to cultural and historical preservation (Stroebe et al., 2017).

Figure 11: Person with Glock 30 at Shooting Range. Noah Wulf, CC BY-SA 4.0 <https://creativecommons.org/licenses/by-sa/4.0>, via Wikimedia Commons.

In certain cultures, gun ownership is deeply rooted in tradition and is perceived as a symbol of individual freedom or heritage, reflecting diverse cultural and traditional motivations for owning firearms (Stroebe et al., 2017). Moreover, owning a gun can be associated with feelings of empowerment, independence, and self-reliance, contributing to the multifaceted nature of motivations for gun ownership (Stroebe et al., 2017).

The occupational motivations for gun ownership are closely tied to the professional responsibilities of individuals working in law enforcement, security, or related fields, highlighting the role of firearms in the professional context (Stroebe et al., 2017). Additionally, concerns about government tyranny and the historical and legal foundations of the right to bear arms contribute to the complex dynamics of motivations for gun ownership (Stroebe et al., 2017). Furthermore, gun ownership is linked to personal identity, values, or lifestyle choices, signifying a sense of belonging to a particular community or subculture, reflecting the intersection of personal identity and gun ownership (Stroebe et al., 2017).

It is crucial to acknowledge the diversity of motivations for gun ownership and the variations in public opinion and cultural attitudes toward firearms across different countries and regions. Understanding the multifaceted nature of motivations for gun ownership is essential for informed policy-making and public discourse on this complex issue (Stroebe et al., 2017).

Recreation and sport are significant aspects of gun ownership, with hunting and sport shooting being prominent activities that enthusiasts engage in. Hunting is a primary recreational purpose for gun ownership, providing individuals with a connection to traditional practices and the outdoors (Diekert et al., 2016). It fosters a connection with nature, wildlife, and the outdoors, and is seen as a way to manage and conserve wildlife populations (Diekert et al., 2016). Responsible and regulated hunting is not only a recreational pastime but also contributes to the sustainable and humane pursuit of game (Diekert et al., 2016). Similarly, sport shooting, including target shooting and competitive shooting events, offers a recreational outlet and builds a sense of camaraderie among participants (Yamane, 2017). These activities emphasize safety, discipline, and adherence to established rules and regulations, contributing to the broader community of shooting enthusiasts (Yamane, 2017).

The reasons for gun ownership are diverse, with self-protection being a commonly cited reason (Barnhorst et al., 2021). However, there is evidence that recreational purposes, such as hunting and sport shooting, play crucial roles in the recreational aspect of gun ownership (Yamane, 2017). A study found that nearly two-thirds of respondents cited recreation as the main reason for owning a firearm, with hunting and sport shooting being the prominent activities (Yamane, 2017). This highlights the significance of recreational activities in shaping individuals' decisions to own guns.

Furthermore, the association between personal ownership of a handgun for protection and self-defence was found to be positively associated with the perceived risk of crime (Stroebe et al., 2017). This suggests that individuals who own guns for self-protection may perceive a higher risk of crime, which could influence their participation in recreational activities such as hunting and sport shooting.

Engaging in target shooting, whether it involves plinking peach cans, perforating paper, shattering clays, or the distinct resonance of bullets striking steel downrange, has become an increasingly popular pastime, and the numbers substantiate this trend (Curcuruto, 2021). Based on the available references, it is evident that a substantial number of individuals participate in recreational shooting activities. Meinke et al. (2017) reported that over 20 million Americans engaged in target shooting-related activities in 2011, confirming regular participation of over 20 million target shooters. This statistic provides a clear indication of the significant participation in recreational shooting within the United States. Furthermore, the study by Temeña et al. (2022) revealed that there is a higher participation rate in recreational activities among female retirees compared to male retirees. This gender-based insight is valuable in understanding the demographic distribution of participants in recreational shooting activities.

Federal data on hunters is primarily derived from the National Survey of Fishing, Hunting, and Wildlife-Associated Recreation, conducted every five years through collaborative efforts by the U.S. Fish and Wildlife Service and the U.S. Census Bureau (RAND Corporation, 2023). As of the 2016 data, approximately 10 million individuals utilized firearms for hunting, with over 50 percent of all hunters engaging in target shooting, and 22 percent visiting shooting ranges (RAND Corporation, 2023). Target shooting also holds popularity as a sport in the United States, with the 2016 survey revealing that 32 million individuals aged six and above participated in firearm target shooting in 2015 (RAND Corporation, 2023).

Curcuruto (2021) reports that in 2020, 56 million Americans participated in target shooting with firearms, marking a substantial 34-percent increase since 2009, as reported by Responsive Management, a survey research firm specializing in attitudes toward natural resource and outdoor recreation issues. Notably, the National Sporting Goods Association asserts that target shooting boasts more participants than soccer, tackle football, and baseball combined.

Numerous factors contribute to the allure of target shooting, including the camaraderie shared with friends and family, skill refinement for enhanced accuracy, preparation for self-protection or home defence, involvement in friendly or professional competitions, and readiness for hunting seasons (Curcuruto, 2021). Target shooting is a versatile activity that appeals to individuals of all ages and skill levels, from novices to seasoned professionals.

Competitive target shooting has a longstanding tradition, dating back to the early days of the Olympics. Shooting was among the original ten Olympic events, with the First Olympiad games in 1896 hosting sixty-one shooters from seven nations (Curcuruto, 2021). Beyond the Olympic stage, target shooting in outdoor clay sports, akin to some Olympic events, has emerged as one of the fastest-growing high school and collegiate sports in the U.S. Organizations like the Scholastic Clay Target Program and USA Clay Target League have experienced a remarkable 25 percent increase in participants, signalling a sustained surge in interest.

The benefits of target shooting extend to conservation efforts, with the firearms and ammunition industry contributing significantly through a 10- to 11-percent excise tax on their products, mandated by the Wildlife Restoration Act of 1937 (Pittman-Robertson). Over the past five years alone, these excise taxes have surpassed $3.5 billion, financing the U.S. Fish and Wildlife Service's Wildlife and Sport Fish Restoration program (Curcuruto, 2021). State wildlife agencies leverage these funds for wildlife management, habitat improvement, research, land acquisition, hunter access, and safety education. Moreover, the excise taxes contribute to the development and maintenance of public shooting ranges (Curcuruto, 2021).

In response to the surge in interest, manufacturers and various groups have taken proactive steps to facilitate the entry of newcomers into target shooting. Since the beginning of 2020, over eight million Americans have become first-time gun owners, with millions expressing a strong interest in making their inaugural gun purchases (Curcuruto, 2021). Recognizing the potential challenges faced by beginners, manufacturers such as Ruger, Smith & Wesson, and Federal Premium, along with organizations like the NRA and IHEA-USA, have disseminated information and instructional videos on firearm safety, regulations, operation, and training through their websites.

Groups like Scouts, 4-H Shooting Sports, and the Izaak Walton League offer introductory courses and leagues, serving as excellent starting points for newcomers. Local shooting ranges and sportsmen's clubs often organize beginner leagues, providing additional options for new gun owners. State and federal wildlife agencies manage over 600 public shooting ranges across the country, making them valuable resources for those seeking guidance.

Research underscores that the most effective way to foster the continued growth of target shooting and make it accessible to all is for experienced shooters to extend invitations to newcomers (Curcuruto, 2021). Therefore, individuals planning a trip to the range are encouraged to invite neighbours, co-workers, or friends, fostering an inclusive environment and enjoying the experience of introducing someone new to the sport.

Moreover, the study by Aksoy et al. (2017) highlighted the positive impact of participating in recreational activities on individuals' quality of life and job satisfaction. This suggests that recreational shooting may contribute to the overall well-being and satisfaction of individuals who engage in this activity. Additionally, the research by Wilson et al. (2022) indicated that participation in organized sports, which may include recreational shooting, is associated with better overall well-being. This further emphasizes the potential positive effects of recreational shooting on individuals' physical and mental well-being.

Number of Guns Owned

The impact of the number of guns an individual owns is influenced by various factors, including the individual's intentions, behaviours, and the context in which the firearms are owned. The purpose of ownership plays a crucial role, as individuals who own multiple guns for recreational activities or as part of a collection may not necessarily pose a higher risk if they handle their firearms responsibly (Bushman et al., 2016). However, the potential for misuse increases with the number of firearms owned, especially if they are not secured properly or if the individual has malicious intentions (Anestis & Houtsma, 2017). Responsible storage and security measures are essential regardless of the number of guns owned, as they can mitigate the risks associated with ownership (Cook & Ludwig, 2006). Additionally, cultural norms and local regulations regarding gun ownership can influence the perception and impact of owning multiple firearms (Anestis & Capron, 2017).

Monitoring and regulation also play a significant role in determining the impact of owning multiple firearms. Stringent background checks and regulations on firearm purchases aim to prevent individuals who pose a risk from acquiring firearms, irrespective of the number they intend to own (Cook & Ludwig, 2004). Furthermore, "red flag" laws have been implemented in some jurisdictions to allow temporary firearm removal from individuals deemed a risk to themselves or others (Rodway et al., 2009).

At the forefront of contentious debates in America stands the issue of gun ownership, uniquely embedded in the country's constitution. Rooted in the historical context of the American Revolution, where an improvised rebel army triumphed over the world's most formidable military force, advocates argue that gun ownership is an integral aspect of American identity (Cheema, 2023). Consequently, the United States boasts the highest number of guns per capita globally, though this statistic can be misleading in gauging actual gun ownership rates among Americans (Cheema, 2023).

The number of guns owned by individuals in the United States is substantial, with estimates indicating that there are approximately 270 million civilian-owned firearms in the country (Yamane, 2017). Between 2015 and 2019, it is estimated that the number of U.S. gun owners increased from 55 to 65 million, and the U.S. firearm stock increased by

60 million guns, from 265 to 326 million (Berrigan et al., 2022). Men are reported to be more likely to own firearms compared to women, with a significantly higher percentage of men stating that they personally owned at least one firearm (Haider & Frank, 2014; Hepburn et al., 2007). Additionally, married men are far more likely to report household gun ownership than married women (Azrael et al., 2000).

A closer examination of gun ownership statistics reveals nuances that challenge conventional perceptions. A Justice Department study from 1997 sheds light on the fact that only 25% of Americans had owned a gun, and a substantial 74% of gun owners possessed more than one firearm. Contrary to intuitive assumptions, the top 20% of gun owners held 55% of all guns, with ten million individuals possessing 105 million guns—an average of ten guns per person (Cheema, 2023). Meanwhile, the remaining 87 million guns were distributed among 34 million people, averaging 2.6 guns per person. In the broader context of the U.S. population in 1994, this indicated that merely 16.7% of Americans owned a firearm (Cheema, 2023).

A prevalent argument in favour of gun ownership emphasizes its role in self-defence against crime and aggression (Cheema, 2023). Proponents contend that banning gun ownership may render ordinary citizens more vulnerable to criminal threats, as criminals could still acquire firearms through illegal channels. The Justice Department's data suggests that 3.1 million individuals might have used guns for defensive purposes, with an estimated total of 23 million incidents. However, refining the criteria for defensive gun use reduces this number to 1.5 million (Cheema, 2023).

Conversely, the study acknowledges that successful defensive gun use can yield inconsistent data when compared to crime statistics. For instance, the data implies that guns enabled potential rape victims to thwart 322 attempts, yet the National Crime Victimization Survey reported 316 total rapes and attempted rapes during the same period (Cheema, 2023). The study introduces scepticism about defensive gun use figures by highlighting factors such as the potential for deterrence, criminals using guns when victims are armed, and the possibility that those reporting gun use may have instigated the situation.

Analysing the broader landscape of crime statistics in the U.S., which recorded around 15 million crimes in 2021, reveals complexities (Cheema, 2023). Nearly half of these were property crimes, including offenses like vandalism, shoplifting, and arson. Assuming that half of these property crimes involved a gun, quantifying the direct impact of gun ownership on total crimes becomes challenging.

Beyond individual ownership, the demand for guns has fuelled a robust industry, with some of the world's largest gun companies headquartered in the U.S. The top three, Vista Outdoor Inc. (NYSE: VSTO), Sportsman's Warehouse Holdings, Inc. (NASDAQ: SPWH), and Smith & Wesson Brands, Inc. (NASDAQ: SWBI), collectively generated approximately $5 billion in revenue in 2021 (Cheema, 2023). The entire industry contributed $51.3 billion to the American economy in 2021. Notable hedge fund gun company stock picks include Axon Enterprise, Inc. (NASDAQ: AXON), DICK'S Sporting Goods, Inc. (NYSE: DKS), and Olin Corporation (NYSE: OLN).

Examining individual companies provides insights into the current state of the industry. Gun companies, like other sectors, have faced challenges such as bloated inventories impacting profitability. For instance, Smith & Wesson Brands, Inc. (NASDAQ: SWBI) experienced a decline in revenue and net income during its fiscal year 2023 due to excess inventory digestion (Cheema, 2023). In contrast, Axon Enterprise, Inc. (NASDAQ: AXON) expanded its global footprint by securing a significant contract to supply tasers to the Maldivian police. Sportsman's Warehouse Holdings, Inc. (NASDAQ: SPWH) faced business challenges, with poor weather and high inflation contributing to a $42 million drop in net sales for the thirteen weeks ending in April, according to its latest earnings report (Cheema, 2023).

To create a comparison between guns per capita and crime rates by country, Cheema (2023) initially utilized data from the Small Arms Survey (SAS) research institute to identify nations with the highest gun ownership per capita. Subsequently, Cheema (2023) collected information on home burglaries worldwide. Ultimately, Cheema (2023) ranked countries common to both datasets based on their guns per capita, presenting burglary statistics per 100,000 for readers to assess and compare. The data from (Cheema, 2023) is tabulated as Table 1 and represented graphically as Figure 12: Number of Guns per Capital Against Number of Home Burglaries Per 100 People derived from Cheema (2023).

Table 1: Burglary statistics per 100,000 against Guns per Capita taken from Cheema (2023).

Rank	Country	Guns Per Capita	Home Burglaries Per 100,000 people
1	United States of America	1.205	527
2	Canada	0.347	429
3	Oriental Republic of Uruguay	0.347	571
4	Republic of Cyprus	0.34	132
5	Iceland	0.317	325
6	Republic of Austria	0.30	119
7	Principality of Liechtenstein	0.288	278
8	Kingdom of Norway	0.288	33
9	Republic of Malta	0.283	197
10	Swiss Confederation	0.276	356
11	New Zealand	0.263	131
12	Kingdom of Sweden	0.231	736
13	Portuguese Republic	0.213	107
14	French Republic	0.196	346
15	Federal Republic of Germany	0.196	105
16	Principality of Monaco	0.196	67
17	Grand Duchy of Luxembourg	0.189	575
18	Commonwealth of The Bahamas	0.188	29
19	Hellenic Republic	0.176	752
20	Republic of Paraguay	0.16	16.7

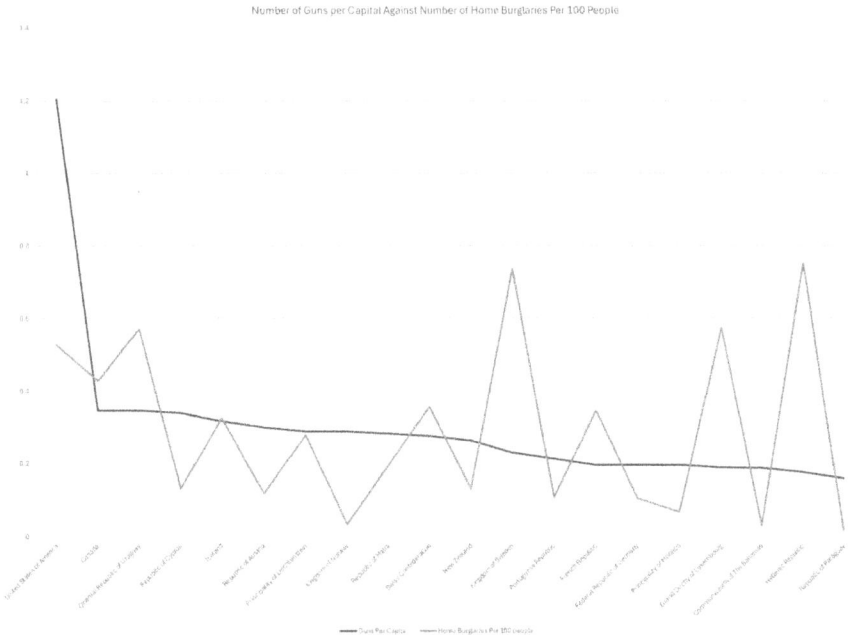

Figure 12: Number of Guns per Capital Against Number of Home Burglaries Per 100 People derived from Cheema (2023).

The comparison of guns per capita and home burglaries in the top 20 countries reveals intriguing variations in the relationship between gun ownership and crime rates.

In the Republic of Paraguay, there is a relatively low crime rate, with approximately 17 guns per capita and only 16.7 burglaries per 100,000 households.

The Hellenic Republic (Greece) presents a contrast with a higher burglary rate of 752 per 100,000 people, despite a guns per capita value of 0.176, indicating a complex impact of gun ownership on crime.

The Commonwealth of The Bahamas exhibits a notably low burglary rate of 29 per 100,000 people and a moderate guns per capita value of 0.188, contributing to its status as a popular financial hub.

Luxembourg, one of the world's most prosperous nations, showcases an interesting dynamic with an approximate guns per capita of 0.189 and a relatively high burglary rate of 575 per 100,000 people.

The Principality of Monaco, despite its small size of two square kilometres, boasts 20 guns per person. However, the burglary rate remains relatively low at 67 incidents per 100,000 people.

In the Federal Republic of Germany, a global economic powerhouse, there are around 20 guns per person, accompanied by a burglary rate of 105 per 100,000 people, highlighting complexities in the relationship between gun ownership and crime.

France, a highly developed nation, maintains nearly 20 guns per capita, while its burglary rate reaches 346 per 100,000 people, showcasing complexities in the interplay between gun ownership and crime.

Portugal demonstrates a balanced scenario with a guns per capita of 0.213 and a burglary rate of 107 per 100,000 people. Mid-level income equality contributes to a $267 billion economy.

Sweden, a prosperous Nordic country, exhibits a contradictory ranking with a high burglary rate of 736 per 100,000 people, coupled with a guns per capita value of 0.231.

New Zealand, an island nation, relies on agriculture and services for economic growth. With 0.263 guns per capita, it experiences a moderate burglary rate of 131 per 100,000 people.

Switzerland, a developed European country with a strong financial system, features 0.276 guns per capita and a burglary rate of 356 per 100,000 people.

The Republic of Malta, with 0.283 guns per capita, demonstrates a relatively low burglary rate of 197 per 100,000 people despite its small size.

Norway, a Nordic European nation with 0.288 guns per capita, maintains a low burglary rate of 33 incidents per 100,000 people, primarily exporting vast amounts of oil.

Despite its small size, Liechtenstein possesses 0.288 guns per capita and experiences a burglary rate of 278 per 100,000 people, contributing to its status as a financial hub.

A landlocked European nation, Austria, displays a balanced scenario with 0.30 guns per capita and a burglary rate of 119 per 100,000 people, contributing to its $479 billion economy.

Iceland, a Nordic European country with 0.317 guns per capita, ranks 12th globally for guns per person. While having a lower burglary rate, it relies primarily on exports of fish and petroleum products.

Cyprus showcases 34 guns per person but ranks low in burglary rates (132 per 100,000 people) with a GDP per capita of $33,807.

Uruguay, a South American country with political stability, exhibits a surprising entry with 0.347 guns per capita and a high burglary rate of 571 per 100,000 people.

Canada maintains ~35 guns per person and a burglary rate of 429 per 100,000 people, emphasizing its high rate of gun ownership.

The United States of America has the highest number of guns per person (1.205) but ranks 13th globally in burglaries, with 527 incidents per 100,000 people.

Responsible Gun Owners Don't Commit Crimes

The statement "responsible gun owners don't commit crimes" is often expressed in discussions around gun ownership. While responsible gun owners are expected to adhere to laws and regulations, it's essential to approach this statement with a nuanced understanding. Responsible gun ownership typically implies individuals who follow legal requirements, practice safe storage, and use firearms in a lawful manner (Azrael et al., 2018). Many gun owners prioritize safety, undergo proper training, and store their firearms securely to prevent unauthorized access (Azrael et al., 2018). These responsible behaviours contribute to the overall goal of minimizing the misuse of firearms (Azrael et al., 2018)).

However, it's important to acknowledge that responsible gun ownership doesn't guarantee immunity from criminal acts. External factors, personal circumstances, mental health issues, or unexpected situations can influence an individual's behaviour, even if they have been responsible gun owners in the past (Webster & Wintemute, 2015). Additionally, accidents or negligence can lead to unintended consequences (Webster & Wintemute, 2015).

The broader conversation around gun control often considers factors such as access to firearms, background checks, mental health evaluations, and the overall regulatory framework (Webster & Wintemute, 2015). Striking a balance between individual rights and public safety is a complex challenge that policymakers aim to address (Webster & Wintemute, 2015).

In summary, while responsible gun ownership is a crucial aspect of firearm safety, it's essential to recognize that no system is foolproof. Society often grapples with finding effective measures to prevent gun-related crimes, considering both the rights of responsible gun owners and the need for public safety.

The attitudes, fears, concerns, and anxieties that influence gun ownership also shape the significance of guns in individuals' lives (Warner & Ratcliff, 2021). Gun ownership is not just about the purchase of a firearm; it encompasses a larger gun culture that maintains distinct and sometimes passionate ideological views of government and individual freedoms (Joslyn & Haider-Markel, 2017). Furthermore, the significance of legal gun ownership to U.S. culture and the political significance of ongoing debates around gun regulation necessitate increased mathematical analysis of gun violence to inform the public (James & Menzies, 2022).

The significance of gun ownership extends beyond mere possession, as it is intertwined with various sociological, psychological, and political factors. For instance, the prevalence of gun ownership has been linked to political identities and voting behaviour in presidential elections, indicating that lack of gun ownership and opposition to guns might be as significant to individual predispositions and judgment as firearm ownership (Joslyn et al., 2017).

The significance of gun ownership also varies across different demographic and regional factors. For example, there is evidence of two partially overlapping subcultures of gun owners, even after controlling for selection into gun-owning household status (Wyant & Taylor, 2007). Additionally, regional differences in gun ownership have been observed, with a higher percentage of individuals in the South reporting owning a gun compared to those in the Northeast (LaPlant et al., 2021).

In the US, the Supreme Court ruled in New York Rifle and Pistol Association v Bruen, affirming the constitutional right of "law-abiding" citizens to publicly carry concealed handguns. However, varying state laws on who is considered "law-abiding" and "responsible" create discrepancies (Berlow, 2023). While many believe concealed carriers should be licensed and trained, 25 states have enacted "constitutional" or "permitless" carry laws, allowing unlicensed individuals to carry loaded firearms in public (Berlow, 2023).

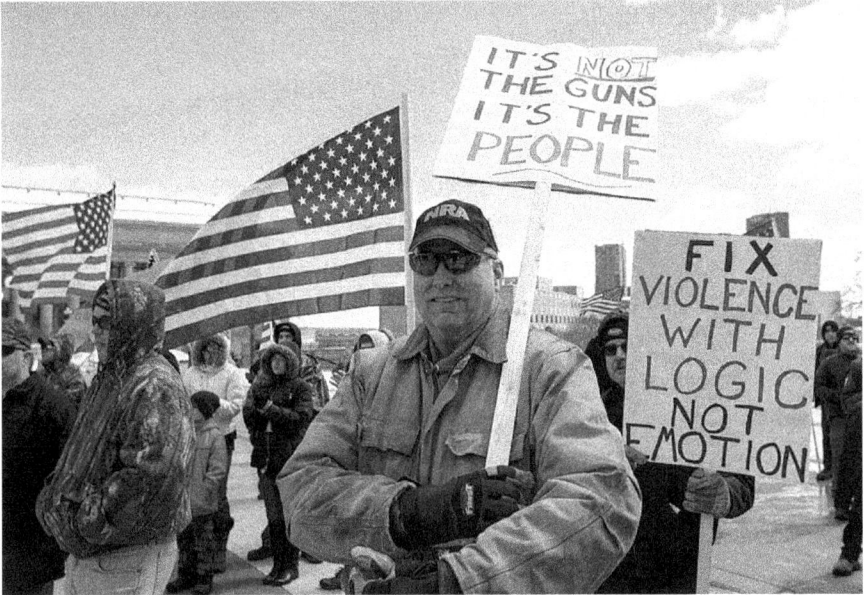

Figure 13: Second Amendment Rally Against Gun Control. About 700 people gathered outside the Minnesota capitol building to denounce all efforts to restrict guns. Speakers called for new laws to protect gun owners like "Stand Your Ground" laws. Fibonacci Blue from Minnesota, USA, CC BY 2.0 <https://creativecommons.org/licenses/by/2.0>, via Wikimedia Commons.

Despite the belief in responsible gun ownership, news of mass murders and gun crimes persists. Thousands of firearms are lost or stolen annually, contributing to crime. Safe storage laws are effective in preventing suicides and accidental injuries, yet half of American firearm owners don't store their guns safely (Berlow, 2023).

Unsecured firearms play a role in unintentional shootings, youth suicides, and averted school shootings (Berlow, 2023). However, only 24 states require secure gun storage. The NRA opposes safe storage mandates and red flag laws designed to temporarily remove guns from potentially dangerous individuals (Berlow, 2023).

While the NRA claims to train millions of "responsible shooters," the quality and effectiveness of the nation's gun training programs remain unclear (Berlow, 2023). Only 60% of gun owners report having formal training, leaving millions potentially untrained. Claims of defensive gun use (DGU) numbers, often touted by the NRA, are contested, with studies showing inconsistencies and lack of reliable data (Berlow, 2023).

Stand-your-ground (SYG) laws, championed by the NRA, have resulted in increased firearm-related homicides and racial bias in adjudication (Berlow, 2023). Despite historical opposition to promiscuous gun carrying, the NRA's influence has expanded concealed carry laws, permitless carry, and SYG laws nationwide.

Stand-your-ground laws, also known as line-in-the-sand or no-duty-to-retreat laws, are legal statutes that bestow upon individuals the right to use force, including deadly force, for self-defence in certain situations without a duty to retreat. Unlike traditional self-defence laws that mandated individuals to retreat from a threat if it was safe to do so before resorting to force, stand-your-ground laws eliminate this duty to retreat. This legal framework empowers individuals to hold their ground and use force, potentially lethal force, if they believe it is necessary to protect themselves or others from imminent harm.

These laws typically encompass key features, such as the absence of a duty to retreat. In traditional self-defence scenarios, individuals were obligated to attempt an escape or avoid a confrontation before resorting to the use of force. Stand-your-ground laws discard this obligation, allowing individuals to confront a threat without the requirement to retreat. The laws also often emphasize the perceived threat to the individual, indicating that if a person reasonably believes they are in danger, they may use force without first attempting to retreat. This shift places importance on the subjective perception of threat, giving individuals greater latitude in determining when to use force in self-defence.

It is crucial to recognize that the specifics of stand-your-ground laws can vary significantly between jurisdictions. The interpretation and application of these laws may differ, contributing to ongoing debates and controversies surrounding their implementation. Proponents argue that these laws empower individuals to protect themselves, emphasizing personal autonomy in self-defence situations. Conversely, critics express concerns about potential misuse of the laws and an associated risk of increased violence. The impact of stand-your-ground laws on public safety and self-defence cases remains a subject of discussion and ongoing research.

The impact of the Bruen ruling on gun violence remains uncertain, but more people are likely to carry guns publicly (Berlow, 2023). In states affected by the decision, a surge in concealed carry permit applications has been observed. The decision may weaken the government's ability to keep guns from potentially irresponsible individuals, marking a significant victory for the NRA, gun manufacturers, and dealers. However, concerns arise about the broader implications for public safety (Berlow, 2023).

Still considering US, an analysis by the University of Pittsburgh reveals that lawful gun owners are responsible for less than a fifth of all gun crimes (Ingraham, 2016). Led by epidemiologist Anthony Fabio, the study focused on 893 firearms recovered from crime scenes in 2008. The findings indicate that in 8 out of 10 cases, the perpetrator was an illegal gun owner, not the lawful owner, raising concerns about how guns transition from legal purchases to crime scenes (Ingraham, 2016).

Over 30% of guns found at crime scenes were stolen, but more than 40% of these stolen guns were only reported as such after being used in crimes (Ingraham, 2016). A worrisome aspect is that for 62% of the recovered guns, the location where the owner lost possession was unknown. Factors contributing to legal firearms entering the black market include theft, carelessness, or determination by thieves. Straw purchases, where someone buys a gun for another person without disclosure, may also play a role (Ingraham, 2016).

While the study supports the argument of gun rights advocates that criminals, not lawful gun owners, are responsible for the majority of gun crimes, it suggests a need to reconsider the dichotomy between "good guys" and "bad guys". The research proposes non-burdensome measures, such as reporting stolen or lost firearms, to prevent legally acquired guns from reaching the wrong hands (Ingraham, 2016).

Previous research indicates that a small fraction of gun dealers contributes to a majority of crime guns. However, a law passed in 2003 prevents sharing information about these dealers with policymakers or researchers, hindering efforts to address the flow of guns from specific dealers to crime scenes (Ingraham, 2016).

United States Gun Ownership Landscape

Laws, Ownership and Use of Firearms in the United States

The foundation of gun ownership in the United States lies in the Second Amendment of the Constitution, which states: "A well-regulated Militia, being necessary to the security of a free State, the right of the people to keep and bear Arms, shall not be infringed" (Masters, 2022).

Firearms hold a significant place in both American society and the country's political discourse. The Second Amendment of the United States Constitution ensures the right to bear arms, with approximately one-third of U.S. adults expressing personal ownership of guns. Concurrently, amidst apprehensions surrounding increasing rates of gun-related fatalities and mass shootings, President Joe Biden has introduced legislation on gun policy. This proposed legislation aims to build upon the bipartisan gun safety bill passed by Congress the previous year (Schaeffer, 2023).

Despite having less than 5 percent of the world's population, the United States possesses 46 percent of the world's civilian-owned guns, making it the leader in firearms per capita, as per the Small Arms Survey (2018). It also holds the highest homicide-by-firearm rate among developed nations. While many gun rights advocates argue that these statistics don't establish a causal relationship, the right to bear arms is not absolute (Masters, 2022).

Congress and state legislatures have the authority to enact controlling legislation, and the U.S. Supreme Court has upheld some firearms restrictions. The Gun Control Act of 1968 imposes restrictions on firearm purchases for individuals under eighteen, convicted criminals, the mentally disabled, and others (Masters, 2022). The Brady Handgun Violence Prevention Act in 1993 mandated background checks for unlicensed individuals buying firearms from federally authorized dealers.

However, some gun laws have faced challenges in the courts. In 2008, the Supreme Court overturned a Washington, DC, law banning handguns, marking the court's first Second Amendment ruling in nearly seventy years (Masters, 2022). While federal law sets the foundation for firearms regulation, states and cities can impose additional restrictions. Studies suggest that states with stricter gun laws, like California or Hawaii, experience fewer gun deaths, though researchers call for further analysis (Masters, 2022).

Despite numerous high-profile mass shootings prompting debates in Congress, legislative efforts have consistently fallen short. Proposed measures, such as an assault weapons ban, expanded background checks, and prohibiting firearm sales to those on federal terrorism watch lists, have faced insufficient support (Masters, 2022).

As of mid-2022, there were no federal laws banning semiautomatic assault weapons, military-style .50 calibre rifles, handguns, or large-capacity magazines (Masters, 2022). Additionally, there was no federal requirement for firearm safety training during gun purchases (Masters, 2022). The federal ban on assault weapons and large-capacity magazines from 1994 to 2004 lapsed as Congress allowed the restrictions to expire.

Gun violence has risen during the COVID-19 pandemic, with approximately nineteen thousand deaths in the U.S. by June 2022, the majority being suicides (Masters, 2022). Mass shootings, defined as those with at least four victims, occurred at a rate of at least one per day.

According to Schaeffer (2023), approximately four in ten U.S. adults indicate residing in households with firearms, with 32% asserting personal ownership of a gun. These figures reveal minimal change since the same inquiry was posed in 2021.

Divergences in gun ownership rates emerge when considering various demographic factors such as political affiliation, gender, and community type. In terms of political allegiance, Republicans and those leaning towards the Republican Party are more than twice as likely as their Democratic counterparts to declare personal gun ownership, with rates at 45% and 20%, respectively. Gender-based disparities are evident, with 40% of men reporting gun ownership compared to 25% of women (Schaeffer, 2023).

Residential location also plays a role, as 47% of individuals residing in rural areas state personal firearm ownership. In contrast, smaller proportions of gun ownership are reported in suburban (30%) and urban (20%) settings. Ethnic and racial differences further contribute to the varied landscape of gun ownership, with 38% of White Americans asserting ownership compared to lesser percentages among Black (24%), Hispanic (20%), and Asian (10%) Americans (Schaeffer, 2023).

Foremost among the motivations cited by gun owners for possessing firearms is personal protection. A significant majority, comprising 72% of gun owners, identifies protection as a major reason for gun ownership. In contrast, lesser proportions attribute their ownership to other factors, with 32% citing hunting, 30% sport shooting, 15% inclusion in a gun collection, and 7% job-related purposes (Schaeffer, 2023).

The landscape of reasons for gun ownership has witnessed only modest changes since our examination of attitudes towards gun ownership and policies in 2017. Back then, 67% of gun owners considered protection a major reason for owning a firearm (Schaeffer, 2023).

Gun owners express notably more positive sentiments regarding the presence of firearms in their households compared to non-owners residing with them. To illustrate, 71% of gun owners express enjoyment in owning a gun, whereas a substantially smaller percentage of non-gun owners within gun-owning households (31%) share this sentiment (Schaeffer, 2023). Furthermore, while 81% of gun owners associate gun ownership with an increased sense of safety, a narrower majority (57%) of non-owners in gun-owning households concur with this perception. Non-owners, in contrast, exhibit a greater propensity to harbor concerns about the presence of a gun at home (27% compared to 12% among owners).

The attitudes towards gun ownership also display variations based on political affiliation, even within the subset of individuals who personally own firearms. Republican gun owners are more inclined than their Democratic counterparts to report feelings of safety and enjoyment associated with gun ownership. Conversely, Democratic gun owners are more likely to express worries about having a firearm in their homes (Schaeffer, 2023).

Non-gun owners hold divergent perspectives on the possibility of owning a firearm in the future. Approximately half (52%) of Americans without firearms presently express an inability to envision themselves owning one, while an almost equal proportion (47%) can envision becoming gun owners at some point (Schaeffer, 2023).

When examining individuals who currently do not own a gun, distinct patterns emerge. Among this group, 56% of men express openness to owning a firearm in the future, while 40% of women share this inclination (Schaeffer, 2023). Moreover, when delving into political affiliations, 61% of Republicans and 40% of Democrats, who presently lack firearm ownership, contemplate the prospect of becoming gun owners. In the realm of racial and ethnic considerations among non-owners, 56% of Black individuals envision themselves owning a gun eventually, a figure that contrasts with smaller percentages observed among White (48%), Hispanic (40%), and Asian (38%) non-owners who harbor similar inclinations (Schaeffer, 2023).

Americans hold divided opinions on the impact of gun ownership on safety, with approximately half (49%) believing that it enhances safety by empowering law-abiding citizens to protect themselves (Schaeffer, 2023). Conversely, an equal share contends that gun ownership diminishes safety by providing widespread access to firearms, contributing to increased misuse. A bar chart illustrates the stark disparities in perspectives regarding whether gun ownership amplifies or diminishes safety in the United States.

Political affiliations significantly shape these views, revealing a pronounced contrast between Republicans and Democrats. While a substantial 79% of Republicans assert that gun ownership increases safety, an almost identical 78% of Democrats argue that it reduces safety (Schaeffer, 2023).

Geographic disparities further influence opinions, particularly between urban and rural Americans. Within urban areas, 64% believe gun ownership diminishes safety, with only 34% asserting its role in increasing safety. Conversely, in rural areas, a significant majority (65%) contends that gun ownership heightens safety, while 33% believe it diminishes safety. Suburban residents, however, exhibit a more evenly divided stance on this issue (Schaeffer, 2023).

An escalating number of Americans express growing concern about the magnitude of gun violence. Currently, six-in-ten U.S. adults assert that gun violence is a very significant problem in the country, marking a notable increase of 9 percentage points from the findings in spring 2022 (Schaeffer, 2023). The June survey reveals that 23% perceive gun violence as a moderately substantial problem, with approximately two-in-ten stating it is either a small problem (13%) or not a problem at all (4%) (Schaeffer, 2023).

Looking towards the future, a substantial 62% of Americans anticipate a rise in the level of gun violence over the next five years. This figure is twice the percentage of those expecting the situation to remain unchanged (31%). A mere 7% anticipate a decrease in the level of gun violence (Schaeffer, 2023).

The prevailing sentiment among a majority of Americans (61%) is that the legal acquisition of a gun in the country is excessively facile. Contrarily, 30% believe that the current ease of legally obtaining a gun is appropriate, while a minor 9% perceive it as too difficult. Notably, non-gun owners express a viewpoint nearly twice as often as gun owners, with 73% of non-owners asserting that it is too easy, compared to 38% of gun owners (Schaeffer, 2023). Conversely, gun owners are more than twice as likely as non-owners to believe the current ease of obtaining a gun is appropriate, with figures at 48% and 20%, respectively (Schaeffer, 2023).

Moreover, partisan and demographic disparities are evident on this matter. A striking 86% of Democrats contend that the legal acquisition of a gun is too easy, in stark contrast to 34% of Republicans expressing the same sentiment. Geographically, a significant majority of urban (72%) and suburban (63%) residents perceive it as too easy, while rural residents exhibit a more divided stance, with 47% asserting it is too easy, 41% claiming it is about right, and 11% deeming it too difficult (Schaeffer, 2023).

Approximately six-in-ten U.S. adults, constituting 58%, express support for more stringent gun laws. An additional 26% contend that the existing gun laws in the United States are appropriately balanced, while 15% advocate for less restrictive gun laws. The percentage of individuals advocating for stricter gun laws has exhibited some variability in recent years. In 2021, 53% endorsed the idea of more stringent gun laws, while in 2019, the figure stood at 60% (Schaeffer, 2023).

In a survey conducted in fall 2022, approximately one-third (32%) of parents with children in K-12 education express significant concern, rating themselves as very or extremely worried about the possibility of a shooting occurring at their children's school (Schaeffer, 2023). Conversely, an equivalent proportion of K-12 parents (31%) indicate low levels of worry, describing themselves as not too or not at all concerned about such an incident, while 37% fall in the middle, expressing a moderate level of worry (Schaeffer, 2023).

Broadening the scope to include all parents with children under 18, encompassing those not currently in school, 63% identify enhancing mental health screening and treatment as a very or extremely effective means of preventing school shootings. This percentage surpasses those who hold similar views about having police officers or armed security in schools (49%), advocating for a ban on assault-style weapons (45%), or implementing metal detectors in schools (41%). In contrast, a mere 24% of parents believe that allowing teachers and school administrators to carry guns in schools would be a very or extremely effective strategy, with half expressing scepticism, deeming it not too or not at all effective (Schaeffer, 2023).

The June 2023 survey reveals that, despite some bipartisan agreement on certain gun policy measures, the majority are sources of political division (Schaeffer, 2023). A noteworthy consensus emerges on two proposals aimed at restricting gun access, with substantial support from both Republicans and Democrats. Specifically, preventing individuals with mental illnesses from purchasing guns garners support from 88% of Republicans and 89% of Democrats, while increasing the minimum age for gun purchases to 21 years receives backing from 69% of Republicans and an even higher 90% of Democrats (Schaeffer, 2023). Additionally, majorities in both parties unite in opposing the allowance of concealed firearms without a permit, with 60% of Republicans and an overwhelming 91% of Democrats expressing opposition.

However, partisan distinctions become evident on other proposals. Democrats, at an 85% majority, favour the prohibition of assault-style weapons and high-capacity ammunition magazines holding more than 10 rounds, while majorities of Republicans (57% and 54%, respectively) oppose these measures.

Conversely, a substantial majority of Republicans support empowering teachers and school officials to carry guns in K-12 schools (74%) and allowing concealed guns in more locations (71%). In contrast, only 27% and 19% of Democrats, respectively, endorse these proposals, revealing significant disparities between the two parties on these issues (Schaeffer, 2023).

Gun ownership aligns closely with perspectives on gun policies. Individuals who possess guns are generally less inclined than non-owners to endorse restrictions on gun ownership, except for a notable exception. Strikingly similar majorities of both gun owners (87%) and non-owners (89%) express support for preventing individuals with mental illness from purchasing guns (Schaeffer, 2023).

Figure 14: Indoor Shooting Range at Sarasota, Florida, USA. Ratha Grimes from Sarasota, FL, United States, CC BY 2.0 <https://creativecommons.org/licenses/by/2.0>, via Wikimedia Commons.

The Second Amendment

The Second Amendment of the United States Constitution has been a subject of ongoing debate, with advocates arguing for the individual's right to own firearms and opponents arguing for the collective right of states to maintain militias (Lee et al., 2017). Scholars have pointed to the legal legacy of the Second Amendment and the American federalist structure that favours gun rights over gun control initiatives, contributing to the exceptional gun culture in the USA (Carlson, 2013). This debate has led to discussions around gun control, with some advocating for the removal of guns from citizens as a solution to violent crime, contrary to the Second Amendment (Ausman & Faria, 2019). Additionally, the interpretation of the right to "keep and bear arms" in the Second Amendment has been influenced by religious language, transforming it into an article of faith in religious nationalism (Dawson, 2019). The ambiguity of the Second Amendment has led to different interpretations of gun rights, making it controversial in American society (Li & Zeng, 2021).

The Second Amendment of the United States Constitution, integrated into the Bill of Rights, stands as a pivotal element in American legal and cultural history. This constitutional provision commences by underscoring the imperative of a well-regulated militia. Rooted in the historical context of the late 18th century, during the drafting and ratification of the U.S. Constitution, the concept of a militia held central importance in the framework of national defence. These militias comprised citizen-soldiers summoned to safeguard the community or the nation.

The articulated purpose of the well-regulated militia is grounded in the necessity for the security of a free state. Reflecting the Founding Fathers' apprehension regarding potential threats to the fledgling nation, they believed that a militia composed of citizens played a crucial role in preserving freedom and fortifying defences against both internal and external threats.

The subsequent segment of the amendment constitutes the core of the Second Amendment. It affirms the right of the people to keep and bear arms, sparking substantial legal and societal debate. This declaration establishes an individual's entitlement to possess and carry firearms.

Concluding with unequivocal language, the amendment asserts that this right "shall not be infringed." Such phrasing accentuates the framers' intention to shield the individual's right to own and carry firearms from undue interference by the government.

The Second Amendment has been a focal point of extensive legal interpretation and debate. A primary area of contention revolves around the connection between the right to bear arms and the well-regulated militia referenced in the amendment. Advocates of an individual's right to bear arms contend that it is an independent right unrelated to militia service. Conversely, critics argue that the amendment primarily addresses the collective right of citizens to participate in a militia and does not prohibit reasonable regulations on firearms ownership.

Over the years, legal rulings, exemplified by the landmark case District of Columbia v. Heller (2008), have affirmed an individual's right to possess firearms for self-defence while permitting certain regulations. The interpretation and application of the Second Amendment persist as subjects of ongoing legal, political, and social deliberations in the United States.

The interpretation of the Second Amendment has implications for public health policy and practice, particularly in relation to firearm violence (Teitelbaum & Spector, 2009). Research has also explored the impact of state firearm laws on homicide rates in different areas, highlighting the need for evidence-based solutions to firearm deaths, especially among youths in the United States (Ranney et al., 2020; Siegel, Solomon, et al., 2019). Additionally, historical analysis has shed light on the ideological origins of the Second Amendment, providing insights into its historical context and development (Shalhope, 1982).

Federal Regulation

In the United States, firearm regulation is a complex issue, with federal laws playing a significant role. The National Firearms Act (NFA) of 1934 and the Gun Control Act of 1968 are two key federal regulations that impose taxes, registration requirements, and licensing of firearm dealers, as well as prohibit certain individuals from owning firearms and require background checks for gun purchases (Mann & Michel, 2016). Additionally, state laws play a crucial role in regulating firearm use, such as laws restricting the intersection of firearms and alcohol, disarming intimate partner violence offenders, and implementing firearm restriction, background checks, and licensing laws to reduce gun violence (Cloud et al., 2022; Galea & Abdalla, 2022; Zeoli et al., 2022).

The effectiveness of these laws in reducing firearm-related mortality and morbidity has been a subject of research. Studies have shown that broadly reducing availability and access to firearms has lowered firearm suicide rates in other countries, but it may not be feasible in the United States (Mann & Michel, 2016). Furthermore, the implementation of state laws, such as disarming intimate partner violence offenders, has been analysed to understand their impact on reducing intimate partner homicide (Cloud et al., 2022). Additionally, the association between state firearm laws and reductions in intimate partner homicide has been studied, indicating the potential effectiveness of firearm restriction laws in reducing gun violence (Zeoli et al., 2022).

The federal gun laws in the United States have evolved over time to address various aspects of firearm regulation. The National Firearms Act (NFA) of 1934 governs the taxation, registration, and transfer of Title II weapons, including machine guns, short-barrelled rifles and shotguns, and other specific categories of firearms (Fontanarosa

& Bibbins-Domingo, 2022). Subsequent acts such as the Gun Control Act of 1968 (GCA) and the Firearm Owners Protection Act (FOPA) have further regulated interstate commerce in firearms and amended provisions related to civilian sale of automatic firearms (Schildkraut & Geller, 2022). Additionally, historical context and legal debates about gun rights and regulation have played a prominent role in shaping federal gun laws (Blocher et al., 2023).

The major federal gun laws in the United States are delineated within various acts:

- National Firearms Act (NFA) (1934): Governing the taxation, registration, and transfer of Title II weapons, this act includes machine guns, short-barrelled rifles and shotguns, explosive ordnance, heavy weapons, suppressors, and disguised or improvised firearms.

- Federal Firearms Act of 1938 (FFA): This mandates a Federal Firearms License (FFL) for gun manufacturers, importers, and sellers, while prohibiting firearm transfers to specific groups, such as convicted felons.

- Omnibus Crime Control and Safe Streets Act of 1968 (1968): Prohibiting interstate trade in handguns, this act raises the minimum age for purchasing handguns to 21.

- Gun Control Act of 1968 (GCA): Primarily focused on regulating interstate commerce in firearms, it restricts interstate transfers unless among licensed manufacturers, dealers, and importers.

- Firearm Owners Protection Act (FOPA) (1986): Amending and partially repealing the Gun Control Act of 1968, this act bars the civilian sale of automatic firearms produced post-enactment and requires ATF approval for their transfers.

- Undetectable Firearms Act (1988): Criminalizing the production, importation, sale, possession, and transfer of firearms with less than 3.7 oz of metal content, this act includes few exceptions.

- Gun-Free School Zones Act (1990): Forbidding unauthorized individuals from possessing firearms in known school zones.

- Brady Handgun Violence Prevention Act (1993): Mandating background checks for most firearm purchasers, contingent on seller and venue.

- Federal Assault Weapons Ban (1994–2004): Prohibiting certain semiautomatics and large-capacity ammunition feeding devices, this ban lapsed in 2004.

- Law Enforcement Officers Safety Act (2004): Granting law enforcement officers and former officers the right to carry concealed firearms nationwide, with exceptions.

- Protection of Lawful Commerce in Arms Act (2005): Shielding firearms manufacturers and licensed dealers from liability for negligence in cases involving crimes committed with their products.

- Bipartisan Safer Communities Act (2022): This act expands background checks, includes juvenile records for purchasers under 21, requires more sellers to have an FFL, allocates funds for state crisis intervention programs, intensifies penalties for arms trafficking and straw purchases, and addresses the "boyfriend loophole."

The current regulatory landscape includes various prohibitions barring fugitives, felons with sentences exceeding one year, and those involuntarily admitted to mental facilities from purchasing firearms, unless their rights are restored. Among the states, forty-four have constitutional provisions akin to the Second Amendment, safeguarding the right to bear arms. Notable exceptions include California, Iowa, Maryland, Minnesota, New Jersey, and New York. Despite New York's lack of constitutional protection, its civil rights laws contain a provision closely resembling the Second Amendment. The U.S. Supreme Court, in McDonald v. Chicago (2010), affirmed the application of Second Amendment protections against state governments. In New York State Rifle & Pistol Association, Inc. v. Bruen, the Supreme Court ruled against imposing "proper cause" or "special need" requirements for concealed carry licenses.

The Gun Control Act of 1968 imposes restrictions on various classes of individuals related to firearms or ammunition, such as buying, selling, using, owning, receiving, shipping, carrying, possessing, or exchanging (Wallin et al., 2021). The prohibitions outlined in the act apply to individuals who have been convicted in any court of a "crime punishable by imprisonment for a term exceeding one year," those who are fugitives from justice, and individuals deemed unlawful users of or addicted to any controlled substance, as defined by the Controlled Substances Act (Wallin et al., 2021). Furthermore, the act extends restrictions to individuals who have been adjudicated as mentally defective or involuntarily committed to any mental institution, illegal aliens unlawfully present in the United States, and those who have been lawfully admitted as aliens under a non-immigrant visa without exemption under 18 U.S.C. § 922(y)(2) (Wallin et al., 2021). Discharged Armed Forces members under dishonourable conditions, individuals who renounce their United States nationality, and those subject to court orders restraining them from harassing, stalking, or threatening an intimate partner or the child of an intimate partner are also subject to these prohibitions (Wallin et al., 2021). Additionally, individuals convicted of a misdemeanour crime of domestic violence fall within the scope of these restrictions (Wallin et al., 2021).

The specific categories outlined in the ATF Form 4473 – Firearms Transaction Record background check form serve as the basis for assessing an individual's eligibility for firearm-related activities (Wallin et al., 2021). According to the US Sentencing Commission, an estimated 5,000 to 6,000 individuals falling into these prohibited categories are convicted annually for unlawfully receiving or possessing a firearm (Wallin et al., 2021). In 2017 alone, more than 25.2 million background checks were conducted as part of the regulatory process (Wallin et al., 2021).

The federal misdemeanour crime of domestic violence firearm restriction has been associated with reductions in firearm intimate partner homicide (IPH) rates (Elizabeth Richardson Vigdor & James A. Mercy, 2006). However, state-level firearm restriction laws targeting misdemeanour crimes of domestic violence have not been significantly associated with either IPH or firearm-related IPH (Wallin et al., 2021). This suggests that the effectiveness of firearm restriction laws may vary between federal and state levels, and further research is needed to understand the impact of these laws across different jurisdictions.

In addition to firearm restrictions, the misuse of firearms is necessary to the occurrence of firearm violence, but there are other contributing factors beyond simply firearms themselves that might also be modified to prevent firearm violence (Branas et al., 2016). This highlights the complexity of addressing firearm violence and the need for comprehensive approaches that consider multiple contributing factors.

Restrictive firearm legislation has been shown to reduce firearm suicides as well as homicides in cross-sectional and longitudinal studies (Kapusta et al., 2007). This indicates that firearm legislation can have a significant impact on reducing firearm-related deaths, supporting the importance of implementing and enforcing effective firearm laws.

Laws restricting access to firearms by domestic violence offenders have been found to prevent intimate partner homicide by restricting access to firearms for individuals subject to restraining orders or convicted of domestic violence misdemeanours (Elizabeth Richardson Vigdor & James A. Mercy, 2006). This underscores the potential of targeted firearm laws in preventing specific types of firearm-related violence.

State Laws

The firearm laws in the United States vary significantly from state to state, resulting in a "patchwork" of regulations (LaPlant et al., 2021). States like California and New York have implemented more restrictive laws, including limitations on magazine capacities, assault weapons bans, and stringent background check requirements, while states like Texas and Florida have more permissive laws (LaPlant et al., 2021).

Research has shown that the expansion of civilian rights to use deadly force in self-defence has had effects on violence and crime, emphasizing the importance of understanding the implications of firearm laws (Yakubovich et al., 2021). Additionally, the enactment of specific laws, such as "Stand Your Ground" self-defence laws, has been associated with changes in unlawful homicides, indicating the potential impact of state laws on firearm-related outcomes (Humphreys et al., 2017).

The patchwork of federal, state, and local regulations has been identified as fertile ground for a thriving national underground firearm market, which supplies most firearms used in interpersonal crimes (Glasser et al., 2022). Additionally, firearm-related morbidity and mortality are concentrated in places with prevalent firearm ownership and less restrictive firearm laws, underscoring the potential for state laws to serve as a layer of protection against firearm-related injuries and deaths (Cloud et al., 2022).

Understanding the complexities of state firearm laws requires consideration of the perspectives of key stakeholders, such as law enforcement officials. Research has explored the perceptions of Texas sheriffs on firearm regulations and mass shootings, providing insights into the practical implications of state firearm laws from the perspective of law enforcement (Meitl et al., 2021). Moreover, the broader socio-political context, including state capacity, political values and culture, temporal political incentives, federalism, and the role of courts, has been highlighted as influential factors in shaping state firearm policies (Silver, 2020).

The gun vary significantly across states, encompassing permit requirements, concealed carry regulations, open carry rules, assault weapons and magazine restrictions, background checks, waiting periods, registration, Stand Your Ground/Castle Doctrine, NFA items, preemption, red flag laws, ammunition restrictions, purchase limits, duty to inform, age restrictions, and peaceable journey laws. These variations necessitate a comprehensive understanding of the specific laws in each state to ensure compliance (D. Webster et al., 2020).

State gun laws have been found to have a substantial impact on firearm mortality rates. For instance, the requirement for background checks on firearm purchases has been associated with a lower homicide rate, emphasizing the potential effectiveness of certain regulations in reducing firearm-related deaths (Kalesan et al., 2016). Additionally, the presence of certain firearm laws in one state has been linked to firearm-related deaths in neighbouring states, highlighting the interconnectedness of state laws and their impact on firearm-related outcomes (Liu et al., 2022).

Moreover, the regulation of assault weapons and high-capacity semiautomatic firearms has been a subject of study, with research investigating the criminal use of such firearms. This includes examining guns recovered by police, guns used in murders of police, and guns used in mass murders, shedding light on the prevalence of criminal activity involving these types of firearms (Koper et al., 2017).

Furthermore, the implementation of red flag laws, which allow for the temporary removal of firearms from individuals deemed a risk to themselves or others, varies across states. This highlights the importance of understanding the presence or absence of such laws in different jurisdictions to address potential risks associated with firearm possession (D. Webster et al., 2020).

The impact of state gun laws on specific outcomes, such as firearm homicides, has been a focus of research. For instance, the mitigating effect of low firearm background check requirements on firearm homicides in border states has been explored, emphasizing the potential influence of varying laws on firearm-related incidents (Ashworth & Kozinetz, 2021).

Figure 15 shows the different approaches and regulations regarding the open carrying of firearms in various jurisdictions. Permissive open carrying denotes a legal environment where individuals can openly carry firearms in public without the need for a specific permit or license. In areas with permissive open carrying laws, individuals enjoy the freedom to openly carry firearms without additional legal requirements beyond general firearm ownership regulations.

In jurisdictions with permissive open carrying but local restrictions, individuals are generally allowed to open carry. However, certain cities or counties may impose additional limitations or regulations. While open carrying is generally permitted, individuals must be aware of and adhere to specific restrictions imposed at the local level.

Licensed open carrying refers to a legal framework where individuals must obtain a specific permit or license to openly carry a firearm in public. In areas with licensed open carrying regulations, individuals are required to go through a formal application process, meet certain criteria, and obtain a permit before openly carrying a firearm.

Anomalous situations may refer to unique or unusual circumstances related to open carrying that do not fit neatly into conventional categories. Anomalous conditions could result from specific legal nuances, exceptions, or temporary conditions that deviate from standard permissive or non-permissive open carrying regulations.

Non-permissive open carrying refers to jurisdictions where open carrying of firearms is generally prohibited or subject to severe restrictions. In areas with non-permissive open carrying laws, individuals may face legal consequences or restrictions if they openly carry firearms without meeting specific criteria, such as having a concealed carry permit.

It is important to note that these terms represent general categories, and the specific regulations may vary widely between different states, countries, or local jurisdictions. Individuals must be aware of and comply with the relevant laws in their specific location.

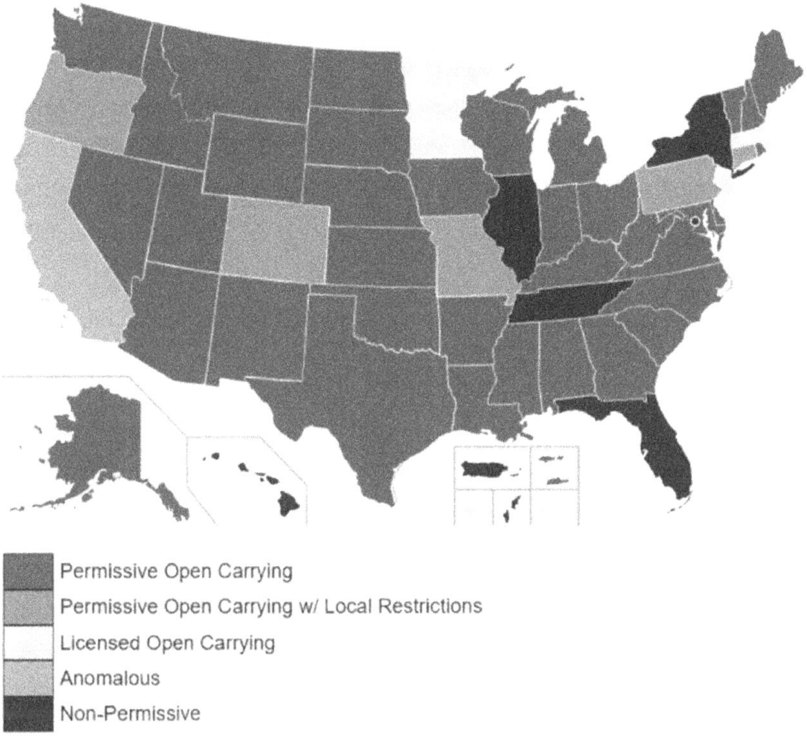

Figure 15: Open Carrying US long guns. Borysk5, CC BY-SA 4.0 <https://creativecommo ns.org/licenses/by-sa/4.0>, via Wikimedia Commons.

The following provides an example of the state-by-state variation:

- Alabama: No state permit is required for the purchase of long guns or handguns, and there is no firearm registration, assault weapon law, or magazine capacity restriction. An owner license is not required. While a permit is needed for concealed carry, Alabama operates as a "shall issue" state for citizens and lawful permanent residents aged 19 or older. Permitless concealed carry became effective on January 1, 2023. Open carry is allowed without a permit, with the condition that handguns must be secured in a holster. The Castle Doctrine/Stand Your Ground law is in place, and the state preempts local restrictions on firearms. There are no restrictions on NFA weapons, no peaceable journey laws, and no background checks required for private sales.

- Alaska: No state permit is required for the purchase of long guns or handguns, and there is no firearm registration, assault weapon law, or magazine capacity restriction. An owner license is not required. A permit is necessary for concealed carry, but Alaska operates as a "shall issue" state for citizens and lawful permanent residents aged 21 or older. Permitless carry took effect on September 9, 2003. Open carry is allowed without a permit. The Castle Doctrine/Stand Your Ground law is in place, and the state pre-empts local restrictions on firearms. There are no restrictions on NFA weapons. Certification for concealed carry must be done within 30 days. There are no peaceable journey laws, and no background checks are required for private sales. A duty to inform law is in place.

- Arizona: No state permit is required for the purchase of long guns or handguns, and there is no firearm registration, assault weapon law, or magazine capacity restriction. An owner license is not required. A permit is needed for concealed carry, but Arizona operates as a "shall issue" state for citizens and lawful permanent residents aged 21 or older. Permitless carry took effect on July 29, 2010. Open carry is allowed without a permit. The Castle Doctrine/Stand Your Ground law is in place, and the state pre-empts local restrictions on firearms. There are no restrictions on NFA weapons. Certification for concealed carry must be done within 60 days. There are no peaceable journey laws, and no background checks are required for private sales.

- Arkansas: No state permit is required for the purchase of long guns or handguns, and there is no firearm registration, assault weapon law, or magazine capacity restriction. An owner license is not required. A permit is needed for concealed carry, but Arkansas operates as a "shall issue" state for citizens and lawful permanent residents aged 21 or older. Permitless carry took effect on August 16, 2013. Open carry is allowed without a permit. The Castle Doctrine/Stand Your Ground law is in place, and the state pre-empts local restrictions on firearms. NFA weapons are restricted. Certification for concealed carry must be done within 15 days. Peaceable journey laws are in place, and no background checks are required for private sales. A duty to inform law is in place.

- California: A partial state permit is required for the purchase of long guns or handguns, and firearm registration is mandatory. California has an assault weapon law and magazine capacity restriction in place. An owner license is not required. While California issues concealed carry permits, they are "may issue," and open carry is allowed in specific circumstances. The Castle Doctrine law is recognized, and the state pre-empts most local restrictions on firearms. NFA weapons are restricted, and certification for concealed carry must be done within 60 days. There are no peaceable journey laws. A ten-day waiting period applies to all firearm purchases, and background checks are required for private sales. California also has a red flag law, requires a background check for ammunition purchases, restricts home-built firearms, and imposes purchase quantity and frequency restrictions.

- Colorado: No state permit is required to purchase long guns or handguns. Firearm registration is not required. There is no specific assault weapon law at the state level, but local restrictions may exist after the repeal of Colorado's statewide firearm preemption law in 2021. Magazine capacity restrictions apply, and magazines holding more than 15 rounds are prohibited after July 1, 2013. No owner license is required. A permit is required for concealed carry of handguns, which is issued by local sheriff offices. Open carry is generally legal without a permit, except in Denver and other posted areas. Concealed carry within a vehicle is allowed without a permit. There is partial state preemption of local restrictions. NFA weapons are not restricted at the state level. Colorado has a red flag law allowing temporary firearm confiscation in specific situations. A waiting period of three days is mandatory for most firearm transfers, effective October 1, 2023.

- Connecticut: A state permit is required to purchase long guns and handguns. Firearm registration is partial, with a de facto registry for handguns and long guns purchased in the state. Assault weapon laws are in place, requiring registration for certain firearms. Magazine capacity restrictions apply, with magazines holding more than 10 rounds prohibited in some areas. No owner license is required. A permit is required for concealed carry, with a two-step permitting process. Open carry is generally illegal as of October 1, 2023. A valid Connecticut pistol permit is required to carry a loaded weapon in a vehicle. The state has a castle doctrine and partial preemption of local restrictions. NFA weapons are not restricted at the state level. Connecticut has a red flag law allowing temporary firearm confiscation. A waiting period of three days is mandatory for most firearm transfers, effective October 1, 2023.

- Delaware: No state permit is required to purchase long guns or handguns. Firearm registration is not required. Assault weapon laws are in place, prohibiting certain firearms. Magazine capacity restrictions apply, limiting magazines to 17 rounds. No owner license is required. A permit is required for concealed carry, with Delaware being de facto shall-issue. Open carry is generally lawful without a permit. Delaware has state preemption of local restrictions, and NFA weapons are restricted. The state has a red flag law allowing temporary firearm confiscation. Background checks are required for private sales.

- District of Columbia: A permit is required to purchase long guns and handguns. An owner license is required, and all firearms must be registered with the Metropolitan Police Department. Assault weapon laws are in place, and possession of magazines holding more than 10 rounds is illegal. NFA weapons are restricted, and peaceable journey laws do not apply. Background checks are required for private sales. The District of Columbia has a red flag law. A waiting period of up to 90 days is mandatory after purchasing a firearm.

- Florida: No state permit is required to purchase long guns or handguns. No waiting period is mandatory, except for a three-day waiting period for some cases. Firearm registration is not required. No assault weapon laws, magazine capacity restrictions, or owner license requirements are in place. Florida has a red flag law allowing temporary firearm confiscation. No permit is required for concealed carry, and open carry is generally banned except for certain protected places and activities. The state has castle doctrine/stand your ground laws, state preemption of local restrictions, and NFA weapons are not restricted. Background checks are not required for private sales. There is an age restriction on firearm sales, prohibiting sales to those under 21 years old.

- Georgia: Georgia's gun laws are characterized by a lack of strict regulations. No state permit is required for the purchase of long guns or handguns, and there is no firearm registration. The state does not have specific assault weapon laws or magazine capacity restrictions. Georgia follows a "shall issue" policy for concealed carry permits, with permitless concealed carry taking effect on April 12, 2022. Open carry is also generally allowed without a permit since the same date. The state has Castle Doctrine/Stand Your Ground laws, state preemption of local restrictions, and does not restrict NFA weapons. Background checks are not mandatory for private sales.

- Hawaii: Hawaii's gun laws involve more stringent requirements. A state permit is necessary for purchasing both long guns and handguns, and firearm registration is mandatory within 5 days of purchase or arrival. The state has no assault weapon laws but imposes magazine capacity restrictions on handguns. No owner license is required, but permits are necessary for both concealed and open carry. Hawaii has "shall issue" policies for concealed carry, although its may-issue law has been impacted by legal decisions. Open carry is generally non-permissive, with exceptions rarely granted. The state restricts NFA weapons, requires background checks for private sales, and has a red flag law.

- Idaho: Idaho's gun laws are notably permissive. No state permit is needed to purchase long guns or handguns, and there is no firearm registration. The state is "shall issue" for concealed carry permits, with permitless carry in effect since July 1, 2016. Open carry is allowed without a permit, and Idaho follows Castle Doctrine/Stand Your Ground laws. The state has preemption of local restrictions, does not restrict NFA weapons, and background checks are not required for private sales.

- Illinois: Illinois has a mix of strict and permissive gun laws. A state permit is required for both long guns and handguns, with the Firearm Owner's Identification card (FOID) needed. Firearm registration is not mandatory. Illinois is a "shall issue" state for concealed carry, with open carry generally prohibited. The state has partial preemption of local restrictions, assault weapon laws, magazine capacity restrictions, and background checks for private sales. NFA weapons are restricted, and there are red flag laws in place. Waiting periods apply after firearm purchases, and there are age restrictions on firearm possession.

- Indiana: Indiana's gun laws are largely permissive. No state permit is required to purchase long guns or handguns, and there is no firearm registration. Indiana is a "shall issue" state for concealed carry, with permitless carry in effect since July 1, 2022. Open carry is generally allowed. The state has Castle Doctrine/Stand Your Ground laws, state preemption of local restrictions, and does not restrict NFA weapons. Background checks are not required for private sales, and Indiana has red flag laws in place.

- Iowa: Iowa's gun laws are relatively lenient. No state permit is required to purchase long guns or handguns, and there is no firearm registration. While a permit is available for acquiring pistols or revolvers, it is not mandatory for firearm purchases. Iowa is a "shall issue" state for concealed carry, with permitless carry in effect since July 1, 2021. Open carry is generally allowed without a permit. The state has Castle Doctrine laws, Stand Your Ground laws, and state preemption of local restrictions. NFA weapons are restricted, and background checks are not required for private sales.

- Kansas: Kansas has relatively lenient gun laws with no state permit required for the purchase of long guns or handguns. Additionally, there is no requirement for firearm registration or an assault weapon law. Magazine capacity restriction and owner licenses are also not mandated. However, a permit is necessary for concealed carry, and Kansas operates as a "shall issue" state for residents aged 21 or older. Notably, permitless carry became effective on July 1, 2015. Open carry does not require a permit. The state has Castle Doctrine/Stand Your Ground laws in effect, and there is preemption of local restrictions. Notably, NFA weapons are not restricted, but the Second Amendment Protection Act limits state enforcement. Certification for concealed carry must occur within 15 days, and there are no peaceable journey laws or background checks required for private sales.

- Kentucky: Kentucky's gun laws are characterized by a lack of requirements for state permits to purchase long guns or handguns, as well as no provisions for firearm registration, assault weapon laws, magazine capacity restrictions, or owner licenses. The state follows a "shall issue" policy for concealed carry permits for residents aged 21 or older. Permitless carry became effective on June 26, 2019. Open carry does not necessitate a permit, and Kentucky adheres to Castle Doctrine/Stand Your Ground laws. State preemption of local restrictions is in place, and there are no restrictions on NFA weapons. Certification for concealed carry must occur within 15 days, and there are no peaceable journey laws or background checks required for private sales.

- Louisiana: Louisiana's gun laws are characterized by the absence of a state permit requirement for purchasing long guns or handguns, as well as no firearm registration, assault weapon laws, magazine capacity restrictions, or owner license requirements. A permit is needed for concealed carry, and Louisiana operates as a "shall issue" state for residents aged 21 or older. Open carry requires a permit. The state has Castle Doctrine/Stand Your Ground laws and preemption of local restrictions. NFA weapons are not restricted, and there are no peaceable journey laws or background checks required for private sales. However, there is a duty to inform law enforcement when carrying without a permit.

- Maine: Maine's gun laws are characterized by the absence of a state permit requirement for purchasing long guns or handguns, as well as no firearm registration, assault weapon laws, magazine capacity restrictions, or owner license requirements. The state has a red flag law in effect, and a permit is necessary for concealed carry, with Maine operating as a "shall issue" state for residents aged 18 or older. Permitless carry became effective on October 12, 2015. No permit is required for open carry, except in certain locations. The state lacks Castle Doctrine/Stand Your Ground laws but has preemption of local restrictions. NFA weapons are not restricted, and certification for concealed carry must occur within 15 days. There are no peaceable journey laws or background checks required for private sales, but there is a duty to inform law enforcement when carrying without a permit.

- Maryland: Maryland's gun laws include a state permit requirement for purchasing both long guns and handguns. While there is no firearm registration for long guns, handgun transfers are recorded with the state. Assault weapon laws and magazine capacity restrictions are in effect, and an owner license (Firearm Identification card) is required. A permit is necessary for concealed carry, and Maryland operates as a "may issue" state with de facto "shall issue" practice. No permit is required for open carry of long guns or antique handguns, but a permit is required for open carry of handguns. The state has limited preemption of local restrictions, and NFA weapons are not restricted except for suppressors. Background checks are required for private sales of regulated firearms, and a red flag law is in effect.

- Massachusetts: Massachusetts has relatively strict gun laws, requiring a state permit for the purchase of both long guns and handguns. There is no firearm registration, assault weapon laws, magazine capacity restrictions, or owner license requirements. Shall issue licenses for concealed carry are issued by local police departments, and a license is required for open carry. The state lacks Castle Doctrine/Stand Your Ground laws and has limited state preemption of local restrictions. NFA weapons are restricted for civilians. Background checks are required for private sales, and a red flag law is in effect.

- Michigan: Michigan's gun laws require a state permit for the purchase of both long guns and handguns. A Handgun Purchase Permit or a Michigan-issued Concealed Pistol License is needed for private handgun purchases. As of 2023, background checks are also required for long guns. Firearm registration is not required for long guns but is necessary for handguns. Michigan does not have an assault weapon law, magazine capacity restrictions, or owner licenses. A permit is required for concealed carry, and Michigan is a "shall issue" state for citizens and lawful permanent residents aged 21 or older. Open carry does not require a permit, except when carrying in a vehicle. The state has Castle Doctrine/Stand Your Ground laws, preemption of local restrictions, and does not restrict NFA weapons. Peaceable journey laws apply, and background checks are required for private sales of handguns. There is also a duty to inform law enforcement when carrying without a permit.

- Minnesota: Minnesota does not require a state permit to purchase long guns but mandates a permit for handguns. There is no firearm registration, assault weapon law, magazine capacity restrictions, or owner licenses. A permit is needed for concealed carry, and Minnesota is a "shall issue" state for residents. Open carry is generally permitted, with restrictions on carrying certain weapons in public places. The state has Castle Doctrine/Stand Your Ground laws, preemption of local restrictions, and some NFA weapons are restricted. Peaceable journey laws are in place, and background checks are required for private sales.

- Mississippi: Mississippi does not require a state permit to purchase long guns or handguns. There is no firearm registration, assault weapon law, magazine capacity restrictions, or owner licenses. Mississippi is a "shall issue" state for concealed carry permits for residents aged 21 or older. Permitless carry took effect on April 15, 2016, and open carry does not require a permit. The state has Castle Doctrine/Stand Your Ground laws, preemption of local restrictions, and does not restrict NFA weapons. Peaceable journey laws do not apply, and there are no background checks required for private sales.

- Missouri: Missouri does not require a state permit for the purchase of long guns or handguns. There is no firearm registration, assault weapon law, magazine capacity restrictions, or owner licenses. Missouri is a "shall issue" state for concealed carry permits for citizens and lawful permanent residents aged 19 or older. Permitless carry took effect on January 1, 2017. Open carry does not require a permit, except localities can pass ordinances restricting it. The state has Castle Doctrine/Stand Your Ground laws and preemption of local restrictions. NFA weapons are not restricted, and peaceable journey laws are in place. Background checks are not required for private sales.

- Montana: Montana does not require a state permit for the purchase of long guns or handguns. There is no firearm registration, assault weapon law, magazine capacity restrictions, or owner licenses. Montana is a "shall issue" state for concealed carry permits for citizens and lawful permanent residents aged 18 or older. Permitless carry took effect on February 18, 2021. Open carry does not require a permit, and the state has Castle Doctrine/Stand Your Ground laws, preemption of local restrictions, and does not restrict NFA weapons. Peaceable journey laws do not apply, and there are no background checks required for private sales.

- Nebraska: Nebraska does not require a state permit for the purchase of long guns but mandates a permit for handguns. There is no firearm registration, assault weapon law, magazine capacity restrictions, or owner licenses. Nebraska is a "shall issue" state for concealed carry permits for citizens and lawful permanent residents aged 21 or older. Permitless carry took effect on September 2, 2023. Open carry does not require a permit. The state has preemption of local restrictions, and some NFA weapons are restricted. Peaceable journey laws do not apply, and background checks are required for private sales of handguns.

- Nevada: Nevada does not require a state permit for the purchase of long guns or handguns. There is no firearm registration or owner licenses. Nevada is a "shall issue" state for concealed carry permits. Open carry does not require a permit, except for certain restrictions. The state has preemption of local restrictions and does not restrict NFA weapons. Peaceable journey laws are in place, and background checks are required for private sales.

- New Hampshire: New Hampshire does not require a state permit for the purchase of long guns or handguns. There is no firearm registration, assault weapon law, magazine capacity restrictions, or owner licenses. New Hampshire is a "shall issue" state for concealed carry permits for residents and non-residents aged 18 or older. Permitless carry took effect on February 22, 2017. Open carry does not require a permit, and the state has Castle Doctrine/Stand Your Ground laws, preemption of local restrictions, and does not restrict NFA weapons. Peaceable journey laws do not apply, and there are no background checks required for private sales.

- New Jersey: New Jersey requires a state permit for the purchase of long guns and handguns. A lifetime purchaser identification card is needed for rifle and shotgun purchases, and a permit is required for each handgun purchase. There is no firearm registration for long guns, but handguns are registered. New Jersey has an assault weapon law, magazine capacity restrictions, and permits are required for concealed and open carry. The state does not preempt local restrictions, and some NFA weapons are restricted. Background checks are required for private sales, and there is a red flag law in effect.

- New Mexico: New Mexico does not require a state permit for the purchase of long guns or handguns, and firearm registration is not mandatory. The state also lacks assault weapon laws or magazine capacity restrictions. Owner licenses are not required for long guns or handguns. However, residents must obtain a concealed carry license on a "shall-issue" basis, involving a criminal history check and a 15-hour handgun safety course. Open carry of loaded firearms is legal in New Mexico without a permit, and loaded firearms may be carried in vehicles without one as well. The state recognizes permits from other states with reciprocity agreements. While there is no duty to inform law enforcement during firearm transport, it is customary to do so. There are no specific laws regarding carrying firearms on college campuses, and no restrictions on NFA weapons. New Mexico has pre-emption of local ordinances, but tribal laws on Native American reservations are not pre-empted. The state has a Castle Doctrine law, though its scope is limited to self-defence situations occurring inside one's home. There is no duty to retreat, and individuals have the right to stand their ground. An opt-out statute allows property owners to prohibit firearms on their premises.

- New York: In New York, a partial state permit is required to purchase handguns, while no permit is needed for long guns. Handgun registration is mandatory, and there is no registration for non-"assault weapon" long guns. Owner licenses are required for handguns, but not for long guns. A concealed carry permit may be issued on a "shall-issue" basis, but open carry is generally not legal, and concealed carry without a permit is a felony. New York has assault weapon laws and magazine capacity restrictions, along with restrictions on Title II (National Firearms Act) weapons. The state has a Castle Doctrine law, pre-empts local restrictions, and some cities have additional regulations. Peaceable journey laws are in effect, and background checks are required for private sales.

- North Carolina: In North Carolina, no state permit is required for the purchase of long guns or handguns, and there is no firearm registration. The state lacks assault weapon laws or magazine capacity restrictions, and no owner license is required. Federal background checks are mandatory for all purchases through firearms dealers, but no background checks are required for private sales. There is no firearm registration, and there are no restrictions on NFA weapons. North Carolina has a Castle Doctrine/Stand Your Ground law in place, pre-empts local restrictions, and has no peaceable journey laws. There is a duty to inform law enforcement during concealed carry.

- North Dakota: In North Dakota, no state permit is required for the purchase of long guns or handguns, and there is no firearm registration. The state lacks assault weapon laws or magazine capacity restrictions, and no owner license is required. No permit is required for open carry or concealed carry (permitless carry). North Dakota has a Castle Doctrine/Stand Your Ground law in place, pre-empts local restrictions, and has no peaceable journey laws. There is a duty to inform law enforcement during concealed carry.

- Ohio: Ohio does not require a state permit for the purchase of long guns or handguns, and there is no firearm registration. The state lacks assault weapon laws or magazine capacity restrictions, and no owner license is required. No permit is required for open carry or concealed carry (permitless carry). Ohio has a Castle Doctrine/Stand Your Ground law in place, pre-empts local restrictions, and has no peaceable journey laws. There is no duty to inform law enforcement.

- Oklahoma: Oklahoma does not require a state permit for the purchase of long guns or handguns, and there is no firearm registration. The state lacks assault weapon laws or magazine capacity restrictions, and no owner license is required. There is no red flag law, and the state prohibits laws allowing firearm confiscation without legal grounds. No permit is required for open carry or concealed carry (permitless carry). Oklahoma has a Castle Doctrine/Stand Your Ground law in place, pre-empts local restrictions, and has no peaceable journey laws. No background checks are required for private sales.

- Oregon: Oregon does not require a state permit for the purchase of long guns, and no handgun permit is required for private sales between family members. The state does not have firearm registration, but records of FFL sales are maintained for 5 years. The minimum age to purchase firearms is 18 for long guns and 21 for handguns. There is no assault weapon ban at the state level. Oregon requires a concealed carry permit, issued on a "shall-issue" basis, and open carry of firearms is legal without a permit. The state pre-empts local restrictions on firearm regulations, and there are no restrictions on NFA weapons. A red flag law allows temporary firearm possession prohibition, and a high-capacity magazine ban is pending due to litigation.

- Pennsylvania: In Pennsylvania, no state permit is required to purchase long guns or handguns, and there is no firearm registration. Although all handgun buyers must undergo a PICS check at the point of sale, the state maintains a "sales database" without creating a registry of firearm ownership. Pennsylvania does not have assault weapon laws or magazine capacity restrictions. There is no owner license requirement. For concealed carry, a License to Carry Firearms (LTCF) is required and issued on a "shall-issue" basis for citizens and lawful permanent residents who are 21 years or older. Open carry without a permit is generally allowed, except in Philadelphia (City of the First Class), where an LTCF is required. The state has Castle Doctrine/Stand Your Ground laws, pre-empts local restrictions, and allows peaceable journey for non-residents with valid carry permits. Background checks are not required for private sales of long guns but are necessary for handguns.

- Rhode Island: In Rhode Island, no state permit is required to purchase long guns, but a permit is needed for handguns. There is no firearm registration, and the state lacks assault weapon laws. Owner licenses are not required. For concealed carry, the state is a hybrid "shall issue" and "may issue" jurisdiction, with licenses granted by local authorities or the state's attorney general's office. Open carry of handguns is allowed only with a pistol permit issued by the attorney general. Vehicle carry is permitted with a valid Rhode Island Pistol Permit. Rhode Island has Castle Doctrine/Stand Your Ground laws, pre-empts local restrictions, and restricts NFA weapons. Peaceable journey laws apply, and background checks are required for private sales, except for active law enforcement officers and those licensed to carry a concealed firearm.

- South Carolina: South Carolina does not require a state permit to purchase long guns or handguns, and there is no firearm registration. The state has no assault weapon laws or magazine capacity restrictions, and no owner license is required. For concealed carry, South Carolina is a "shall issue" state for citizens and lawful permanent residents who are 21 years or older. Open carry is allowed without a permit for long guns, while individuals with a concealed weapon permit can openly carry handguns. South Carolina has Castle Doctrine/Stand Your Ground laws, pre-empts local restrictions, and does not restrict NFA weapons. There are no peaceable journey laws or background check requirements for private sales.

- South Dakota: In South Dakota, no state permit is required to purchase long guns or handguns, and there is no firearm registration. The state does not have assault weapon laws or magazine capacity restrictions, and no owner license is required. South Dakota is a "shall issue" state for concealed carry permits, available to citizens and lawful permanent residents who are 18 years or older. Enhanced permits are available to those 21 or older. South Dakota has Castle Doctrine/Stand Your Ground laws, pre-empts local restrictions, and does not restrict NFA weapons. There are no peaceable journey laws, and background checks are not required for private sales.

- Tennessee: Tennessee does not require a state permit for the purchase of long guns or handguns, and there is no firearm registration. The state lacks assault weapon laws or magazine capacity restrictions, and no owner license is required.

Tennessee is a "shall issue" state for concealed carry permits, available to citizens and lawful permanent residents who are 18 years or older. Enhanced permits are issued to those who complete a training course. Tennessee allows permitless open carry for handguns, and there is no duty to inform law enforcement during encounters. The state has Castle Doctrine/Stand Your Ground laws, pre-empts local restrictions, and does not restrict NFA weapons. There are no peaceable journey laws, and background checks are not required for private sales.

- Texas: In Texas, no state permit is required to purchase long guns or handguns, and there is no firearm registration. The state lacks assault weapon laws or magazine capacity restrictions, and no owner license is required. Texas is a "shall issue" state for concealed carry permits, available to citizens and lawful permanent residents who are 21 years or older. Permitless carry for those 21 and older took effect on September 1, 2021. Texas allows open carry without a permit for long guns, but handguns must be carried in a holster. The state has Castle Doctrine/Stand Your Ground laws, pre-empts local restrictions, and does not restrict NFA weapons. Texas recognizes peaceable journey laws, and background checks are not required for private sales.

- Utah: Utah does not require a state permit for the purchase of long guns or handguns, and there is no firearm registration. The state lacks assault weapon laws or magazine capacity restrictions, and no owner license is required. Utah is a "shall issue" state for concealed carry permits, available to citizens and lawful permanent residents who are 18 years or older. Permitless carry for those 21 and older took effect on May 5, 2021. Utah allows open carry without a permit for those 21 or older. The state has Castle Doctrine/Stand Your Ground laws, pre-empts local restrictions, and does not restrict NFA weapons. Utah recognizes peaceable journey laws, and background checks are not required for private sales.

- Vermont: Vermont does not require a state permit for the purchase of long guns or handguns, and there is no firearm registration. The state lacks assault weapon laws and has magazine restrictions for long guns and handguns. No owner license is required, and Vermont allows permitless carry for citizens and lawfully admitted aliens. Vermont permits open carry without a permit, and the state pre-empts local restrictions. Vermont legalized suppressors on June 17,

2015. Background checks are required for private sales, and Vermont has red flag laws and storage requirements. The waiting period for firearm transfers is 72 hours, exempting transfers without background checks.

- Virginia: No state permit is required to purchase long guns or handguns. There is no firearm registration requirement, except for fully automatic firearms (machine guns), which must be registered with the state police. No owner license is required, but proof of age and citizenship is needed for firearm purchases. Concealed carry permits are issued in a "shall issue" manner to residents and non-residents. Training options are restricted starting January 1, 2021. Open carry is generally allowed without a permit, but certain cities and counties have exceptions for specific firearms. Virginia has state pre-emption for most firearm laws, but local governments have expanded power to ban firearms in certain areas. Assault weapons are regulated, requiring proof of age and citizenship for purchase. Magazine capacity restrictions apply to magazines capable of holding more than 20 rounds, defining firearms as assault weapons. Background checks are required for private sales, with penalties for noncompliance. Virginia has a red flag law, allowing a judge to issue an Extreme Risk Protective Order for temporary firearm confiscation.

- Washington: Partial state permits are required to purchase pistols or semiautomatic rifles, with proof of completing a recognized firearm safety training program for the latter. Firearm registration is partial, with retail dealers required to record and report sales. No owner license is required. Washington is a "shall-issue" state for concealed carry permits, with no training requirements. Open carry is allowed without a permit, with some restrictions in vehicles. Washington has state pre-emption for firearm laws, with some exceptions in Seattle and Edmonds. Assault weapons are regulated, and magazine capacity restrictions apply. NFA weapons are partially restricted. Background checks are required for private sales. Washington has a red flag law for Extreme Risk Protective Orders.

- West Virginia: No state permit is required to purchase long guns or handguns. No firearm registration or assault weapon laws exist. No magazine capacity restrictions apply. No owner license is required. West Virginia is a "shall-issue" state for concealed carry permits, with permitless carry in effect since May 24, 2016. Open carry is allowed without a permit. West Virginia has Castle Doctrine/Stand Your Ground laws and state pre-emption for firearm laws. NFA weapons are not restricted, and background checks are not required for private sales.

- Wisconsin: No state permit is required to purchase long guns or handguns. No firearm registration, assault weapon laws, or magazine capacity restrictions apply. No owner license is required. Wisconsin is a "shall-issue" state for concealed carry permits, with no training requirements. Open carry is allowed without a permit. Wisconsin has Castle Doctrine/Stand Your Ground laws and state pre-emption for firearm laws. NFA weapons are not restricted, and background checks are not required for private sales.

- Wyoming: No state permit is required to purchase long guns or handguns. No firearm registration, assault weapon laws, magazine capacity restrictions, or owner license requirements exist. Wyoming is a "shall-issue" state for concealed carry permits, with permitless carry in effect since July 1, 2011. Open carry is allowed without a permit. Wyoming has Castle Doctrine/Stand Your Ground laws and state pre-emption for firearm laws. NFA weapons are not restricted, and background checks are not required for private sales.

The gun laws in various United States Territories are as follows:
- In American Samoa, a permit is necessary for the purchase of long guns or ammunition, and the registration of firearms is obligatory. Civilian possession of handguns is prohibited, and stringent assault weapon laws extend to banning all handguns and centrefire firearms. Additionally, concealed carry is strictly illegal, and individuals opting for open carry must possess a valid License to Possess, limited to shotguns and rimfire rifles. Notably, National Firearms Act (NFA) weapons, including explosive devices, machine guns, and silencers, are prohibited in this territory.

- Guam enforces a permit requirement for the purchase and possession of firearms, coupled with mandatory firearm registration and owner licenses. Concealed carry permits are issued through a "shall issue" policy, while open carry necessitates a Firearm Owner's Identification (FOID). Guam adheres to Castle Law provisions and prohibits certain NFA weapons such as short-barrelled rifles (SBR), short-barrelled shotguns (SBS), machine guns, and silencers.

- In the Northern Mariana Islands, permits are mandatory for the purchase of guns or ammunition, although firearm registration has been ruled unconstitutional. The jurisdiction also experienced the invalidation of assault weapon bans. Magazine capacity restrictions are in place, and while concealed carry is prohibited, lawful open carry is permitted under specific conditions. Notably, National Firearms Act (NFA) weapons, including short-barrelled shotguns, machine guns, and suppressors, are prohibited.

- Puerto Rico requires a permit for taking possession of firearms, with mandatory firearm registration and owner licenses. As of January 1, 2020, concealed carry permits follow a "shall issue" policy, while open carry remains prohibited. The territory enforces restrictions on National Firearms Act (NFA) weapons and mandates background checks for private sales.

- In the U.S. Virgin Islands, permits are obligatory for the purchase of any firearm or ammunition, accompanied by mandatory firearm registration. The jurisdiction prohibits assault weapons and .50 BMG rifles, while magazine capacity restrictions are in place. Obtaining concealed carry permits involves a stringent process, and open carry is strictly prohibited. Additionally, National Firearms Act (NFA) weapons, including automatic firearms and short-barrelled shotguns, are prohibited in the U.S. Virgin Islands.

Concealed Carry Laws

Concealed carry laws in the United States vary widely among states, with some states having relatively few restrictions on issuing permits, while others have more stringent requirements such as demonstrating a specific need or completing extensive training (Tomislav Victor Kovandzic et al., 2005). States can be categorized as "Shall-Issue" or "May-Issue," with the former issuing permits to applicants who meet certain criteria, and the latter having more discretionary authority in issuing permits (Tomislav Victor Kovandzic et al., 2005). The expansion of shall-issue concealed handgun laws in the United States has been attributed to low-collective security in states, drawing on the thesis of the new criminologies of everyday life and the conceptualization of sovereign subjects (Steidley, 2019).

Research has shown that only about 1% of the adult population has concealed hand-gun permits, while survey research indicates that at least 8% of adults carry a gun for protection each year (Tomislav Victor Kovandzic et al., 2005). This suggests a significant gap between the number of permits issued and the actual prevalence of concealed carry for protection. Additionally, the political conservatism and the proportion of hunters in the population have been consistently related to permitting, indicating a potential cultural norm that values and cherishes gun ownership (Thompson & Stidham, 2010).

The influence of fear of crime, gender, and southern cultural tradition on the frequency of carrying firearms for protection against criminal victimization has been examined, highlighting the psychological and sociological factors that contribute to concealed carry behaviours (Bankston et al., 1990). Furthermore, the availability of data and the state's culture surrounding firearm prevalence and violent crime rates have been considered in research, emphasizing the importance of understanding the broader context in which concealed carry laws operate (Carter & Binder, 2016).

The impact of concealed carry laws on crime rates has been a subject of debate, with studies examining the effects of right-to-carry laws on violent crime and crime deterrence (Kovandzic & Marvell, 2003; Smith & Petrocelli, 2018). These studies have contributed to the ongoing discourse on the relationship between concealed carry laws and public safety, addressing concerns about the potential effects of deregulation on crime rates.

Background Checks

The federal background check system in the United States, known as the National Instant Criminal Background Check System (NICS), is a crucial tool for screening potential gun buyers. However, there are gaps in the system, and not all sales are subject to background checks, particularly private sales and those at gun shows.

The National Instant Criminal Background Check System (NICS), implemented by the Federal Bureau of Investigation (FBI), plays a pivotal role in this process by scrutinizing potential gun buyers through comprehensive databases containing information on criminal history, mental health records, and other disqualifying factors (Rozel & Mulvey, 2017). However, limitations and gaps persist, as not all firearm transactions are subject to background checks, particularly private sales and transactions at gun shows (Castillo-Carniglia et al., 2017). This exemption for private sales has raised concerns about individuals acquiring firearms without undergoing comprehensive vetting, potentially evading the system designed to prevent firearms from reaching individuals with disqualifying factors (Castillo-Carniglia et al., 2017).

Research has shown that background checks are strongly correlated with other measures of firearm sales, including tax revenue from firearm sales, per capita gun ownership, and the net total of guns manufactured, imported, and exported (Brownstein et al., 2020). Furthermore, studies suggest that federal and state background check laws can reduce gun-related crimes and firearm deaths in the adult population as well as reduce adverse outcomes of firearm ownership (Levine & McKnight, 2017). Additionally, the implementation of background checks, particularly those related to mental health, has been associated with lower firearm suicide deaths (Timsina et al., 2020). It is important to note that rates of firearm injury and mortality are far higher in the United States compared to other high-income nations, emphasizing the significance of effective background check policies in reducing firearm-related harm (Silver et al., 2018).

Open Carry

Open carry laws in the United States have a significant impact on firearm regulations, contributing to the diverse patchwork of state-level policies that shape the nation's approach to gun rights. These laws govern the visibility of firearms in public spaces, determining whether individuals are allowed to openly carry firearms without concealment. The regulations surrounding open carry vary widely across states, reflecting diverse perspectives on gun rights and public safety Yakubovich et al., 2021).

Some states have permissive open carry laws, allowing individuals to openly carry firearms without the need for a separate permit. In these jurisdictions, residents can exercise their right to bear arms openly, making the presence of firearms visible to others. Conversely, other states impose restrictions on open carry, requiring individuals to obtain a permit before openly carrying a firearm in public. These permits often involve background checks and, in some cases, training requirements, aiming to balance individual gun rights with public safety and responsible firearm ownership. Additionally, a subset of states outright prohibits open carry, regardless of whether individuals possess a permit or not, often rooted in considerations of public safety and the potential for intimidation or panic associated with visible firearms (Rosengart, 2005).

The nuances in open carry laws underscore the decentralized nature of firearm regulation in the U.S., with individual states retaining considerable autonomy in shaping policies that align with their unique cultural, social, and political contexts. These divergent approaches fuel ongoing debates regarding the impact of open carry on public safety, individual rights, and law enforcement practices (McClellan & Tekin, 2016).

Advocates for permissive open carry laws argue that they empower law-abiding citizens to openly exercise their Second Amendment rights and promote a culture of self-reliance. On the other hand, critics express concerns about increased public anxiety, the risk of confrontations, and challenges for law enforcement in distinguishing between law-abiding citizens and potential threats (Schell et al., 2020). As the United States continues to grapple with questions surrounding gun rights and regulations, open carry laws remain a focal point of discussion and legislative action, reflecting ongoing efforts to strike a balance between individual freedoms and societal safety (Blau et al., 2016).

Castle Doctrine and Stand Your Ground

The legal concepts of Castle Doctrine and Stand Your Ground represent distinct elements of self-defence laws in the United States. The Castle Doctrine, applied in several states, allows individuals to use deadly force to defend themselves within their homes, with no duty to retreat when faced with a threat (Foshee et al., 1999). On the other hand, Stand Your Ground laws extend the right to use deadly force to public spaces, eliminating the duty to retreat before using force in self-defence (Foshee et al., 1999). These laws have sparked debates about potential misuse, escalation of violence, and racial disparities in their application.

The application of Stand Your Ground laws has raised concerns about the potential for increased violence and the difficulty in determining the reasonableness of a person's belief in the necessity of using force (Foshee et al., 1999). Additionally, research has shown that emotional valence and arousal significantly affect safety attention, mediating safety attention levels and personal factors (Wang, 2021). This is relevant as it highlights the psychological aspects that may influence individuals' responses in self-defence situations.

Furthermore, the discussion of therapeutic responses to domestic violence and the controversies surrounding them is pertinent to the debates about the potential misuse and escalation of violence related to self-defence laws (Brown & James, 2014). Theorizing about violence also provides a comprehensive understanding of the broader implications of self-defence laws and their impact on society (Stanko, 2006).

Gun Ownership in the United States

Understanding gun ownership in America goes beyond merely identifying individuals who own or do not own guns. Some Americans who do not personally own guns reside with someone who does or have owned guns in the past. Additionally, many individuals who currently do not own guns, including those who have never owned one, express openness to gun ownership in the future (Parker et al., 2017).

Among American adults, three in ten claim to currently own a gun, and an additional 11% state that they do not personally own a gun but live with someone who does (Parker et al., 2017). Among those who do not presently own a gun, approximately half express the possibility of owning one in the future.

Gun ownership exhibits gender, racial, and geographical variations. Men are more likely than women to be gun owners, with white men showing a particularly high likelihood of gun ownership. In rural areas, 46% identify as gun owners, compared to 28% in suburban areas and 19% in urban settings (Parker et al., 2017). Political affiliations also play a role, with Republicans and Republican-leaning independents being more than twice as likely as Democrats and their counterparts to claim gun ownership (44% vs. 20%).

For many gun owners, exposure to firearms occurred during childhood, with about two-thirds stating that there were guns in their households while growing up. Additionally, 76% report that they fired a gun for the first time before turning 18. Among non-gun owners, although fewer grew up in gun-owning households, a substantial share (40%) experienced this, and 61% have fired a gun (Parker et al., 2017).

Gun owners cite various reasons for ownership, with the majority having more than one reason. Protection ranks highest, with 67% stating it as a major reason for owning a gun. About 38% mention hunting as a major reason, while 30% point to sport shooting, including target, trap, and skeet shooting. Fewer individuals cite gun collection (13%) or their job (8%) as major reasons for owning a gun.

Two-thirds of gun owners possess more than one gun, and 29% own five or more. Handguns or pistols are prevalent among 72% of gun owners, followed by rifles (62%) and shotguns (54%). Among those owning a single gun, the majority (62%) own a handgun or pistol, while fewer possess a rifle (22%) or a shotgun (16%) (Parker et al., 2017).

The estimated sales of firearms in the United States have shown a consistent increase in the 21st century, with a significant surge in 2020 during the COVID-19 pandemic. This surge is evidenced by a substantial increase in the number of background checks for firearm purchases, indicating a spike in gun sales (Levine & McKnight, 2017). The FBI's National Instant Background Check System (NICS) has played a crucial role in monitoring these trends (Levine & McKnight, 2017).

Estimates on gun ownership in the U.S. have been derived from polling conducted by organizations such as the General Social Survey (GSS), Harris Interactive, and Gallup (Reeping et al., 2019). However, disparities in results across different polls have raised concerns about their reliability (Reeping et al., 2019). Despite these challenges, it was estimated that U.S. civilians owned 393 million firearms in 2018, with 40% to 42% of households having at least one gun (Reeping et al., 2019). The General Social Survey poll indicated a long-term decline in the percentage of Americans and households claiming ownership of guns, with household ownership declining from around 50% in the late 1970s and early 1980s to 32% by 2015 (Reeping et al., 2019).

Gun ownership rates exhibit variations across geographic regions, demographic disparities, and political affiliations (Celinska, 2007). For instance, gun ownership rates vary from approximately 25% in the Northeastern United States to 60% in the East South Central States (Celinska, 2007). Additionally, demographic disparities are evident, with 49% of men reporting gun ownership compared to 33% of women, 44% of whites owning guns compared to 24% of non-whites, and 56% of those in rural areas owning guns compared to 40% of suburbanites and 29% of urban dwellers (Celinska, 2007). Political affiliation is another influencing factor, with 53% of Republicans owning guns compared to 36% of independents and 31% of Democrats (Celinska, 2007). Criticism of surveys like the GSS survey revolves around their inability to offer sufficient macro-level detail to draw conclusions on the relationship between overall firearm ownership and gun violence (Khubchandani & Price, 2020). While some studies found no correlation between overall firearm ownership and gun violence, others revealed positive correlations between gun ownership and homicide rates in the United States (Khubchandani & Price, 2020).

The number of guns manufactured for the U.S. market has been a topic of interest due to its implications for public safety and policy. The ATF's Annual Firearms Manufacturing and Exportation Report provides insights into the production of firearms for the U.S. market (Smart et al., 2020). Historical ATF data and U.S. International Trade Commission import reports indicate that over 494 million firearms have been produced for the U.S. market since 1899, excluding exports by domestic manufacturers and military firearms (Smart et al., 2020). The surge in gun production in recent years, with a record 22.5 million guns in the U.S. market in 2021, reflects a significant increase compared to previous years (Smart et al., 2020). The majority of guns produced are handguns, constituting 57% of firearm production in 2021, indicating a shift from historical trends where rifles and shotguns predominated (Smart et al., 2020).

The relationship between gun production and gun deaths has been a subject of study. Research suggests a correlation between increased gun production and rising gun deaths, particularly in the context of suicides (Lang & Lang, 2021). However, it is important to note that correlation does not imply causation, and factors such as household gun ownership levels may have a more significant impact on gun deaths than overall gun production (Lang & Lang, 2021). Additionally, the impact of mass shootings on gun policy has been studied, indicating that these events evoke large policy responses (Lang & Lang, 2021).

While the ATF provides valuable data on gun production, there are limitations to consider. The production figures do not account for how many firearms exit circulation each year, and factors such as attrition, including rust, breakage, confiscation, and illegal export, contribute to the reduction in the number of guns in circulation (Smart et al., 2020). Furthermore, the ATF data does not encompass 3D-printed guns and most guns assembled from kits until recently, as they were not required to be reported (Smart et al., 2020).

The United States has experienced a significant surge in firearm manufacturing in recent years. From 1986 to 2008, the annual average production stood at 3.8 million firearms, soaring to an average of 8.4 million per year from 2009 to 2018, with a peak in 2016 at 11.5 million firearms (Fowler et al., 2015). This growth is primarily attributed to rifle and pistol production, constituting nearly 76 percent of firearms manufactured between 2009 and 2018 (Fowler et al., 2015). The surge in the gun manufacturing industry is further evidenced by the remarkable 255 percent increase in the number of licensed gun manufacturers from 2009 to 2018, reaching nearly 12,600 by 2018 (Fowler et al., 2015). This growth was widespread across the nation, with variations in the size of the gun manufacturing industry from state to state (Bräuer et al., 2016). Despite numerous gun manufacturers, a few major companies concentrate on the lion's share of total gun production (Fowler et al., 2015).

The surge in firearm manufacturing has also been associated with legislative factors. Fleegler et al. (2013) highlighted the impact of firearm legislation on firearm-related fatalities in the United States, indicating the relevance of regulatory measures in shaping the industry. Additionally, Gopal and Greenwood (2017)studied the effects of mass shootings on stock prices of firearm manufacturers, shedding light on the economic implications of such events on the industry.

The significant increase in firearm imports to the United States has been a notable trend in recent years. The annual average of imported firearms rose from 1.5 million from 1986 to 2008 to 4.2 million from 2008 to 2018, primarily driven by imports of handguns and rifles (Fowler et al., 2015).. These imports primarily originate from 15 countries, with Austria being the leading supplier, providing over 5 million firearms, primarily handguns, from 2013 to 2018. Other significant handgun suppliers include Brazil, Croatia, and Germany, while Canada, Italy, and Turkey export a substantial number of rifles and shotguns to the United States (Fowler et al., 2015).

The regulation of firearms imports is a shared responsibility between the Bureau of Alcohol, Tobacco, Firearms and Explosives (ATF) and U.S. Customs and Border Protection (CBP). Importers must obtain a license from ATF, pay a $50 annual fee, and undergo a background check. Import licenses, valid for three years, witnessed a 53 percent increase from 735 in 2009 to 1,127 in 2018, with over 40 percent of these licenses in 2018 held by individuals or businesses in just six states: Florida, Texas, California, Virginia, Pennsylvania, and Arizona (Fowler et al., 2015).

Furthermore, a ban on importing most models of foreign-made semiautomatic assault rifles was implemented in response to a 1989 executive action following a school shooting in Stockton, California. Despite concerns about lax enforcement and innovation by foreign manufacturers, attempts to narrow the definition of unlawful "non-sporting" firearms have largely failed, maintaining the ban (Fowler et al., 2015).

Gun exports from the United States have experienced significant changes in terms of destination countries and types of firearms exported. The U.S. Census Bureau data from 2014 to 2018 indicates a shift in the primary countries receiving exported firearms from the United States, with Canada emerging as the largest recipient of U.S. long guns, importing over $350 million worth from 2014 to 2018. Additionally, there has been a notable change in the types of firearms exported, with rifle and pistol exports growing to constitute more than 75 percent of the total from 2005 to 2018, compared to the pre-1995 period when revolvers and shotguns accounted for nearly 60 percent of exported firearms (Moore, 2017).

The regulatory change implemented by the Trump administration in January 2020, which shifted export controls for certain firearms and their ammunition from the U.S. Department of State to the U.S. Department of Commerce, has raised concerns about weakened oversight. This change has increased the risk of exported goods reaching criminal organizations or human rights violators, as the Commerce Department employs less robust protocols. Furthermore, the rule change removed congressional oversight of potential arms transfers, amplifying concerns about the increased use of U.S. weapons in global armed conflicts and human rights abuses (Moore, 2017).

In light of these developments, it is crucial to consider the potential implications of such shifts in gun exports. The concerns raised about weakened oversight and the increased risk of U.S. weapons reaching criminal organizations or human rights violators highlight the need for robust monitoring and control mechanisms in the export of firearms. Additionally, the removal of congressional oversight of potential arms transfers underscores the importance of ensuring transparency and accountability in the export of firearms to mitigate the risk of their involvement in global armed conflicts and human rights abuses (Moore, 2017).

The expansion of the U.S. gun industry is mirrored by the growth in the number of licensed individuals operating as gun dealers. From close to 47,500 in 2009, the number of licensed gun dealers rose to over 55,900 by 2018, marking an 18 percent increase (Parsons et al., 2020). Notably, this rise surpassed the 6.6 percent growth in the U.S. population during the same period, suggesting that the increase in gun dealers is primarily industry-driven (Parsons et al., 2020).

States like Texas, Pennsylvania, Ohio, Florida, Michigan, and California house the highest numbers of licensed gun dealers, while Wyoming, Montana, Alaska, North Dakota, and South Dakota boast the highest rates of gun dealers per 100,000 residents (Parsons et al., 2020).

Current federal law mandates that individuals "engaged in the business of dealing in firearms" must obtain a license from ATF. Qualifying for this license requires legal eligibility for firearm possession, a background check, fingerprint submission, and a $200 fee for a three-year license (Parsons et al., 2020). ATF investigators then conduct a quali-fication interview and inspection. However, existing regulations provide vague guidance on what constitutes being "engaged in the business," allowing unscrupulous individuals to exploit this ambiguity and sell guns at high volumes without obtaining a license. In 2016, ATF updated guidance for gun sellers, indicating that a license is necessary for those repetitively buying and selling firearms with the principal motive of making a profit (Parsons et al., 2020).

The number of licensed gun dealers does not entirely illuminate the extent of the retail market in guns, as dealers are not required to report the volume of their sales to ATF. Current federal law prohibits ATF from maintaining a comprehensive list of gun sales, leaving background checks using the National Instant Criminal Background Check System as a proxy measure for assessing the scale of gun sales. From 1999 to 2008, an annual average of 7.7 million background checks for gun sales occurred, rising to 13 million from 2009 to 2018 (Parsons et al., 2020). However, these figures likely underrepresent the full scope of gun sales, omitting sales facilitated by unlicensed sellers.

Range of firearms in the United States

The range of firearms available for sale in America caters to various preferences and purposes. Handguns, including pistols and revolvers, are popular choices for self-defence and concealed carry (Bellesiles, 1998). Rifles, such as bolt-action, semi-automatic, and lever-action, are commonly used for hunting, sport shooting, and self-defence (Bellesiles, 1998). Shotguns, known for their versatility, are also used for hunting and home defence (Bellesiles, 1998). Additionally, modern sporting rifles like AR-15 style rifles are popular for civilian use, including sport shooting and home defence (Bellesiles, 1998). Specialized firearms, such as submachine guns and machine guns, are designed for rapid-fire and are commonly used by military and law enforcement. Antique and collectible firearms, including muzzleloaders and single-shot firearms, are popular among historical reenactors and black powder enthusiasts.

The availability of firearms has been cited as a major reason for America's uniquely lethal brand of violence, contributing to a firearm homicide rate approximately 24 times higher than comparable high-income nations (Semenza et al., 2021). It's important to note that firearm regulations vary by state, and federal regulations apply to certain types of firearms, such as fully automatic weapons. Background checks and waiting periods may be required for firearm purchases from licensed dealers to ensure compliance with local, state, and federal laws when purchasing and owning firearms (Belleslies, 1998).

Handguns, including pistols and revolvers, are handheld firearms with distinctive features. Pistols have a single chamber and come in designs like semi-automatic, single-shot, or revolvers. Revolvers are known for their simplicity and reliability, featuring a rotating cylinder with multiple chambers.

Long guns encompass rifles and shotguns, each serving different purposes. Rifles, with their long barrels, are designed for accuracy and distance. They come in various action types, such as bolt-action, semi-automatic, and lever-action, and are commonly used for hunting, sport shooting, and self-defence. Shotguns, with smooth or rifled barrels, fire shells containing multiple pellets (shot) or a single slug. They are versatile and find use in hunting, sport shooting, and home defence.

Modern sporting rifles, exemplified by AR-15 style rifles, are often referred to as "black rifles." These firearms are known for their modular design and are popular for civilian use, including sport shooting and home defence.

Specialized firearms, such as submachine guns, machine guns, and derringers, cater to specific needs. Submachine guns are automatic firearms designed for rapid-fire, using pistol-calibre ammunition and are commonly used by military and law enforcement. Machine guns, capable of sustained rapid fire, are heavily regulated and restricted in the civilian market. Derringers, small and compact handguns designed for concealed carry, often have limited capacity.

Antique and collectible firearms include muzzleloaders and single-shot firearms. Muzzleloaders are firearms loaded from the muzzle, requiring powder, projectile, and primer. They are popular among historical reenactors and black powder enthusiasts. Single-shot firearms, whether antique or replicas, are designed to fire one round at a time, contributing to the diversity of firearms available for collectors and enthusiasts.

Gun Related Crime in the United States

According to recent data from the Centers for Disease Control and Prevention (CDC) presented in an analysis by the Violence Policy Center (VPC), states with the highest overall rates of gun deaths in the United States tend to have weak gun violence prevention laws and higher rates of gun ownership. Conversely, states with the lowest overall gun death rates typically have strong gun violence prevention laws and lower rates of gun ownership (Violence Policy Center, 2022).

The VPC analysis focuses on gun deaths, including homicides, suicides, and fatal unintentional shootings, in the year 2020, the most recent year for which data is available. The analysis reveals a correlation between the stringency of a state's gun laws and its gun death rate. The states with the five highest gun death rates in 2020 were Mississippi, Wyoming, Louisiana, Alaska, and Missouri, all characterized by lax gun violence prevention laws and higher rates of gun ownership. On the other hand, the states with the lowest gun death rates were Hawaii, Massachusetts, New Jersey, Rhode Island, and New York, all of which boast robust gun violence prevention laws and lower rates of gun ownership (Violence Policy Center, 2022).

In 2020, the total number of Americans killed by firearms was 45,222, representing a significant 14 percent increase from 2019. The national gun death rate surged from 12.10 per 100,000 in 2019 to 13.73 per 100,000 in 2020. This increase was primarily driven by a spike in gun homicides, rising by 34 percent from 2019 to 2020, while firearm suicide deaths experienced a more modest 1.5 percent increase (Violence Policy Center, 2022).

In 2022, the United States experienced 45,222 gun-related deaths, a per capita rate significantly higher than that of other industrialized nations (Amnesty International, 2024). The successive administrations in the United States have allowed gun violence to evolve into a human rights crisis, exacerbated by the absence of measures such as a national firearm registry for monitoring gun ownership. Legal provisions across all states permit individuals to carry concealed firearms in public, with only California, Florida, Illinois, and the District of Columbia imposing general bans on the open carrying of firearms.

An alarming trend is the increasing number of firearm suicides among Black, Latino, and Asian teenagers, with data from the Centers for Disease Control revealing a staggering 120% surge from 2011 to 2020 (Amnesty International, 2024). Additionally, the United States has witnessed a disturbing rise in mass shootings, defined as incidents where four or more victims are killed or injured. In 2022 alone, there were 46 school shootings, surpassing any yearly count since 1999 and causing profound harm to children who either witness the violence or find themselves cowering in classrooms, attempting to seek refuge from it (Amnesty International, 2024).

The year 2021 saw an unprecedented 683 mass shootings in the United States, marking a record high. Among the deadliest incidents in recent years were the 2015 nightclub shooting in Orlando, resulting in 49 deaths and 53 injuries; the 2017 concert shooting in Las Vegas, claiming 60 lives and injuring 411; and the 2019 store shooting in El Paso, where 23 people lost their lives and 23 were wounded (Amnesty International, 2024).

Statistics on Daily Gun Violence in America highlight the pervasive impact of firearms on individuals across all age groups in the United States. On a daily basis, a staggering 327 people fall victim to gun-related incidents, encompassing a range of outcomes (Brady United, 2024). Among them, 117 individuals lose their lives due to gunshot injuries, while 210 manage to survive. Tragically, 46 individuals are murdered, and 67 succumb to gun suicide (Brady United, 2024).

When focusing on children and teens aged 1-17, the daily toll is alarming, with 23 young lives affected by gun violence (Brady United, 2024). Six of them tragically lose their lives, and 3 are victims of murder, while 17 endure the aftermath of surviving gunshot injuries. Additionally, 8 children and teens are intentionally shot by someone else but manage to survive, and 2 face the devastating impact of either gun suicide or attempted suicide. Furthermore, 8 youngsters become unintentional victims in family fire incidents, involving improperly stored or misused guns found in homes.

Moving beyond daily statistics, the annual gun violence impact in the United States paints an even graver picture (Brady United, 2024). Annually, a staggering 117,345 individuals are shot, with 42,654 losing their lives to gun violence. This includes 16,651 murder victims and 24,569 individuals who succumb to gun suicide. Among survivors, 76,725 individuals bear the physical and emotional scars of gunshot injuries (Brady United, 2024).

For children and teens aged 1-17, the annual toll reaches 7,957, comprising 2,029 young lives lost to gun violence. This includes 1,130 murdered children and teens and 732 individuals who succumb to gun suicide (Brady United, 2024). The statistics further reveal the prevalence of intentional shootings, unintentional incidents, and the distressing reality of family fire situations. These statistics underscore the urgent need for comprehensive measures to address gun violence and its devastating impact on individuals, families, and communities across the United States.

The VPC emphasizes the urgent need for attention from policymakers in addressing the escalating firearm homicide rates. The calculated state gun death rates consider the total number of gun deaths per 100,000 people, providing a standard method for comparing fatal levels of gun violence across states.

States with "weak" gun violence prevention laws, as defined by the VPC, are those that contribute minimally or not at all to federal law, featuring permissive regulations on carrying firearms openly or concealed in public (Violence Policy Center, 2022). Conversely, states with "strong" gun violence prevention laws are defined by the addition of substantial state regulations absent from federal law, including restrictions on particularly hazardous firearms, setting safety standards for firearms, requiring a permit to purchase a firearm, and imposing limitations on carrying firearms openly or concealed in public.

In 2022, the enduring impact of the COVID-19 pandemic persisted, reflecting in the near-record levels of gun deaths (Brownlee, 2022). Across the nation, communities grappled with the dual challenges of escalating gun homicides and suicides. Despite these challenges, the year also witnessed a significant milestone in firearms legislation, as Congress passed the first gun reform law in decades, coinciding with a groundbreaking Supreme Court ruling that expanded gun rights.

Among the noteworthy figures from 2022, an estimated 20,138 firearm deaths (excluding suicides) were recorded. This represented a slight decline compared to the record-breaking year of 2021. The Gun Violence Archive, monitoring these statistics since 2014, encompassed various incidents such as murders, accidental shootings, and homicides deemed legally justified by law enforcement. Preliminary data from the Centers for Disease Control indicated over 48,000 firearm homicides and suicides in 2021, marking a historical high (Brownlee, 2022). The age-adjusted gun death rate of 14.8 per 100,000 people was the highest since 1993.

In a landmark case, the U.S. Supreme Court voted 6 to 3 in New York State Rifle and Pistol Association v. Bruen. For the first time, the court acknowledged an individual's right to carry loaded guns in public. The June ruling prompted several states with stricter standards on carrying guns in public to loosen their permitting rules and introduced a new constitutional test for evaluating cases involving gun restrictions (Brownlee, 2022).

The number of federally licensed gun dealers operating nationwide reached 71,600, with a notable increase of 2,000 registrations in the last five years. This statistic underscored the ongoing importance of Federal Firearms Licenses (FFLs), requiring dealers to conduct background checks on all gun sales and maintain detailed records (Brownlee, 2022).

Over the last decade, there was a concerning 120 percent increase in the firearm suicide rate among Black teenagers. Data analysed by The Trace, based on Centers for Disease Control data, revealed a doubling of suicide rates among Black, Latino, and Asian teenagers (Brownlee, 2022). This trend suggested narrowing disparities as suicide rates among young Black and brown individuals worsened.

The Bipartisan Safer Communities Act, a comprehensive gun reform law, allocated $1.5 billion for various initiatives. This included $750 million for states to enhance or enact red flag laws and other crisis intervention programs, $250 million for community-based violence intervention initiatives, and $200 million for improving the national background check system (Brownlee, 2022). Additional funds supported school safety, police, and mental health programs.

Despite an overall decline, Americans purchased 16.5 million guns in 2022, marking the second yearly decrease since the peak in 2020 (Brownlee, 2022). Gun sales had surged in 2020 amid concerns over COVID-19, racial injustice protests, social unrest, and the presidential election. However, this decline was not uniform, with record highs reported in Oregon following the approval of a ballot referendum.

In 2022, there were 648 mass shootings, ranking as the second-highest on record, just behind 2021. While mass shootings (four or more shot) slightly decreased, mass murders (four or more people killed) increased by 30 percent, from 28 in 2021 to 36 in 2022 (Brownlee, 2022).

On K-12 school property, 332 people were shot in 2022, marking a 46 percent increase. This set records for both the number of people shot and the number of incidents, as reported by the K-12 School Shooting Database, which includes all gun violence incidents on school properties (Brownlee, 2022).

A record-setting 1,060 people were shot and killed by police in 2022, surpassing the previous record set in 2021. The relatively stable trend of around 1,000 people shot and killed by police annually saw a slight increase in recent years (Brownlee, 2022).

In 2022, at least 35 transgender and gender non-conforming people were killed (Brownlee, 2022). This count is listed as "at least" due to the underreporting of deaths and misgendering. Notably, two trans individuals, Daniel Aston and Kelly Loving, were shot and killed in the Club Q mass shooting in Colorado Springs.

Despite the potential benefits of red flag laws, there were zero red flag petitions filed by law enforcement in Colorado's most populous county. These Emergency Risk Protection Orders allow temporary gun seizures from individuals deemed a danger to themselves or others. The lack of law enforcement involvement contrasted with the eight petitions approved between late 2020 and November 2021, all of which were filed by family and friends (Brownlee, 2022).

In 2022, four states repealed concealed carry permit requirements. Alabama, Georgia, Indiana, and Ohio passed permitless carry laws, allowing residents to carry concealed handguns in public without a license (Brownlee, 2022). This followed the trend set in 2021 when six states passed similar permitless carry laws.

IMPACT OF GUN CONTROL POLICIES IN THE USA

Gun Control Policies that Could Reduce the Incidence of violent crime and mass shootings

Gun control policies aimed at reducing violent crime and mass shootings encompass a range of measures, each with its own rationale and potential impact. Research has shown that the effectiveness of these policies can vary based on factors such as implementation, enforcement, and cultural attitudes toward firearms (D. W. Webster et al., 2020). For instance, comprehensive background check (CBC) policies have been associated with an increase in firearm background checks in certain states, indicating potential impact on regulating firearm acquisition (Castillo-Carniglia et al., 2017). Additionally, state background checks for gun purchase have been linked to changes in firearm deaths, suggesting a potential influence on overall firearm-related mortality rates (Sen & Panjamapirom, 2012b).

The impact of community violence on social outcomes, such as standardized test performance and fear of victimization, has been documented, highlighting the broader societal implications of gun violence (Sharkey et al., 2014; Stroebe et al., 2017). Mass shootings have also been found to influence public support for gun control measures, indicating a potential shift in attitudes and policy preferences following such events (Kantack & Paschall, 2019). Moreover, the risk of gun violence to children and youth has been a significant concern, emphasizing the need for policies and interventions to protect vulnerable populations (Simpson & Rohan, 2023).

Innovative interventions beyond traditional gun laws have been proposed to address gun violence, reflecting the evolving strategies to mitigate its impact (Branas et al., 2021). Additionally, the assessment of gun safety policy by gun owners has been studied, shedding light on the underlying principles and detailed opinions that shape attitudes toward firearm regulations (Grene et al., 2023). Moreover, efforts to keep guns from high-risk persons through background checks and gun violence restraining orders have been explored as part of state-level initiatives (Vernick et al., 2017).

Morral (2023b) presents a summary of findings from studies exploring the consequences of mental health-related prohibitions on gun ownership and their implications for violent crime, total homicides, and firearm homicides. The key points can be categorized as follows:

- Limited Evidence on Reduction of Violent Crime: The evidence indicates that prohibitions linked to mental illness might have a mitigating effect on violent crime. However, the strength of this association is constrained, and the evidence falls short of being conclusive.

- Inconclusive Effects on Total Homicides and Firearm Homicides: The text underscores the uncertainty surrounding the impact of mental health-related prohibitions on total homicides and firearm homicides. Studies employing comparable methodological rigor reveal inconsistent evidence or merely suggestive effects.

- Background Checks and Mental Illness Records: One study (Sen & Panjamapirom, 2012a) scrutinized the outcomes of background checks encompassing mental illness records on total homicides and firearm homicides. The findings suggest a potential correlation between these background checks and a decrease in both types of homicides, with the reduction in total homicides achieving statistical significance.

- NICS Reporting Changes: Another study (Swanson et al., 2013) delved into the repercussions of alterations in reporting gun-disqualifying mental health records to the National Instant Criminal Background Check System (NICS). This study identified a statistically significant reduction in violent crime arrest rates for individuals with a disqualifying mental health condition in Florida.

- Methodological Concerns: The text raises notable methodological concerns, particularly with the study conducted by (Sen & Panjamapirom, 2012a). These concerns revolve around potential biases or limitations in the study design.

The overarching conclusion is that there is limited evidence supporting the notion that certain state or federal mental health-related prohibitions on gun ownership may diminish violent crime (Morral, 2023b). Nevertheless, the evidence regarding the impact on total homicides and firearm homicides is regarded as inconclusive.

It is important to acknowledge that while these studies offer insights into the potential ramifications of mental health-related gun ownership prohibitions, the limitations and uncertainties in the evidence should be duly considered when formulating conclusions or shaping policy decisions (Morral, 2023b).

Charbonneau (2023a) offers an overview of research findings related to the impact of background checks on violent crime, with a specific focus on firearm-related homicides. The discussion encompasses various aspects, including the effects of dealer background checks, universal background checks, studies and methodologies employed in the research, and the limitations associated with these studies.

The examination of dealer background checks reveals inconclusive evidence regarding their effects on violent crime and total homicides (Charbonneau, 2023a). However, there is moderate evidence suggesting that dealer background checks may contribute to a reduction in firearm homicides.

Similarly, the evaluation of universal background checks presents a nuanced picture. While there is moderate evidence indicating a potential decrease in total homicides due to these laws, the evidence concerning their impact on firearm homicides is limited.

Charbonneau (2023a) delves into the complexity of studies and methodologies utilized in researching the subject. It emphasizes the diverse findings across studies, highlighting the uncertainty of effects in some cases and indicating reductions in firearm homicides in others.

Specific attention is given to studies on dealer background check laws, particularly those pertaining to the 1994 Brady Act. The inconsistent findings from these studies, along with mixed results from examinations of state-mandated dealer background checks, underscore the need for careful interpretation of their implications (Charbonneau, 2023a).

The discussion extends to studies on universal background check laws, which exhibit varying findings across different states and cities. Some studies suggest reductions in both firearm and total homicides following the implementation of these laws, contributing to the overall complexity of the relationship.

Background checks for private sales are also explored, revealing uncertain findings and variations dependent on the time frame and covariates considered in different studies. Some studies even indicate a potential increase in firearm homicides associated with private-seller background checks.

Charbonneau (2023a) further examines the components of background check records, discussing the comprehensiveness of these checks, including factors such as restraining orders, mental illness, and fugitive status. Studies suggest that more comprehensive background checks may be associated with fewer total and firearm homicides.

Expert opinions are highlighted as a crucial aspect of understanding the potential effects of background checks on violent crime outcomes (Charbonneau, 2023a). The passage emphasizes the importance of considering these expert perspectives in the broader analysis.

Lastly, the limitations of the studies are discussed, including issues such as model overfitting, lack of control groups, and potential confounds. The passage concludes by emphasizing the overall complexity of the relationship between background checks and violent crime, with evidence varying based on different factors and methodologies used in studies (Charbonneau, 2023a). It acknowledges the passage as a synthesis of various studies and underscores the subjectivity inherent in interpreting the information, prompting a call for further research and consideration of diverse perspectives.

The assessment of ten studies on dealer background checks reveals uncertain results concerning their effects on homicides and violent crime rates. While certain components, such as mental illness checks and restraining order checks, show evidence of effectiveness in reducing violent crime, the overall effects remain inconclusive (Charbonneau, 2023a). Specifically, studies examining the overall effect on firearm homicides provide moderate evidence that dealer background checks may contribute to a reduction in such incidents.

In the context of universal background checks, six studies scrutinize their impact on homicides. The findings present uncertain effects, with variations in outcomes based on the specific laws implemented. Notably, a significant reduction in homicides in U.S. cities is observed after the implementation of universal background checks, contrasting with uncertain effects in rural areas. Regarding firearm homicides, ten studies indicate varying associations, including both reductions and increases. While some studies report significant reductions in firearm homicides associated with universal background checks, others suggest increases or uncertain effects. The evidence regarding universal background checks' impact on firearm homicides remains limited, despite the diverse findings in the literature (Charbonneau, 2023a).

The analysis underscores the complex and nuanced nature of the relationship between background checks and crime. While certain components of background checks show promise in reducing violent crime, the overall effects, especially concerning firearm homicides, present a diverse and sometimes contradictory picture. The evidence suggests a need for further investigation and comprehensive evaluation before definitive conclusions can be drawn regarding the efficacy of background checks in mitigating crime (Charbonneau, 2023a).

Smucker (2023a) conducted a thorough examination of studies focused on appraising the repercussions of firearm prohibitions associated with domestic violence on a range of outcomes within the realm of violent crime. The subsequent paragraphs elucidate the principal findings and conclusions derived from these investigations.

DVRO Policies and Intimate Partner Homicide: The evidence strength pertaining to state laws instituting firearm prohibitions for individuals subjected to DVROs is classified as moderate. Studies have consistently shown that these laws yield moderate evidence indicating a significant reduction in both total and firearm-related intimate partner homicides. The findings suggest that firearm prohibitions for individuals under DVROs can effectively reduce both total and firearm-related intimate partner homicides (Smucker, 2023a).

Domestic Violence Misdemeanour Policies and Intimate Partner Homicide: In contrast, the evidence strength in the context of state firearm prohibitions linked with domestic violence misdemeanours is characterized as inconclusive. The data concerning the impact of these prohibitions on overall or firearm-related intimate partner homicides remains inconclusive, with variations apparent across different studies. Therefore, the impact of state firearm prohibitions associated with domestic violence misdemeanours on intimate partner homicides remains uncertain.

Prohibitions Associated with Stalking Offenses and Intimate Partner Homicide: The strength of evidence for prohibitions associated with stalking offenses is classified as limited for stalking misdemeanours and inconclusive for stalking convictions (Smucker, 2023a). Limited evidence suggests that prohibitions associated with stalking misdemeanours may contribute to an increase in total intimate partner homicides, while evidence for stalking convictions remains inconclusive. This indicates that the impact of stalking-related prohibitions on intimate partner homicides is not well-established.

Other Violent Crime Outcomes: The evidence strength in this category is designated as limited. Limited evidence indicates that firearm prohibitions related to domestic violence may lead to a reduction in both total and firearm-related homicides within specific subgroups, with variations contingent on the type of prohibition and the demographic under consideration. This suggests that the impact of firearm prohibitions on other violent crime outcomes is not as well-documented as in the context of intimate partner homicides (Smucker, 2023a).

Methodological Concerns: Several studies raise methodological concerns, encompassing issues related to study design or data analysis, which may impinge upon the reliability of their findings. These concerns highlight the need for rigorous research methodologies to ensure the validity and reliability of the evidence presented.

Overall Assessment: The findings furnish nuanced insights into the intricate relationships between firearm prohibitions associated with domestic violence and various outcomes in violent crime. The strength of evidence exhibits variability across different outcomes, underscoring the imperative for further research to address inconclusive findings (Smucker, 2023a). This summary, while providing a high-level overview, underscores the necessity for a more profound understanding through an examination of the specific studies and their methodologies.

The evidence strength varies across different policies related to domestic violence and intimate partner homicide, highlighting the need for continued research to elucidate the impact of firearm prohibitions on these outcomes. The nuanced nature of the findings emphasizes the importance of considering methodological concerns and conducting further in-depth studies to enhance our understanding of the complex relationships between firearm prohibitions and violent crime outcomes (Smucker, 2023a).

Smucker (2023b) explores the effects of firearm surrender laws on violent crime, specifically focusing on intimate partner homicides. The overall findings are presented in a nuanced manner, revealing inconclusive evidence regarding the impact of laws requiring prohibited possessors to surrender firearms on violent crime in general and intimate partner homicides in particular.

The summary indicates inconclusive evidence regarding the general effects of firearm-surrender laws on violent crime and intimate partner homicides. However, when combined with expanded firearm prohibitions, firearm-surrender laws exhibit moderate evidence of reducing firearm-involved intimate partner homicides, along with limited evidence suggesting a reduction in overall intimate partner homicides (Smucker, 2023b).

Six studies are discussed, all centred around surrender laws related to domestic violence. These studies, conducted over various periods and focusing on different aspects of firearm-surrender policies, contribute to the overall analysis. Noteworthy among them are Elizabeth Richardson Vigdor and James A Mercy (2006), Zeoli and Webster (2010), Díez et al. (2017), Raissian (2016), and Knopov et al. (2019). Each study explores different dimensions of the relationship between firearm surrender laws and violent crime, offering insights into their varied effects.

Throughout the analysis, Smucker (2023b) emphasizes methodological rigor. Smucker (2023b) notes concerns related to study design, data analysis, and potential biases that could impact the reliability of findings. These considerations are crucial for interpreting the results and understanding the limitations of the studies.

The included forest plot presents estimates of the standardized effect sizes (or IRRs) for each outcome associated with firearm-surrender laws. The IRRs, along with confidence intervals, provide a statistical measure of the impact of these laws on various violent crime outcomes (Smucker, 2023b).

Smucker (2023b) concludes with a summary of the overall findings reiterating the inconclusive evidence for the effects of surrender laws alone on violent crime. However, when surrender laws are combined with expanded prohibitions against firearm ownership for specific categories, there is a suggestion of moderate evidence for reducing firearm-involved intimate partner homicides and limited evidence for reducing all intimate partner homicides (Smucker, 2023b).

In essence, Smucker (2023b) underscores the complexity of the relationship between firearm-surrender laws and violent crime, emphasizing the need for careful consideration of methodological factors and the combined effects of policies for a more comprehensive understanding.

Charbonneau (2023b) scrutinizes the influence of Child-Access Prevention (CAP) laws on violent crime, with a particular focus on firearm homicides and assault injuries among young people (Charbonneau, 2023b). Child-access prevention laws demonstrate a favourable trend in reducing firearm homicides or firearm assault injuries among young individuals. Notably, at least three studies, devoid of significant methodological weaknesses, consistently observed suggestive or significant effects in the same direction, utilizing multiple independent datasets (Charbonneau, 2023b).

The evidence regarding the impact of child-access prevention laws on total homicides and other violent crimes remains inconclusive (Charbonneau, 2023b). Studies with comparable methodological rigor produced inconsistent findings concerning the policy's effect on these outcomes. In some instances, a single study reported uncertain or suggestive effects, contributing to the overall ambiguity of the evidence.

The analysis encompasses eight quasi-experimental studies, providing insights into the effects of CAP laws on violent crime. These studies delve into specific facets such as firearm homicides, negligent storage provisions, school shootings, workplace homicides, and assault injuries (Charbonneau, 2023b). Each study contributes to the nuanced understanding of the multifaceted impact of CAP laws.

Certain studies prompt methodological concerns, shedding light on issues such as overfitting, lack of adjustment for clustering, low power to detect rare outcomes, and potential violations of linear probability model assumptions (Charbonneau, 2023b). These concerns are important for interpreting the reliability and validity of the findings derived from the studies.

While supportive evidence is identified for the positive impact of child-access prevention laws in reducing firearm homicides or firearm assault injuries among young individuals, the evidence regarding their effects on total homicide rates and other violent crimes remains inconclusive. A comprehensive evaluation of several studies, each characterized by its unique strengths and weaknesses, contributes to a nuanced understanding of the intricate dynamics surrounding the impact of CAP laws on different aspects of violent crime (Charbonneau, 2023b).

The analysis conducted by Schell (2023) delves into the repercussions of Child-Access Prevention (CAP) laws on unintentional firearm injuries and deaths across various age groups, encompassing both children and adults. The summarized findings highlight the impact of these laws on distinct demographics.

Concerning Child-Access Prevention Laws and Children, the study unearths supportive evidence implying an association with a reduction in unintentional firearm injuries and deaths. Notably, at least three studies, distinguished by robust methodologies, consistently reveal suggestive or significant effects moving in the same direction (Schell, 2023). This consistency is maintained across multiple independent datasets, reinforcing the credibility of the findings.

Transitioning to the examination of Child-Access Prevention Laws and Adults, the evidence suggests a more circumscribed impact, indicating a potential decrease in unintentional firearm injuries and deaths among adults. While one study adhering to inclusion criteria reported a significant effect on outcomes, no contradictory evidence surfaced in studies boasting equivalent or stronger methodologies (Schell, 2023).

The expansive spectrum of Studies Reviewed comprises seven studies that met the inclusion criteria. These studies systematically explored the effects of CAP laws on unintentional injuries or deaths, catering to diverse age groups. Analytical approaches included state and time fixed-effects models, covering negligent storage provisions, reckless provision laws, felony CAP laws, and misdemeanour CAP laws.

Despite the valuable insights gleaned from the studies, Methodological Concerns cast a shadow, with certain studies raising issues such as overfitting, lack of adjustment for clustering, and potential violations of linear probability model assumptions. These concerns emerge as critical facets, demanding consideration for a nuanced interpretation of the findings (Schell, 2023).

Concluding the analysis, the findings underscore supportive evidence for child-access prevention laws effectively reducing unintentional firearm injuries and deaths among children (Schell, 2023). Nevertheless, the evidence regarding their impact on young adults or adults remains confined, marked by limitations. The amalgamation of studies, characterized by varying strengths and methodologies, collectively contributes to a comprehensive understanding, suggesting that CAP laws might indeed exert a positive influence on mitigating unintentional firearm injuries and deaths across diverse age groups.

Smart (2023b) assesses the effects of Child-Access Prevention (CAP) laws on suicide, presenting key findings related to young people, adults, and the total population.

For young people, there is moderate evidence that CAP laws reduce total suicides, supported by at least two studies with significant effects in the same direction and no contradictory evidence found. However, evidence for the overall impact of CAP laws on total suicides is inconclusive, with studies showing inconsistent results (Smart, 2023b).

Regarding firearm self-injuries among young people, there is supportive evidence that CAP laws reduce such incidents, including firearm suicides, suicide attempts, and non-suicidal self-injuries (Smart, 2023b). At least three studies with robust methodologies found suggestive or significant effects in the same direction using multiple independent datasets.

The analysis includes 11 quasi-experimental studies, five of which are new in this edition. These studies examine various aspects of CAP laws, such as negligent storage provisions and reckless provision laws. Methodological concerns arise in some studies, highlighting issues like overfitting, lack of adjustment for clustering, and potential violations of linear probability model assumptions (Smart, 2023b).

Several studies attempt to isolate the effects of specific provisions of CAP laws, including those related to negligent storage and reckless provision. Findings suggest reductions in firearm suicides and injuries among young people but also reveal limitations in data quality and potential biases in effect size estimates.

The research provides moderate evidence that CAP laws reduce total suicides among young people, while evidence for their impact on total suicides in the general population remains inconclusive (Smart, 2023b). The analysis emphasizes the importance of considering methodological concerns and variations in study findings when interpreting the effects of CAP laws on firearm-related outcomes among different age groups.

The analysis by Morral (2023d) evaluates the effects of waiting periods on violent crime, focusing on total homicides and firearm homicides. The key findings indicate that waiting periods may decrease total homicides, with moderate evidence supporting this relationship. Two or more studies, at least one free from serious methodological weaknesses, found significant effects in the same direction. Contradictory evidence was not identified in studies with equivalent or stronger methods (Morral, 2023d).

Further, waiting periods may decrease firearm homicides, but the evidence for this relationship is limited (Morral, 2023d). At least one study meeting inclusion criteria, without significant methodological weaknesses, reported a significant effect on the outcome. No studies with equivalent or stronger methods provided contradictory evidence.

The analysis incorporates six studies assessing the effects of waiting periods on violent crime. Ludwig and Cook (2000) compared states that implemented waiting periods in 1994 (due to the Brady Act) with states that did not. However, methodological concerns led to the discounting of evidence, considering the possibility of overfitting in the model.

Studies specifically examining waiting periods' impact on violent crime include Mustard (2001), Roberts (2009), Hepburn et al. (2004), Edwards et al. (2018), and Luca et al. (2017). Mustard's findings on the effects of waiting periods on police officer deaths had uncertain results. Roberts highlighted declines in intimate partner homicide associated with waiting periods of two to seven days, while longer or shorter waiting periods showed only suggestive effects. Hepburn et al. found suggestive negative effects on homicides, while Edwards et al. found uncertain effects on total homicides but suggestive effects on decreasing firearm homicides. Luca, Malhotra, and Poliquin reported significant reductions in total and firearm homicide rates among adults aged 21 or older.

The research provides moderate evidence that waiting periods may reduce total homicides and limited evidence that they may reduce firearm homicides (Morral, 2023d). Methodological concerns in some studies are acknowledged, emphasizing the need for careful interpretation of the findings.

Smart (2023e) explores the impact of waiting periods on suicide, considering both total suicides and firearm suicides. The key findings indicate that waiting periods may decrease total suicides, but the evidence for this relationship is limited. At least one study meeting inclusion criteria, without significant methodological weaknesses, reported a significant effect of waiting periods on total suicides. No studies with equivalent or stronger methods provided contradictory evidence (Smart, 2023e). Waiting periods may decrease firearm suicides, and the evidence for this relationship is moderate. Two or more studies, at least one free from serious methodological weaknesses, found significant effects in the same direction. Contradictory evidence was not identified in other studies with equivalent or stronger methods (Smart, 2023e).

The analysis involves four studies assessing how waiting-period laws influence suicide. Cook and Ludwig (2013) provided results comparable to an earlier paper (Ludwig & Cook, 2000). However, methodological concerns in the earlier paper led to the discounting of evidence (Smart, 2023e).

Recent studies by Edwards et al. (2018) and Luca et al. (2017) built on Ludwig and Cook's work, estimating the effects of waiting periods on suicide rates. Edwards et al. found significant negative effects on firearm suicides and suggestive negative effects on total suicides associated with any purchase delay. Luca, Malhotra, and Poliquin found significant negative effects on total and firearm suicide rates of laws imposing a mandatory delay on handgun purchases or a permitting system with waiting periods (Smart, 2023e).

A study by Anestis and Anestis (2015) compared national suicide trends with those in South Dakota and the District of Columbia after changes in waiting-period laws. Although the descriptive evidence is limited, it suggested an increase in suicide rates following the repeal of a waiting-period law in South Dakota and a decrease following an extension of the waiting period in the District of Columbia.

The research indicates limited evidence that waiting periods may reduce total suicides and moderate evidence that they may reduce firearm suicides. Methodological concerns in some studies are acknowledged, emphasizing the importance of careful interpretation of the findings.

Smart (2023d) delves into the impact of minimum age requirements on suicide, with a specific focus on firearm-related suicides among young individuals. In examining this complex issue, the study draws several noteworthy conclusions.

The findings suggest that implementing minimum age requirements for purchasing a firearm might contribute to a reduction in firearm suicides among young people (Smart, 2023d). The evidence supporting this correlation is considered moderate. Notably, two or more studies, with at least one demonstrating robust methodology, consistently reported significant effects in the same direction. Importantly, there was a lack of contradictory evidence from studies employing equivalent or more rigorous methods.

On the other hand, the analysis indicates a level of uncertainty regarding the effects of higher minimum age requirements for purchasing a firearm on total suicides (Smart, 2023d). The evidence in this regard is inconclusive, with studies of comparable methodological rigor yielding inconsistent findings. In some instances, a single study identified uncertain or suggestive effects, adding complexity to the overall picture.

Similarly, the assessment of higher minimum age requirements for possessing a firearm reveals uncertain effects on total suicides. The evidence remains inconclusive, with studies of similar methodological rigor providing inconsistent findings or suggesting uncertain effects on total suicides. As in the previous case, the inclusion of a single study reporting uncertain or suggestive effects contributes to the ambiguity surrounding this relationship (Smart, 2023d).

Despite the uncertainties in total suicides, the analysis suggests that higher minimum age requirements for possessing a firearm may have a limited impact on decreasing firearm suicides among young people. In this case, at least one study, meeting predefined inclusion criteria and characterized by robust methodology, reported a significant effect of the policy on reducing firearm suicides. Importantly, there was an absence of contradictory evidence from studies with equivalent or stronger methods.

This comprehensive analysis involves eight quasi-experimental longitudinal studies, with three studies presenting novel findings. Contributions from Marvell (2001), Webster et al. (2004), Kappelman and Fording (2021), Antonio Rodríguez Andrés and Katherine Hempstead (2011), Gius (2015), Rosengart et al. (2005), Siegel, Pahn, et al. (2019), and Raifman et al. (2020) collectively offer diverse perspectives on the impact of minimum age requirements on suicide.

Certain studies, such as those by Kappelman and Fording (2021), Siegel, Pahn, et al. (2019), and Raifman et al. (2020), suggest a potential association between both minimum age purchase and possession laws, featuring higher age limits than federal law, and substantial reductions in firearm suicides among individuals aged 24 or younger. However, it is crucial to acknowledge lingering uncertainties, with some studies indicating inconsistent or suggestive effects (Smart, 2023d). Careful interpretation is essential due to variations in study methodologies, highlighting the importance of addressing potential overfitting concerns in certain models.

Regarding minimum age requirements for purchasing a firearm, Webster et al. (2004) reported uncertain effects of minimum purchase age laws (ranging from ages 16 to 21) on suicides among those aged 14–17 and 18–20. Rosengart et al. (2005) found uncertain effects of laws requiring a minimum age of 21 to purchase a firearm on suicides and firearm suicides across all age groups. Antonio Rodríguez Andrés and Katherine Hempstead (2011) found that laws banning firearm purchases by minors were linked to significantly lower suicide rates among males aged 15–44. Kappelman and Fording (2021) and Raifman et al. (2020) both observed reductions in firearm suicides associated with higher minimum ages of purchase than required by federal law.

The evidence on how higher minimum age requirements for purchasing a firearm affect total suicides is inconclusive. However, studies focusing on laws setting 21 as the minimum age for firearm purchase provide moderate evidence suggesting that such laws may reduce firearm suicides among young people.

Concerning minimum age requirements for possessing a firearm, Marvell (2001) found uncertain effects of laws banning handgun possession by juveniles on suicide rates among those aged 15–19. Webster et al. (2004) reported uncertain effects of minimum possession age laws (ranging from ages 14 to 21) on suicides and firearm suicides among those aged 14–17. Siegel, Pahn, et al. (2019) found suggestive negative effects of these laws on total suicide rates and significant negative effects on firearm suicide rates. Rosengart et al. (2005) found uncertain effects of laws setting a minimum handgun possession age of 21 on suicides overall and among those aged 20 or older, with a suggestive effect indicating potential increases in suicides among those under age 20. Gius (2015) reported only uncertain effects of state minimum age of possession laws on firearm suicides among those aged 19 or younger. Kappelman and Fording (2021) found a significant effect of laws with a higher minimum age of handgun possession than required by federal law in reducing firearm suicides among those aged 24 and younger.

The evidence for how minimum age requirements for possessing a firearm affect total suicides is inconclusive, while there is limited evidence suggesting that higher minimum age requirements for possession may reduce firearm suicides among young people.

Analysis by Morral (2023a) on the effects of licensing and permitting requirements on suicide reveals limited evidence indicating that such requirements may decrease total suicides and firearm suicides among adults. The evidence is based on at least one study meeting inclusion criteria and devoid of significant methodological weaknesses. However, the impact of licensing and permitting requirements on total suicides and firearm suicides among minors remains inconclusive, with studies of comparable methodological rigor yielding inconsistent evidence or single studies reporting uncertain or suggestive effects (Morral, 2023a).

The review encompasses five U.S.-based longitudinal studies, including new findings from Alexander D McCourt et al. (2020). Webster et al. (2004) examined the effects of firearm policies on suicides among teens (aged 14–17) and young adults (aged 18–20) from 1976 to 2001, finding that permit-to-purchase laws significantly increased total suicide rates among those aged 18–20, primarily driven by a 22-percent increase in firearm suicides. However, the results were uncertain for non-firearm suicides and younger age groups. Antonio Rodríguez Andrés and Katherine Hempstead (2011) reported mixed results, associating permitting requirements with reduced suicide rates among men aged 45 or older but increased rates for men aged 15–24. (Crifasi et al., 2015)used a synthetic control approach, suggesting a reduction in firearm suicide rates in Connecticut after the implementation of permit-to-purchase laws. Alexander D McCourt et al. (2020) provided similar findings with a 33-percent decrease in firearm suicides in Connecticut and a 24-percent increase in Missouri after the repeal of permit-to-purchase requirements. Lastly, Luca et al. (2017) indicated that handgun permit requirements were associated with significantly reduced rates of total and firearm suicides for adults aged 21 or older.

The analysis finds limited evidence supporting the idea that licensing and permitting requirements may decrease total suicides and firearm suicides among adults, while the evidence regarding their impact on minors is inconclusive Morral (2023a). The studies suggest varying effects, with careful consideration required due to methodological limitations and potential confounding factors.

The analysis on the effects of assault weapon and high-capacity magazine bans on mass shootings by Smart (2023a) presents inconclusive evidence regarding the impact of assault weapon bans, while suggesting that high-capacity magazine bans may decrease mass shootings to a limited extent.

Assault weapon bans show uncertain effects on mass shootings, with studies of comparable methodological rigor yielding inconsistent evidence or single studies reporting uncertain or suggestive effects (Smart, 2023a). The analysis includes six studies examining the effects of state or federal assault weapon bans on multiple-victim shooting incidents or casualties. Gius (2015) focused on public mass shootings, indicating that state assault weapon bans had a statistically significant but smaller effect on reducing mass shooting death rates, with uncertain effects on injuries. Luca et al. (2017) found uncertain effects of state assault weapon bans on the probability of mass shooting incidents occurring, serving as a robustness check for their primary focus on the effects of mass shootings on gun policy. D. W. Webster et al. (2020) provided uncertain evidence that assault weapon bans were associated with mass shooting incidents or deaths.

For high-capacity magazine bans, evidence suggests a limited decrease in mass shootings. Klarevas et al. (2019) found that state-level high-capacity magazine bans were associated with fewer mass shootings and deaths in incidents involving a high-capacity magazine, with suggestive reductions in overall mass shooting incidents and deaths. D. W. Webster et al. (2020) reported significant or suggestive associations between state high-capacity magazine bans and lower rates of mass shooting incidents.

The analysis finds inconclusive evidence for the effect of assault weapon bans on mass shootings and limited evidence suggesting that high-capacity magazine bans may reduce mass shootings to some extent (Smart, 2023a). The studies highlight varying effects, with caution warranted due to methodological limitations and potential biases.

Gun Control Policies that Could Increase the Incidence of violent crime and mass shootings

The debate surrounding gun control policies is multifaceted, with critics raising concerns about potential unintended consequences and the efficacy of certain measures. Critics argue that stricter gun regulations may deter law-abiding citizens from acquiring firearms for self-defence, leaving them vulnerable to criminal activity (D. W. Webster et al., 2020). Additionally, critics suggest that assault weapons bans may be more symbolic than practical, as individuals intent on causing harm can find alternative means, potentially impacting overall crime rates minimally (Koper et al., 2017). Restrictions on magazine capacity might lead to increased firearm ownership, potentially facilitating quicker reloading and firing, negating the intended effects of such restrictions (Siegel et al., 2020). Waiting periods for firearm purchases could hinder law-abiding citizens from promptly obtaining a weapon for self-defence, particularly in urgent situations (Liu et al., 2022).

Critics also argue that universal background checks may not effectively prevent criminals from obtaining firearms, potentially burdening law-abiding citizens without a proportional reduction in crime (Balakrishna & Wilbur, 2021). Concerns about due process have been raised regarding red flag laws, as individuals could face temporary firearm removal without adequate legal safeguards (Wintemute, 2012). Sceptics of firearm registration and licensing express concerns that such measures might create a framework for future gun confiscation efforts, contributing to resistance against these policies (Donohue, 2022). Critics argue that solely focusing on community-based violence prevention programs without addressing the immediate availability of firearms might be insufficient in preventing mass shootings (Collins et al., 2018).

These arguments highlight the complexity of the issue, emphasizing the need to consider various perspectives and potential implications of gun control policies. The effectiveness of each measure can be influenced by factors such as implementation, enforcement, and cultural attitudes toward firearms (D. W. Webster et al., 2020). It is crucial for policymakers to strike a balance between reducing the risks of gun-related violence and respecting individual rights, considering public opinion, legal considerations, and the political landscape (Abelow et al., 2020).

Analysis by Smart (2023c) of the effects of concealed-carry laws on violent crime reveals a complex landscape. There is supportive evidence indicating that shall-issue concealed-carry laws may increase both total and firearm homicides. This relationship is affirmed by at least three studies with robust methodologies, demonstrating suggestive or significant effects consistently in the same direction across multiple independent datasets. However, for permitless-carry laws, evidence on their effects on total homicides is inconclusive, with studies of comparable methodological rigor yielding inconsistent evidence or single studies reporting only uncertain or suggestive effects (Smart, 2023c). Concerning violent crime, there is limited evidence suggesting that shall-issue concealed-carry laws may increase it, as at least one study meeting the inclusion criteria reported a significant effect, and no studies with equivalent or stronger methods provided contradictory evidence (Smart, 2023c).

The research on the impact of shall-issue laws on violent crime intensified in 1997 following analyses by Lott and Mustard (1997), asserting that states adopting shall-issue laws experienced significant decreases in various crime rates. Subsequent studies, listed in the analysis, critically examined and responded to these findings, leading to inconclusive results and the acknowledgment of methodological issues. Notable reviews by the National Research Council (NRC) and the Community Preventive Services Task Force, both in 2005, echoed the uncertainty in determining the effect of shall-issue laws on violent crime due to methodological sensitivities and statistical imprecision (Smart, 2023c).

The early studies were marred by significant problems, such as inaccuracies in county crime data, exclusion of counties with undefined arrest rates, errors in shall-issue state classifications, lack of control for serial correlation, and overfitting of statistical models with an excessive number of covariates (Smart, 2023c). Most of these issues were later addressed by authors and were improved upon in subsequent studies.

Since 2004, research efforts have focused on refining methodologies and addressing earlier limitations. Studies using county-level, state-level, and city-level data have contributed to the understanding of concealed-carry laws' impact on violent crime. However, the complexity of this issue persists, and the evolving nature of research aims to provide more accurate insights into the relationship between concealed-carry laws and violent crime outcomes (Smart, 2023c).

County-level studies on the impact of shall-issue laws on crime data face challenges due to significant shortcomings in the reporting of crime statistics to the FBI by numerous county police agencies. The abrupt changes in addressing missing data in the early 1990s further complicate comparisons between earlier and later data. Despite these issues, some analyses have continued using county-level crime data or alternative sources like the CDC's National Vital Statistics System for evaluating the effects of such laws.

Roberts (2009) utilized FBI's Supplementary Homicide Reports to examine intimate partner homicide rates, finding that may-issue laws significantly increased such homicides compared to shall-issue laws. Aneja et al. (2011) corrected errors in previous analyses and found no statistically significant effects of shall-issue laws on seven crime rates. Moody (2001) contested the methodology of Aneja, Donohue, and Zhang, presenting an updated hybrid model suggesting that shall-issue laws reduced trends in rape and murder rates.

Durlauf et al. (2016) explored the sensitivity of analyses regarding shall-issue laws' impact on violent crime, highlighting the importance of population weights and model specifications. Crifasi et al. (2018) examined the effects of shall-issue laws on homicides in large, urban counties, finding a significant increase in firearm homicide rates.

State-level studies present a mixed picture. Hepburn et al. (2004) found uncertain effects of shall-issue laws on state homicide rates. Rosengart et al. (2005) and Martin Jr and Legault (2005) provided varying results, with some indicating an increase in firearm homicides associated with shall-issue laws. Gius (2014) found higher gun-related murder rates in states with more-restrictive policies. Donohue et al. (2019) reported uncertain effects on murder rates but significant increases in violent and property crime rates.

Synthetic control methods were employed by Donohue, Aneja, and Weber (2019) to estimate effects over time, suggesting that states with shall-issue laws experienced elevated rates of violent crime. Siegel, Pahn, et al. (2019), found significant increases in homicide rates with shall-issue laws but uncertain effects for permitless-carry laws. Shi and Lee (2018) explored various crime rates, finding mixed results for shall-issue laws' effects, with some indicating immediate increases in crime.

Studies also investigated the impact of concealed-carry laws on specific outcomes, such as workplace homicides, assaults on police officers, and campus crime rates. Doucette et al. (2019) reported significant increases in firearm workplace-related homicides associated with more-permissive concealed-carry laws. Sabbath et al. (2020) found that additional restrictive concealed-carry provisions reduced workplace homicide rates.

Overall, the studies present a complex and sometimes conflicting picture of the effects of shall-issue laws on various crime rates, with methodological considerations and data limitations influencing the results.

Several city-level studies have investigated the impact of shall-issue laws on rates of violent crime, including homicide, robbery, assault, and rape. Tomislav V Kovandzic et al. (2005) conducted an analysis on 189 large U.S. cities from 1980 to 2000, finding uncertain effects for all violent crime outcomes. La Valle (2013) analysed data from 56 cities spanning 1980–2010, suggesting that shall-issue laws significantly reduced gun homicides but showed conflicting results when compared with another study (La Valle & Glover, 2012). Siegel et al. (2020) focused on medium-to-large cities and nonurban areas between 1991 and 2016, indicating a significant reduction in firearm homicides in cities after the repeal of stringent may-issue laws. Smith and Petrocelli (2019) examined the impact of concealed-carry deregulation in Arizona, finding uncertain effects on violent crime outcomes in Tucson.

Three studies examined the relationship between unmarried fertility or abortions and violent crime, including shall-issue laws as covariates. Donohue III and Levitt (2001), (Lott Jr & Whitley, 2007), and Kendall and Tamura (2010) provided varying results on the effects of shall-issue laws on violent crime rates. Zimmerman (2014) studied private security measures, including shall-issue laws as a covariate, finding that these laws led to higher rates of murder and assault. Manski and Pepper (2018) investigated shall-issue effect estimates under different assumptions, concluding that causal effects were not well identified. Strnad (2007) used Bayesian model comparison techniques to reanalyse the effects of shall-issue laws, suggesting little or no effect on most outcomes.

Among the 22 studies without serious methodological concerns, the evidence on the impact of shall-issue laws on violent crime is mixed. For total homicides, the literature provides supportive evidence that shall-issue laws increase total homicides, especially in studies including data beyond 2000 Smart (2023c). Regarding firearm homicides, there is supportive evidence that shall-issue laws increase these rates. For robberies, assaults, and rapes, the available studies provide inconclusive evidence on the effects of shall-issue laws Smart (2023c). Additionally, evidence on overall violent crime is inconclusive, with some studies suggesting an increase. The sensitivity of results to model specification and varying study methodologies highlight the complexity of assessing the impact of shall-issue laws on violent crime Smart (2023c).

The analysis, as presented by Morral (2023c), of the effects of Stand-Your-Ground (SYG) laws on violent crime reveals mixed findings. The overall impact on total homicide rates is considered moderate, with evidence suggesting that SYG laws may lead to an increase in total homicides. This conclusion is drawn from multiple studies, at least one of which was methodologically robust, consistently showing significant effects in the same direction. However, the certainty of these findings is somewhat undermined by potential methodological weaknesses in some studies (Morral, 2023c).

Similarly, the evidence regarding the influence of SYG laws on firearm homicides is supportive, indicating that these laws may contribute to an increase in firearm homicide rates. Multiple studies, not compromised by significant methodological weaknesses, consistently demonstrate effects in the same direction, using independent data sets. The association between SYG laws and overall violent crime rates, however, is deemed limited. One study meeting the inclusion criteria reported a significant effect of SYG laws on overall violent crime rates, but contradictory evidence was lacking among studies with equivalent or stronger methodologies (Morral, 2023c).

Sixteen studies were identified in the analysis, with nine contributing new findings. Cheng and Hoekstra (2013) study, conducted from 2000 to 2010, found a significant association between SYG laws and a 6 to 11 percent increase in homicide rates. Gius (2016) analysed a longer time series (1980–2011) and identified significant increases in murder rates associated with SYG laws. (McClellan & Tekin, 2017) study from 1999 to 2010 indicated an 8-percent increase in firearm homicides. Other studies, including those focusing on subsets such as workplace homicides, provided uncertain or mixed associations with SYG laws.

In summary, the analysis suggests that SYG laws may moderately increase total homicide rates, offer supportive evidence for an increase in firearm homicides, and show limited evidence for an impact on overall violent crime rates (Morral, 2023c). The findings underscore the complexity of assessing the consequences of SYG laws and highlight the need for further research to better understand their nuanced effects on different aspects of violent crime.

Effectiveness

The effectiveness of gun control policies in the USA is a multifaceted and contentious issue, influenced by various factors such as the specific policies implemented, their enforcement, cultural attitudes towards firearms, and the overall context of crime and violence. Several measures have been implemented to address this issue, each with its own effectiveness and challenges, as discussed above.

Background checks for gun purchases have been relatively effective in screening out prohibited buyers, aiming to prevent individuals with criminal records or mental health issues from acquiring firearms legally. However, challenges in enforcement and incomplete databases have allowed some individuals to slip through the system (Sen & Panjamapirom, 2012b). The effectiveness of the previous federal assault weapons ban (1994-2004) is debated, with some studies suggesting a limited impact on overall crime rates, as perpetrators could switch to non-banned firearms. The challenges lie in the contentious definition of "assault weapons" and potential loopholes in the regulation of specific firearm features (Rosengart, 2005).

Waiting periods, which aim to provide a cooling-off period and conduct background checks, have a debated impact on overall crime rates. While they might prevent impulsive purchases, critics argue that they can be an inconvenience for law-abiding citizens and may not significantly deter criminals (Liu & Wiebe, 2019). States with permissive concealed carry laws argue that armed citizens can deter crime. However, studies on the impact of concealed carry on crime rates are inconclusive and depend on various factors. Critics express concerns about the potential for increased firearm-related incidents and accidents (Callcut et al., 2019).

Red flag laws, allowing temporary firearm removal from individuals deemed a risk, aim to prevent potential violence. While they can be effective, concerns about due process have been raised, and their effectiveness depends on the proper identification of individuals at risk and the legal safeguards in place (Lang, 2016). Gun buyback programs aim to reduce the number of firearms in circulation but have limited impact on overall crime rates, as they often attract law-abiding citizens rather than criminals. These programs may not reach the most at-risk populations or address the illegal acquisition of firearms (LaPlant et al., 2020).

Programs focused on addressing root causes of violence have shown promise, but their impact on reducing mass shootings is not direct. Long-term success may require addressing broader societal issues beyond gun control (Vernick et al., 2017). Ensuring background checks for all gun sales aims to close loopholes, but enforcement challenges and resistance to universal checks pose obstacles. The effectiveness depends on compliance and the ability to prevent private sales without checks (Collins et al., 2018).

Everytown Research & Policy (2024) discusses a comparison of gun policies and gun violence rates across U.S. states. States with stronger gun laws tend to have lower rates of gun violence. The analysis ranks states based on 50 key gun safety policies and their corresponding gun violence rates per 100,000 residents. The top-performing states in terms of gun law strength include California, New York, and Illinois, while states like Kansas, Missouri, and Alaska are considered national failures in terms of gun safety (Everytown Research & Policy, 2024).

The analysis emphasizes that if all states adopted the gun safety measures of the national leaders, approximately 298,000 lives could be saved in the next decade. The study categorizes states into different tiers based on their gun law strength and gun violence rates, highlighting a clear correlation between strong gun laws and fewer deaths.

Everytown Research & Policy (2024) advocates for core foundational laws, such as background checks, Extreme Risk laws, secure gun storage requirements, and rejecting Shoot First (Stand Your Ground) and permitless carry laws. It suggests that these measures are crucial for effective gun violence prevention.

Additionally, the analysis notes the impact of neighbouring states' weak laws on a state's vulnerability, citing the "iron pipeline" phenomenon where traffickers bring guns from states with weaker laws to those with stronger regulations (Everytown Research & Policy, 2024). The role of high gun ownership rates in contributing to gun violence is also discussed.

Everytown Research & Policy (2024) underscores the importance of time for new laws to have an impact, citing examples of states that have recently strengthened their policies and may see positive effects in the coming years. It also emphasizes the need for federal laws to complement state efforts, pointing out existing gaps in the federal system.

GUN OWNERSHIP AND CONTROL IN CANADA

Canadian Gun Control Landscape

Gun ownership is relatively high in Canada, with approximately thirty-five firearms per hundred residents, ranking the country fifth globally in this aspect (Masters, 2022). Despite the substantial number of firearms, Canada does not face a comparable level of gun violence. Similar to the United States, Canada's federal government establishes gun restrictions, with the option for provinces, territories, and municipalities to add supplementary regulations. The history of Canada's gun laws reveals a pattern of responses to incidents of gun violence (Masters, 2022).

A pivotal event occurred in 1989 when a student armed with a semiautomatic rifle killed fourteen students and injured many others at a Montreal engineering school (Masters, 2022). This tragedy led to significant gun reforms, including the implementation of a twenty-eight-day waiting period for purchases, mandatory safety training courses, more thorough background checks, bans on large-capacity magazines, and increased restrictions on military-style firearms and ammunition (Masters, 2022).

In Canada, firearms are categorized into three classes: nonrestricted weapons (ordinary rifles and shotguns), restricted weapons (handguns, semiautomatic rifles or shotguns), and prohibited weapons (automatic weapons). Ownership of fully automatic weapons is illegal unless registered before 1978 (Masters, 2022).

Changes to the law in 1995 mandated individuals to obtain a license for purchasing guns and ammunition, along with registering all firearms. However, in 2012, the registration requirement for nonrestricted guns was eliminated, and associated public records were expunged (Masters, 2022). Following a mass shooting at a Quebec City mosque in 2017, the government enacted a bill to reinstate the registration of nonrestricted firearms and allow background checks to consider events from over five years ago (Masters, 2022). In response to Canada's deadliest mass shooting in 2020, where a gunman killed twenty-two people, Prime Minister Justin Trudeau announced a ban on "assault-style" firearms (Masters, 2022). The legislation also compelled owners of now-prohibited firearms to either participate in a buyback program or adhere to a stringent storage regimen (Masters, 2022).

The Canadian firearms regulations, established by the federal Criminal Law Amendment Act of 1977, are aimed at controlling the possession and use of various types of firearms. The law prohibits automatic weapons and sawed-off shotguns and rifles, reserving them primarily for police and military use. Handguns face restrictions, requiring a registration certificate for possession and a permit, issued under limited circumstances, for carrying. Only specific individuals, including police, gun club members, collectors, and those demonstrating a need for self-protection, can obtain a certificate (Rose, 1994).

Hunting rifles and shotguns are subject to acquiring a firearms acquisition certificate, with a 28-day waiting period and a fee (Rose, 1994). The law prohibits individuals with certain criminal records or a history of violence or mental disorders associated with violence from obtaining this certificate. Court-ordered possession bans, ranging from 10 years to life, may be imposed for individuals convicted of serious crimes or deemed a safety risk (Rose, 1994).

The law grants police extensive search and seizure powers concerning prohibited and restricted firearms, allowing warrantless searches and inspections. Illegal possession or transfer of prohibited or restricted weapons can result in imprisonment, with varying terms depending on the offense. The minimum age for firearm possession is 18, with exceptions for supervised minors.

The Canadian Constitution lacks specific protections for gun owners (Rose, 1994). The Criminal Law Amendment Act classifies firearms into prohibited, restricted, and non-restricted categories. Firearms acquisition certificates are mandatory for obtaining any firearm, and registration certificates are required for restricted firearms. Permits for carrying restricted firearms are issued for specific purposes and durations. Businesses involved with firearms must obtain annual permits, and firearm storage and handling must adhere to specified regulations (Rose, 1994).

Appeals processes are in place for those aggrieved by decisions of firearms officers or issuing authorities (Rose, 1994). The law emphasizes secure storage of firearms and imposes penalties for reckless handling. Various saving provisions exempt individuals from prosecution in certain circumstances, such as acquiring prohibited weapons through judicial sales.

Canada classifies firearms into three main categories: Non-Restricted, Restricted, and Prohibited. Non-Restricted firearms generally include long guns, such as hunting rifles and shotguns, while Restricted firearms encompass specific handguns and semi-automatic firearms. Prohibited firearms include certain handguns, fully automatic firearms, and others. The Canadian Firearms Act of 1995 established the classification of firearms into Non-Restricted, Restricted, and Prohibited categories, with specific criteria for each category (Langmann, 2012). This legislation covers all firearms and has been in place since 1995, providing a model for incremental firearms control (Langmann, 2012). The Act has been associated with preventing or containing various types of firearms deaths, including those among youth, and has been credited with a decline in male firearm suicide rates in Quebec (Burrows et al., 2013).

The Canadian Medical Association (CMA) and the Canadian Paediatric Society (CPS) have supported classifying non-powdered firearms capable of causing injury as firearms under Canada's Firearms Act (1995) (Saunders et al., 2022). This highlights the importance of comprehensive firearms regulations in addressing the burden of firearm injuries in Canadian children and youth (Saunders et al., 2022).

In Canada, the rate of firearm ownership is lower than that of the USA, but high compared with other upper-income countries (Austin & Lane, 2018). The relatively strict federal gun control laws in Canada have been associated with preventing firearm injuries in Canadian youth (Austin & Lane, 2018). Additionally, the Canadian approach to handgun regulation has been deemed consistent with respect for the autonomy of persons, prevention of harms, and social justice (Vernick et al., 2007).

In Canada, individuals are required to obtain a firearms license from the Royal Canadian Mounted Police (RCMP) in order to own and possess firearms. There are two main types of licenses: the Possession and Acquisition License (PAL) for individuals wanting to buy, own, and use firearms, and a Restricted PAL (RPAL) for those seeking to acquire restricted firearms.

The primary license for individuals aspiring to buy, own, and use firearms is known as the Possession and Acquisition License (PAL). This license allows holders to possess non-restricted firearms, which typically include long guns such as hunting rifles and shotguns. Additionally, individuals with a PAL can acquire firearms, subject to the applicable legal and regulatory requirements.

For those who wish to acquire restricted firearms, a specialized license, namely the Restricted Possession and Acquisition License (RPAL), is required. The RPAL is an extension of the PAL, tailored specifically for individuals seeking ownership of restricted firearms. Restricted firearms encompass a range of specific handguns and semi-automatic firearms, and their ownership is subject to more stringent regulations due to their inherently higher potential for misuse or harm.

The process of obtaining either the PAL or RPAL involves a thorough vetting procedure conducted by the RCMP. This includes comprehensive background checks, criminal record verifications, and considerations for mental health issues. Applicants are also required to successfully complete the relevant Canadian Firearms Safety Course (CFSC) or the Canadian Restricted Firearms Safety Course (CRFSC), depending on the type of license sought. These safety courses provide essential education on responsible firearm handling, storage, and use, ensuring that license holders are well-informed and competent in their firearm-related activities.

The Possession and Acquisition License and its restricted counterpart, the RPAL, reflect Canada's commitment to balancing individual rights with public safety considerations. By implementing a structured and regulated licensing system, the Canadian government aims to mitigate potential risks associated with firearm ownership while allowing law-abiding citizens to engage in responsible firearm-related activities.

The process of obtaining a firearms license in Canada involves stringent measures to ensure the safe storage and transport of firearms, the purchase of ammunition, and rifle training (Ajdacic-Gross et al., 2006). The licensing laws in Canada are designed to ensure the safe and responsible ownership and use of firearms within the country.

The licensing laws in Canada have been subject to ethical and legal debates, particularly in comparison to the United States' approach to handgun regulation. Canada's licensing laws have been challenged as potentially infringing on an individual's "right" to own a gun, despite the possibility of owning firearms, particularly rifles and shotguns, for many individuals (Vernick et al., 2007). This highlights the complex ethical and legal considerations surrounding firearms licensing in Canada.

Research has shown that firearms licensing data may not be a reliable proxy for firearm access, and there is a lack of recent survey data available about ownership and storage practices in Canada (Toigo et al., 2023). This emphasizes the need for ongoing research and data collection to inform and evaluate firearms licensing policies and their effectiveness in ensuring public safety.

The registration of firearms is mandatory in Canada, and all firearms must be registered with the Canadian Firearms Program (CFP). Non-restricted firearms are typically associated with the possession license, while restricted firearms must be individually registered. The Canadian Firearms Program (CFP) was established in 1995, and since its implementation, there has been a significant reduction in firearm-related suicides and intimate partner homicides (Snider et al., 2009). The program includes background checks, licensing, references, psychological questionnaires, prohibition of paramilitary style rifles, and magazine capacity restrictions to decrease the incidences and deaths from mass shootings (Langmann, 2022). Additionally, Bill C-51 introduced mandatory record-keeping by arms dealers, enacted a ban on fully automatic firearms, and required Firearm Acquisition Certificates (FACs) for rifles and shotguns (Bennett, Karkada, Erdoğan, et al., 2022).

Research has shown that restrictive firearms regulations in Canada contributed to a decrease in suicides, but firearm registration remains a contentious issue (Burrows et al., 2013). The implementation of legislation does not always decrease the total number or the overall suicide rate, as seen in other countries (Kennedy et al., 2021). However, since 2000, suicide rates in Quebec have declined strikingly, particularly among teenagers and young adult men, indicating the potential impact of firearms regulation on declining rates of male suicide (Gagné et al., 2010).

Data from Canada from 1969 to 1985 showed that the passage of a stricter firearms control law in 1977 was associated with a decrease in the use of firearms for homicide but an increase in the use of all other methods for homicide (Leenaars & Lester, 1994). This suggests that while firearms legislation may impact the use of firearms for homicide, it may also lead to a shift in the methods used for committing homicides.

To ensure the safe and responsible use of firearms, individuals in Canada are required to undergo a thorough process before obtaining a firearms license. This process includes background checks, such as criminal record checks and considerations for mental health issues, as well as the completion of the Canadian Firearms Safety Course (CFSC) for non-restricted firearms or the Canadian Restricted Firearms Safety Course (CRFSC) for restricted firearms. These measures are in place to prevent individuals with a history of criminal activity or mental health issues from obtaining firearms, thereby promoting public safety and reducing the risk of firearm-related incidents (Castillo-Carniglia et al., 2017; Jennissen et al., 2021; Price & Norris, 2010; D. W. Webster et al., 2020).

The background checks for firearm licensing in Canada involve a comprehensive review of various types of data, including criminal history through fingerprints, to identify conditions that prohibit firearm possession. This approach goes beyond relying solely on the information provided by the applicant, ensuring a more thorough assessment of an individual's eligibility to possess firearms (D. W. Webster et al., 2020).

States may maintain mental health databases that are utilized to determine firearm eligibility, and this information may be forwarded to the National Instant Criminal Background Check System. This demonstrates the consideration of mental health issues in the background check process for firearm licensing, aligning with the goal of preventing individuals with serious mental illness from obtaining firearms (Price & Norris, 2010).

In addition to background checks, the completion of the Canadian Firearms Safety Course (CFSC or CRFSC) is a crucial requirement for obtaining a firearms license in Canada. This course provides essential knowledge and skills related to firearm safety, handling, and operation, ensuring that individuals are equipped to use firearms responsibly and in accordance with the law (Jennissen et al., 2021; Wintemute, 2013).

The Canadian Firearms Safety Course (CFSC) serves as a comprehensive educational program integral to the Canadian firearm licensing process. Mandatory for individuals seeking a Possession and Acquisition License (PAL) to own and use firearms, including non-restricted firearms like hunting rifles and shotguns, the course aims to equip participants with the essential knowledge and skills for the safe and responsible handling of firearms.

Within the CFSC, participants are instructed on fundamental Firearm Safety Rules, emphasizing principles such as treating every firearm as loaded, maintaining a safe direction, and being conscious of the target and its surroundings. The curriculum also delves into the diverse Types of Firearms, elucidating their components and functionalities to foster an understanding of the distinct characteristics and capabilities of various firearms (Royal Canadian Mounted Police, 2024).

Ammunition forms a critical component of the course, where participants gain insights into identifying, handling, and safely storing different types of ammunition. This knowledge is paramount for ensuring the secure and effective use of firearms. Practical guidance is provided on Loading and Unloading firearms, covering proper techniques for handling ammunition, inserting and removing magazines, and maintaining the firearm in a safe condition when not in use.

Participants are educated on the Safe Handling and Storage of firearms, receiving information on securing firearms to prevent unauthorized access, utilizing locked containers for storage, and implementing precautions to avoid accidents (Royal Canadian Mounted Police, 2024). While the CFSC is not a marksmanship training course, it introduces participants to the Fundamentals of Marksmanship, including principles like aiming, trigger control, and breath control.

Legal and Ethical Considerations are integral to the curriculum, offering insights into Canadian firearm laws and regulations. Participants learn about their legal responsibilities as firearm owners, encompassing licensing requirements, storage regulations, and rules for firearm transportation.

Typically delivered by certified instructors approved by the Royal Canadian Mounted Police (RCMP), the CFSC comprises both theoretical and practical components. Participants are required to pass a written and practical exam, demonstrating their comprehension of the material. Successful completion of the CFSC is a prerequisite for obtaining a Possession and Acquisition License (PAL) in Canada.

The implementation of comprehensive background check (CBC) laws, as well as handgun purchaser licensing laws, has been shown to have an impact on firearm-related incidents. Studies have examined the effects of these laws on firearm homicide and suicide rates, highlighting the potential of such regulations to contribute to reducing firearm violence (Castillo-Carniglia et al., 2017; Irvin et al., 2014; Alexander D. McCourt et al., 2020).

Moreover, there is support among federally licensed firearms retailers for background check requirements on all firearm transfers and selected criteria for denying the purchase of handguns based on criminal convictions, alcohol abuse, and serious mental illness. This reflects the recognition of the importance of stringent background checks and denial criteria in promoting responsible firearm ownership and preventing the acquisition of firearms by individuals with disqualifying factors (Wintemute, 2013).

To ensure the secure storage and transportation of firearms, it is essential to implement measures that limit access to unauthorized individuals. Secure storage practices, such as storing firearms unloaded and locked up using locking devices like gun safes or cable locks, are crucial for preventing unauthorized access and theft (Pallin & Barnhorst, 2021). Additionally, formal firearms training has been linked to improved firearm storage practices, emphasizing the importance of training covering safe handling, safe storage, and theft prevention (Berrigan et al., 2019). It has been suggested that safe storage could reduce the risk of firearms being lost due to burglary or theft, which occurs frequently in the US (Kellermann et al., 2000). Furthermore, the use of locking devices to limit ready access to firearms for unauthorized users is emphasized for safe storage (Bandel et al., 2023).

In the context of suicide prevention and interpersonal violence, recommendations include voluntary, temporary out-of-home firearm storage and secure storage at home to reduce firearm access during times of risk (Barnard et al., 2021). Studies have also highlighted the importance of firearm storage in preventing injury and death, with a focus on reducing intentional and unintentional injuries and deaths from firearms (Rivara et al., 1997). Moreover, research has shown that most firearms that were stolen were properly stored in gun safes, indicating the effectiveness of secure storage in preventing theft (Lakomaa, 2014).

The relationship between insecure storage, firearm theft, and subsequent acts of violence and injury has been emphasized, reinforcing the need to educate firearm owners to secure their weapons and enforce security laws (Walters, 2000). Additionally, legislative action and measures to reduce migration of firearms across state borders have been proposed as part of an overarching strategy to prevent firearm-related deaths, highlighting the importance of comprehensive firearm legislation (Liu et al., 2022).

The Canadian government has implemented gun bans in response to public safety concerns, aiming to reduce the risk of gun violence and ensure public safety. These bans have been a subject of extensive research and analysis. For instance, a study by Fleming et al. (2018) highlights the successful lobbying efforts of the Coalition for Gun Control in Canada, which led to the implementation of the Firearms Act of 1995. Additionally, Schwartz (2022) demonstrates the utility of a framework through an evaluation of the 2020 assault-style weapons ban in Canada, emphasizing the systematic scoping review of the literature on the impact of assault-weapons bans. Furthermore, Ulrich (2022) emphasizes the role of the government in addressing the broad harms of gun violence and the associated racial disparities, indicating the necessity of government intervention in combating this issue.

The study by Stroebe et al. (2021) sheds light on the belief of a substantial proportion of Canadian handgun owners in the need for self-defence, which poses a challenge to the Canadian government's attempt to outlaw handgun ownership. This highlights the complexities and challenges associated with implementing gun bans in Canada. Additionally, the research by Koper et al. (2017) discusses the federal government's ban on assault weapons from 1994 to 2004, indicating the historical context of gun bans in Canada.

The study by Newman and Hartman (2017) demonstrates that increased proximity to mass shootings is associated with heightened public support for stricter gun control, indicating the influence of public sentiment and events on the implementation of gun control measures. Additionally, Ulrich (2019) emphasizes the need for a public health approach to address gun violence, highlighting the multifaceted nature of combating this issue.

In Canada, the legality of self-defence with a firearm is a complex and contentious issue. The Criminal Code recognizes self-defence with a firearm, but it is very restricted, and the use of force with a firearm is legal only if the accused can prove that their life was in danger (Ajdacic-Gross et al., 2006). The Firearms Act of 1995 provides a legal framework for the acquisition, possession, and carrying of restricted or prohibited firearms for protection from other individuals when police protection is deemed insufficient, although this situation is extremely rare (Ajdacic-Gross et al., 2006). Additionally, there has been intensive public debate concerning firearms in Canada over the past two decades, particularly regarding the effectiveness of gun control legislation.

Furthermore, there have been efforts to address the burden of firearm injuries, especially in children and youth, in Canada. The Canadian Medical Association and the Canadian Paediatric Society have published statements supporting the classification of non-powdered firearms capable of causing injury as firearms under Canada's Firearms Act (Saunders et al., 2022). Moreover, the Canadian law of self-defence has become more permissive in important respects, raising questions about its implications and potential risks (Weisbord, 2020). Additionally, amendments to the homicide provisions in the Criminal Code have reframed the law of self-defence and provocation, but without explicit consideration for the circumstances of women who kill abusive partners (Edwards & Koshan, 2023).

Firearm Ownership in Canada

The data from Royal Canadian Mounted Police (2019) for the year 2019 presents the number of individual firearms possession and acquisition licences in Canada, broken down by different provinces and territories. The total number of Possession and Acquisition Licences (PAL) in Canada was 2,219,344, with a total population of 37,811,399. This equates to approximately 5.87 licences per 100 people across the country.

In Alberta, there were 326,519 firearm licences among a population of 4,384,982, resulting in approximately 7.45 licences per 100 people. British Columbia had 310,193 licences among a population of 5,130,251, translating to approximately 6.05 licences per 100 people. Manitoba had 93,425 licences among a population of 1,374,081, resulting in approximately 6.80 licences per 100 people. New Brunswick had 70,958 licences among a population of 780,631, equating to approximately 9.09 licences per 100 people. Newfoundland and Labrador had 77,116 licences among a population of 523,847, resulting in approximately 14.72 licences per 100 people.

The Northwest Territories had 6,022 licences among a population of 45,189, translating to approximately 13.33 licences per 100 people. Nova Scotia had 77,017 licences among a population of 976,495, equating to approximately 7.89 licences per 100 people. Nunavut had 3,859 licences among a population of 38,625, resulting in approximately 9.99 licences per 100 people. Ontario had 628,714 licences among a population of 14,638,247, translating to approximately 4.29 licences per 100 people. Prince Edward Island had 6,530 licences among a population of 158,778, equating to approximately 4.11 licences per 100 people. Quebec had 497,862 licences among a population of 8,542,198, resulting in approximately 5.83 licences per 100 people. Saskatchewan had 113,143 licences among a population of 1,176,427, translating to approximately 9.62 licences per 100 people. Finally, Yukon had 7,986 licences among a population of 41,648, equating to approximately 19.17 licences per 100 people. This data is represented graphically as Figure 16.

Licences per 100 people

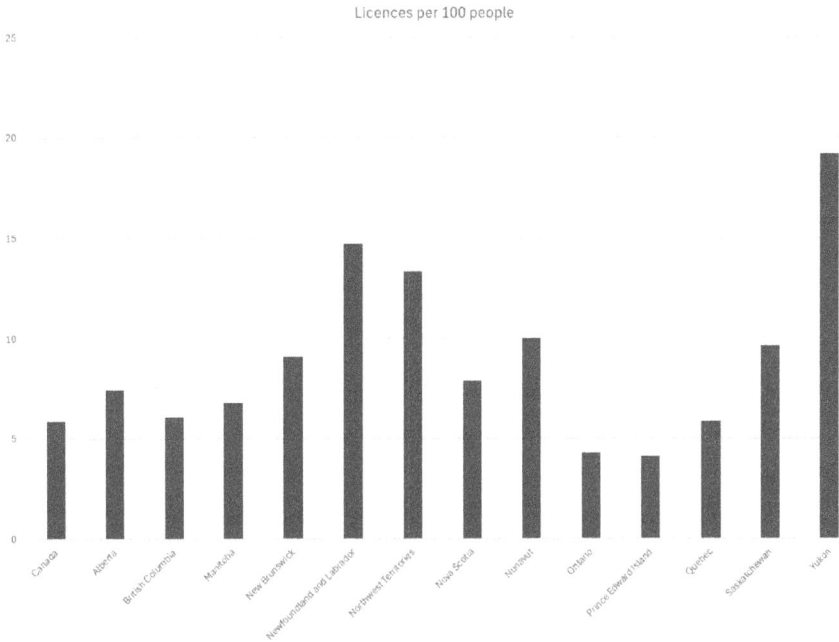

Figure 16: Individual firearms licences in Canada, 2019.

This data provides a comprehensive overview of the distribution of individual firearms licences across different regions of Canada, offering insights into the prevalence of firearm ownership relative to the population in each jurisdiction. The variations in the number of licences per 100 people across the provinces and territories reflect the differing attitudes towards firearm ownership and regulations in these regions. The high number of licences per 100 people in Newfoundland and Labrador, the Northwest Territories, Nunavut, and Yukon may indicate a greater cultural acceptance or reliance on firearms in these areas, potentially influenced by factors such as hunting traditions, geographic isolation, or specific socio-economic conditions. Conversely, the lower number of licences per 100 people in Ontario and Prince Edward Island may suggest a relatively lower prevalence of firearm ownership in these regions, possibly influenced by urbanization, stricter regulations, or differing cultural attitudes towards firearms.

Firearms in Canada are categorized into prohibited, restricted, non-restricted, and antique classes based on the specifications outlined in Part III of the Criminal Code.

Prohibited: Prohibited firearms include handguns with a barrel length less than 105 millimetres or designed for .25 or .32 calibre ammunition. Rifles and shotguns are also prohibited if altered to have a barrel length less than 457 millimetres or an overall length less than 660 millimetres. Firearms with fully automatic fire capability, "converted auto-matics," and those prescribed by specific regulations fall into this category.

The Government of Canada, as of May 1, 2020, has implemented a prohibition on over 1,500 models of assault-style firearms and certain components of newly prohibited firearms, including the upper receivers of M16, AR-10, AR-15, and M4 patterns. New maximum thresholds for muzzle energy (greater than 10,000 Joules) and bore diameter (20 mm bore or greater) have been established, rendering firearms exceeding these limits prohibited (Public Safety Canada, 2024). To provide a transition period, a Criminal Code amnesty is currently in effect until October 30, 2025. This amnesty aims to shield individuals or businesses lawfully possessing newly prohibited firearms at the time of the prohibition from criminal liability as they work towards compliance with the new regulations.

The specific categories of firearms classified as prohibited under the Criminal Code, effective May 1, 2020, encompass various models, with changes from non-restricted or restricted classifications to prohibited. Examples include M16, M4, AR-10, AR-15 rifles, Ruger Mini-14 rifle, Vz58 rifle, M14 rifle, Beretta CX4 Storm carbine, Robinson Armament XCR rifle, CZ Scorpion EVO 3 carbine and pistol, SIG Sauer SIG MCX and SIG Sauer SIG MPX carbine and pistol, and Swiss Arms Classic Green and Seasons Series rifles. Notably, the upper receiver of the AR-15 rifle is also prescribed as a prohibited device (Public Safety Canada, 2024).

Furthermore, firearms with specific physical characteristics are prohibited due to their potential power exceeding safe civilian use. This includes firearms with a bore diameter of 20mm or greater, such as grenade launchers, and firearms capable of discharging a projectile with a muzzle energy greater than 10,000 Joules, exemplified by sniper rifles (Public Safety Canada, 2024).

Restricted: Federal laws in Canada impose strict restrictions on transporting restrict-ed or grandfathered firearms in public. While prohibited or restricted firearms are gen-erally prohibited in public spaces, exceptions exist for authorized transportation (ATT) for specific purposes. These include transfer to a new owner, transportation to a range, training course, repair shop, or gun show. Some individuals may receive an authorization to carry (ATC) for specific reasons, such as licensed trappers, protection against wildlife in remote areas, guarding valuables, or imminent danger to life (rarely issued).

Restricted firearms include handguns, firearms with a barrel length less than 470 millimetres, capable of semi-automatic discharge, and those with reduced overall length by folding or telescoping. Firearms prescribed as restricted by specific regulations are also included.

Non-restricted: Non-restricted firearms encompass those not falling into prohibited or restricted categories.

Antique: Antique firearms, exempt from the Possession and Acquisition License (PAL) requirement, include various categories designed before 1898. This includes cartridge-firing long arms and handguns chambered in obscure large-calibre rimfire cartridges, single-shot cartridge-firing centrefire rifles, rimfire smoothbore shotguns, centrefire cartridge handguns with no longer widely available calibres, and muzzleloading (black powder) handguns and cap-and-ball revolvers. Modern replicas of non-cartridge-firing long guns with specific ignition mechanisms are also considered antiques if designed before 1898.

The number of registered handguns in Canada witnessed a substantial 71% increase from 2010 to 2020, reaching around 1.1 million, as reported by the federal government (Williams, 2022). A 2017 Small Arms Survey approximated the civilian possession of firearms in Canada at 12.7 million, with an estimated ratio of 34.7 firearms per 100 people (Williams, 2022).

Gun ownership is concentrated, with more than 2.2 million people holding gun licenses in 2020, according to the Royal Canadian Mounted Police (Williams, 2022). Ontario and Quebec, the two most densely populated provinces, housed the majority of license holders, followed by the western provinces of Alberta and British Columbia. A 2019 Angus Reid survey revealed that the majority of guns in Canada are situated in rural areas and primarily used for hunting and recreational shooting (Williams, 2022).

In terms of gun violence, Canada exhibits a firearm homicide rate of 0.5 per 100,000 people, notably lower than the United States' rate of 4.12, as stated by the University of Washington's Institute for Health Metrics and Evaluation in a 2021 analysis (Williams, 2022).

Canada has experienced notable mass shootings in its history, including incidents in 1989 at Ecole Polytechnique in Montreal, 1992 at Concordia University, 2006 at Dawson College in Montreal, 2016 in La Loche, Saskatchewan, 2017 at a mosque in Quebec City, and 2020 in Portapique, Nova Scotia (Williams, 2022).

Despite these incidents, a March 2021 survey by Leger found that 66% of respondents supported stricter gun control in Canada (Williams, 2022). However, gun rights advocates, such as the Canadian Coalition for Firearms Rights, opposed the latest measures, denouncing the new legislation as a "massive sucker punch" (Williams, 2022). Alberta's chief firearms officer, Teri Bryant, criticized the proposed freeze on handgun sales, considering it an "enormous intrusion" into property rights and private lives, characterizing it as "virtue signalling" by the government (Williams, 2022). She advocated for hiring more firearms officers to ensure prompt and thorough vetting instead (Williams, 2022).

Impact of Gun Control Policies in Canada

Gun control has been a topic of significant interest and debate, particularly in countries such as Canada. Several studies have examined the impact of gun control on various aspects of society, including homicide rates, gun violence, and cultural attitudes towards firearms. The impact of gun control in Canada can be analysed from various perspectives, taking into account factors such as public safety, crime rates, and the balance between individual rights and collective security.

The Canadian approach, which includes comprehensive background checks, licensing, and restrictions on certain types of firearms, aims to prevent individuals with criminal intent or mental health issues from acquiring firearms (Barney & Schaffner, 2019). Additionally, gun control measures in Canada are designed to mitigate the risk of mass shootings, with efforts to ban certain types of assault-style firearms and implement stricter licensing requirements contributing to reducing the potential for large-scale violence (Luca et al., 2019). These measures contribute to public safety by regulating the possession and use of firearms, fostering a sense of security among the general population (Barney & Schaffner, 2019). However, critics argue that gun control measures may disproportionately affect law-abiding gun owners and infringe on individual rights, emphasizing the need to balance the preservation of legitimate uses of firearms, such as for sport or hunting, with the need for public safety (Sato & Haselswerdt, 2022).

In the context of Canada, Sheptycki (2009) indicates that gun control legislation has had a positive effect on reducing gun-related crime in the country, although a residual level of gun-related crime still persists. This suggests that while gun control measures have been effective to some extent, there are still challenges that need to be addressed. Additionally, Fleming et al. (2018) highlighted the successful lobbying efforts of the Coalition for Gun Control in Canada, which led to the implementation of the Firearms Act in 1995. This demonstrates the potential for advocacy and policy changes to influence gun control measures in the country.

Stricter gun control measures in Canada have been associated with relatively lower rates of gun-related crimes compared to countries with laxer regulations, such as the United States (Barney & Schaffner, 2019).

Snider et al. (2009) emphasized the potential impact of weakening gun laws in Canada, suggesting that such changes could lead to a significant increase in firearm-related mortality and injury. This underscores the importance of maintaining and strengthening existing gun control regulations to mitigate potential adverse outcomes.

In contrast, Klein (2019) highlighted the differences in attitudes towards firearms between Canada and the United States, indicating that gun ownership became synonymous with American identity, while Canadian women's liberationists were not necessarily aware of Canada's distinct attitudes towards firearms. This comparison underscores the influence of cultural and societal factors on gun control attitudes and policies.

DeKeseredy (2019) revealed that nearly 50% of domestic homicides involving firearms in Canada occurred in rural communities, despite these communities accounting for less than 20% of the country's population. This highlights the need for targeted interventions and policies to address gun-related violence in rural areas. Overall, the synthesis of these studies suggests that gun control measures in Canada have had a positive impact on reducing firearm-related homicides and crime. However, there are ongoing challenges, particularly in rural communities, and the potential consequences of weakening gun laws should be carefully considered to prevent an increase in firearm-related mortality and injury.

Internationally, Canada is often cited as an example of a country with effective gun control policies that strike a balance between individual freedoms and public safety (Luca et al., 2019). Comparisons with other nations highlight the diverse approaches to gun control and their varying impacts on crime rates and public safety (Luca et al., 2019). While these measures aim to enhance public safety and prevent firearm-related crimes, ongoing efforts are required to address emerging challenges and strike a balance between individual rights and collective security (Barney & Schaffner, 2019).

Canadians, Dare et al. (2023) suggests, are traditionally proud of their world's longest undefended border with the United States, find comfort in an imagined wall shielding them from American gun politics. However, recent amendments to Canada's gun control legislation, aimed at permanently banning military-style assault weapons, face challenges.

Introduced in response to rising firearm violence and supported by public health science, the amendments were withdrawn in February 2023 due to political impasse and opposition influenced by well-organized gun lobby groups (Dare et al., 2023). The retreat raises concerns about eroding distinctions between Canada and the U.S. on gun issues, highlighting a historical shift in gun control policies and public health imperatives.

Despite having no constitutional right to bear arms, Canada has experienced an erosion of gun control laws, with a high rate of gun ownership and increasing firearm-related incidents. Recent legislative efforts, such as Bill C-21, aim to address gun violence comprehensively, including freezing handgun sales, tackling cross-border smuggling, and restricting non-powder firearms. The withdrawn assault weapons ban, originally responding to a mass shooting, is seen as pivotal in preventing future incidents (Dare et al., 2023).

The influence of the gun lobby, echoing tactics of the U.S. National Rifle Association (NRA), raises concerns (Dare et al., 2023). Social media amplifies disinformation campaigns, targeting physicians advocating for evidence-based gun control. Dare et al. (2023) posits that despite valid criticisms of how the assault weapons amendments were introduced, the public health imperative supporting bans on weapons designed for maximum harm remains strong. Scientific evidence suggests that comprehensive bans decrease mass shootings and fatalities (Dare et al., 2023).

In a study by Bennett, Karkada, Erdogan, et al. (2022) a total, 1,479 articles underwent screening, leading to the inclusion of 18 studies. Among these, ten studies focused on the impact on homicides, revealing that 5 reported a decrease during the post-legislation period. One study indicated a shift from firearms to alternative methods of homicide among individuals aged 15–24 years. Evaluating suicides, eleven studies were conducted, with 9 showing a reduction in suicide rates. However, eight of these studies uncovered evidence of substitution from firearms to other means of suicide. Examining accidental deaths, two studies found no discernible benefits post-legislation. The available evidence on the effectiveness of Canadian firearms legislation in reducing homicide and accidental death rates remains inconclusive (Bennett, Karkada, Erdogan, et al., 2022). While a decrease in firearm-related suicide rates was noted, the presence of method substitution suggests the need for a re-evaluation of existing laws. Establishing an improved, evidence-based national framework for gun violence prevention may be beneficial (Bennett, Karkada, Erdogan, et al., 2022).

GUN OWNERSHIP AND CONTROL IN THE UNITED KINGDOM

UK Gun Control Landscape

The evolution of modern gun control measures in the United Kingdom (UK) can be traced back to significant acts of violence that led to public outcry and subsequent legislative action. One such event was the 1987 Hungerford massacre, where a lone gunman carried out a six-hour shooting spree, prompting the introduction of the Firearms (Amendment) Act ("Firearms (Amendment) Act 1997," 2013). This legislation expanded the list of prohibited weapons, including specific semiautomatic rifles, and imposed stricter registration requirements for other firearms. The impact of such incidents on public attitudes and subsequent policy changes has been a subject of extensive research (Frey & Kirk, 2021).

The aftermath of the Hungerford massacre and similar events has led to a re-examination of the effect of mass shootings on public support for gun control (Barney & Schaffner, 2019). It has been observed that such incidents have a profound impact on attitudes toward gun restrictions, often resulting in the implementation of far-reaching gun control policies, as seen in the case of the Dunblane massacre in 1996, which led to the banning of private ownership of handguns in Great Britain (Frey & Kirk, 2021).

The issue of gun control is highly politicized, even among gun owners, indicating that firearms have become political symbols with meanings that extend beyond mere self-interest in protecting ownership status (Burton et al., 2021). The polarization of attitudes toward gun policy, including gun control, has been a subject of interest, with studies seeking to explore the relationship between firearm knowledge and support for different categories of gun control measures (Kruis et al., 2021). Furthermore, the roots of the gun control debate have been found to be racialized, with portrayals of gun violence tapping into latent racial biases among certain groups (Walker et al., 2020). This racial dimension adds complexity to the discourse surrounding gun control and highlights the multifaceted nature of the issue.

In the context of the United Kingdom, the impact of mass shootings on gun policy has been a topic of investigation, with research focusing on the legislative response to such events and the effectiveness of gun control measures in reducing gun violence (Luca et al., 2019). The role of interest groups and their influence on gun legislation has also been examined, shedding light on the dynamics that shape the development and implementation of gun control policies (Richards, 2017). The public's perception of gun control legislation and the disconnect between public opinion and actual legislation have been areas of interest, with researchers attributing this gap to differences in engagement between supporters and opponents of stronger gun control (Aronow & Miller, 2016). Additionally, the media's coverage of armed attacks, framing them either as mass shootings or terrorism, has implications for public perception and policy responses (Hoffman & Jengelley, 2020).

The UK has implemented some of the most stringent control measures on public access to firearms, particularly in response to tragic events such as the 1996 Dunblane school massacre. Following this incident, the UK banned private ownership of handguns, with exceptions in Northern Ireland, the Channel Islands, and the Isle of Man, each having its legislation (Frey & Kirk, 2021). Additionally, Scotland imposes additional licensing for airguns, which is distinct from England and Wales (Frey & Kirk, 2021). The effectiveness of stringent firearms legislation as an evidence-based public health strategy to reduce firearm-related deaths is debated, and available scientific evidence is not conclusive (Gjertsen et al., 2013). However, there is evidence that firearm control policies have been associated with reduced firearm mortality rates in the United States (Kalesan et al., 2016). Furthermore, the introduction of legislation restricting ownership and access to firearms has been linked to significant decreases in firearm-related suicides, particularly among youth (Beautrais et al., 2006). These findings suggest that restrictive firearms regulations can have a positive impact on reducing firearm-related deaths.

The UK's response to the Dunblane massacre reflects a broader trend in countries such as the UK and the US, where there has been an increase in the regulation of firearms and a limitation of personal freedoms in response to perceived risks, such as terrorist attacks (Kupfer, 2015). This indicates that the UK's approach to firearms legislation is part of a larger global trend in addressing public safety concerns. Moreover, there is evidence that firearm control legislation, including a "cooling-off" period before firearm purchase, has been associated with reduced suicide rates, especially among younger adult men (Cantor & Slater, 1995). This suggests that firearm control legislation can have a positive impact on reducing firearm-related suicides.

Mass shootings are extremely rare in the UK, with only five major civilian-initiated shootings recorded in British history, including the Hungerford massacre (1987), Monkseaton shootings (1989), Dunblane massacre (1996), Cumbria shootings (2010), and Plymouth shooting (2021) (Khorram-Manesh et al., 2019). Concerns about the availability of illegal firearms have been sporadic, and there have been occasional incidents linked to frustrated men promoting toxic masculinity and antifeminism, such as the Isla Vista killings in 2014, the Toronto Van attack in 2018, the Hanau shootings in early 2020, and the Plymouth shooting in the UK in August 2021 (Vu et al., 2021). Research has also delved into the professionalism of co-offending groups committing violent firearms offenses in the UK, aiming to understand these groups in terms of their level of professionalism (Caddick & Porter, 2011).

The Dunblane tragedy in 1996, which resulted in the loss of sixteen schoolchildren, led to a significant shift in the UK's gun laws. The public outcry following this mass shooting fuelled the Snowdrop Petition campaign, ultimately resulting in the enactment of the UK's strictest gun laws, particularly the banning of handguns. This legislative change was accompanied by the implementation of a temporary gun buyback program, which was credited with removing tens of thousands of illegal or unwanted guns from circulation. The impact of such gun buyback programs has been a topic of interest in various studies. Research by Leigh and Neill (2010) found that a buyback in Australia led to a substantial drop in firearm suicide rates, indicating a potential positive effect of such programs on reducing firearm-related deaths. Additionally, a study by Kuhn et al. (2002) provided insights into the implementation of buyback programs in Milwaukee County, highlighting the practical aspects of such initiatives.

Furthermore, the effectiveness of gun control laws in the UK has been a subject of investigation. Ceylan et al. (2002) discussed the strict gun control laws in the UK, emphasizing the regulations around air weapons. They noted that despite stringent laws, most conventional air weapons in the UK do not require a license, raising questions about the efficacy of existing regulations. In contrast, (Ferrazares et al., 2021) presented findings suggesting that gun buyback programs in the US have had limited impact on reducing gun crime or firearm-related violence. This perspective adds a layer of complexity to the discourse surrounding the effectiveness of such initiatives.

The approach to policing in the UK differs significantly from that in the United States and other countries, as a majority of police officers in the UK do not carry firearms, in contrast to their counterparts elsewhere. Instead, only specially trained police units, responding to specific emergencies or operations, are armed. This approach aligns with the concept of policing by consent rather than by force (Phillips, 2020). The UK's policy on firearms aligns with the emphasis on de-escalation and policing by consent, reflecting a different approach to law enforcement compared to countries where firearms are more readily available, such as the US (Hobson et al., 2022). The historical examination of police firearms in the UK suggests that the use of firearms by officers has been a subject of scholarly inquiry, reflecting the unique approach to firearms within the UK police force (Phillips, 2020).

The decision to arm police officers is a critical one, as it directly impacts public safety and the nature of law enforcement. Research findings suggest that officers heavily rely on dispatched information when making decisions to use deadly force in ambiguous situations (Taylor, 2019). This reliance on information and the decision-making process underscores the significance of the UK's approach to firearms, as it reflects a deliberate effort to limit the use of deadly force and emphasize de-escalation. The use of de-escalation techniques in conflict situations and their effectiveness is discussed in Skiba (2020), recognising that it is essential to acknowledge that if a situation persists in escalating and de-escalation proves impossible or ineffective, individuals must have a strategy to safeguard themselves in the event that the worst-case scenario materializes.

In the context of the UK, the role of firearms in policing is also intertwined with broader societal and political dynamics. The development of dedicated police gang/firearm units in English cities, such as Trident in London, reflects the influence of policy transfer from the US and the recognition of specific challenges related to firearms and organized crime (Fraser & Atkinson, 2014). Additionally, the perception of firearms among police officers can be influenced by factors such as membership in pro-gun associations, highlighting the multifaceted nature of attitudes towards firearms within law enforcement (Borba & Gomes, 2021).

The gun control framework in the United Kingdom is known for its strict regulations, contributing to lower levels of gun homicide compared to other developed nations. Handguns are generally prohibited, with exceptions for police, military personnel, and those granted special permission. Military-style weapons are also banned. The licensing process for other firearms involves stringent checks, including criminal record, mental health, and references. A "good reason" such as job requirements or sport is necessary, while self-defence is not considered valid. Licenses must be renewed every five years, and stringent storage requirements are in place to prevent unauthorized access. Participation in gun clubs is permitted without a certificate if engaged in target shooting under specific conditions. Unlawful possession of a firearm carries a mandatory minimum prison sentence of five years, underscoring the strict enforcement of gun laws.

The legal framework surrounding firearms in the United Kingdom has evolved significantly since the enactment of the Firearms Act in 1968. This seminal legislation consolidated existing firearms laws into a single statute and introduced several key provisions that have shaped the country's approach to gun control. Subsequent amendments and additional acts have further refined and expanded upon these regulations, addressing specific concerns and incidents related to firearms. This comprehensive review will provide a detailed analysis of the key laws, regulations, and licensing guidance pertaining to firearms in the UK from 1968 to the present day.

The Firearms Act of 1968 marked a significant milestone in the regulation of firearms in the UK. Enacted with the aim of consolidating existing firearms legislation, this act introduced several important provisions that continue to influence the country's approach to gun control. One of the key aspects of this legislation was the requirement for individuals to obtain Firearms Certificates for rifles and handguns. To be granted such certificates, applicants were required to demonstrate good character, provide a valid reason for firearm possession, and ensure secure storage of the firearms. Additionally, the act introduced the Shotgun Certificate, which imposed less stringent requirements compared to the Firearms Certificate. This allowed individuals to possess any number of shotguns without the need for a specific reason and without storage restrictions. The Firearms Act of 1968 served as the foundational legal framework for gun control in the UK until the tragic events of the 1987 Hungerford massacre prompted further legislative action.

In response to the escalating concerns surrounding firearms following the Hungerford massacre, the UK government enacted the Firearms (Amendment) Act of 1988. This legislation imposed additional restrictions on shotguns, specifically prohibiting pump-action and self-loading rifles. Furthermore, military weapons firing explosive ammunition were brought under tighter control, reflecting the government's efforts to address the evolving landscape of firearm-related risks and threats.

The year 1997 witnessed significant changes to firearms legislation in the UK, particularly in response to the tragic events at Dunblane. The Conservative government introduced the Firearms (Amendment) Act 1997, which imposed restrictions on handguns, confining their possession to approved clubs and banning larger calibre handguns. Subsequently, the Labour government enacted the Firearms (Amendment) (No 2) Act 1997, which effectively prohibited civilian handgun ownership, with limited exceptions for muzzle-loading guns and starting pistols. These legislative measures underscored the government's commitment to addressing public safety concerns and mitigating the risks associated with civilian handgun ownership.

The early 2000s saw the introduction of additional legislative measures aimed at addressing specific aspects of firearm possession and use. The Anti-Social Behaviour Act of 2003 criminalized the possession of air weapons or imitation firearms in public places, reflecting the government's efforts to curb the misuse of such weapons in public settings. Subsequently, the Violent Crime Reduction Act of 2006 prohibited the sale, manufacture, import, modification, and transfer of Realistic Imitation Firearms (RIFs), while still permitting their ownership. Notably, airsoft guns were exempt from these restrictions, and face-to-face transactions became mandatory for air weapons, reflecting the government's nuanced approach to regulating different types of firearms and their associated activities.

The year 2010 witnessed the enactment of the Crime and Security Act, which introduced provisions aimed at safeguarding public safety in relation to airguns. Specifically, the act made it an offense to store airguns in a manner that allowed unauthorized access by individuals under the age of 18, reflecting the government's commitment to preventing unauthorized access to potentially dangerous firearms by minors.

In 2014, the College of Policing issued the Authorised Police Practice - Guide to Firearms Licensing, which mandated police refusal or revocation of firearms licenses for applicants or holders with records of domestic violence, drug and alcohol abuse, or mental illness. This guidance underscored the importance of considering an individual's background and behavioural history when assessing their suitability for firearm ownership, reflecting the government's commitment to ensuring responsible firearm licensing practices.

The year 2015 saw the introduction of the Air Weapons and Licensing (Scotland) Act, which mandated licensing for all airguns exceeding one joule in power in Scotland. This legislation reflected the Scottish government's efforts to introduce specific regulations tailored to the unique context of airgun ownership and use within the country.

In 2016, the British Medical Association issued guidance to GPs, obligating them to document firearms license applications in patients' notes and inform the police of any concerning factors until notified of the person's loss of weapons. This guidance underscored the role of healthcare professionals in contributing to the assessment of individuals' suitability for firearm ownership, reflecting the government's recognition of the importance of involving medical professionals in the licensing process. Furthermore, in 2016, Crimestoppers established the Gun Safety Line, a phone line that allows individuals to anonymously report concerns about the behaviour of gun owners, whether legal or illegal. This initiative reflected the government's commitment to engaging the public in efforts to promote responsible firearm ownership and usage, while also addressing potential risks associated with firearms in the community.

The Offensive Weapons Act 2019 outlined proposed amendments to Section 5 (Prohibited Weapons) of the 1968 act during the Bill stage, introducing three new categories: bump stocks, "Rapid Firing" MARS and Lever-release rifles (distinct from legally permissible lever-action rifles), and "High Muzzle Energy" firearms generating over 10,000ft/lb muzzle energy (National Rifle Association, 2020). The ban on bump stocks, triggered by the 2017 Las Vegas shooting, aimed to prevent their importation for use with illegal firearms, despite their limited impact on the UK legal market. MARS and Lever-release firearms, seen as a "loophole" allowing rapid firing, were reclassified under Section 5, with a compensation scheme for owners initiated in December 2020 ahead of the March 2021 enforcement. The proposal regarding high muzzle energy firearms, targeting .50BMG calibre rifles, did not make it into the final Act, and various proposed amendments, addressing firearm restrictions and airgun licensing in England and Wales, were not adopted. Public consultation in December 2020 evaluated air weapons and high muzzle energy firearms, with the results published in July 2022 (National Rifle Association, 2020).

The evolution of firearms laws, regulations, and licensing guidance in the UK from 1968 to the present day reflects the government's ongoing commitment to addressing public safety concerns, mitigating the risks associated with firearm ownership and usage, and promoting responsible firearm licensing practices. The legislative measures and guidance introduced during this period have been shaped by specific incidents, evolving societal attitudes towards firearms, and the government's recognition of the need to adapt regulations to address emerging challenges. As the landscape of firearm-related risks continues to evolve, it is likely that further legislative and regulatory measures will be introduced to ensure the continued safety and security of the public in relation to firearms.

The UK law categorizes a firearm as a lethal barrelled weapon, a prohibited weapon according to section 5, a relevant component part, or an accessory designed or adapted to reduce the noise or flash caused by firing the weapon. The definition of a "lethal barrelled weapon" includes any barrelled weapon capable of discharging a shot, bullet, or other missile with kinetic energy of more than one joule at the muzzle. This definition encompasses various items under firearms legislation, while airsoft guns with muzzle energy below 1 joule are not classified as firearms but are subject to separate restrictions under the Violent Crime Reduction Act 2006 (Wightman et al., 2013).

The Firearms Act 1968, which forms the basis of firearms legislation in the UK, categorizes firearms under different sections. By default, firearms fall under "Section 1," allowing private individuals to hold them with a Firearm Certificate containing appropriate conditions. This certificate is granted based on demonstrating membership of a Home Office Approved target club or engaging in hunting or pest-control work. However, further legislation may impose different restrictions on specific firearm types (Wightman et al., 2013).

The legislation also includes provisions for re-classification of certain firearms. For example, airguns deemed "not especially dangerous" can be held without a license in England and Wales, while most shotguns are held on a Section 2 Shotgun Certificate. Prohibited Weapons defined under Section 5 of the 1968 Act include machine guns, most semi-automatic rifles, most handguns, tasers, incapacitating sprays, and certain types of ammunition. Additionally, antiques and firearms of particular historic or technical value may be held by collectors or museums, even if they would normally be prohibited under Section 5 (Wightman et al., 2013).

The possession of ammunition for firearms is restricted to the holder of a Firearm Certificate authorized to possess that type of ammunition. However, shotgun cartridges can be legally possessed by anyone over the age of 15 without a license, provided the cartridges contain 5 or more shots (Wightman et al., 2013).

It is important to note that the Scottish Parliament does not have legislative authority over firearms, except for air guns since 2012. In Northern Ireland, firearms regulation is devolved to the Northern Ireland Assembly and is primarily regulated by the Firearms (Northern Ireland) Order 2004, which differs from the law in Great Britain. For instance, most handguns remain classified as Section 1, not Section 5 (prohibited weapons) in Northern Ireland (Wightman et al., 2013).

Firearm Ownership in the United Kingdom

The United Kingdom has specific regulations regarding firearms, including rifles, pistols, shotguns, and airguns. The law classifies most long firearms with rifled barrels under Section 1, allowing them to be held with a Firearm Certificate. This includes various types of rifles such as single-shot, bolt-action, Martini-action, lever-action, and revolver rifles in any calibre (Haw et al., 2004). However, self-loading and pump-action rifles are restricted to .22 rimfire calibre. Prohibited rifles encompass fully-automatic rifles, select-fire rifles, self-loading and pump-action rifles (except in .22 rimfire calibres), MARS, and Lever-release rifles (Haw et al., 2004).

Pistols and revolvers are subject to specific regulations, with most being prohibited in Great Britain, except for certain exceptions such as those used for humane dispatch or possessing historical significance (Haw et al., 2004). The legislation has led to the emergence of a market for "long-barrelled revolvers" and "long-barrelled pistols," which are permissible under certain conditions (Haw et al., 2004). Additionally, certain models of blank-firing starting pistols that can be easily converted to fire live ammunition may face restrictions or require a Firearm Certificate (Haw et al., 2004).

Shotguns are also regulated, with specific criteria for permitted types, including single-, double-, or triple-barrelled shotguns, as well as those with lever-action, pump-action, or semi-automatic action and a fixed magazine capacity of no more than 2 cartridges (Haw et al., 2004). Shotguns with a detachable magazine or larger fixed magazine are considered firearms and require a Section 1 Firearm Certificate (Haw et al., 2004).

Airguns are exempt from the requirement of a Firearm Certificate or Shotgun Certificate, except in Scotland where a certificate is now required (Haw et al., 2004). However, regulations exist regarding the acquisition, purchase, possession, and use of airguns, including age limits and restrictions on online or mail-order sales (Haw et al., 2004).

The legislation also addresses ammunition, with certain types being prohibited for civilians, including explosive, incendiary, noxious, and armour-piercing ammunition (Haw et al., 2004). The quantity of ammunition a Certificate Holder may possess is determined by Certificate conditions on a per-calibre basis (Haw et al., 2004).

Securing a license is a complex and lengthy procedure that initiates with the completion of an application form, wherein individuals are required to provide specific reasons for desiring a firearm, emphasizing the necessity to demonstrate a "good reason". This justification may involve professional or sporting requirements, as a mere desire to own a particular type of firearm is insufficient. Moreover, applicants must substantiate their eligibility for a firearms certificate and establish that they pose no threat to public safety or peace (BBC, 2021).

The involvement of independent referees is integral, as they are expected to furnish confidential character statements offering detailed insights into the applicant's mental state, home environment, and attitude towards firearms. Law enforcement officers conduct thorough checks on the Police National Computer to identify any criminal record, with individuals having served prison sentences exceeding three years being permanently barred from holding a firearms license (BBC, 2021). In cases where applicants declare relevant medical conditions, such as neurological disorders or mental health issues, communication with general practitioners (GPs) may be necessary. GPs are also contacted post-certification, allowing them to raise concerns and append notes to the medical records of firearm certificate holders (BBC, 2021).

Ultimately, senior officers must ascertain that individuals seeking shotgun licenses have secure storage facilities, typically in the form of a dedicated gun cabinet. Each certificate remains valid for a duration of five years (BBC, 2021).

Chief police officers retain the authority to revoke or decline the renewal of a license. This action can be taken if it is determined that the license holder is no longer trustworthy. In the fiscal year 2020/21, 306 firearm certificates were revoked in England and Wales, while in 2019/20, 49 firearms certificates were revoked in Scotland. Additionally, failure to utilize the firearm or acquire one by the certificate's expiration may also result in non-renewal of the license.

As per the data for England and Wales in 2021, there were 156,033 individuals certified to possess firearms, collectively owning 617,171 weapons. Additionally, there are shotgun certificates accounting for 1.4 million shotguns (BBC, 2021). Statistics pertaining to Scotland indicate that in 2020, 25,983 certificate holders possessed a total of 70,839 firearms (BBC, 2021). Furthermore, 46,703 individuals in Scotland are certified to hold shotguns, encompassing 133,037 weapons under this scheme (BBC, 2021).

Individuals in Northern Ireland have the option to obtain firearms certificates for various purposes, such as sports and pest control. In 2020, the number of firearm certificate holders reached 55,441 (BBC, 2021). In contrast to other parts of the UK, handguns are not prohibited in Northern Ireland. Notably, Northern Ireland stands as the sole region within the UK where gun ownership for self-defence purposes is permitted. Individuals can apply for a "personal protection weapon" certificate, which is granted when there is a perceived "real and immediate risk" to the individual, and possessing a firearm is deemed "reasonable, proportionate, and necessary to protect the life of the applicant" (BBC, 2021).

Gun Related Crime in the UK

Statistics regarding police-recorded firearm offenses are published by the Office for National Statistics (ONS) in the Crime in England & Wales bulletin, while gun-related crime statistics can be found in the ONS publication titled "Offences involving the use of weapons: data tables" (Allen & Burton, 2022).

For the year ending March 31, 2021, non-air firearms, which include handguns, shotguns, and rifles, constituted 69% of all recorded firearm offenses, while air firearms, such as air rifles, accounted for the remaining 31%. (Allen & Burton, 2022). During this period, police in England & Wales recorded a total of 5,709 non-air firearm offenses, marking a 14% decrease from the 6,622 offenses reported in 2019/20 (Allen & Burton, 2022).

In terms of homicides, the data indicates that there were 35 shooting-related homicides in the same period, constituting 6% of all homicides. Among these victims, 11% were female, and 89% were male (Allen & Burton, 2022).

Analysing the types of firearm offenses, the Criminal damage and Violence Against Person (VATP) categories collectively represented 31% and 29% of both air and non-air firearms offenses, respectively. Possession of weapons and Robbery accounted for 15% and 12% of offenses, respectively (Allen & Burton, 2022).

Examining the types of firearms used, handguns remained the most frequently used non-air firearm, comprising 37% of such offenses in 2020/21 (Allen & Burton, 2022). This marked a 7 percentage point decrease from 44% in 2010/11. Rifles remained the least common non-air firearms type, representing approximately 1% of all offenses over the period (Allen & Burton, 2022).

In terms of firearm offenses by Police Force Area, the Metropolitan Police Service (MPS) recorded the highest number of non-air firearm offenses in 2020/21, making up 22% of all such offenses in England and Wales (Allen & Burton, 2022). Compared to 2019/20, the MPS reported a 27% decrease in non-air weapon offenses, dropping from 1,765 to 1,281 (Allen & Burton, 2022). West Midlands Police had the highest rate of non-air firearm offenses at 24.5 per 100,000 population, followed by South Yorkshire Police at 20.8 in the year ending March 31, 2021 (Allen & Burton, 2022).

The number of firearm offences in London from 2015 to 2023 exhibited fluctuations, with the year 2022/23 recording 1,085 firearm offences, representing a slight increase from the 1,071 offences in 2021/22 (Statista, 2023d). It is noteworthy that the latter marked the year with the fewest firearm offences in the provided time period. The years 2020/21 and 2021/22, however, saw a significant decrease in firearm offences, which could potentially be attributed to the COVID-19 lockdowns (Statista, 2023d). This trend is consistent with the overall crime rate in London, which decreased from 102.4 crimes per 1,000 people in 2019/20 to 83.3 in 2020/21, before rising to 92.8 in 2021/22 and 100.9 in the most recent reporting year (Statista, 2023d).

In the context of firearm homicides, the United Kingdom stands out for its stringent gun laws, resulting in relatively low levels of gun crime and firearm homicides. In 2021/22, only four percent of homicides in England and Wales were attributed to shootings, a stark contrast to the United States, where 85.7 percent of homicides in 2021 were gun-related (Statista, 2023d). The predominant method of killing in England and Wales homicides was the use of a sharp instrument, constituting 41 percent of homicides in the 2020/21 reporting year.

Turning to the financial aspect of law enforcement, the policing budget for London in the fiscal year 2023/24 reached £4.53 billion, indicating an increase from £4.44 billion in the previous fiscal year (Statista, 2023d). This marks the sixth consecutive year of London's police budget increasing, in contrast to the period between 2013/14 and 2018/19, when it remained around £3.3 billion. Interestingly, it was even smaller than the budget in 2012/13, which stood at £3.62 billion. These budget increments align with an ongoing recruitment drive for police officers, as evidenced by the increase in the number of police officers in London from 31,087 in 2018 to 34,868 in 2022 (Statista, 2023d).

Many argue that the gun control approach in the UK offers several valuable lessons and insights that could be beneficial for other countries to consider. The UK's strict legislation, particularly its restrictions on firearm types, stringent licensing processes, and ban on handguns for the general public, has contributed to enhancing public safety (D. W. Webster et al., 2020). The emphasis on public safety is a central tenet of the UK's gun control strategy, designed to minimize the risk of gun-related violence and protect citizens (Hemenway & Miller, 2013). Additionally, the UK's firearm licensing process involves rigorous background checks, including criminal records, mental health assessments, and character references, ensuring that individuals granted gun ownership do not pose a threat to public safety (Prickett et al., 2014). By restricting access to certain types of firearms and imposing controls on their possession and use, the UK aims to reduce the potential for gun-related crimes.

The enforcement of firearm storage requirements, such as the need for a secure gun cabinet, has also contributed to preventing unauthorized access and enhancing overall safety (Schenck et al., 2022). Furthermore, the UK's commitment to regular evaluation and re-evaluation of its gun control laws ensures their ongoing effectiveness and allows for adjustments to address emerging challenges or changing societal dynamics (Kleck et al., 2016). Lastly, the importance placed on public awareness and education regarding gun ownership and safety in the UK can contribute to promoting responsible gun ownership and informing the public about the potential risks associated with firearms, thus contributing to a safer society (Kruis et al., 2021).

These lessons from the UK's gun control approach are valuable; however, it is important to note that each country's approach to gun control must be tailored to its unique social, cultural, and legal context. What works in one country may not be directly transferable to another. Therefore, while these lessons offer valuable insights, they should be adapted and implemented with careful consideration of local circumstances (Sycafoose, 2014).

GUN OWNERSHIP AND CONTROL IN AUSTRALIA

Australian Gun Control Approach

Australia boasts over 3.5 million registered firearms, with an average of four firearms per licensed owner, as reported by the University of Sydney's GunPolicy.org in data released for 2021 (Black, 2022). In addition to the registered firearms, an estimated 260,000 illegal firearms contribute to a national total approaching 3.8 million guns, as indicated by GunPolicy.org. Approximately three out of every 100 Australians hold a licensed gun ownership status (Black, 2022).

Munslow (2017) identifies that the permissible number of firearms a person may possess is not explicitly defined and varies based on the specific type of shooting activities involved. For instance, a rabbit or fox hunter might require a .22 Rimfire for short-range shots, a .17 HMR or Magnum for slightly longer distances, a varmint rifle like a .220, .223, or .22/250, and potentially a heavier varminter like a .243 for windy days (Munslow, 2017). Different scenarios, such as pig hunting or various types of deer hunting, would warrant a similar consideration for suitable firearms. From a practical standpoint, having at least two rifles serving the same purpose is justifiable for hunters, given the challenges of extensive travel and the inability to check firearm zero in remote locations (Munslow, 2017). This precaution becomes crucial as most firearms lack backup sights, and hunters often operate without professional guides or the option to borrow a replacement gun in case of malfunctions, emphasizing the importance of a 'genuine need' with due regard to public safety, recognizing that the greater the number of firearms, the more scrutiny the 'genuine need' may face (Munslow, 2017).

The turning point for contemporary gun control in Australia occurred with the tragic Port Arthur massacre of 1996, where a young man, armed with a semiautomatic rifle, perpetrated the nation's deadliest mass shooting, resulting in the loss of thirty-five lives and injuries to nearly two dozen others. In response to this horrifying event, the conservative-led national government swiftly implemented substantial modifications to the country's gun laws in collaboration with various states and territories responsible for firearm regulation. Following the Port Arthur massacre in 1996, the federal government of Australia persuaded all states and territories to implement tough new gun control laws that made it illegal to own particular types of firearms (Chapman et al., 2015). The shock of the 1996 Port Arthur massacre galvanized Australia to cascade a transformational rejection of gun culture across society, leading to substantial changes in gun laws that significantly restrict the use and ownership of weapons (Brown, 2016). The Australian governments united to remove semi-automatic and pump-action shotguns and rifles from civilian possession as a key component of gun law reforms (Chapman et al., 2015).

The impact of these legislative changes was significant. After the implementation of the National Firearms Agreement (NFA) in 1996, there were no mass firearm killings in Australia, confirming the important role of this legal initiative in preventing such tragedies (Hu & Tkebuchava, 2022). The reforms also led to faster falls in firearm deaths, firearm suicides, and a decade without mass shootings, demonstrating the effectiveness of the legislative changes in reducing gun-related violence (Chapman et al., 2015). Furthermore, there were dramatic reductions in firearm-related suicides after the implementation of strong regulatory reforms in Australia (Etzersdorfer et al., 2006). The comprehensive firearm laws, such as the NFA, limited public firearm ownership through regulations and a government buy-back program of guns from individual owners, contributing to the decrease in gun-related violence (Quenzer et al., 2021).

The impact of the gun law reforms in Australia was also observed in the reduction of mass shooting incidents, firearm death rates, suicides, and homicides, indicating the effectiveness of the legislative changes in addressing various forms of gun-related violence (Brown, 2016). The decline in suicide in Australia coincided with a reduction in the availability of lethal means, highlighting the role of stricter firearm laws in reducing suicides (Solmi et al., 2017). Additionally, gun control laws in South Australia led to significant decreases in suicides using firearms, in comparison with other Australian states without similar gun laws in place, where there was an increase in suicide rates (Ruby & Sher, 2013).

The National Agreement on Firearms in Australia, implemented in 1996, had a significant impact on firearm-related outcomes. The agreement led to the removal of approximately 650,000 assault weapons from public circulation, constituting about one-sixth of the national stock (Taylor & Li, 2015). It enforced licensing and registration, mandated firearm safety courses, and required licensees to demonstrate a "genuine need" for a specific type of firearm (Taylor & Li, 2015). The implementation of the National Firearms Agreement (NFA) was associated with a significant decline in firearm suicide rates, particularly in younger males (Chapman et al., 2015; Gilmour et al., 2018). Additionally, the NFA led to declines in both gun-death rates and mass shootings related to firearms (Chapman et al., 2015; Webster, 2016). The introduction of strict gun control laws and the buyback of firearms facilitated by the NFA had a positive impact on reducing firearm deaths and homicides (Koo et al., 2017; Xin et al., 2014).

Despite these achievements, concerns arose in 2017 when there was a surge in gun sales, prompting warnings from Australian gun control advocates about potential relaxations in gun laws in certain states and territories. The discourse on gun safety was also shaped by the tragic suspected murder-suicide of a family of seven in Western Australia, marking the country's most severe mass shooting in two decades. Presently, Australia has a higher number of guns in circulation than before the Port Arthur massacre, even though the overall ownership has declined over the same period.

Australia's gun laws predominantly fall under the purview of its states and territories, while the federal government oversees the regulation of gun importation. In the final two decades of the 20th century, prompted by several high-profile killing sprees, the federal government collaborated with all state governments to implement more stringent firearms legislation.

The National Firearms Agreement (NFA) of 1996 in Australia was a significant milestone in the country's history, particularly in response to the tragic Port Arthur Massacre. The NFA led to a comprehensive overhaul of gun laws, including federally funded gun buybacks, voluntary surrenders, and state government-initiated gun amnesties. This initiative resulted in the collection and subsequent destruction of over a million firearms, contributing to a decline in firearm deaths and suicides (Chapman et al., 2015). The impact of the NFA was substantial, with studies showing faster declines in firearm deaths and suicides following its implementation (Chapman et al., 2015). Additionally, the NFA was associated with a significant decline in firearm suicide rates, particularly in younger males (Koo et al., 2017). The Australian Firearms Buyback, a key component of the NFA, also had a notable effect on reducing gun deaths (Lee & Suardi, 2010).

The NFA's influence extended beyond immediate outcomes. It played a pivotal role in reshaping attitudes about guns over time (Shapira et al., 2021). Furthermore, the NFA's impact on rates of homicide, suicide, and mass shootings in Australia has been a subject of extensive research, with evidence supporting its effectiveness in reducing these incidents (Brown, 2016). The NFA also became a part of Australia's national identity, with commemorative events reflecting its significance in the country's history (Frew & White, 2015).

The structure of firearm legislation in Australia operates within a framework established through national agreements following significant shooting incidents at Port Arthur in 1996 and Monash University in 2002. The Australian state and territory governments, represented by the Australian Police Ministers' Council (APMC) and Council of Australian Governments (COAG), crafted three pivotal agreements that have shaped contemporary firearm laws. These agreements include the National Firearms Agreement (1996), the National Firearm Trafficking Policy Agreement (2002), and the National Handgun Control Agreement (2002).

To possess or use a firearm, an individual must obtain a firearm license. License holders are obligated to demonstrate a "genuine reason" for holding a firearm license (excluding self-defence) and must not be classified as a "prohibited person." Furthermore, all firearms must be registered to the owner by serial number.

The regulation of firearm ownership, possession, and use is primarily governed by individual state and territory laws across Australia. In New South Wales, the Firearms Act 1996 and Weapons Prohibition Act 1998, along with associated regulations, dictate these aspects. Similarly, Victoria adheres to the Firearms Act 1996 and associated regulations, while Queensland follows the Weapons Act 1990 and associated regulations. Other states, such as Western Australia, South Australia, Tasmania, Northern Territory, and the Australian Capital Territory, each have their respective legislation and associated regulations governing firearms.

On the federal level, the importation of firearms is subject to stringent restrictions outlined in Regulation 4F and Schedule 6 of the Customs (Prohibited Imports) Regulations 1956 (Cth). This dual-tiered system, combining national agreements and individual state and territory legislation, forms the comprehensive legislative structure governing firearms in Australia.

The National Firearms Agreement in Australia categorizes firearms into distinct categories with varying levels of control. Category A includes rimfire rifles, shotguns, and air rifles. Category B encompasses centrefire rifles, muzzleloading firearms, and certain shotguns. Category C includes pump-action or self-loading shotguns and semi-automatic rimfire rifles. Category D covers all self-loading centrefire rifles, certain shotguns, and semi-automatic rimfire rifles with over ten rounds. Category H pertains to handguns owned for genuine reasons. Category R/E includes restricted weapons like military firearms and certain antique firearms, subject to varying regulations across states (Ozanne-Smith et al., 2004).

The implementation of the National Firearms Agreement in Australia has been associated with a significant decline in firearm suicides, especially in younger males (Chapman et al., 2015). The rates of total firearm deaths, firearm homicides, and firearm suicides all at least doubled their existing rates of decline after the revised gun laws (Chapman et al., 2015). The resultant National Firearms Agreement is considered the most radical gun safety legislation introduced into any country in recent history (McLeod et al., 2021). The agreement mandated the government to buy back certain types of firearms from civilians (Phillips et al., 2013). To be eligible for a Category H Licence, a target shooter must undergo a probationary period, participate in a minimum number of shooting sessions, and provide a fingerprint record when applying for a permit.

Licensing procedures involve the issuance of firearms licenses by individual states, granted for legal purposes such as hunting, sport shooting, pest control, collecting, and for farmers and farm workers. Renewal of licenses is mandatory every 3 or 5 years, with exceptions in the Northern Territory, South Australia, and Queensland, where it extends to 10 years. Full license eligibility requires individuals to be at least 18 years old.

Junior licenses, available from 12 years of age in Victoria and New South Wales (or 11 in Queensland), permit firearm use for instructional purposes or participation in sport or target shooting competitions. Convicted offenders and those with a history of mental illness are ineligible for licenses.

In May 2018, Victoria implemented firearm prohibition orders targeting individuals intending to possess, use, or carry firearms for unlawful purposes, resulting in immediate surrender of any firearm or related item and license cancellation.

Individuals or businesses engaged in firearm-related activities, such as buying, selling, or trading firearms or ammunition, must secure a firearm dealer's license. Firearms repairers are required to hold a firearms repairer's license, both subject to annual renewal.

In Queensland, adherence to firearm laws requires individuals to obtain a valid firearms license for legal possession or use of firearms in the state. This mirrors the regulations in NSW, where firearm registration is also mandatory. The Weapons Act 1990 (QLD) and Weapons Regulation 2016 (QLD) stipulate that individuals must demonstrate a "legitimate reason" to qualify for a firearms license. Acceptable reasons include sports or target shooting, recreational shooting, weapon collection, or occupational requirements. Queensland categorizes firearms licenses into A through H, each allowing possession of specific firearms contingent upon a lawful purpose. For instance, a category H license necessitates providing substantial reason and proof of necessity. The Queensland Police, authorized by the Firearms Act Qld, manage the issuance and oversight of firearm licenses in the state.

To secure a firearms license in Queensland (Criminal Defence Lawyers Australia, 2022a), one must complete a Qld firearms license application through the Qld firearms registry. The eligibility criteria include being at least 18 years old, with the provision for a minor firearms license for individuals aged 11-17 under strict conditions. Other prerequisites involve completing a firearms safety course in Queensland within the last 12 months (Qld firearms training), ensuring adequate secure storage for the firearm, having a lawful reason for firearm possession, and undergoing an assessment by the Queensland Commissioner of Police as a "fit and proper person" based on conviction record and health conditions.

Individuals convicted of firearms-related or drug offenses, violent acts, or crimes related to weapons face a mandatory five-year prohibition from obtaining a firearm license in Queensland. Certain firearm offenses, such as public possession of a short firearm without reasonable cause, can result in obligatory imprisonment. Firearm licenses in Queensland are generally valid for five years, and penalties for illegal possession or use of firearms without a license, according to section 50 of the Weapons Act, range from two to thirteen years in prison, depending on the type and quantity of firearms involved.

Replica firearms, including gel blasters, do not fall under the category of "firearms" or "weapons" in Queensland and do not require a license or registration. However, specific rules apply, such as keeping them out of sight during transport and securely storing them when not in use.

The Queensland firearms license conditions code, code AR1, authorizes the licensee to possess and use registered weapons for purposes like storage, manufacturing, modifying, or repairing weapons. This aligns with Schedule 2 of the Weapons Regulation 2016 (Qld). The license also allows for conducting business at specified premises and mandates secure storage unless otherwise authorized by law.

Various locations, such as the Brisbane Gun Club and Qld Firearms Training, offer the Queensland firearms safety course. While applicants can apply online, physical attendance is mandatory to complete the course. The safety course certificate, valid for 12 months, is a prerequisite for applying for a firearm license in the desired category.

Transporting firearms in Queensland requires compliance with specific storage conditions, such as using a locked boot, a metal container fixed to the vehicle, or a securely closed container out of sight. Leaving a firearm in an unlocked vehicle without a valid license holder present is strictly prohibited.

In Victoria, the possession and use of firearms are governed by The Firearms Act 1996. A valid firearms license is a prerequisite for possessing or using a firearm in Victoria. The license category specifies the allowable reasons for firearm use. The licensing process, managed by the Licensing and Regulation Division of Victoria Police, aligns with the firearm licensing laws in NSW.

To obtain a firearms license in Victoria (Criminal Defence Lawyers Australia, 2022a), residents must fulfill various requirements, including being a resident of Victoria, being at least 18 years old (or between 12-18 years for a junior firearms license), being considered "fit and proper," not being a "Prohibited Person," having a genuine reason for needing the firearms license, and completing an approved firearms safety course in Victoria.

The Victorian Firearms Registry, a branch of Victoria Police, maintains a database of all registered firearms in the state. Categories A, B, C, D, E, and H classify firearms licenses, each allowing specific types of firearms. Penalties for possessing illegal firearms in Victoria depend on the type and severity of the offense, ranging from summary to indictable offenses, with corresponding imprisonment terms.

Licenses in Victoria, categorized into various types, such as A, B, C, D, and E, specify the allowable firearms and purposes. Category A includes airguns, non-semi-automatic rimfire rifles, and certain shotguns, while Category B covers non-automatic or semi-automatic centrefire rifles and specific shotguns. Penalties for firearm offenses in Victoria vary, with summary offenses attracting up to 2 years in prison and indictable offenses, including dealing with category E long-arms and handguns, carrying higher penalties.

Address changes in Victoria necessitate notification to the Victoria Police firearms registry to avoid serious penalties. The possession or display of imitation firearms is illegal without approval, although toy firearms do not require a license. Antique firearms can be legally possessed under a firearm collector's license.

Renewal of firearm licenses in Victoria involves application to the Chief Commissioner, with costs varying based on the license type. To obtain a firearm license in Victoria, completion of a firearm safety course and test is mandatory.

Transporting firearms in Victoria follows similar storage and safety requirements as in NSW. Specific conditions imposed on firearm licenses in Victoria are outlined in schedule 2 of the Firearms Act 1996, requiring compliance for lawful possession and use.

Under section 112D of the Firearms Act 1996, the Chief Commissioner of Police in Victoria can prohibit individuals aged 14 or above from acquiring, possessing, carrying, or using firearms. Violating such prohibitions can result in up to 10 years of imprisonment.

Firearms in Victoria must be registered with Victoria Police. Notable firearm dealers in the area, such as Clayton Firearms Victoria and Melbourne Gun Works, provide a range of firearms, including used and second-hand options.

Firearm laws in the Australian Capital Territory (ACT) are enforced by the ACT Police force, responsible for issuing firearm licenses and permits. Possession or use of a firearm without a license is illegal and carries imprisonment penalties, varying based on firearm classification.

Every firearm in the ACT must be registered, with possession of an unregistered firearm resulting in criminal charges. To acquire a firearm, residents must obtain a 'permit to acquire' from the ACT firearms registry, demonstrating a genuine reason, being over 18, deemed a suitable person, providing identification, meeting storage requirements, and proving ACT residency.

Legitimate reasons for firearm ownership in the ACT include sport/target shooting, recreational hunting, firearms collection, and organizational needs. Five main license categories (A, B, C, D, and H) dictate permissible firearms, and license holders must present their license upon police request. On-the-spot inspections can be conducted by ACT police under the Firearms Act 1996 (ACT).

Firearm regulations in South Australia mandate possession of a registered firearm and a firearms license under specific categories. Justifying a genuine need for the firearm is crucial, with acceptable reasons ranging from sports shooting to security work. Each license category corresponds to certain types of firearms, and eligibility criteria include age, carrying the license when carrying the firearm, lack of prior violent convictions, absence of intervention orders, and freedom from physical or mental impairment.

TAFE firearm safety training courses, available online, are a prerequisite for eligibility in South Australia. The South Australia Police firearms branch issues firearm licenses, which are renewed at participating Post Offices. Penalties for unauthorized firearm possession or use depend on the license category and firearm type, ranging from imprisonment to fines as per the Firearms Act South Australia (Firearms Act 2015 (SA)).

A permit to acquire a firearm is also required in South Australia for lawful ownership. Unlike most other states, replica firearms in Western Australia do not require a license, but responsible use and display are mandatory.

Firearms legislation in Western Australia is governed by The Firearms Act 1973 (WA). Possession, carry, or use of a firearm requires a license or permit, with a genuine reason as a prerequisite. Compliance with storage rules is mandatory, and penalties for non-compliance depend on the firearm type and offense nature.

Applying for a firearm license in Western Australia involves demonstrating a genuine reason, completing a firearms safety awareness test, and submitting necessary documentation. Replica firearms do not require a license in Western Australia, and strict conditions govern their transport. Temporary permits are required for travellers bringing firearms to WA.

Firearm regulations in the Northern Territory follow the Firearms Act 1997 (NT), requiring a license and registration for legal firearm possession or use. Penalties for illegal possession or use vary based on the firearm and license category, with specific reasons justifying ownership.

License categories in the NT range from A to H, with eligibility criteria such as age, absence of domestic violence orders, and completion of an approved firearms safety course. A permit to acquire is also mandatory in addition to a firearm license.

The Firearms Act 1996 (Tas) governs firearm laws in Tasmania, making a firearms license a legal requirement for possession or use. Conditions for obtaining a license include age, genuine reason, fitness as a responsible person, completion of a firearms safety course, and absence of recent violent convictions.

Firearm licenses in Tasmania are categorized into A, B, C, D, and H, each allowing specific firearm types for designated purposes. Personal protection or self-defence is not recognized as a genuine reason for firearm ownership. Firearms must be registered, and penalties for unregistered firearms involve imprisonment and fines.

In NSW, firearm possession or use necessitates a firearms license or permit, firearm registration, and a separate permit to acquire. Compliance with the Firearms Act 1996 (NSW) and Weapons Prohibition Act 1998 (NSW) is mandatory, with severe penalties for offenses.

Obtaining a firearms license in NSW requires demonstrating a genuine reason and, for specific license categories, a special need. A legitimate reason is necessary for a firearms permit, with all firearms requiring registration. The Firearms Registry manages the database, accessible to Australian police officers. Non-compliance can result in cancellation of registration and confiscation, with penalties ranging from imprisonment to fines.

Address changes must be promptly updated, and imitation firearms are illegal without approval. Antique firearms require a collector's license. Renewal of firearm licenses involves application to the Chief Commissioner, with costs varying. A firearm safety course and test are mandatory, and transportation must adhere to specific conditions.

In summary, each Australian state and territory has distinct firearm laws and licensing procedures, emphasizing genuine reasons, safety, and responsible ownership. Understanding and adherence to these regulations are crucial to legal firearm possession and use.

Although firearm categories remain consistent across all states and territories in Australia, storage requirements vary from one jurisdiction to another. While the specifications for safes, lockers, or cabinets designed for firearm storage may differ slightly, it is the individual's responsibility to ensure that all firearms are securely locked away in a designated gun safe when not in use. This also applies to the storage of ammunition. The information provided below serves as general guidance, and applicants and licensees should familiarize themselves with the current legislation and requirements specific to their state or territory.

In the Australian Capital Territory (ACT), firearm owners are personally responsible for ensuring the security and safekeeping of their firearms to prevent unauthorized access. Failure to comply with safekeeping laws may result in the seizure of firearms by the police (ACT Policing, 2023). Storage guidelines from the ACT Firearms Registry should be followed, with specific requirements based on firearm categories and quantities.

Different regulations apply to various categories of firearms and their quantities. For Category A and B firearms (up to 10 firearms), a metal lockable container is required, with firing mechanisms stored separately in another lockable container. For Category A and B firearms exceeding 10, as well as Category C, D, and H firearms, storage in a metal, concrete, or brick safe is mandatory.

Category A and B firearms (up to and including 10 firearms) must be stored in either a metal lockable container with a separate lockable metal drawer or container for firing mechanisms or a security container constructed of recognized hardwood and lined with steel sheeting. The container must be bolted to the floor or wall with a minimum of two suitable anchor bolts, unless the container's empty mass is 150 kilograms or more.

Category A and B firearms (in excess of 10 firearms), Category C, D, and H firearms must be stored in a metal or concrete or brick safe. Specific construction standards apply, including structural grade mild steel for metal safes and minimum thickness requirements. Safes must be fitted with secure door mechanisms and fixed securely to the building structure.

Changes to the ACT Firearms Regulations in 2018 mandate that license holders with more than 10 registered firearms must store them in a metal, brick, or concrete safe securely mounted on a wall or floor. Collectors' firearms have additional requirements, with specific conditions for temporarily disabling Category A or B firearms and permanently disabling Category C and D firearms. Display requirements also exist, and transactions must be arranged through approved firearms dealers or club armourers.

Firearm legislation in New South Wales (NSW) imposes clear responsibilities on firearm owners for safe storage, with different requirements based on license categories. Regardless of the license type, individuals must ensure that firearms are securely stored, preventing loss, theft, or access by unauthorized persons. Paintball permit holders with a firearms license can store their paintball markers and firearms in the same safe storage setup, provided it meets higher safety standards set out in the Firearms Act 1996.

Under section 39 of the Firearms Act 1996, all license holders in NSW must ensure secure storage of their firearms, taking reasonable steps to prevent loss, theft, or unauthorized access. Firearms stored outside an inhabited dwelling must be in an approved safe, individually secured with a lock, and equipped with an off-site monitored alarm. The premises should also have an intruder alarm and duress facilities, monitored off-site.

For Category A and B firearms, additional safe storage requirements exist under Section 40 of the Firearms Act 1996. Firearms must be stored in a locked, approved receptacle made of hard wood or steel when not in use. If the receptacle weighs under 150 kilograms, it must be fixed to prevent easy removal. Specific standards for locks, construction, and securing points apply, as determined by the Commissioner.

License holders must allow police inspections of safe storage facilities at mutually agreed times, facilitating requests by the police for inspections. Alternative storage arrangements can be approved by the Commissioner. Category C, D, and H license holders must store firearms in a locked steel safe approved by the Commissioner, securely bolted to the premises, with ammunition stored separately in a locked container.

Failure to meet these requirements can result in fines or imprisonment. The Commissioner provides a list of approved safes and locking mechanisms, ensuring compliance with Section 41(1) of the Act.

The ability to meet safe storage requirements is crucial for obtaining a firearm license in the Northern Territory (NT). Licenses will not be issued without adequate storage facilities. Approved commercial gun cabinets and safes are available, and self-built cabinets are allowed if they meet security standards.

For Category A/B firearms, recommended metal thickness is 3.0mm or more, with specific design features. The receptacle must be secured with provision for bolt down points, and if it weighs over 150kg when empty, bolting is not necessary. Category C/D/H firearms have higher thickness requirements for the safe door and overall structure. Secure mounting to a wall or floor is mandatory.

Combination cabinets meeting requirements for Category A/B firearms can be used for Category H firearms, with specific design criteria for the internal compartment. The internal cabinet must provide double thickness on the front and sides and be securely fixed to the wall or floor.

In Queensland, firearm owners are obligated to take reasonable precautions to ensure the safe storage of firearms, preventing theft, loss, and unauthorized access. Failure to secure firearms can result in penalties exceeding $10,000 or imprisonment according to Section 60 of the Weapons Act 1990.

For safe storage of Category A, B, and C firearms, specific requirements include a rigid structure made of solid steel or solid timber with no holes or perforations. Acceptable materials are specified, excluding aluminium or alloys. Containers weighing less than 150kg when empty must be securely attached to a permanent building. The container must have a robust combination lock, keyed lock, or keyed padlock, and firearms must be unloaded and the bolt removed or action broken for storage. Ammunition must be stored separately in a locked container.

Storage requirements for Category D, H, and R firearms involve a rigid structure made of solid steel, securely bolted to a building. Similar lock and firearm handling requirements apply. If more than 30 firearms are stored, additional regulations come into effect.

In South Australia, the Firearms Act and Regulations emphasize the privilege of possessing and using firearms with public safety as a priority. The minimum storage standards, outlined in Schedule 1 of the Firearms Regulations 2017, aim to make it challenging for criminals to access firearms.

Firearms and ammunition should be stored securely at the owner's primary residence or, if used for work, at the place of employment. Storage facilities are subject to inspection by police, and it is an offense to refuse access for inspection. Category A and B firearms must be stored in a locked steel cabinet or container that meets specific standards. Additional requirements include secure fixing to the building structure if the container weighs less than 150kg.

For Category C, D, and H firearms, as well as Category A and B firearms exceeding ten, an approved steel safe is necessary. Minimum thickness requirements for doors, sides, and back apply, along with secure fixing to the building structure. For collectors, additional requirements exist, including storage in an approved steel safe or a substantially built, lockable wooden cabinet.

Firearm owners in South Australia must seek approval for storage facilities, with inspections conducted by police. Compliance with the Firearms Regulations 2017 is essential to maintaining a firearms license.

The Firearms Act 1996 in Tasmania requires firearm owners to take reasonable steps to ensure firearms are not stolen, lost, or misused. Safe storage is crucial to meeting this obligation. All firearms must be stored in an approved security container when not in use. Ammunition must be stored separately in a secure container.

Category A and B firearms can be stored in a container with walls and doors at least 2mm thick. The container must be secured to the structure of the building. For Category C, D, and H firearms, as well as Category A and B firearms exceeding 10, a gun safe approved by the Commissioner of Police is necessary. Additional requirements include secure fixing to the building structure.

Category C, D, and H firearms must be individually secured within the safe. Collectors may have additional conditions for storage. Regular inspections by police may occur to ensure compliance with the Firearms Act 1996.

In Victoria, firearm storage requirements are governed by the Firearms Act 1996. Owners are responsible for preventing theft, loss, or unauthorized access to firearms. Secure storage is a condition of licensing, and failure to comply may result in the cancellation of the license.

Category A and B firearms must be stored in a locked container constructed of hardwood, metal, or another material approved by the Chief Commissioner. The container must be securely anchored to the structure if it weighs less than 150kg when empty. Category C, D, and H firearms require a metal safe, and specific construction standards apply. The safe must be bolted to the structure and weigh at least 150kg when empty.

Additional regulations exist for collectors, dealers, and primary producers, with storage requirements tailored to each category. Police may inspect storage facilities, and non-compliance may lead to penalties, including imprisonment.

Western Australia has strict regulations regarding the storage of firearms, with owners required to take all reasonable precautions to prevent loss, theft, or unauthorized access. Specific storage requirements are outlined in the Firearms Regulations 1974.

Category A and B firearms must be stored in a locked metal container or gun safe that meets certain standards. The container or safe must be securely fixed to the structure if it weighs less than 150kg when empty. Ammunition must be stored separately in a locked container. Category C, D, and H firearms require a metal safe, and additional regulations apply to collectors, dealers, and primary producers.

Police may inspect storage facilities, and compliance with storage regulations is essential for maintaining a firearms license. Failure to meet storage requirements may result in fines or imprisonment.

Firearm storage regulations in Australia are designed to prioritize public safety by ensuring that firearms are securely stored and inaccessible to unauthorized individuals. While there are consistent national categories for firearms, each state and territory has its own specific storage requirements and regulations.

Effects of Policy on Firearm Ownership and Use

The Australian federal 12-month amnesty and buyback scheme, which took place from October 1996 to September 1997, was a significant government adjustment to gun control regulations, resulting in the repurchase of a large number of newly prohibited firearms (Lee & Suardi, 2010). The scheme led to the repurchase of 659,940 firearms, including semiautomatic and pump-action rifles and shotguns, and a subsequent buyback in 2003 resulted in the destruction of 68,727 handguns (Lee & Suardi, 2010). This initiative was one of the most massive government adjustments to gun control regulations in the developed world in recent history (Lee & Suardi, 2010). The impact of the buyback scheme was substantial, with approximately 20 percent of Australia's firearms estimated to have been retrieved during the buyback (Lee & Suardi, 2010).

The National Firearms Agreement (NFA) in Australia, implemented in response to the 1996 Port Arthur mass shooting, led to a significant decline in household firearm ownership rates. Lee and Suardi (2010) highlighted the impact of the NFA, which introduced strict gun laws, resulting in a notable decrease in firearm ownership. This is supported by (Chapman et al., 2015), who emphasized that the removal of rapid-firing firearms from civilians can effectively reduce mass shootings, firearm homicides, and firearm suicides. Additionally, (Bailey et al., 2019) indicated that while national trends in firearm deaths remained steady from 1999 to 2014, data from 2015 onwards showed increases in both fatal and non-fatal firearm-related injuries, suggesting a potential correlation with the decline in firearm ownership rates.

According to the data provided by GunPolicy.org (2023), the percentage of Australians holding a gun license has decreased by 48% from 1997 to 2020. In 1997, there were 6.52 licensed firearm owners per 100 population, which dropped to 3.41 licensed gun owners per 100 people by 2020. The number of Australians holding a gun license has decreased from 1.2 million in 1997 to 868,000 in 2020. However, the decline in gun licenses does not necessarily mean there are fewer guns in the country. The rate of registered firearms per 100 population has increased by 1.7% over the last 25 years, with an estimated 3.5 million registered firearms now in civilian possession, averaging four per owner. Additionally, an estimated 260,000 illegal firearms are believed to be in the grey market. Polling data indicates a decrease in gun ownership across households, suggesting that while fewer people are choosing to own guns, existing gun owners are accumulating more firearms. The population of Australia has grown by 40% in the same period, further diluting the proportion of gun owners. This data underscores the continued impact of Australia's firearm policies, implemented in the wake of the 1996 Port Arthur Massacre.

Using data as of 2020, GunPolicy.org (2023) outlines that the total number of guns (licit and illicit) held by civilians in Australia has steadily increased from 2.5 million in 1997 to 3.78 million in 2020. However, the rate of private gun ownership per 100 people has seen a slight decline from 17.59 in 1996 to 14.83 in 2020.

The number of handguns in civilian possession decreased from 192,000 in 2005 to 120,790 in 2010. In a comparison of private gun ownership in 206 countries, Australia ranked 26th for the number of privately owned guns and 46th for the rate of private gun ownership. The percentage of households in Australia owning one or more guns also decreased from 25% in 1988 to 6.2% in 2005. Specifically, the ownership of rifles and shotguns in households decreased to 12.5% and 6.9%, respectively, in 1992. The ownership of handguns also declined from 1.6% in 1989 and 1994 to 0.3% in 2005. The number of licensed gun owners has significantly dropped from 1.2 million in 1997 to 868,110 in 2020. Consequently, the rate of licensed firearm owners per 100 people declined from 6.52 in 1997 to 3.41 in 2020. The number of registered guns has risen from 2.5 million in 1997 to 3.52 million in 2020, and the rate of registered guns per 100 people dropped from 17.59 in 1996 to 13.81 in 2020.

Lastly, the estimated number of unregistered and illicit firearms ranged between 250,000 in 2007 and 267,579 in 2010. The rate of such firearms per 100 people also fluctuated around 1.08 to 1.31 from 2006 to 2016. Despite the decrease in the number of shooters and firearm owners in Australia, the number of guns has increased, indicating a higher number of guns per gun owner. In 1997, the rate of gun ownership was 2.1 guns per owner, whereas in 2019, it rose to 3.9 guns per owner. This change has had significant implications for the gun industry. If the ratio of guns per owner had remained at 2.1, there would have been 1.45 million fewer guns in 2016, equating to approximately $1.45 billion in lost sales, considering an estimated price of $1,000 per gun. The motives for ownership include hunting and sport, pest control by primary producers, and collecting. Despite this, there has been a decline in the number of people engaging in sporting shooting and hunting, and the overall number of gun owners has fallen. Yet, those who do own guns are now buying almost twice as many as they did two decades ago (Browne, 2019).

Since the implementation of the National Firearms Agreement in 1996, Australia has experienced a significant decrease in both the number and rate of homicides, including murder and manslaughter. The initial years following the enactment of the law saw a slight increase in the number of homicides, with a peak in 1999, but this was followed by a decline to a record low in 2007, and this low rate has been maintained through 2013. In fact, by 2013, there were 23% fewer homicides than in 1996. As Australia's population has increased over this period, the nation's homicide rate has fallen even more, from 1.6 per 100,000 in 1995-96 to 1 per 100,000 in 2013-14 (Kiely, 2017).

Moreover, firearm-related homicides have also significantly decreased since the implementation of the 1996 gun law, with a remarkable 57% decrease from 1989-90 to 2013-14. While there is no consensus on whether these decreases are directly due to the gun laws, some evidence suggests a correlation. A study by scholars at the University of Sydney in 2006 found that gun fatalities decreased more rapidly after the gun law passed, with no fatal mass shootings in the following decade and accelerated declines in firearm deaths, particularly suicides (Kiely, 2017).

The total number of annual deaths resulting from firearms in Australia has seen a substantial decline from 685 in 1979 to 229 in 2019. The annual rate of all gun deaths per 100,000 population has also reduced significantly from 4.70 in 1980 to 0.90 in 2019 (GunPolicy.org, 2023). In terms of gender breakdown, male deaths due to firearms, which generally constitute the majority of gun deaths, decreased from 220 in 2007 to 211 in 2019. The annual rate of male gun deaths per 100,000 population fell from 2.12 in 2007 to 1.67 in 2019. In contrast, female gun deaths remained relatively low, with 17 in 2007 and 18 in 2019. The annual rate of female gun deaths per 100,000 population also remained low, going from 0.16 in 2007 to 0.14 in 2019. The overall data suggests a marked decrease in gun-related deaths in Australia over several decades.

The total number of annual firearm homicides in Australia has significantly decreased from 123 in 1988 to 34 in 2020. Over the same period, the annual rate of firearm homicides per 100,000 population also saw a major decline, from 0.74 in 1988 to 0.13 in 2020. In 2019, 16% of all homicides were committed with a firearm, which is a decrease from the 25% reported in 1995. Looking at gender breakdown, in 2019, there were 30 male and 9 female firearm homicides. The annual rate of male firearm homicide per 100,000 was 0.24, and for females, it was 0.07. This data indicates a considerable reduction in firearm homicides for both genders over the years.

The annual number of unintentional shooting deaths has declined significantly from 30 in 1988 to 4 in 2019. The annual rate of unintentional shooting deaths per 100,000 population also decreased from 0.18 in 1988 to 0.02 in 2019. In 2019, there were 3 unintentional male shooting deaths and 1 female, with respective rates of 0.02 and 0.01 per 100,000 population. Over the years, there has been a substantial decrease in unintentional male shooting deaths from 40 in 2000 to 3 in 2019. For females, the number of unintentional shooting deaths has generally remained low, with zero reported in most years since 2009.

The evidence suggests that Australia's National Firearms Agreement of 1996 has had a significant impact on reducing both the number and rate of homicides, including firearm-related deaths. While there may not be a consensus on the direct causation, various studies have indicated a correlation between the implementation of the gun laws and the observed decline in firearm-related deaths. The decrease in firearm homicides, suicides, and unintentional shooting deaths, as well as the absence of fatal mass shootings, all point to the potential effectiveness of the legislation. Further research and analysis are necessary to fully understand the complex factors contributing to these trends, but the data overwhelmingly supports the positive impact of Australia's gun laws on reducing gun-related deaths.

In contrast, Edward (2021) discusses the Australian gun control measures implemented through the National Firearms Agreement (NFA) following the Port Arthur massacre in 1996. While proponents argue its success, critics, such as James Walsh from the Shooting Industry Foundation of Australia, contend that studies reveal no significant reduction in firearm-related deaths, challenging the efficacy of the NFA (Edward, 2021). Homicide data suggests a pre-existing downward trend in Australia, and some argue that the NFA did not impact this trend significantly.

Comparisons with the United States, where gun laws vary between states, reveal complexities. Edward (2021) questions the applicability of the Australian model to the U.S., emphasizing constitutional differences and the distinct cultural significance of gun ownership. The large number of firearms in the U.S. and the protection of individual rights make a similar gun buyback scheme challenging.

Edward (2021) also criticizes the impact of the NFA on shooting sports, limiting the competitiveness of Australian shooters globally. Despite the NFA, violent crimes persist, and a black market for guns exists, raising doubts about the overall effectiveness of the gun control measures. Critics argue that a more fruitful approach would involve addressing issues related to violent criminals and flaws in the criminal justice system rather than targeting law-abiding gun owners.

Further, in the period leading up to March 2022, both New South Wales (NSW) and Victoria, Australia's most populous states, have experienced a surge in illegal firearm-related incidents, including high-profile shootings. NSW reported 10 firearm murders and 84 firearm assaults, marking the deadliest year since 2018 (Boaz, 2022). In Victoria, as of September 1, 2022, there were already 10 firearm assault deaths, representing a 25% increase compared to the fatalities in 2020 and 2021 (Boaz, 2022).

Authorities in various jurisdictions, including Victoria, have initiated measures to combat the proliferation of illegal firearms. These efforts include the establishment of task forces, a National Firearms Amnesty that began on July 1, 2021, and the creation of an illegal guns unit by the Victorian government in January of the previous year. To proactively address illicit firearm trafficking, Victoria Police employ firearms prohibition orders (FPOs), with more than 1,550 currently active (Boaz, 2022).

Despite the implementation of FPOs, the effectiveness of these orders in reducing serious crimes is under scrutiny. In 2019, a year after the introduction of FPOs, Victoria recorded a nine-year high in firearm assault deaths (Boaz, 2022). However, Victoria Police contend that FPOs are a valuable tool in curbing firearm-related crime, citing examples such as no non-fatal injury shootings being linked to outlaw motorcycle gangs in 2021 (Boaz, 2022).

FPOs empower law enforcement to ban individuals associated with organized crime from interacting with firearms. Those served with an FPO must surrender their firearms immediately and can be subjected to police searches without a warrant if there is reason to suspect firearm possession. In NSW, 118 such searches were conducted in the current year, resulting in the seizure of 211 firearms (Boaz, 2022).

Despite these efforts, the scale of the challenge is immense. The Australian Criminal Intelligence Commission (ACIC) estimates that there are at least 260,000 illegal firearms circulating in Australia, with a potential high-end estimate reaching 600,000 (Boaz, 2022). The figures, produced in 2016, remain largely consistent, indicating that the seizures made by authorities represent only a fraction of the illegal firearms market (Boaz, 2022).

Gun Ownership and Control in Germany

Gun Control in Germany

Throughout Germany's history, the nation's approach to gun control has undergone significant transformations, leading to the establishment of the strict regulations in place today (Proctor, 2023a). The evolution of firearms laws in the federal republic has shaped the parameters governing the purchase, ownership, and use of guns, delineating the eligibility criteria and the contexts in which firearms can be utilized. Notably, the Weimar Republic marked a period characterized by stringent firearm regulations, setting the stage for subsequent shifts in gun control laws during the Nazi era (Proctor, 2023a).

During the Weimar Republic, firearm rules were characterized by a strict regulatory framework, bearing resemblance to contemporary gun control laws. The ownership of guns was limited to individuals over the age of 20, with stringent restrictions imposed on the general populace, except for government and railway employees. Consequently, gun ownership in Germany during this period was relatively low, reflecting the impact of the stringent firearm regulations enforced by the Weimar Republic (Proctor, 2023a).

The ascendancy of the Nazi party in Germany heralded a significant departure from the firearm regulations of the Weimar Republic. The enactment of the German Weapons Act of 1938 ushered in a paradigm shift, expanding the scope of gun ownership to a broader segment of the population, contingent upon meeting specific conditions. Notably, the 1938 legislation completely deregulated the sale and acquisition of rifles and shotguns, with regulations exclusively targeting handguns (Proctor, 2023a). Furthermore, the possession of ammunition was liberalized, and the minimum age for firearm acquisition was lowered from 20 to 18. This legislative overhaul resulted in the relaxation of gun ownership restrictions for hunters, government personnel, and NSDAP members, signifying a marked departure from the stringent regulations of the Weimar Republic (Proctor, 2023a).

However, despite the apparent liberalization of gun laws under the Nazi regime, marginalized groups, particularly Jewish individuals, were systematically deprived of the right to purchase firearms. The discriminatory regulations targeting Jewish individuals extended beyond the prohibition of acquiring and possessing guns, encompassing restrictions on employment in weapons and ammunition manufacturing facilities, as well as engaging in arms trade (Proctor, 2023a). The enactment of the Regulations Against Jews' Possession of Weapons, a complementary legislation to the 1938 law, further exacerbated the oppression of Jewish individuals, prohibiting them from possessing any form of weapons, including knives, truncheons, and ammunition. This discriminatory legislation, which came into force the day after Kristallnacht, exemplified the targeted and systematic deprivation of the right to bear arms for oppressed groups during the Nazi era (Proctor, 2023a).

Germany's strict gun control laws are regulated by the German Weapons Act, which aligns with the European Firearms Directive. This federal statute comprehensively governs the handling, acquisition, storage, commerce, and maintenance of firearms and ammunition (Krüsselmann et al., 2021). The law requires individuals to possess a weapons possession card (Waffenbesitzkarte) to own or purchase a firearm and a weapons license (Waffenschein) to use or carry a loaded firearm. However, the use of guns for private self-defence is restricted, and the possession card only allows for the transportation of firearms, requiring them to be unloaded and locked in a case when in public (Krüsselmann et al., 2021).

According to the German Ministry of the Interior, there are approximately 5.5 million legally owned firearms in Germany, possessed by 1.4 million individuals. The distribution of firearms includes 1.5 million sport shooters, 400,000 hunters, 300,000 collectors, and 900,000 individuals who own inherited firearms. The possession of firearms for sport shooting, such as in *Figure 17*, and hunting, as shown in *Figure 18*, is permitted under specific conditions, such as holding a hunting license (Jagdschein) for hunters.

Additionally, there is a minor firearms certificate (Kleiner Waffenschein) for carrying lower-powered weapons, including starting pistols and flare guns.

Figure 17: Professor Dr. Volker Blüm, founder and initiator of the Field Target shooting discipline in Germany on the "green". Peter Suttner, CC BY-SA 3.0 <http://creativecomm ons.org/licenses/by-sa/3.0/>, via Wikimedia Commons.

In response to a school shooting, German weapons expert Holger Soschinka emphasized the strictness of Germany's weapons laws, asserting that they are sufficient (Krüsselmann et al., 2021). However, critics argue that the laws are too lenient, with one anti-weapons group claiming that the law is unconstitutional as it prioritizes the interests of sport shooters over people's right to life and physical integrity (Krüsselmann et al., 2021).

The German National Gun Registry, established in 2012, provides insights into the prevalence of firearms in the country. Despite the strict regulations, the estimated number of firearms in circulation, both legal and illegal, could be as high as 45 million. This indicates a significant number of firearms in Germany, raising concerns about their potential misuse and the need for stringent control measures.

The development of firearm laws in Germany has been influenced by historical events and public debates. The Federal Weapons Act of 2002, along with subsequent amendments, introduced significant changes such as increased age requirements for licensed hunters and competition shooters, psychological evaluations for individuals under 25, and routine verifications of safe firearms storage. These changes were partly a response to incidents like school shootings in Erfurt, Emsdetten, and Winnenden, leading to a public debate attributing blame to various elements of youth culture, society, and private gun ownership (Schell et al., 2020).

Current firearm laws in Germany have undergone significant developments since the aftermath of World War II. Initially, even German police officers were prohibited from carrying firearms, and private ownership was not reinstated until 1956. The legal landscape resembled the 1928 Law on Firearms and Ammunition. Substantial revisions occurred in 1972 with the enactment of the Federal Weapons Act, a response to the Red Army Faction's terror activities. Further modifications were introduced in 2002, and subsequent amendments in 2008 and 2009 resulted from a public debate following school shootings in Erfurt, Emsdetten, and Winnenden.

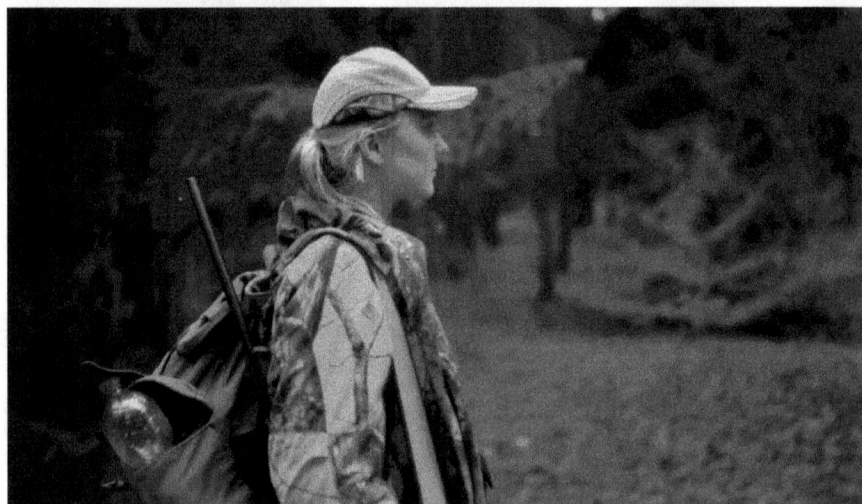

Figure 18: Huntress on her way to the hunting stand in a forest near Magdeburg, Saxony-Anhalt, 2019. flutertv, CC BY 3.0 <https://creativecommons.org/licenses/by/3.0>, via Wikimedia Commons.

The 2002 Weapons Act raised age requirements for licensed hunters and competition shooters. Additionally, it mandated psychological evaluations for individuals under 25 seeking large-bore firearms, assessing personal adequacy. The first amendment in 2008 aimed to prohibit specific weapons, including airsoft guns and tasers, from public places, allowing exceptions for professional or ceremonial use and private premises. The second amendment in 2009 introduced routine verifications of firearms storage and tightened conditions for continuous necessity. A constitutional complaint challenged the law, alleging a violation of home inviolability.

The weapons law excludes military and police use, with identity cards permitting carrying for these entities. However, strict controls govern the issuance of guns and ammunition within the military. Firearms in Germany exceeding 7.5 Joule muzzle energy require a valid ownership license. The Federal Weapons Act employs a two-tiered approach to licensing, and suppressor possession aligns with the associated firearm's licensing requirements. Sports shooters face restrictions on magazine capacity, limiting long weapon magazines to 10 rounds during sports shooting, although acquiring and possessing any magazine for any firearm remains legal without a license.

In Germany, the possession of firearms is regulated by the requirement to obtain a firearms ownership license, known as Waffenbesitzkarte or WBK. This license is mandatory for individuals who wish to purchase and handle firearms, and it imposes certain restrictions and responsibilities on the license holders. The issuance of firearms ownership licenses is subject to specific criteria and is categorized into different types based on the intended use of the firearms, such as competitive shooting, hunting, and collecting.

The firearms ownership license grants individuals the right to purchase firearms and handle them on their own property, as well as on any private property with the property owner's consent. However, when transporting firearms on public premises, the licensed firearm must be unloaded and stored in a stable, fully enclosing, locked container. This requirement ensures the safe and secure transportation of firearms in public spaces. Additionally, the license does not entitle the owner to shoot the weapon or carry it on public premises without the prescribed container.

Furthermore, individuals holding firearms ownership licenses are obligated to obtain mandatory insurance and provide a secure means of storing the firearms on their premises, typically in the form of a weapons locker. These measures are in place to ensure the safe and responsible ownership of firearms, minimizing the risk of unauthorized access and potential misuse. The issuance of firearms ownership licenses is contingent upon meeting specific criteria outlined in the German Weapons Act (WaffG). These criteria include being at least 18 years of age, demonstrating trustworthiness, personal adequacy, expert knowledge, and establishing the necessity for obtaining the license. Additionally, inheritors of legal firearms may obtain a permit without demonstrating expert knowledge or necessity, although the firearm must be blocked by an arms dealer in the absence of these requirements. It is important to note that an inheritor's license does not include the right to acquire or handle ammunition.

However, certain individuals are prohibited from obtaining a firearms ownership license, including convicted felons, individuals with a history of mental disorders, and those deemed unreliable, such as individuals with a history of drug or alcohol addiction, as well as known violent or aggressive persons. These restrictions are in place to prevent firearms from falling into the hands of individuals who may pose a risk to public safety.

The firearms ownership licenses are issued in three color-coded varieties, each catering to different purposes and necessities. These categories include licenses for competitive shooting, hunting, and collecting, each with specific regulations and limitations tailored to their respective activities.

For individuals engaged in competitive shooting, membership in registered gun clubs is a prerequisite, and they must demonstrate regular practice and participation in competitions to qualify for a green license. This license allows the purchase of specific types and quantities of firearms, with additional approvals required for further acquisitions. Similarly, individuals involved in hunting must pass the German hunter's exam and obtain a hunters' license to purchase long guns and handguns for hunting purposes, with specific regulations regarding approvals and registration. Collectors and firearms experts are issued a red license, which allows the purchase of various firearms, subject to specific themes for collectors and expertise requirements for firearms experts.

Gun Ownership and Use in Germany

Gun ownership in Germany is a prevalent practice, with approximately 1 million individuals legally possessing firearms, contributing to a total of 5.4 million firearms across the federal states (Proctor, 2023a). The country ranks as the fourth most armed nation globally, indicating a significant presence of firearms within its borders. The primary motivations behind firearm ownership in Germany are related to sporting activities and hunting pursuits. However, amidst this scenario, there is an ongoing debate among German politicians regarding the necessity for stricter regulations on gun ownership (Proctor, 2023a).

Germany's National Weapons Registry provides data indicating the existence of 5.4 million legally owned firearms in the country, reflecting a substantial prevalence of firearms among the populace. This places Germany among the top nations in terms of firearm ownership globally. Despite this high number of firearms (Proctor, 2023a), Germany maintains one of the lowest rates of gun-related deaths worldwide. Nevertheless, the occurrence of several mass shootings in recent years has ignited discussions concerning the need for further restrictions on the availability of firearms throughout the country.

In the context of gun crime, Germany's stringent regulations contribute to relatively lower levels of gun-related criminal activities compared to countries with more lenient gun laws. On average, approximately 155 individuals fall victim to gun-related fatalities annually in Germany, primarily attributed to criminal activities (Proctor, 2023a). Additionally, sporadic incidents involving the use of firearms, such as mass shootings like the 2023 Hamburg shooting and terrorist attacks like the 2020 Halle synagogue attack, have occurred, underscoring the potential risks associated with firearm ownership (Proctor, 2023a).

Despite variations in laws and regulations across different regions within Germany, particularly in Bavaria, firearms and weapons are subject to uniform regulations consistent with the rest of the country (Proctor, 2023a). Notably, Munich has been the site of several significant mass shooting incidents, including the tragic massacre of Israeli athletes during the 1972 Munich Olympics and the 2016 Munich mass shooting, resulting in nine fatalities and 27 injuries (Proctor, 2023a). Consequently, the issue of firearms control holds significant importance for many residents of Munich, reflecting the broader societal concerns regarding gun ownership and its implications.

Furthermore, Germany has made substantial contributions to the global firearms industry, with the country being the origin of some of the most renowned firearms worldwide (Proctor, 2023a). Notably, the MP5, a widely utilized machine gun, is manufactured by the German firm Heckler and Koch, showcasing Germany's influence in the production of firearms. Additionally, the Heckler and Koch VP9 pistol and the historically significant Karabiner 98K are among the notable German-made firearms, further highlighting the country's impact on the global firearms landscape (Proctor, 2023a).

In Germany, the legal framework governing firearms is based on a clear distinction between weapons and war weapons, with the latter being specifically listed in the War Weapons Control Act. The possession or use of war weapons, which include fully automatic rifles, machine guns (unless they are antiques from World War II or earlier), or barrels or breeches for such weapons, is strictly prohibited under German law (Knight, 2022). Additionally, pump-action shotguns are also banned under the Weapons Act.

Furthermore, some semi-automatic weapons are categorized as war weapons, although not all fall under this classification (Knight, 2022).

The regulations also extend to firearms that are banned from sporting use in Germany. These firearms may not be purchased with a license issued for sporting use, but they are allowed on hunters' and collectors' licenses. This category includes handguns with a barrel length of less than 7.62 cm (3 inches), semi-automatic long guns with a built-in magazine with a capacity of more than 10 rounds, and semi-automatic firearms that closely resemble a prohibited firearm (Knight, 2022). The latter is determined based on specific criteria such as barrel length, design, and ammunition specifications.

Certain firearms do not require a license for ownership by individuals over 18 years of age. This includes single-shot percussion firearms developed before 1 January 1871 and muzzle-loaders with a flintlock or earlier design (Knight, 2022). However, the purchase of black powder or similar substances for the actual use of these firearms does require a license.

In Germany, prohibited firearms may only be owned by individuals with a special license from the Federal Criminal Police Office, which is typically granted to manufacturers, exporters, and collectors in rare cases (Knight, 2022). Prohibited firearms include those defined as "war weapons" by the law, fully automatic firearms, pump-action shotguns with specific characteristics, firearms designed to resemble everyday objects for concealment, and certain handguns made after January 1, 1970, that fire ammunition with specific calibre restrictions (Knight, 2022).

The issuance of firearms carry permits is subject to stringent requirements. Applicants must be at least 18 years old, demonstrate reliability and personal aptitude, possess specialized knowledge, establish a need for the permit, and have liability insurance for personal injury and property damage of at least €1 million (Knight, 2022). These permits allow licensees to publicly carry legally owned weapons, with provisions for concealed or open carrying (Knight, 2022). However, they are typically only issued to individuals with a particular need for carrying a firearm, such as private security personnel, celebrities, politicians, and persons living under a raised threat level. Licensed hunters, on the other hand, do not require a permit to carry loaded weapons while hunting or unloaded weapons while directly traveling to and from such activities (Knight, 2022).

In 2002, Germany introduced a small firearms carry permit, known as Kleiner Waffenschein, which allows the public carrying of gas pistols (both blank and irritant types) and flare guns. Unlike the full firearms carry permit, the small firearms carry permit does not require a demonstration of expert knowledge, necessity, or mandatory insurance (Knight, 2022). The only prerequisites for obtaining this permit are legal age, trustworthiness, and personal adequacy. However, carrying these types of firearms on public property still requires the permit, and carrying them at public events is prohibited (Knight, 2022).

In the process of applying for a gun license in Germany, individuals are required to demonstrate their reliability, personal aptitude, specialized knowledge, and need for possessing a firearm (Knight, 2022). The responsibility of processing these applications lies with the local authorities, specifically the public order office (Ordnungsamt) or the police, depending on the applicant's place of residence. The verification of reliability and personal aptitude is a crucial aspect of the application process, and it involves assessing various criteria as stipulated by the law.

One of the key determinants of an applicant's reliability and personal aptitude is their criminal record. According to the law, individuals who have been convicted of a crime within the last ten years are considered unreliable or lacking in personal aptitude. Additionally, circumstances that suggest a potential for reckless use of weapons, such as being associated with banned or unconstitutional organizations, engaging in activities deemed a threat to Germany's foreign interests, or being subjected to preventive police custody multiple times in the last five years, can also lead to a negative assessment of reliability and personal aptitude. Furthermore, dependence on alcohol, drugs, or mental illness are factors that are taken into consideration when evaluating an individual's personal aptitude for possessing a firearm (Knight, 2022)

Specific requirements are in place for individuals under the age of 25 who are applying for their first gun license (Knight, 2022). They are mandated to provide a certificate of "mental aptitude" from a public health officer or psychologist, further emphasizing the stringent measures in place to assess personal aptitude.

In addition to demonstrating reliability and personal aptitude, applicants are also required to exhibit specialized knowledge in the handling and use of firearms. This can be achieved through the successful completion of a state examination that covers legal and technical aspects of firearms, safe handling, and shooting skills. Furthermore, individuals can also demonstrate specialized knowledge by undergoing training related to firearms, such as hunting license examinations, gunsmith's trade examinations, or gaining three years of full-time employment in the gun or arms trade (Knight, 2022). Completion of specific training courses involving firearms, culminating in an examination, is also recognized as a means of demonstrating specialized knowledge. Additionally, officially recognized shooting associations have the authority to conduct their own examinations to verify an applicant's specialized knowledge (Knight, 2022).

Furthermore, the law stipulates that applicants must establish a need for possessing a firearm, which is defined as "personal or economic interests meriting special recognition." This need can be demonstrated in various capacities, including but not limited to being a hunter, marksman, traditional marksman, collector of weapons or ammunition, weapons or ammunition expert, endangered person, weapons manufacturer, weapons dealer, or a member of a security firm (Knight, 2022). Moreover, individuals who can prove that they are at an increased risk of being the victim of a crime may also be considered to have a legitimate need for carrying a firearm. Additionally, members of shooting associations and clubs can substantiate their need for a gun license by providing a certificate from an association of sports shooters confirming the necessity of possessing firearms to maintain their tradition (Knight, 2022).

Gun Related Crime

Germany has implemented stringent gun control measures with the primary objective of safeguarding public safety and mitigating the potential for gun-related violence. These measures have led to relatively low rates of private gun ownership in comparison to other nations, attributable to the strict regulations and comprehensive background checks governing firearm possession (Butts et al., 2015). The regulations contribute to a diminished prevalence of firearms within the general populace, impacting the overall landscape of gun ownership in the country. Furthermore, the stringent regulations on gun ownership are designed to deter the misuse of firearms and diminish the likelihood of gun-related violence (Branas et al., 2009). Germany has adapted its gun control laws to address potential loopholes and bolster public safety, particularly in response to high-profile incidents of mass violence, such as school shootings (Reeping et al., 2019). These legal adjustments encompass heightened age requirements, psychological assessments, and restrictions on specific categories of firearms, aiming to mitigate the risk of mass shootings and similar acts of violence.

It is imperative to acknowledge that while Germany has implemented stringent gun control measures, the overall safety and crime rates in any country are influenced by a multitude of factors. Therefore, the impact of gun control should be contextualized within the broader societal, economic, and cultural landscape that shapes crime and public safety (Ulrich, 2022). In the year 2018, Germany witnessed 1,209 incidents of gun violence, leading to 137 fatalities and 904 individuals sustaining injuries (Castillo, 2023). In 2022, approximately 4,092 individuals faced firearm threats in Germany, and around 4,442 people were shot with various types of firearms, marking an uptick compared to the preceding year (Statista, 2023a). Ongoing evaluations and adaptations to gun control laws may be implemented in response to evolving challenges and societal requirements (Boine et al., 2022).

APPROACH TO GUN CONTROL IN SWITZERLAND

Switzerland's Gun Control Landscape

S witzerland's approach to gun control is deeply rooted in its cultural and historical context, setting it apart from many other nations. The country is renowned for its high rate of gun ownership, with firearms being deeply ingrained in Swiss culture, often associated with the tradition of militia service. This unique approach to gun control is characterized by several key points, including firearm ownership, the militia tradition, licensing and registration, background checks, low gun crime rates, and its international comparison with other European countries (Proctor, 2023b). Switzerland boasts one of the highest rates of firearm ownership globally, with a significant portion of its population owning guns. It is not uncommon for Swiss citizens to keep firearms at home, and the Swiss government estimates that there are approximately 2 to 3 million guns in civilian possession in a country of around 8 million people (Proctor, 2023b).

The Swiss militia system plays a pivotal role in shaping the country's approach to gun control. Under this system, Swiss citizens undergo military training and are entrusted with keeping their military-issued firearms at home (Proctor, 2023b). Upon completing their mandatory military service, individuals often have the option to retain their service weapons. This practice significantly contributes to the widespread availability of firearms among the civilian population.

While gun ownership is prevalent in Switzerland, the country has regulations in place to govern the acquisition and possession of firearms. Individuals generally need to obtain a license to purchase firearms, and certain types of weapons, such as automatic firearms, are subject to stricter controls (Proctor, 2023b). Although registration of firearms is mandatory, it is not as comprehensive as in some other countries. Prior to acquiring a firearm, individuals in Switzerland are subjected to background checks, which encompass an evaluation of the individual's criminal record and mental health. However, the requirements for obtaining a firearm are generally less stringent compared to some other European countries (Proctor, 2023b).

Despite the widespread ownership of firearms, Switzerland experiences relatively low rates of gun crime. This is attributed to the country's strong tradition of responsible gun ownership, with the connection between guns and the militia system fostering a culture of discipline and safety (Proctor, 2023b).

Switzerland's approach to gun control diverges significantly from that of many other European countries. While the country has established regulations, its emphasis on individual responsibility and the militia tradition sets it apart in terms of gun culture and ownership (Proctor, 2023b). In Switzerland, the possession and use of firearms are governed by a comprehensive legal framework. Most individuals seeking to purchase weapons are required to obtain a weapons acquisition permit, which entails meeting specific conditions such as being over 18 years of age, having no criminal record related to violence, and not being deemed a threat to themselves or others. Additionally, individuals wishing to carry weapons in public places must obtain a permit, which is typically granted to those working in law enforcement, private security, or defence, and requires passing an examination to demonstrate proficiency in firearm handling.

Swiss law categorizes weapons into three groups: those that must be declared, those requiring a permit, and illegal weapons. Firearms such as pistols, revolvers, and semi-automatic rifles with a small magazine necessitate a weapons acquisition permit, which can be obtained from the cantonal weapons office. On the other hand, larger or more dangerous weapons, including machine guns and automatic blades, are illegal in Switzerland, with exemptions only granted in extreme circumstances by applying to the cantonal weapons authority (Proctor, 2023b).

Transporting firearms within Switzerland does not require a permit, but it is mandatory to ensure that no ammunition is present in the firearms during transportation. Importing firearms from other countries necessitates obtaining an import permit, with the European Weapons Pass not being accepted as a valid import permit in Switzerland (Proctor, 2023b).

Switzerland's legislation concerning weapons, including the Weapons Law (WG, LArm) and Weapons Act (WV, OArm), has undergone significant revisions in response to international agreements and domestic referendums. The country's adherence to the Schengen Treaty, effective as of 12 December 2008, prompted adjustments to its weapons laws. Furthermore, in 2019, the Swiss population voted in a referendum to incorporate the European Firearms Directive, an addition to the Schengen agreement, leading to further modifications in the legislation. Additionally, the Act on Personal Military Equipment (VPAA, OEPM) governs the handling of military equipment, particularly personal weapons used by military personnel.

The scope of the law encompasses various categories of weapons, each subject to specific regulations. Firearms, such as pistols, revolvers, rifles, pump guns (Vorderschaftrepetierer), lever-action rifles, and self-loading guns (shotguns and rifles), fall under its purview. Additionally, air and CO2 guns with a muzzle energy of at least 7.5 joules, or those posing a risk of confusion with a firearm, are regulated. Imitation and blank firing guns (Schreckschuss) and airsoft guns are also included when there is a potential for confusion with real firearms. Furthermore, the law addresses the handling of certain bladed weapons, including butterfly knives, throwing knives, switchblade or automatic knives with a total length greater than 12 cm and blade length exceeding 5 cm, as well as daggers with a symmetrical blade less than 30 cm. Devices intended to cause harm, such as batons (Schlagrute), throwing stars, brass knuckles, and slings with armrest, are also covered. Moreover, electric shock devices and irritant-containing spray products listed in Annex 2 of the weapons ordinance (WV/OArm) are regulated, with the exception of pepper spray.

The legislation also explicitly prohibits certain categories of weapons. This includes automatic firearms and military launching devices for ammunition, projectiles, or missiles with explosive effects, along with their essential or specially designed components. Additionally, automatic firearms modified to semi-automatic firearms and their essential components are prohibited, with exceptions for Swiss army firearms acquired directly from military authorities and components essential for maintaining their functionality. The law also restricts the ownership of specific semi-automatic centrefire weapons, such as handguns and small firearms equipped with high-capacity loading devices, as well as semi-automatic small firearms that can be shortened to a length of less than 60 cm without losing functionality. Firearms resembling everyday objects and their essential components, grenade launchers, laser devices, night-vision devices, silencers, and certain types of knives are also prohibited. Furthermore, the law addresses the possession of shock rods or stun guns, throwing stars, buttstock-equipped slingshots, tasers, and concealed firearms designed to resemble everyday objects.

Carrying firearms in public or outdoor spaces, including off-duty militia members carrying non-issued weapons, requires a gun carrying permit (Waffentragbewilligung in German, permis de port d'armes in French, and permesso di porto di armi in Italian), as per Article 27 of the Weapons Act (WG/LArm). These permits are typically granted to private citizens in specific occupations like security. Although it's uncommon, individuals in military service or sport shooters may be seen carrying unloaded rifles. The issuance of such exceptional permits is highly selective.

However, there are specific situations where carrying firearms is permissible without a permit, such as holding a valid hunting license, participating in a demonstration related to a historical event, engaging in a secure perimeter shooting competition for airsoft guns, or being an airport security officer, border patrol officer, or game warden in the course of their employment. Additionally, any licensed gun holder may transport an unloaded firearm for special situations.

To obtain a carrying permit, three conditions must be met (Article 27, Section 2 WG/LArm): fulfilling the conditions for a buying permit, providing plausible justification for carrying firearms to protect oneself or others from a specified danger, and passing an examination demonstrating weapon handling skills and knowledge of lawful weapon use. The permit is valid for five years, subject to surrender or revocation, and applies only to the specified firearm type.

For renewing a firearms license, individuals passing the practical test less than three years ago are exempt from retaking it. There is also no need to retake the theory test if legal provisions remain unchanged, and there is sufficient knowledge of the legal conditions for using a weapon (Article 48, Section 4 WV/OArm).

Regarding the transportation of guns in public, specific requirements must be met, such as transporting unloaded guns separately from ammunition and using a valid purpose for transportation. Examples include travel to or from marksmanship courses, hunting, military purposes, army warehouses, displaying the gun to a potential buyer, or during a change of residence.

The EU firearm ban, an amendment to the European Firearms Directive, introduces restrictions on firearm possession and acquisition. Swiss law needs to incorporate these changes due to Switzerland's Schengen Area membership. The directive includes an exemption allowing target shooters to possess one firearm used during mandatory military service if converted to semi-automatic only. This exemption was challenged by the Czech Republic before the European Court of Justice, and a referendum in Switzerland supported the stricter EU restrictions on semi-automatic weapons.

Army-issued arms and ammunition collection have been integral to the Swiss military's militia structure. Swiss soldiers, traditionally part of a militia trained to swiftly respond to foreign threats, undergo basic military training around age 20 and remain in reserve until approximately age 30 (or 34 for officers). Until 2007, militia members were provided 50 rounds of ammunition for their military weapons in sealed ammo boxes, audited regularly by the government for emergency response capability.

In December 2007, the Swiss Federal Council halted the distribution of ammunition to soldiers, requiring the return of previously issued rounds. By March 2011, over 99% of the ammunition had been retrieved. Specialist militia members, responsible for safeguarding sensitive sites, were allowed to retain military-issued ammunition at home, while others could access ammunition from military armories during emergencies. Upon completing their service, militia members could purchase their converted semi-automatic Stgw 90 and select equipment, contingent on a weapon acquisition permit and participation in specified federal exercises.

The government supports rifle training and competitions for interested adolescents, subsidizing the sale of military-issued ammunition at licensed shooting ranges. Ammunition sold to minors must be used immediately at the range under supervision. The Swiss Army maintains strict adherence to lawful military conduct, evident in cases such as the 2005 prosecution of recruits reenacting Abu Ghraib torture scenes, including charges related to the improper use of service weapons.

Recreational shooting is prevalent in Switzerland and encouraged by the government, particularly for militia members. The annual Eidgenössisches Feldschiessen, the world's largest rifle shooting competition, saw about 200,000 attendees before the turn of the century, with participation decreasing to 130,000 in 2012. Additionally, private shooting ranges offer gun rentals for enthusiasts.

Figure 19: Alterwil Feldschiessen (Alterwil Field Shooting) 2022. SwissBloke, CC BY-SA 4.0 <https://creativecommons.org/licenses/by-sa/4.0>, via Wikimedia Commons.

The Swiss attribute their success in avoiding mass shootings to strict gun regulations and a robust approach to firearm training. Notably, Switzerland has not experienced a mass shooting since 2001, and in 2016, it recorded only 47 attempted homicides involving firearms. The country boasts over 2 million privately owned guns among its 8.3 million residents, resulting in an overall low murder rate (Brueck, 2023).

The National Rifle Association (NRA) often references Switzerland as evidence that stringent gun control measures are unnecessary. The Swiss, however, have specific regulations governing gun use. The country places significant emphasis on firearm training, holding an annual shooting contest for adolescents aged 13 to 17, known as Zurich's Knabenschiessen (Brueck, 2023). This tradition, dating back to the 1600s, promotes accuracy, and winners are crowned Schutzenkonig, or king/queen of marksmen (Brueck, 2023).

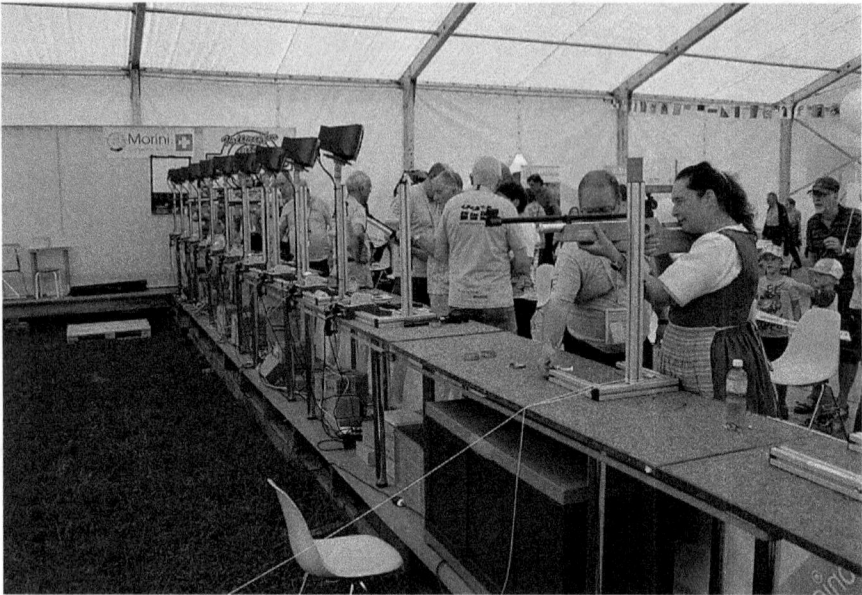

Figure 20: 10-metre shooting range for everyone in the tent of the Swiss Shooting Sports Association at the Unspunnen Festival. Pakeha, CC BY-SA 4.0 <https://creativecommon s.org/licenses/by-sa/4.0>, via Wikimedia Commons.

Switzerland's unique approach to gun ownership is tied to its concept of "armed neutrality." Having remained neutral in international conflicts since 1815, many Swiss view gun ownership as a patriotic duty to defend their homeland. Unlike the United States, Switzerland mandates military service for men, providing them with a pistol or rifle and requisite training between ages 18 and 34 (Brueck, 2023). After service, individuals can purchase and retain their weapons with a permit.

Switzerland's borders are strategically designed for defence, featuring numerous demolition points. Approximately a quarter of Swiss gun owners use their weapons for military or police purposes. Despite the decline in privately owned guns over the past decade, Switzerland maintains a balance between civilian firearm ownership and public safety (Brueck, 2023).

Gun sellers in Switzerland adhere to strict licensing procedures. Local authorities decide on permits, keeping detailed records, while laws prevent those with criminal convictions or violent tendencies from owning guns (Brueck, 2023). The Swiss also prioritize happiness, health, and good governance, consistently ranking among the world's happiest countries.

However, Switzerland faces challenges, including one of the highest rates of gun violence in Europe, with suicides being the predominant cause of gun-related deaths. The introduction of federal gun regulations in 1999 aimed to address rising crime rates, aligning Swiss laws with European Union standards (Brueck, 2023). Though Switzerland is not without flaws, its unique combination of responsible gun ownership, strict regulations, and cultural factors contributes to its distinct approach to firearms (Brueck, 2023).

Gun ownership in Switzerland

Gun ownership in Switzerland is a unique phenomenon that distinguishes the country from its neighbouring European counterparts. The prevalence of gun ownership in Switzerland can be attributed to the nation's longstanding tradition of military conscription, which has fostered a culture of familiarity and comfort with firearms (Proctor, 2023b). Despite the high rate of gun ownership, Switzerland maintains relatively low levels of gun-related crime, with a significant portion of the population engaging in shooting sports (Proctor, 2023b).

Switzerland boasts a notably high rate of gun ownership, with approximately 2.3 million registered firearms in a population of 8.7 million (Proctor, 2023b). This equates to nearly one in four individuals in the country possessing a firearm, although some estimates suggest even higher figures. Consequently, Switzerland ranks among the countries with the highest rates of gun ownership globally, with statistics indicating it as the third-highest in terms of the number of guns per 100,000 residents, trailing behind only the United States and Yemen (Proctor, 2023b).

According to the 2017 Small Arms Survey, the civilian-held firearms in Switzerland are estimated to be around 2,332,000, equating to approximately 27.6 guns per 100 residents based on the country's population of 8.4 million (Alpers et al., 2022). Alternative assessments suggest an even higher figure, with some estimates reaching up to 4,500,000 privately held firearms, resulting in an estimated 54.5 guns per 100 people in 2017. A 2004-05 International Crime Victims Survey (Dijk et al., 2007) indicated that about 28.6% of Swiss households possessed firearms, and 10.3% owned handguns, reflecting the second-highest percentage of firearm ownership in Europe.

The relationship between gun ownership and the Swiss Army is a distinctive aspect of the country's firearm culture. As part of the national service, the Swiss Army conscripts soldiers and provides them with training in the use of weapons for military purposes. Unlike many other nations, Swiss legislation permits soldiers to retain their firearms at home, albeit without the accompanying ammunition. This practice is unique and contributes to the prevalence of firearms in Swiss households (Proctor, 2023b).

While Switzerland does not mandate general gun ownership for its citizens, the obligation for many able-bodied men between the ages of 18 and 65 to undergo military service results in a significant number of individuals being required to maintain their service weapons in good condition at home (Proctor, 2023b). This requirement is contingent on the possibility of being called into active duty, rather than a blanket mandate for all citizens to own firearms.

Despite the high prevalence of gun ownership, Switzerland maintains a relatively low incidence of gun-related violence (Proctor, 2023b). The country's homicide rate stands at approximately 0.55 per 100,000 inhabitants, reflecting one of the lowest rates of gun crime globally. In 2020, only 47 homicides were committed with firearms, underscoring the rarity of gun-related violence in Switzerland (Proctor, 2023b).

Although Switzerland has stringent regulations in place to ensure that only individuals with proper permits can obtain firearms, the country has experienced rare instances of serious gun crimes, including mass shootings. Notably, the most recent large-scale mass shooting occurred in 2001, when an individual perpetrated a violent attack in the cantonal parliament of Zug, resulting in multiple casualties (Proctor, 2023b). This tragic event prompted heightened security measures, such as the installation of X-ray scanners in parliamentary buildings, to mitigate the risk of similar incidents in the future (Proctor, 2023b).

Buying guns in Switzerland involves obtaining a weapon acquisition permit (art. 8 WG/LArm). Citizens and foreigners holding a C permit, aged 18 or above, without a curator, not deemed a danger to themselves or others, and lacking a criminal record with convictions for violent crimes are eligible to request this permit. Foreign nationals residing in Switzerland without a settlement permit must provide an official attestation from their home country confirming their authorization to acquire the weapon. However, individuals with citizenship from specific countries, unless granted exceptional authorization, are excluded from buying, selling, and owning weapons.

To apply for a permit, individuals need to submit essential documentation to the cantonal weapon bureau, including a valid official identification or passport copy and the official attestation for eligible foreign nationals. Additionally, a written contract is required for every transfer of a weapon or essential weapon component without a weapons acquisition permit (art. 10 WG/LArm), with both parties obligated to retain the contract for at least ten years.

The contract must encompass details such as the seller's and buyer's personal information, weapon specifics (kind, manufacturer, label, calibre, weapon number), and the date and place of transfer. Moreover, it should include the official identification of the acquiring person and information on data processing in compliance with privacy policies. This information must be forwarded to the cantonal weapon registration bureau within 30 days for inclusion in the registry, excluding CO_2 and airsoft guns from this requirement (art. 11 WGLArm).

In the context of Swiss firearms regulations, various categories of firearms are subject to different acquisition permit requirements as outlined in the Weapons Act (WG) and the Weapons Ordinance (WV). The categories include antique firearms, firearms that can be acquired without acquisition permits, firearms requiring a shall-issue acquisition permit, firearms necessitating a may-issue exceptional acquisition permit, and firearms eligible for a shall-issue exceptional acquisition permit for sport shooters, as well as a may-issue exceptional acquisition permit for collectors and for weapons other than firearms and their accessories.

Antique firearms, as defined by the regulations, pertain to firearms manufactured before 1870. These firearms are governed solely by Articles 27 (carrying) and 28 (transportation) of the Weapons Act. Notably, no acquisition permit is needed for antique firearms. The next category encompasses firearms that can be acquired without acquisition permits. This includes single-shot and multi-barrel hunting rifles, replicas of single-shot muzzle loaders, manual repetition rifles designated by the Federal Council for specific purposes, single-shot rabbit slayers, compressed air and CO_2 weapons meeting specific energy criteria or resembling real firearms, as well as imitation, blank cartridge, and airsoft weapons that can be mistaken for real firearms due to their appearance. These firearms fall under the purview of Article 10 of the Weapons Act and do not require an acquisition permit.

Moving on, the category of firearms requiring a shall-issue acquisition permit encompasses semi-automatic centrefire weapons such as handguns and small firearms equipped with low-capacity loading devices, revolvers, lever-action rifles, pump-action rifles, and self-loading shotguns with a specific capacity. Article 8 of the Weapons Act stipulates the acquisition of these firearms with a shall-issue acquisition permit. The subsequent category pertains to firearms that necessitate a may-issue exceptional acquisition permit. This includes automatic firearms, military launching devices, and their components, as well as certain semi-automatic centrefire weapons, semi-automatic small firearms with specific features, firearms resembling everyday objects, and grenade launchers. The issuance of this permit is contingent upon professional requirements, protection duties, recreational target shooting, collecting, national defence needs, educational, cultural, research, or historical purposes as outlined in Article 28c of the Weapons Act.

Furthermore, there exists a category for firearms eligible for a shall-issue exceptional acquisition permit for sport shooters. This category includes automatic firearms modified to semi-automatic firearms and certain semi-automatic centrefire weapons. Notably, proof of regular use or membership of a club needs to be provided after 5 and 10 years, specifically for the first weapon purchased with this type of permit. This provision is detailed in Article 28d of the Weapons Act and Article 13c of the Weapons Ordinance. Moreover, the regulations also delineate a category for firearms eligible for a may-issue exceptional acquisition permit for collectors. This category encompasses automatic firearms, military launching devices, certain semi-automatic centrefire weapons, and semi-automatic small firearms with specific features. The issuance of this permit is contingent upon proof that the firearms are kept in a secure location and protected from unauthorized access, as specified in Article 28e of the Weapons Act.

Lastly, there is a category for weapons other than firearms and their accessories that can be acquired with a regular may-issue exceptional acquisition permit. This category includes knives, daggers, striking and throwing devices (excluding batons), electrical shock devices, and weapon accessories. The acquisition of these weapons is subject to professional requirements, use for industrial purposes, compensating for physical handicaps, or collecting, as outlined in Article 28b of the Weapons Act.

The process of buying ammunition in Switzerland is subject to specific legal regulations, similar to those for purchasing firearms. According to the Swiss Weapons Act and its Ordinance, individuals seeking to buy ammunition must adhere to certain requirements. These include providing official identification demonstrating that the individual is over 18 years old, as well as presenting a recent criminal record, a valid weapons acquisition permit, or a European Firearms Pass if requested by the seller (Filindra, 2020). Additionally, there are restrictions on the acquisition and possession of certain types of ammunition, such as armour-piercing bullets, those containing explosive or incendiary devices, and projectiles that release harmful substances . However, there are exceptions for the acquisition of ammunition during shooting events and range practice, and individuals under the age of 18 may obtain ammunition for immediate shooting under supervision.

Furthermore, the Swiss Weapons Act allows for the reloading of ammunition, and while there are no specific limitations on the quantity of ammunition an individual can own and store under federal law, cantonal ordinances may impose restrictions, such as the limit of 300kg of ammunition in Zürich without appropriate paperwork.

The storage of weapons, essential weapon components, ammunition, and ammunition components in Switzerland is governed by specific regulations outlined in Article 26 of the Weapons Act (WG/LArm).

Firstly, these items must be securely stored in a safe place, ensuring protection against unauthorized access by third parties. Additionally, in the event of a weapon loss, immediate reporting to the police is mandatory to address the situation promptly.

Special requirements apply to automatic firearms or those converted to semi-automatic status, as stipulated in Article 47 of the Weapons Ordinance (WV/OArm). For such firearms, the bolt-carrier-group must be kept separate from the rest of the firearm and securely locked, introducing an extra layer of precautionary measures.

The majority of firearm-related deaths in Switzerland are attributed to suicides, with shooting oneself with a firearm accounting for 21.5% of suicides in the period of 2001–2012, with a significant gender imbalance of 29.7% for male suicides compared to 3.0% for female suicides (Vuorio et al., 2015). On the other hand, gun crime in Switzerland is relatively limited, with a low homicide rate of 0.50 per 100,000 population in 2016, making Switzerland one of the countries with the lowest homicide rates globally. Out of the recorded homicides in 2016, 20.3% were committed with a gun, with 16 completed homicides involving firearms, the majority of which were committed with handguns. Additionally, for the period of 2009–2016, on average 16.5 out of 49.4 completed homicides were committed with a firearm, with handguns being the most commonly used type of firearm.

The correlation between the presence of firearms in households and the increased risk of suicide has been extensively documented. Switzerland has one of the highest firearm suicide rates globally, with a rate of 2.5 per 100,000, trailing behind Finland at 2.7 and the United States at 7. In 2022, out of the 220 firearm-related deaths in Switzerland, 200 were attributed to suicide. This alarming statistic has raised significant concerns among organizations dedicated to suicide prevention. According to an information sheet published by the association Stop Suicide, the ready availability of a highly lethal method such as firearms significantly elevates the risk of both suicide attempts and completed suicides (Turuban & Stegmüller, 2024).

In terms of "gun culture" in Switzerland, the gun ownership culture is deeply rooted in a sense of patriotic duty and national identity (Bachmann, 2012). The Swiss take pride in their right to own and carry firearms, with guns being considered a fun and wholesome recreational activity. Switzerland ranks high in gun ownership per capita, but the country maintains a low violent-crime rate. The tradition of having a "gun in every closet" is linked to a historical belief that Switzerland could be invaded, necessitating an armed citizenry. Despite occasional challenges to widespread gun ownership, Swiss laws regulating gun sale, ownership, and licensing are considered stringent. The Swiss emphasize a culture of responsibility and safety, instilled from a young age, contributing to their low crime rates despite widespread gun ownership. The societal focus on responsibility and community support is seen as a key factor in deterring gun violence in Switzerland (Bachmann, 2012).

The low crime rate in Switzerland, despite the widespread availability of firearms, and the inapplicability of the Swiss approach to the current American context, can be attributed to the deeply ingrained culture of responsibility and safety that is deeply rooted in Swiss society and transmitted across generations (Bachmann, 2012). Children as young as 12 are involved in local gun groups, where they are taught marksmanship. The Swiss Shooting Sports Association oversees approximately 3,000 clubs with 150,000 members, including a youth division (Bachmann, 2012). While many members store their firearms and ammunition at home, others opt to keep them at the club. Remarkably, despite the easy accessibility of handguns and rifles, there have been no reported instances of club members using their firearms for criminal activities, as stated by Max Flueckiger, the association's spokesperson (Bachmann, 2012).

GUN CONTROL IN JAPAN

Gun Laws in Japan

Japan is renowned for having some of the most stringent gun control measures in the world. The Japanese approach to gun control is characterized by a combination of rigorous regulations, a focus on public safety, and a cultural context that differs significantly from many Western countries. This comprehensive approach encompasses various key aspects of gun control in Japan. The firearms law in Japan explicitly prohibits the possession of firearms and swords, with limited exceptions. Citizens are allowed to possess firearms for hunting and sport shooting, subject to a rigorous licensing process.

Except for law enforcement and the military, individuals in Japan are prohibited from purchasing handguns or rifles (Kopel, 1992). Those involved in hunting or target shooting are limited to shotguns and airguns under specific conditions. The police conduct thorough checks on the ammunition inventory of gun license holders to ensure no unaccounted-for shells or pellets. Prospective gun owners are required to undergo an official safety course, covering aspects like gun maintenance, loading and unloading methods, shooting from various positions, and target practice for stationary and moving objects (Kopel, 1992). Licenses are valid for three years, and when not in use, all guns must be securely stored (Kopel, 1992). Even possession of a starter's pistol is strictly regulated.

The stringency of gun laws is reflected in the low crime rate in Japan. In 1985, handguns were involved in only 209 crimes, with a significant portion attributed to organized crime groups (Kopel, 1992). Japanese citizens appear to willingly comply with gun laws, and there is no mandatory minimum penalty for unauthorized firearm possession. The pressure to conform and the internalized willingness to do so are more pronounced in Japan compared to the United States. Japan's strong spirit of conformity not only contributes to its low crime rate but also explains the widespread acceptance of strict gun control (Kopel, 1992). It is acknowledged that a gun ban similar to Japan's would be incompatible with America's deeply ingrained gun culture, which has existed for over 300 years, emphasizing individual liberties in contrast to Japan's authoritarian philosophy of government.

To obtain a firearm license, Japanese citizens must undergo a thorough background check and a series of exams, including a written test and a shooting range test. The types of firearms allowed are also restricted, primarily to shotguns and air guns, with handguns being highly regulated and difficult to obtain. In addition to stringent licensing require-ments, Japan imposes strict storage regulations for firearms. Gun owners are required to store their firearms securely, typically involving the use of separate locked containers for guns and ammunition. Ammunition control is another crucial aspect of Japan's gun control measures.

This process includes passing a shooting-range test with a minimum score of 95%, undergoing a mental health evaluation at a hospital, and a comprehensive background check involving interviews with family and friends.

The sale of ammunition is tightly controlled, with buyers required to show their firearm license when purchasing ammunition. Furthermore, Japan enforces stringent background checks for firearm ownership. Applicants undergo a comprehensive back-ground check, including criminal and mental health records, to ensure that only individ-uals meeting the strict criteria are granted firearm licenses. Mandatory training is also a fundamental component of Japan's gun control framework. Prospective gun owners are required to attend classes on firearm safety and handling, and they must pass practical exams at shooting ranges to demonstrate their proficiency.

Moreover, individuals in Japan must provide specific reasons for wanting to own a firearm, such as sports shooting or hunting, as self-defence is not considered a valid reason for ownership. The renewal and monitoring of firearm licenses are also integral to Japan's gun control system. Firearm licenses must be renewed regularly, and authorities monitor gun owners to ensure continued adherence to regulations.

Gun licenses in Japan have a unique expiration policy, as they require renewal every three years, accompanied by the repetition of license tests (Faria, 2012). After a decade of owning a shotgun, license-holders become eligible to apply for a rifle (Faria, 2012). Japan is historically recognized as the pioneer in implementing gun laws, as it initiated the earliest gun buyback program in 1685, setting a global precedent (Faria, 2012). This early initiative underscores Japan's longstanding commitment to stringent gun control measures.

Each prefecture is allowed to operate a maximum of three gun shops, and the purchase of new cartridges requires the submission of expended cartridges. A "prefecture" is an administrative division or region in some countries, typically found in East Asia, including Japan. It is a geographical area that is given a certain degree of administrative and governmental authority. In Japan, for example, prefectures are the country's primary administrative units, each headed by a governor. They serve as the equivalent of states or provinces in other countries. The term may have different meanings or administrative structures in various countries, but it generally refers to a specific level of administrative division.

Additionally, new magazines can only be acquired through the exchange of old ones. In the event of a gun owner's death, their relatives are obligated to surrender the firearms. Off-duty police officers are not permitted to carry weapons, and on-duty officers, except for special squads, rarely use firearms. Arrests are typically made without the use of firearms, and police officers are expected to be proficient in judo.

The rarity of gun ownership in Japan is evident, with a reported rate of 0.6 guns per 100 people in 2007 (Faria, 2012). This statistic highlights the strict regulations and limited prevalence of firearms in the country. Furthermore, instances of mass killings in Japan typically involve assailants resorting to knives or alternative methods rather than guns (Faria, 2012). This trend aligns with the country's low rate of gun-related violence, as evidenced by the recording of only six gun deaths in 2014.

Former Japanese Prime Minister Shinzo Abe, aged 67, was fatally shot on July 8. 2022, in Nara, Japan, with a makeshift firearm while campaigning for the Liberal Democratic Party (LDP). This event was particularly surprising given Japan's reputation for emphasizing gun safety, as the country has implemented strict regulations on gun sales and ownership for many years.

Despite having a population exceeding 125 million, Japan experiences significantly lower rates of gun violence and overall violent crime compared to global averages. The annual gun death rates in Japan typically remain in the single digits. In 2019, the World Health Organization reported only nine firearm-related deaths. Concurrently, the U.S.

Census Bureau estimated a firearm ownership rate of 0.16 per 100 people in Japan during the same year.

An in-depth analysis of the historical context of weapon ownership in Japan reveals a lack of cultural support for widespread gun ownership, with weapons traditionally being reserved for the ruling class (Kopel, 1990). Additionally, the Japanese societal emphasis on communalism, as opposed to individualism, has facilitated the acceptance of strict gun control laws. The Japanese government's active promotion of a social environment conducive to gun control, along with the homogeneity of the Japanese population, has contributed to the low crime rate and general disinterest in gun possession (Kopel, 1990). Kopel (1990) ultimately asserts that while there is room for improvement in the firearms policy of the United States, the adoption of the Japanese system is impractical due to the differing social contexts. Kopel (1990) suggests that while gun limitations may contribute to low crime rates as part of a comprehensive social control system, the fundamental answer lies in the Japanese tradition of submission to authority and trust in the government, which distinguishes Japan from the United States.

Firearm and Sword Possession Control Law

The Swords and Firearms Possession Control Law, enacted in 1958 and subject to multiple revisions, is a comprehensive Japanese legislation governing firearms, firearm parts, ammunition, and bladed weapons (Alleman, 2000). Initially introduced to establish safety regulations preventing harm associated with the possession and use of firearms and swords, the law has evolved over time to address changing societal needs and incidents (Alleman, 2000).

Historically, gun and sword control in Japan dates back to the late 16th century, with efforts by Toyotomi Hideyoshi to disarm peasants and quell uprisings (Library of Congress, 2017). Stricter controls on civilian gun ownership emerged during the Meiji Restoration, and after World War II, the Swords and Firearms Possession Control Law was enacted in 1958, aiming to prevent gang-related conflicts involving guns and swords (Library of Congress, 2017).

The law covers various aspects, including the possession, use, import, discharge, conveyance, receipt, and sale of firearms and firearm parts (Library of Congress, 2017). Notably, handguns are completely prohibited, and the law retains restrictions on swords and bladed weapons. Amendments, prompted by incidents involving guns, have been implemented, such as import bans and changes in the age requirement for owning hunting rifles (Library of Congress, 2017).

The impact on Japanese society is profound. Due to stringent firearm control measures, gun ownership is exceptionally low, resulting in minimal gun-related crimes. Over the past three decades, the highest recorded annual gun-related deaths were 39 in 2001, with subsequent years experiencing as few as four such deaths (Library of Congress, 2017). Japanese culture, marked by historical influences, views weapons as symbols of rulers rather than the ruled. Consequently, firearms are generally perceived as inherently dangerous and subject to strict control (Kopel, 1993; Library of Congress, 2017).

Law enforcement practices reflect the societal stance on firearms. Police stations house guns in secured cases, yet their use is rare (Kopel, 1993). Even during events like student riots involving Molotov cocktails, the police refrain from employing guns, opting for alternative measures such as body armour.

Organized crime, notably Yakuza syndicates, still utilize older handgun models like the Walther P38 and Tokarev pistols, often smuggled from China, Russia, and North Korea. The preference for these antiquated firearms is attributed to their lower cost compared to modern alternatives on the black market and the Yakuza's cultural inclination toward traditional Japanese swords. Huang et al. (2010) provide insights into Chinese narcotics trafficking and the involvement of transnational criminal syndicates. They propose that there is little evidence linking transnational human smuggling and drug trafficking to traditional organized criminal syndicates such as the Triad society. This suggests that the Yakuza's reliance on antiquated guns smuggled from China may be related to their involvement in transnational criminal activities, including drug trafficking.

Furthermore, Liu (2019) discusses narcotics trafficking networks in North Korea and identifies North Korea as a source of methamphetamine distributed by various criminal groups, including the Japanese Yakuza. This supports the claim that the Yakuza syndicates smuggle antiquated guns from North Korea, indicating their involvement in criminal activities in the region. In addition, Martin (2012) discusses the practices of smuggling syndicates, highlighting their tactical methods of infiltrating or appropriating existing mobilities, including commodity flows. This sheds light on the Yakuza's potential involvement in smuggling operations to acquire the antiquated guns from China, Russia, and North Korea.

Pros And Cons of Japanese Gun Control Policy

Japan's gun control policy has contributed to significantly lower rates of gun-related crimes compared to countries with more permissive gun laws. The strict regulations on firearm ownership and usage have been effective in reducing the incidence of gun violence within the country. According to a study by the National Police Agency of Japan, the number of gun-related crimes in Japan is remarkably low, with only a few hundred cases reported annually. This stands in stark contrast to countries with less stringent gun control policies, where gun crime rates are substantially higher. The data clearly indicates that Japan's approach to gun control has resulted in a safer society with fewer incidents of gun violence.

One of the notable advantages of Japan's gun control policy is its effectiveness in preventing mass shootings. Incidents involving multiple casualties, which are tragically common in countries with lax gun laws, are rare in Japan. The stringent regulations and thorough background checks for firearm ownership have acted as a deterrent against individuals with malicious intent obtaining firearms for mass shooting purposes. This has contributed to a sense of security and safety within the Japanese society, as the risk of mass shootings is significantly lower compared to countries with less strict gun control measures.

The emphasis on gun control in Japan has significantly contributed to public safety. With fewer firearms in circulation due to strict regulations, the risk of accidents, suicides, or criminal misuse of guns is notably reduced. This has resulted in a safer environment for the general public, as the limited availability of firearms has minimized the potential for firearm-related incidents. The data from the Ministry of Health, Labour and Welfare in Japan supports this, showing a lower rate of firearm-related accidents and suicides compared to countries with less stringent gun control policies.

Japan's gun control policy aligns with the country's cultural values, where weapons are traditionally viewed as symbols of rulers rather than the ruled. This cultural perspective fosters a sense of harmony and societal aversion to widespread gun ownership. The policy reflects and reinforces the cultural norms and values of the Japanese society, contributing to a cohesive and harmonious social environment. The cultural alignment of the gun control policy with traditional values has been instrumental in shaping a society where the prevalence of firearms is minimal, and the focus is on non-violent conflict resolution.

The strict regulations on firearm ownership and acquisition in Japan make it challenging for criminals to obtain firearms legally. This limitation has contributed to the overall lower crime rates in the country, as the barriers to accessing firearms act as a deterrent for criminal activities involving guns. The data from the National Police Agency of Japan indicates a lower incidence of firearm-related crimes committed by individuals with illegally obtained firearms, further supporting the effectiveness of the policy in limiting the availability of firearms to criminals.

One of the primary criticisms of Japan's gun control policy is the potential limitation it imposes on an individual's right to self-defence. The stringent measures and restrictions on firearm ownership may leave individuals feeling vulnerable in situations where immediate police intervention is not feasible. This limitation has sparked debates regarding the balance between public safety and individual rights, particularly in cases where individuals perceive the need for self-defence in the absence of accessible firearms.

The cultural aversion to firearms in Japan, reinforced by the stringent gun control policy, has the potential to limit personal freedoms for individuals who view gun ownership as a legitimate aspect of self-expression or a hobby. The policy imposes a particular cultural perspective on the populace, which may conflict with the views and values of individuals who do not align with the prevailing cultural norms. This has led to discussions about the impact of the policy on individual freedoms and the imposition of a specific cultural viewpoint on the entire society.

Despite the strict controls on firearm ownership and circulation, there have been instances of organized crime groups, such as the Yakuza syndicates, acquiring firearms through smuggling. This highlights a potential loophole in the system that determined criminals can exploit to obtain firearms illegally. The presence of organized crime groups obtaining firearms through illicit means raises concerns about the effectiveness of the policy in preventing criminal access to firearms and the need for additional measures to address smuggling and organized crime activities related to firearms.

Enthusiasts interested in sports shooting may find the strict regulations in Japan limiting their ability to pursue this hobby. The stringent licensing requirements and adherence to rigorous procedures for firearm ownership have been cited as deterrents for individuals interested in sports shooting. This has raised discussions about the balance between public safety and the preservation of legitimate recreational activities, particularly in cases where the regulations pose significant barriers to participation in sports shooting.

In situations where immediate self-defence is necessary, individuals without access to firearms might be less prepared to protect themselves or others. This concern has been raised in the context of emergencies where police response times are delayed, and individuals may perceive a lack of adequate means to defend themselves. The potential lack of preparedness due to limited access to firearms has sparked discussions about alternative measures for self-defence and the implications of relying solely on law enforcement for protection in critical situations.

It is important to note that the assessment of the pros and cons of Japanese gun control policy is influenced by individual perspectives, societal values, and the cultural context in which the policy is implemented. The evaluation of the policy's impact encompasses a range of factors, including public safety, individual rights, cultural considerations, and the effectiveness of the measures in preventing firearm-related incidents. As such, a comprehensive analysis of the policy requires a nuanced understanding of the diverse perspectives and implications associated with gun control in Japan.

GUN CONTROL IN BRAZIL, SOUTH AFRICA AND RUSSIA

Gun Control in Brazil

B razil leads the world in number of firearm deaths and ranks sixth by country in rate of firearm deaths per 100,000 people (Malta et al., 2020). In Brazil, the ownership and possession of firearms are regulated by specific criteria and background checks. Citizens are required to obtain a gun license, and there are restrictions on the types of firearms civilians can own. The regulations aim to ensure that only individuals who meet certain requirements and pass thorough checks are allowed to possess firearms.

In Brazil, civilian gun ownership is allowed under specific regulations. Individuals seeking firearm ownership must be at least 25 years old and register their weapons with the Federal Police (Harrison et al., 2023). The permitted firearms include handguns and semiautomatics, with assault weapons prohibited for civilians. According to legislation from 2019, gun permits, which cost $26, are valid for ten years and require renewal. Penalties for illegal firearm possession range from one to three years in prison (Harrison et al., 2023). Additionally, Brazilian law prohibits the manufacture, sale, and import of toys or replicas resembling real firearms (Harrison et al., 2023). Additionally, background checks are conducted to assess an applicant's criminal record. These requirements are in place to ensure that individuals seeking gun ownership meet certain standards and do not pose a risk to public safety.

While citizens can purchase guns, obtaining carry permits for taking the weapon outside the home is a challenging process. Applicants must provide a written justification for carrying, demonstrate a clean criminal record, undergo a mental health evaluation by an approved psychologist, and show evidence of proper gun training (Harrison et al., 2023). These permits are valid for five years and are selectively authorized for armed forces, police, prison guards, security officials, and certain transportation personnel. Civilian-owned firearms are restricted in specific locations such as schools, government buildings, churches, and sports complexes (Harrison et al., 2023).

Common reasons for owning a firearm in Brazil include self-defence, target shooting, and sports shooting. The perception of personal safety is often cited as a motivation for gun ownership. Understanding the reasons behind gun ownership is crucial in shaping policies and regulations related to firearms in the country.

All firearms in Brazil must be registered with the Federal Police. The registration process involves providing details about the firearm, the owner, and the purpose for ownership. This registration system is designed to keep track of firearms and their owners, contributing to the overall regulation of gun ownership in the country.

Former President Bolsonaro, known for his pro-gun stance, implemented over 40 decrees during his tenure, weakening gun control measures (Harrison et al., 2023). The changes included increasing the allowable number of firearms from four to six, permitting the carrying of up to two guns in public, doubling ammunition purchases for certain weapons, and easing licensing requirements for collectors and hunters (Harrison et al., 2023). Legal firearm purchases in Brazil surged by 65 percent during Bolsonaro's term, with 1.6 million of the 3 million registered civilian guns acquired in his tenure (Harrison et al., 2023). However, estimates from the Insper Institute suggest the actual number of firearms in the country could be 10 to 15 times higher than the registered figure (Harrison et al., 2023).

Upon assuming office in January 2023, President Luiz Inácio Lula da Silva, who previously implemented extensive gun control measures during his first term (2003–2007), has begun repealing many of Bolsonaro's pro-gun actions (Harrison et al., 2023). Lula issued a decree requiring gun owners to register their firearms in a government database by the end of March, 2023, imposing legal consequences for non-compliance, including prison or fines. By March 21, 2023, only 60 percent of gun owners had reportedly complied.

Brazilian President Luiz Inácio Lula da Silva also recently enacted a decree that tightens regulations on civilian access to firearms in Brazil, aiming to reverse the pro-firearms policies implemented by his predecessor, Jair Bolsonaro (Bridi, 2023). The decree reduces the allowable number of guns for personal safety from four to two, limits the permitted ammunition per gun from 200 rounds to 50, and mandates documentation demonstrating the necessity of firearm possession (Bridi, 2023).

Furthermore, the decree restricts civilians from owning 9 mm pistols, reserving them for members of the police and military. During Bolsonaro's presidency (2019-2022), he advocated for the rights of "good citizens" to protect their families and assets, leading to a relaxation of rules on gun and ammunition ownership. Despite lacking a constitutional right to bear arms, Bolsonaro asserted that "an armed populace will never be enslaved" (Bridi, 2023).

The estimated number of guns in civilian hands surged to 2.9 million during Bolsonaro's term, according to the Instituto Sou da Paz, a non-profit monitoring public security in Brazil (Bridi, 2023). While this figure remains considerably lower than in the United States, the rate of homicides in Brazil remained stable during Bolsonaro's presidency. In 2022, the number of homicides was approximately 47,500, similar to the 2019 rate, as reported by the Brazilian Forum on Public Safety (Bridi, 2023).

The 2023 Brazilian Yearbook of Public Security reports a significant increase in registered gun owners in Brazil, reaching nearly 800,000, a substantial rise from the less than 120,000 recorded in 2018 when Mr. Bolsonaro assumed office (Wright, 2023). It's noteworthy that Brazil lacks a constitutional right to bear arms. In response to concerns about inadequate oversight, the responsibility for supervising civilian weapons is transitioning from the army to Brazil's federal police (Wright, 2023).

Brazil faces significant challenges related to high levels of violence, and the presence of illegal firearms is a major concern. Efforts to combat the circulation of illegal firearms are ongoing, and addressing the issue of illegal firearms is crucial in enhancing public safety and reducing violence in the country. The monthly count of shootings in Rio de Janeiro spanning from 2021 to 2023 reveals that in 2022, the city experienced a total of 3,587 recorded incidents (Statista, 2023b). Notably, March stood out as the month with the highest number of shootings across all three years, constituting around 10 percent of the annual total in 2022, with 357 occurrences. Conversely, the lowest count of shootings within the specified period transpired in July 2023, registering 214 cases (Statista, 2023b).

Gun crime in Brazil has been a significant public health and safety concern, with a high number of intentional violent deaths caused by firearms. According to the Brazilian Public Safety Yearbook, in 2020, 47,773 people suffered intentional violent deaths in

Brazil, with 72.5% of these deaths being caused by guns (Maia et al., 2022). The concern over firearm violence and death in Brazil has led to changes beyond national legislation, as evidenced by previous studies reporting success in reducing the burden of gun deaths through policy changes in Brazil and other countries (Malta et al., 2020; Mokdad et al., 2018). Additionally, between 2000 and 2009, Brazil reduced the number of deaths from firearms after implementing the Disarmament Statute and national campaigns for voluntary firearm surrender in 2004 (Wanzinack et al., 2018).

The impact of gun crime in Brazil extends to various aspects of society, including the involvement of police officers, women of fertile age, and adolescents. A study conducted in Brazil revealed that almost 70% of deaths among women of fertile age were caused by guns (Nascimento et al., 2018). Furthermore, perceived experiences of community violence among adolescents in Brazil have been a subject of concern, reflecting the broader impact of gun crime on the population (Moraes et al., 2021). Additionally, the repercussions on work, health, and family relationships of police officers wounded by gunshot injuries in Brazil highlight the multifaceted consequences of gun violence (Maia et al., 2022)..

The issue of gun crime in Brazil is also intertwined with socio-environmental determinants of health, as evidenced by a systematic literature review that aimed to improve the understanding of violence, focusing on the analysis of the relation between socioeconomic factors and homicide rates in Brazilian capitals (Rodrigues et al., 2021). Furthermore, the presence of armed dealers with formidable stocks of guns and ammunition highlights the paradox of the legitimate monopoly of violence in Brazil and the unbreakable logistics that continually brings firearms and ammunition to the gangs active in the favelas (Barcellos & Zaluar, 2014).

The political landscape and attitudes towards firearms in Brazil have also played a significant role in shaping the discourse around gun crime. Gun control has been a relevant political issue in Brazil for over twenty years, and the attitude of Brazilian federal police officers towards firearms has been a subject of research, reflecting the complex dynamics surrounding firearm control in the country (Borba & Gomes, 2021; Sanjurjo, 2021). Moreover, reviewing ethnographic work on criminal governance groups in Brazil alongside judicial documents detailing the links between the government and militia operatives indicates that criminal governance finds ideological support and functional resonance in the administration (Funari, 2021).

Gun Control in South Africa

The prevalence of firearm-related harm in South Africa is a significant public health concern, with the country having one of the highest firearm-related homicide rates in the world (Otieno et al., 2015). The criminal use of firearms is widespread and a major contributing factor to the high homicide rate in the country (Banwari, 2017). Furthermore, the prevention of violence, including firearm-related injuries and deaths, is a major public health priority in South Africa, necessitating an intersectoral response (Norman, 2007).

The Firearms Control Act 60 of 2000 in South Africa plays a crucial role in regulating the possession of firearms by civilians. This act imposes several conditions for the possession of a firearm, including a competency test, background checking of the applicant, inspection of the owner's premises, and licensing of the weapon by the police (Meel, 2018). However, there have been challenges in the implementation of this act, as evidenced by the delays in processing competency certification, new licenses, and renewal of existing licenses by the police, with waiting periods exceeding two years from the date of application (Matzopoulos et al., 2016). The Central Firearms Registry has implemented a turnaround strategy to address these challenges, resulting in a significant improvement in the processing period for new licenses, with the maximum processing time now set at 90 days Engelbrecht et al. (2017).

The implementation of the Firearms Control Act of 2000 has been associated with a decrease in gunshot-related injury deaths, indicating that stricter gun control measures have contributed to this decline (Matzopoulos et al., 2016). Furthermore, the act has been publicized as a significant contributor to saving lives and enhancing safety in South Africa (Meel, 2018). This is supported by evidence showing a decrease in firearm homicides following the implementation of reformed gun control legislation and firearm amnesties in South Africa (Swart et al., 2015).

In South Africa, individuals or permanent residents, typically over the age of 21 (though exceptions may apply based on demonstrated need), seeking to own firearms must obtain a license for each individual firearm. The maximum allowable number of firearms per individual is four, and there is a limit of 200 rounds of ammunition per license. However, individuals achieving 'dedicated status' through a registered shooting club can potentially license an unlimited number of firearms, with ammunition limits also lifted (Mathews et al., 2019). Prohibited firearms encompass fully automatic firearms, certain projectile-launching devices, and altered firearms without proper authorization (Mathews et al., 2019).

Semi-automatic firearms, including rifles and shotguns, are not inherently prohibited. However, obtaining them requires a business license, a restricted firearms license for self-defence, or dedicated hunting and shooting licenses. Notably, there is no official magazine capacity restriction for semi-automatic rifles. Handguns of all firing actions, except fully automatic, are legally allowed under all licenses, and there is no specific magazine capacity restriction for handguns.

Legally owned firearms can be carried in public without an additional permit, provided they are appropriately holstered or stored in designated holders. Handguns must be carried in a holster attached to the person or in a suitable holder, while other firearms must be carried in a holder designed for that purpose. The firearm must be completely covered, and the individual carrying it must maintain effective control.

According to official statistics, over the period spanning 2020 to 2021, in excess of 12,900 individuals were apprehended for the unlawful possession of firearms (Magome & Mosamo, 2022). The Democratic Alliance party has raised concerns, claiming that over the five years leading up to 2022, more than 3,400 police firearms were reportedly unaccounted for. In response to a series of shootings in July 2022, resulting in 22 fatalities and involving weapons like AK-47 rifles, South Africa Police Minister Bheki Cele announced plans for a comprehensive search, conducting house-to-house operations to locate illegal firearms (Magome & Mosamo, 2022).

Certain places are designated as prohibited areas or firearm-free zones (FFZ) under the Control of Access to Public Premises and Vehicles Act of 1985. The Firearms Control Act of 2000 allows for the application and granting of FFZ status by the Minister of Police under Section 140. Distinct from voluntary Gun Free Zones (GFZ), FFZs are legally enforced and violations can result in severe penalties, including up to 25 years in prison. Police are empowered to search buildings or premises, individuals, and seize firearms or ammunition within an FFZ based on reasonable suspicion.

An important development occurred on May 7, 2004, when the Minister of Police issued Notice 749 of 2004, declaring all schools and learning institutions, including higher education institutions, as firearm-free zones. However, as of the latest available information, no FFZs have been declared by the Minister.

In the context of firearm regulation, there are various types of licenses and permits that individuals can obtain in order to possess firearms for different purposes. These licenses and permits are outlined in detail in the relevant legislation, specifically in chapter 6, sections 13, 15, and 16. Each type of license or permit is tailored to specific needs and activities, and the issuance of these licenses and permits is subject to certain criteria and conditions as stipulated by the Registrar.

The first type of license is the "Licence to possess firearm for self-defence" as provided for under chapter 6, section 13. This license allows the holder to possess specific types of firearms, namely a shotgun that is not fully or semi-automatic, or a handgun that is not fully automatic. The issuance of this license is contingent upon the individual's demonstration of a genuine need for a firearm for self-defence and an inability to satisfy that need through alternative means. The Registrar has the authority to issue this license to natural persons who meet these criteria.

The second type of license is the "Licence to possess firearm for occasional hunting and sports-shooting" as outlined in chapter 6, section 15. This license permits the possession of handguns that are not fully automatic, as well as rifles or shotguns that are not fully or semi-automatic. It is intended for natural persons who engage in occasional hunting or sports shooting activities, and who may not be official members of recognized hunting or shooting clubs. The Registrar is empowered to issue this license to eligible individuals.

The third type of license is the "Licence to possess firearm for dedicated hunting and dedicated sports-shooting" under chapter 6, section 16. This license allows the holder to possess a wider range of firearms, including handguns that are not fully automatic, rifles that are not fully automatic, shotguns that are not fully automatic, and semi-automatic shotguns. To qualify for this license, the applicant must be a dedicated hunter or sports person, and their application must be supported by a sworn statement or solemn de-claration from the chairperson of an accredited hunting association or sports-shooting organization, or a delegated representative. This statement attests to the applicant's mem-bership in the relevant association or organization. Furthermore, there is a specific license for "professional hunting" under chapter 6, section 16, which is tailored for individuals engaged in professional hunting activities. This license likely has specific requirements and conditions that are distinct from those of other licenses, given the professional nature of the hunting activities involved.

In addition to the various licenses for firearm possession, there are also permits related to ammunition. The "Permit to possess ammunition in private collection" allows the holder to possess firearms ammunition, and it is particularly relevant for individuals who have firearms in their private collection. This permit is distinct from licenses for firearms and is specifically focused on the possession of ammunition. Moreover, there is a provision for a "Licence to possess firearm in private collection" which allows the holder to possess firearms in a private collection. This license is likely intended for individuals who collect firearms as a hobby or for other legitimate purposes, and it may have specific criteria and conditions related to the maintenance and use of firearms in a private collection.

Additionally, there is a "Licence to possess firearm for business purposes" which permits the possession of firearms for specific business-related activities. This license is applicable to various entities and individuals engaged in specific business activities such as security companies, accredited firearms trainers, professionals involved in theatrical, film, or television productions, accredited professional hunters, and individuals accredited for other business purposes as determined by the Registrar. The issuance of this license is subject to the discretion of the Registrar and likely involves stringent criteria and conditions to ensure the responsible and lawful use of firearms for business purposes.

In terms of gun ownership, as of March 2015, South Africa recorded approximately 1.8 million licensed civilian gun owners, constituting a mere 3.4% of the country's 51.8 million population (Gun Free South Africa, 2024). To put it differently, among a group of 100 individuals, only 3 possess a firearm. This figure marks a decline from the statistics of 1999, which reported slightly over 2 million (2,027,411) gun owners, reflecting a ratio of 5 gun owners per 100 people.

In terms of registered firearms, just over 3 million (3,081,173) were documented for civilian ownership, resulting in a ratio of 5.9 guns per 100 people (Gun Free South Africa, 2024). This represents a 14% decrease from the figures in 1999 when 3.5 million (3,554,336) guns were registered to civilians, equating to a ratio of 8.3 firearms for every 100 people (Gun Free South Africa, 2024). The gradual reduction in both the number of licensed gun owners and registered firearms over this period underscores a notable shift in the prevalence of civilian firearm ownership in South Africa (Gun Free South Africa, 2024).

The assertion that gun crime is predominantly associated with illegal firearms often leads to the belief that addressing the issue involves strategies such as amnesties, buy-back programs, police operations, and intelligence efforts to seize illegal guns. Contrary to this perception, the majority of guns used in crimes were initially legally manufactured, indicating that legal firearms can enter the illicit weapons market in South Africa.

Three primary avenues contribute to the influx of legal guns into the illegal pool of weapons in South Africa. Firstly, legal guns may be smuggled from neighbouring countries, although research suggests that this occurrence is relatively low, with a more significant likelihood of guns being smuggled to neighbouring countries instead (Gun Free South Africa, 2024). Secondly, fraudulent activities, corruption, and lax enforcement of the Firearms Control Act result in individuals who are not considered 'fit and proper' being issued firearm certificates, licenses, permits, or authorizations (Gun Free South Africa, 2024).

However, the most substantial source of illegal guns in South Africa arises from the loss and theft of firearms from both civilians and state institutions. Despite some inconsistencies in statistics, data reveals that firearm loss and theft constitute a significant challenge, with civilians losing between 15 and 28 guns daily, and police officers losing between 2 and 5 guns daily from 2011 to 2014 (Gun Free South Africa, 2024).

Gun Free South Africa (2024) posits that given the prevalence of gun loss and theft, a viable approach to mitigate the diversion of legal guns to the illegal market involves implementing stringent regulations in the gun licensing process. This emphasizes the importance of addressing the vulnerabilities in the licensing system to prevent unauthorized access to firearms, contributing to the overall reduction of illegal firearms in circulation (Gun Free South Africa, 2024).

Considering the impact of South African gun control approaches, the impact of South Africa's gun laws, particularly the Firearms Control Act (FCA) of 2000, on reducing gun-related violence is a complex and multifaceted issue. The FCA, signed into law by President Thabo Mbeki, introduced stringent measures such as detailed motivations for gun ownership, strict background checks, and psychological evaluations for applicants. Additionally, it was accompanied by a firearms amnesty and police operations to capture illegal weapons. Matzopoulos et al. (2016) presented surveillance data from South Africa's five major cities from 2001 to 2005, the period for which comprehensive injury mortality surveillance data were available, and indicated a decrease in gun-related deaths following the implementation of the FCA (Matzopoulos et al., 2016).

Research indicates that the FCA was associated with a decrease in gun-related deaths, particularly in the years immediately following its enactment. However, there are contrasting views on whether this decline can be solely attributed to the new firearm policies. While some argue that the decrease in gun murders can be linked to the FCA, others contend that the decline was already underway before the law came into full effect. Nevertheless, there is evidence to suggest that the FCA had a positive impact on reducing gun-related violence, particularly in the context of intimate partner femicide and female homicides (Matzopoulos et al., 2016).

Comparative studies with other countries, such as the United States, provide valuable insights into the impact of gun laws on violent crime. Research in the US has shown that more lenient gun laws can lead to an increase in murders, particularly in states that passed stand-your-ground laws, indicating the importance of stringent firearm regulations in reducing violent crime (Copelyn, 2022). Similarly, evidence from Colombia, where restrictions on carrying firearms were implemented in specific cities, demonstrated a significant decrease in gun murders, highlighting the potential effectiveness of such policies in reducing lethal violence (Copelyn, 2022).

In the South African context, the issue of concealed carry permits has also been a point of contention (Copelyn, 2022). While current laws allow citizens to carry concealed firearms with a permit, concerns have been raised about the potential implications of a well-armed population in a society where violence is often the first resort for conflict resolution. Epidemiologists have highlighted the role of firearms in escalating disputes and contributing to the lethality of conflicts, emphasizing the need for comprehensive measures to address the root causes of violence (Copelyn, 2022).

One of the significant impacts of gun control policies in South Africa is the reduction in legal firearm ownership. The implementation of stricter measures, including limitations on the number of firearms individuals can own, has led to a decrease in legal firearm ownership. This reduction is aimed at preventing legal guns from falling into the wrong hands and being used in criminal activities. However, despite efforts to control legal firearm ownership, challenges persist in preventing the loss and theft of firearms, contributing to the presence of illegal guns in criminal activities. Strict enforcement and improved regulation of the licensing process are essential to address this issue effectively.

In terms of public safety, the impact of gun control policies is evident in the debate around citizens' ability to defend themselves. Stricter regulations on firearm ownership may impact the perceived right to self-defence, with proponents arguing that reducing the number of guns in circulation enhances overall public safety. Moreover, criminal elements often use illegal firearms in violent activities. The effectiveness of gun control policies is measured, in part, by their ability to curb the availability of illegal firearms, making it more challenging for criminals to acquire weapons.

The regulatory measures associated with gun control policies play a crucial role in determining their impact. The licensing process, which includes stringent background checks, mental health evaluations, and regular license renewals, contributes to a more robust system that aims to keep firearms out of the hands of those who pose a risk. Additionally, the establishment of firearm-free zones, particularly in sensitive areas such as schools and government buildings, is intended to enhance public safety and prevent potential incidents of gun violence in specific locations.

Public perception and compliance also significantly influence the impact of gun control policies. The success of these policies depends on the level of public acceptance and compliance. Public awareness campaigns and education about the importance of responsible firearm ownership can contribute to greater adherence to regulations. Furthermore, changes in political leadership may lead to shifts in gun control policies, influencing the overall impact on gun ownership and use.

Gun Control in Russia

The history of gun ownership in Russia has undergone significant fluctuations, transitioning from an armed populace during the monarchy to near complete disarmament under the Soviet Union. Presently, Russian laws pertaining to gun ownership stand in stark contrast to those in the United States, and despite numerous restrictions, gun culture in Russia remains a prevalent trend (Anguilano, 2018).

The right to self-defence holds significant importance in Russian law, with the constitution guaranteeing individuals the right to defend their property. Anguilano (2018) emphasizes this constitutional right, stating that individuals are permitted to defend their lives using any means at their disposal, including various weapons, as outlined by the law. Russian citizens have the legal right to possess firearms for various purposes such as hunting, sport-shooting, pest control, self-defence, and collecting. The authorized firearms in Russia encompass handguns and non-military-style rifles, excluding assault rifles like AK-47s, AR-15s, or FN-FALs. World Population Review (2024) identifies that there are 17.6 million civilian firearms in Russia, at a rate of 12.3 guns per 100,000 people.

As of 2023, the regulations stipulate that handguns using live ammunition are not permitted for concealed carry in public. Instead, only handguns using rubber bullets are allowed for self-defence purposes (Stetsenko et al., 2022). There is an exception to this law, which allows for the possession and concealed carry of commemoration pistols with special engravings. These pistols are permitted to use live ammunition and can be used for self-defence, provided the recipient is 21 years of age or older and possesses a valid firearms permit (Stetsenko et al., 2022).

Furthermore, the regulations prohibit rifles and shotguns with barrels less than 500 mm (20 in) long, as well as firearms that shoot in bursts or have a capacity of more than 10 rounds, except for use on gun ranges (Stetsenko et al., 2022). Additionally, suppressors are generally prohibited and require special government permission for possession (Stetsenko et al., 2022). The law also limits individuals from possessing more than ten guns, including up to five shotguns and up to five rifles, unless they are part of a registered gun collection (Stetsenko et al., 2022).

Eligibility for purchasing a firearm in Russia necessitates individuals to be over the age of 18 and to pass rigorous background checks. Those with a history of mental illness or substance abuse are disqualified from firearm ownership. The scrutiny of background checks, particularly concerning the mental health of potential buyers, is stringent. Furthermore, the Federal Assembly is contemplating legislation to penalize doctors who misdiagnose or provide inaccurate documentation for mentally ill patients seeking to purchase firearms (Anguilano, 2018). Detailed records are maintained regarding the type of gun, its intended purpose, and calibre, with magazine capacity limited to no more than 10 rounds. The issue of barrel length of firearms has been a recurring concern in the country, with some organizations advocating for the legalization of short-barrelled weapons (Anguilano, 2018).

In the context of illicit weapons in Russia, Anguilano (2018) indicates that the Ministry of Internal Affairs previously estimated the number to range from five to 25 million pieces. Although Russia has experienced a significant decrease in terrorist activities since the 1990s, gun-related crimes have steadily increased, reaching a peak of 5400 incidents in 2015 (Anguilano, 2018). Conversely, as of April 2017, an estimated 4.5 million Russians were legally in possession of approximately 7.3 million firearms. However, this figure represents only about 3 percent of the population, with the vast majority remaining unarmed (Anguilano, 2018).

Gun control laws in Russia are characterized by strict regulations governing the possession and use of firearms. These regulations are primarily established and enforced through federal laws, outlining a detailed process for obtaining a firearm license. The key points regarding gun control in Russia encompass licensing and registration, types of firearms allowed, ownership purposes, background checks, age restrictions, ammunition regulations, storage requirements, gun-free zones, and regulations for prohibited persons.

Licensing and registration form the cornerstone of firearm regulation in Russia. Individuals seeking to own and use firearms legally must obtain a license, which is issued for specific types of firearms and purposes, such as self-defence, hunting, or sports shooting. Furthermore, firearms must be registered with the authorities, ensuring accountability and oversight of their ownership and use. In terms of the types of firearms allowed, Russia generally prohibits civilian ownership of automatic and semi-automatic firearms. However, handguns, shotguns, and certain types of rifles are permitted for civilian ownership, subject to proper licensing and registration.

Background checks constitute a fundamental component of the licensing process, encompassing thorough assessments of applicants' criminal records and mental health history. Individuals with a history of domestic violence or mental health issues may be denied a firearm license based on the findings of these background checks. Age restrictions are also integral to Russia's gun control laws. The minimum age for obtaining a firearm license is typically 18 for long guns (rifles and shotguns) and 21 for handguns, reflecting the government's emphasis on responsible firearm ownership. Ammunition purchase and possession are subject to regulation in Russia, with buyers often required to present their firearm license when acquiring ammunition. This additional layer of oversight ensures that individuals purchasing ammunition are authorized firearm owners.

Although an initial license is not obligatory for firearm acquisition, first-time buyers must undergo a background check and participate in firearms safety courses. Additionally, firearms need to be officially registered with the Russian National Federal Police. A Public Carry Permit is mandatory for individuals wishing to carry firearms openly in public spaces.

The secure storage of firearms when not in use is mandated by law in Russia, with specific requirements outlined to prevent theft or unauthorized access. These storage requirements are designed to promote responsible firearm ownership and enhance public safety. Certain locations, such as schools and government buildings, are designated as gun-free zones in Russia, where the possession of firearms is prohibited. This designation contributes to the maintenance of safe and secure environments in these sensitive areas. Moreover, individuals with specific occupations or affiliations, such as law enforcement or security personnel, may be subject to distinct regulations governing their firearm ownership, reflecting the varying contexts in which fire.

Violating Russian gun regulations can result in severe consequences, including up to four years of imprisonment for the unlawful possession or sale of firearms, up to two years for carrying a firearm while under the influence, and up to three years for negligent storage or mishandling of a firearm leading to injury or death. Furthermore, individuals convicted of a firearm-related offense may face a permanent prohibition on owning firearms.

Sport-shooting and hunting are immensely popular pastimes in Russia. With an estimated population of around 110 million people, there are approximately 35,340,900 registered firearms and 4,041,000 issued Public Carry permits as of 2015 (Anon, 2024). Russia stands as one of the leading nations in firearm ownership across Eastern Europe, Asia, and even North America, aligning with the Slavic heritage tradition of widespread firearm possession (Anon, 2024).

Key advocates for gun rights in Russia include prominent organizations such as the Motherland Rifle Coalition and the Russian National Shooters Organization (Anon, 2024). Other noteworthy associations supporting firearm enthusiasts include the Smoothbore Federation and the Hunters and Fishers Association (Anon, 2024).

From 2015 onwards, there has been a gradual decrease in the number of criminal acts in Russia involving firearms, gas weapons, ammunition, explosives, and explosive devices (Statista, 2023c). In 2021, the recorded crimes in this category amounted to 3.5 thousand, showcasing a decline from the initial period of observation when over five thousand offenses of this nature were reported across the country (Statista, 2023c).

VARYING PERSPECTIVES

Extent of Gun Ownership Globally

The Small Arms Survey conducted a comprehensive study on the global distribution of firearms across 230 countries in 2018, encompassing various types of firearms and ownership by civilian, military, and law enforcement groups (Austin, 2018). The report revealed a significant increase in the estimated global firearms stockpile, reaching over 1 billion firearms, marking a 17% surge over the past decade. The majority of these firearms, approximately 85%, are held by civilians, including individuals, private security firms, non-state armed groups, and gangs. In comparison to the Small Arms Survey's 2007 report, the current findings indicate a substantial rise in civilian firearm ownership, with the United States standing out as a significant contributor to this surge, possessing nearly 40% of the world's firearms despite having only 4% of the global population (Austin, 2018).

The report also delves into the specific dynamics of firearm ownership in the United States, highlighting that the country has witnessed a consistent increase in civilian firearm acquisition, averaging around 14 million guns annually over the last five years (Austin, 2018). This surge in firearm ownership is further exemplified by the estimation that American civilians possess a staggering 393 million firearms, translating to approximately 121 firearms for every 100 residents. Moreover, the Pew Research Center's findings revealed that firearm ownership varies across different age groups, with one-third of Americans over 50 owning a gun, compared to 28% among 18- to 29-year-olds (Austin,

2018). Additionally, the prevalence of firearms in the US is underscored by the fact that 42.3% of US hunters/shooters reported owning at least one AR-15 platform (M16-style) rifle (Austin, 2018).

The report also sheds light on the global distribution of firearms, with the United States leading in civilian firearm ownership, followed by India and China. However, when analysed in terms of the number of weapons per 100 residents, Yemen, Montenegro, and Serbia emerge as the top three, following the US. Furthermore, the study highlights the significant presence of firearms in law enforcement and military stockpiles, with Russia, China, and India featuring prominently in these categories (Austin, 2018).

The report emphasizes the challenges associated with regulating and controlling the proliferation of small arms, particularly in developing countries and those affected by conflict. It underscores the need for accurate data and effective governance to address the multifaceted implications of widespread firearm ownership, including human rights abuses, criminal activities, insurrection, and violence. The longevity of firearms, such as revolvers and AK-47 assault rifles, further complicates the regulation and control of these weapons, with some firearms capable of remaining functional for several decades. (Austin, 2018).

The widespread ownership of firearms, particularly by civilians, private security firms, and non-state armed groups, has direct implications for public safety. The presence of a large number of firearms can contribute to an increased risk of accidents, crime, and violence. This is supported by research indicating that areas with higher rates of firearm ownership tend to have higher rates of firearm-related deaths and injuries. Additionally, the accessibility of firearms can lead to their misuse, posing a threat to public safety and security. Therefore, addressing the distribution and ownership of firearms is crucial in mitigating these risks and ensuring the well-being of communities.

The surge in the global firearms stockpile raises concerns about the potential for increased violence and human rights abuses. Firearms are often associated with criminal activities, armed conflict, and human rights violations. The proliferation of weapons in the hands of non-state armed groups and gangs can exacerbate these issues, leading to heightened levels of violence and insecurity within communities. Furthermore, the availability of firearms can empower individuals or groups to infringe upon the human rights of others, perpetuating a cycle of violence and abuse. Thus, addressing the distribution and use of firearms is essential in upholding human rights and preventing further escalation of violence.

In regions affected by conflict, the presence of a significant number of firearms in the hands of various actors, including non-state armed groups, can perpetuate instability and contribute to prolonged conflicts. This situation can hinder the enjoyment of social rights, such as the right to live in a peaceful and secure environment. Research has shown that the availability of firearms can prolong conflicts and make post-conflict recovery more challenging. Moreover, the unchecked proliferation of small arms can fuel insurrection and hinder efforts to establish sustainable peace and security. Therefore, addressing the distribution and use of firearms is crucial in promoting stability and safeguarding social rights in conflict-affected regions.

Austin (2018) emphasizes the challenges associated with regulating and controlling the proliferation of small arms. Effective governance and regulation are essential for safeguarding social rights. Governments play a crucial role in implementing policies that balance individual rights with the broader interests of public safety and security. This involves enacting and enforcing laws and regulations that govern the acquisition, possession, and use of firearms, as well as implementing measures to prevent illicit trafficking and unauthorized access to firearms. Additionally, governments have a responsibility to provide oversight and accountability in the management of firearms to ensure that they do not pose a threat to social rights and public safety.

Firearm ownership patterns within communities, as highlighted in the report, can impact the overall well-being of individuals. The prevalence of firearms may create an environment of fear and insecurity, affecting community cohesion and mental health. Research has shown that living in areas with high levels of firearm ownership can contribute to heightened levels of stress and anxiety among residents (Austin, 2018). Additionally, the presence of firearms can impact social interactions and community dynamics, potentially leading to a breakdown of trust and cohesion. Therefore, addressing the distribution and ownership of firearms is essential in promoting community well-being and fostering a sense of security and belonging among residents.

Accurate data on firearm ownership is crucial for informed policymaking. Governments and international organizations need reliable information to develop and implement policies that protect social rights while addressing the challenges associated with widespread firearm ownership. This involves establishing comprehensive systems for collecting and analysing data on firearm ownership, use, and related incidents. By utilizing data-driven approaches, policymakers can better understand the impact of firearms on public safety, security, and human rights, and tailor interventions and regulations accordingly. Therefore, investing in robust data collection and analysis is essential in formulating effective policies to address the implications of firearm distribution on social rights.

Austin (2018) underscores the need for international collaboration to control the illicit trade of firearms. Cooperation between nations is essential to address the transnational nature of small arms proliferation and its impact on social rights globally. This involves sharing information, resources, and best practices to combat the illicit trade of firearms and prevent their unauthorized transfer across borders. Additionally, international collaboration can facilitate the implementation of common standards and regulations to govern the global trade in firearms, thereby reducing the risk of diversion to illicit markets and non-state actors. Therefore, fostering international collaboration is crucial in addressing the cross-border implications of firearm distribution and promoting the protection of social rights on a global scale.

Basis for variation in Approaches to Gun Control

Approaches to gun control vary significantly around the world due to a complex interplay of historical, cultural, legal, political, and socio-economic factors. This diversity in approaches can be attributed to several key reasons, each of which contributes to the unique circumstances and attitudes towards firearms in different nations.

Historical Context plays a crucial role in shaping a country's approach to gun control. The Colonial Legacy is one such factor, as countries with a history of colonization may have inherited or adapted the gun control practices of their colonizers. For example, former British colonies often have regulatory frameworks influenced by British gun control laws. Additionally, Independence and Revolutions have also played a significant role in shaping attitudes and regulations regarding firearms. Nations that underwent revolutions or wars for independence may have developed specific attitudes and regulations regarding firearms, often influenced by the role of firearms in achieving independence or in post-independence governance.

Cultural Factors also significantly impact the diversity in approaches to gun control. Societal attitudes towards firearms are often shaped by cultural traditions, historical events, and perceived values associated with gun ownership. For instance, in countries where hunting or sport shooting is deeply ingrained in the culture, regulations may be more permissive for these purposes. Furthermore, traditions and values within a society can influence the perception of firearms and the need for regulation.

Legal Frameworks, including constitutional rights and statutory laws, are critical in shaping a country's approach to gun control. The presence or absence of constitutional provisions related to gun ownership, such as the Second Amendment in the United States, can significantly influence legal frameworks. Moreover, the specific laws enacted by governments, including the type of firearms allowed, licensing procedures, and restrictions, contribute to the overall approach to gun control within a country.

The Political Climate, including political ideologies and public opinion, also plays a pivotal role in shaping gun control policies. Different political groups may have varying stances on individual rights, public safety, and the role of the state, which in turn influences the development and implementation of gun control measures. Governments often respond to public sentiment, and attitudes toward guns may be influenced by historical events, crime rates, or high-profile incidents, further shaping the political climate surrounding gun control.

Public Safety Concerns, such as crime rates and terrorism, are additional factors contributing to the diversity in approaches to gun control. Countries experiencing high crime rates may adopt stricter measures to control firearms in an effort to enhance public safety. Similarly, nations facing security threats may implement stringent regulations to prevent the illicit flow of weapons and combat terrorism, further influencing their approach to gun control.

Social and Economic Factors also play a significant role in shaping attitudes towards gun control. Societies with significant income disparities may grapple with issues related to illegal firearms and crime, impacting the stringency of gun control measures. Additionally, the level of urbanization can influence the perception of guns, with urban areas often having different concerns and priorities compared to rural areas, thus impacting the approach to gun control.

International Relations and Historical Incidents are also influential in shaping a country's approach to gun control. International agreements, pressure, or collaborations can impact a country's approach to gun control, as nations may align their policies with global efforts to combat illicit arms trafficking. Moreover, high-profile incidents, such as mass shootings, can lead to changes in gun control policies as governments respond to public demands for increased safety measures, further shaping the historical and societal context of gun control.

Economic Interests, particularly the presence and influence of the firearms industry, can affect gun control policies. Countries with a significant firearms manufacturing sector may have different considerations than those without, as economic interests intersect with regulatory frameworks and public policy.

Purchasing a Gun

To emphasise the difference between gun control approaches and to provide further context, we can consider an article by Carlsen and Chinoy (2019) who outline the basic steps for how most people buy a gun in 16 different countries. The process of purchasing a firearm varies significantly across different countries, with each nation implementing its own set of regulations and requirements to ensure responsible gun ownership. This following, based on the outlines provided by Carlsen and Chinoy (2019) aims to provide a comprehensive overview of the basic steps involved in purchasing a firearm in 16 different countries, namely the United States, Japan, New Zealand, South Africa, Mexico, Australia, Austria, Canada, India, Germany, Britain, Brazil, Russia, Israel, China, and Yemen. By examining the specific procedures and regulations in each country, this comparison seeks to highlight the diversity of approaches to firearm acquisition and the underlying factors that shape these processes, which in turn is reflective of the country's gun control culture and policy.

- United States: In the United States, the process of purchasing a firearm involves several key steps. First, individuals are required to pass an instant background check, which considers factors such as criminal convictions, domestic violence history, and immigration status. Following the successful completion of the background check, individuals can proceed to purchase a gun. It is important to note that while federal law mandates background checks for purchases from licensed dealers, private sales do not always require such checks, leading to variations in the application of this regulation across different states. Additionally, some states impose additional buying restrictions, including waiting periods and expanded background checks, further contributing to the complexity of the firearm purchasing process in the United States.

- Japan: In Japan, the process of acquiring a firearm is characterized by a comprehensive set of requirements and assessments. Prospective gun owners are first

required to undergo a firearm class and pass a written exam, which is conducted periodically throughout the year. Subsequently, individuals must obtain a
doctor's note affirming their mental fitness and absence of a history of drug
abuse. The next step involves applying for a permit to undergo firing training,
which may take up to a month to obtain. Following this, applicants are required
to undergo a thorough review of their criminal history, gun possession record,
employment status, involvement with organized crime groups, personal debt,
and relationships with friends, family, and neighbours. Additionally, individuals
must apply for a gunpowder permit, undergo a one-day training class, pass a firing test, and obtain a certificate from a gun dealer specifying the desired firearm.
Furthermore, individuals seeking a gun for hunting purposes are required to
apply for a hunting license. The process culminates in the purchase of a gun,
which is preceded by the acquisition of a gun safe and an ammunition locker
that comply with safety regulations.

- New Zealand: In the aftermath of tragic mass shootings, New Zealand implemented stringent gun regulations, including the requirement for individuals to
  pass a background check that encompasses criminal, medical, mental health,
  and domestic violence records. Additionally, applicants are mandated to provide
  character references and undergo a home security inspection to ensure proper
  firearm storage. The approval process for a firearms license in New Zealand
  may extend over several weeks or months, reflecting the meticulous scrutiny
  applied to each application. Notably, the country enacted a law prohibiting the
  possession of most semiautomatic weapons following a devastating shooting incident, underscoring the government's commitment to enhancing gun control
  measures. Despite the stringent regulations, New Zealand does not mandate
  the registration of most firearms, distinguishing its approach from that of some
  other countries.

- South Africa: In South Africa, the process of purchasing a firearm involves
  joining an accredited hunting or shooting club or providing documentation to
  substantiate the need for self-defence. Prospective gun owners are then required
  to complete firearm safety training, including a written test and practical assessment, and furnish two employers, friends, or community leaders as references.
  The subsequent steps include undergoing fingerprinting, passing a review of

criminal behaviour, history of domestic violence and drug abuse, and in some cases, participating in interviews with family and neighbours. Additionally, individuals are mandated to purchase a gun safe that complies with safety regulations and allow the police to inspect their storage. The application process culminates in a federal review, which may extend over several months, before individuals can proceed to purchase a gun.

- Mexico: In Mexico, the process of purchasing a firearm entails obtaining a letter from local authorities confirming the absence of a criminal record, submitting a letter demonstrating employment status and income, and passing a background check that considers criminal history, employment, and current gun ownership. Notably, individuals seeking to purchase a gun in Mexico are required to travel to Mexico City, where the only authorized store for gun sales is located. Following this, applicants must undergo fingerprinting before completing the purchase of a firearm.

- Australia: In Australia, the process of acquiring a firearm involves joining and regularly attending a hunting or shooting club or providing evidence of being a collector. Prospective gun owners are then required to complete a course on firearm safety and operation, including a written test and practical assessment, and arrange firearm storage that complies with safety regulations. The subsequent steps include passing a review that considers criminal history, domestic violence, restraining orders, and arrest history, with authorities potentially conducting interviews with family and community members. Individuals seeking to acquire a specific type of weapon must apply for a permit, with a mandatory waiting period of at least 28 days before purchasing the approved fir

- Austria: In Austria, the process of purchasing a firearm varies depending on the type of firearm being sought. To acquire a handgun or semiautomatic rifle, individuals must demonstrate that they are in serious physical danger, pass a review of their criminal history, complete a mental health survey, and undergo a psychological and physical test. Additionally, applicants are required to complete a course on safe gun handling and storage and install safe gun storage before purchasing the firearm. Notably, individuals purchasing a hunting rifle in Austria are subject to different requirements, including passing a written exam and shooting test, as well as a mandatory waiting period of three days before collecting the firearm.

- Canada: In Canada, the process of purchasing a firearm involves several key steps, including proving participation in an approved shooting club or range or demonstrating status as a gun collector to acquire a handgun. Additionally, individuals seeking to purchase any type of gun must complete a safety course and pass both a written and practical test, provide two references, and apply for a permit, with a mandatory waiting period of 28 days before the processing of the application commences. The subsequent steps include passing a background check that considers criminal record, mental health, addiction, and domestic violence history before proceeding to purchase a gun. Notably, individuals purchasing a handgun in Canada are required to register the firearm with the police before taking it home, further emphasizing the stringent regulations governing firearm acquisition in the country.

- India: In India, the process of acquiring a firearm involves joining a shooting club or demonstrating a threat to oneself or one's property. Prospective gun owners are then required to attend a practical training course on firearm handling and shooting, obtain a certificate of physical and mental health from a doctor, and affirm the presence of a safe place to store the firearms. The subsequent steps include passing a review that considers three years of tax returns, criminal history, mental health history, and domestic violence, with interviews conducted with the applicant, their family, and neighbours. Notably, the specific steps involved in acquiring a firearm in India may vary depending on the enforcement practices of local officials, reflecting the decentralized nature of firearm regulations in the country.

- Germany: In Germany, the process of purchasing a firearm involves joining a shooting club, obtaining a hunting license, demonstrating status as a gun collector, or proving that one's life is threatened. Prospective gun owners are then required to demonstrate specialized knowledge of firearms, potentially involving a written exam and practical demonstration of safe handling, and submit a certificate of mental fitness if they are under 25 years of age. Additionally, individuals must arrange proper firearm storage and pass a background check that considers criminal history, mental health, and drug addiction. The subsequent steps include applying for a permit to purchase a specific gun, which may entail an additional short background review, before proceeding to purchase the firearm.

- Britain: In Britain, the process of acquiring a firearm involves joining a shooting club or documenting hunting arrangements, requesting a character reference, arranging proper firearm storage, and passing a background check that includes a police interview at the applicant's home. Notably, the storage arrangements of the firearm may be subject to inspection as part of the application process, reflecting the emphasis on responsible firearm ownership in the country.

- Brazil: In Brazil, the process of purchasing a firearm entails writing a statement justifying the need for a gun for self-defence, completing a course on firearm handling, obtaining a statement from an accredited psychologist certifying mental fitness, and confirming the absence of a criminal record or ongoing criminal investigation. Following these steps, individuals can proceed to purchase a gun, which must be registered with the federal police. Additionally, individuals are required to fill out an online form to transport the gun and return to the dealer to pick up the firearm, reflecting the comprehensive nature of the firearm acquisition process in Brazil.

- Russia: In Russia, the process of acquiring a firearm involves obtaining a hunting license or providing a justification for the need for a gun for self-defence. Prospective gun owners are then required to pass a test covering relevant laws, handling, and first-aid skills, obtain a doctor's note affirming the absence of mental illness or history of drug abuse, attend a firearm safety and handling class, and pass an exam. The subsequent steps include applying for a license, passing a background check, and proceeding to purchase a gun, reflecting the stringent regulations governing firearm acquisition in Russia.

- Israel: In Israel, the process of acquiring a firearm involves joining a shooting club or demonstrating residence or employment in a dangerous area authorized for gun ownership. Prospective gun owners are then required to obtain a doctor's note affirming the absence of mental illness or history of drug abuse, install a gun safe, and release their criminal and mental health history to the authorities. The subsequent steps include purchasing a gun and a limited supply of bullets, usually around 50, and demonstrating proficiency in using the firearm at a firing range before taking it home. Notably, certain professions, including those in security, research, and pest control, may have facilitated access to firearms in Israel, reflecting the nuanced approach to firearm acquisition in the country.

- China: In China, the process of acquiring a firearm involves establishing a specific reason for possessing a firearm, such as for hunting or sports shooting, and arranging for the storage of the gun at a designated location. Prospective gun owners are then required to demonstrate knowledge of safe gun use and storage, pass a background check that considers mental illness, criminal record, and domestic violence, before proceeding to purchase a gun, reflecting the stringent regulations governing firearm acquisition in China.

- Yemen: In Yemen, the process of acquiring a firearm is characterized by a relatively informal approach, with individuals able to purchase guns from gun markets or online sellers. Despite the existence of laws mandating the acquisition of guns from licensed dealers and registration with the authorities, enforcement of these regulations is limited, contributing to a high rate of gun ownership in the country.

The process of purchasing a firearm varies significantly across different countries, with each nation implementing its own set of regulations and requirements to ensure responsible gun ownership. The diverse approaches to firearm acquisition reflect the complex interplay of cultural, historical, and legal factors that shape the regulation of firearms in different parts of the world. By examining the specific procedures and regulations in 16 different countries, this paper has provided a comprehensive overview of the basic steps involved in purchasing a firearm, shedding light on the nuanced and multifaceted nature of firearm acquisition processes globally.

EFFECTIVE GUN CONTROL POLICIES

Rating System for Effective Gun Control Policies

The criteria for an effective gun control policy encompass a range of factors that have been extensively studied and debated in academic literature. One crucial aspect is the public's support for specific strategies intended to keep guns away from dangerous individuals, such as mandatory background checks for all types of gun purchases, mental health screenings, and mandatory gun education (Kruis et al., 2021). Additionally, it is important to address misconceptions, such as the assumption that mental illness causes gun violence, and to understand the complex interplay between mental illness and gun crime (Metzl & MacLeish, 2015). Furthermore, the assessment of gun owners' underlying principles and detailed opinions is essential for developing policies that are mutually agreed upon and effective (Grene et al., 2023).

An effective gun control policy should consider the benefits, opportunities, costs, and risks associated with different interventions, and prioritize strategic criteria through a rigorous analytic network process (Vargas et al., 2021). It is also important to consider the impact of firearm laws on non-firearm deaths, as evidenced by a systematic review and meta-analysis that evaluated the effects of various gun policies on firearm homicides and suicides (Smart et al., 2020).

Public opinion and the framing of gun control policies play a significant role in their effectiveness. Understanding the public's perception of gun control, as well as the deliberate issue linkage between gun control and confidence in law enforcement, is essential (Miller, 2018). Additionally, the self-protection/crime control perspective and the rhetoric used by gun policy organizations are important factors to consider when formulating effective policies (Merry, 2015; Wozniak, 2016). Furthermore, correcting misperceptions of gun policy support can foster intergroup cooperation between gun owners and non-gun owners, highlighting the importance of communication and education in policy implementation (Susmann et al., 2022). Additionally, the effectiveness of value-based messages in engaging gun owners on firearm policies and the impact of mass shootings on gun policy are crucial considerations (Boine et al., 2022; Luca et al., 2019).

The impact of gun legislation on firearm-related fatalities, the deterrence effects of gun laws, and the direct and moderating effects of mass shooting anxiety on political and policy attitudes are also important factors to consider (Fleegler et al., 2013; Joslyn & Haider-Markel, 2018; Oliveira & Neto, 2015). Moreover, the role of identity in predicting opposition to gun control and the importance of gun policy to individuals' attitudes should be taken into account (Lacombe et al., 2019).

In addition to public opinion and framing, the role of protests and institutional tools in influencing gun policy, as well as the portrayal of characters in the gun policy debate, are important aspects to consider (Merry, 2017; Sato & Haselswerdt, 2022). Furthermore, the impact of gender on policy preferences, the influence of individualism and collectivism on attitudes toward gun control, and the framing and policy change after shooting rampages are all relevant to the development of effective gun control policies (Celinska, 2007; Hurka & Nebel, 2013; Stucky et al., 2008).

Finally, the effectiveness of legislation controlling gun usage and the reduction of gun-related deaths through comprehensive gun control legislation are crucial considerations in formulating effective policies (Kwon & Baack, 2005).

On the basis of the notions above and extensive discussions throughout this book, an effective gun control policy typically encompasses several key criteria to enhance public safety while balancing individual rights. These criteria may include:

1. Comprehensive Background Checks:

   ◦ Require thorough background checks for all individuals seeking to purchase firearms. This should include criminal history, mental health evaluations, and other relevant factors.

2. Licensing and Registration:

   ◦ Implement a licensing system that mandates individuals to obtain a license before owning a firearm. This process should involve an application, veri-fication of good reason, and periodic renewals. Registering firearms can aid law enforcement in tracking ownership.

3. Restrictions on Firearm Types:

- Place restrictions on the types of firearms available for civilian ownership, particularly those with high capacity or rapid-fire capabilities. Banning certain military-style weapons can help reduce the potential for mass shootings.

4. Waiting Periods:

- Institute mandatory waiting periods between the time of purchase and the actual acquisition of a firearm. This provides additional time for background checks and may prevent impulsive acts of violence.

5. Safe Storage Requirements:

- Enforce strict guidelines for the secure storage of firearms, such as the use of lockboxes or gun safes. Proper storage helps prevent accidents, theft, and unauthorized access.

6. Education and Training:

- Implement educational programs on responsible gun ownership, safety, and storage. Mandatory training courses for firearm owners can promote a culture of responsible gun use.

7. Red Flag Laws:

- Introduce "red flag" laws that allow temporary firearm removal from individuals deemed a risk to themselves or others based on evidence of mental health issues or other concerns. Such laws empower law enforcement to act preventatively.

8. Limits on Ammunition Sales:

- Set restrictions on the sale and possession of high-capacity magazines and certain types of ammunition. Limiting the firepower available to individuals can reduce the severity of potential incidents.

9. Universal Background Checks for All Sales:

   ○ Close loopholes in background check requirements, ensuring that all
     firearm sales, including private sales and those at gun shows, are subject to
     thorough background checks.

10. Regular Policy Evaluation:

   ○ Establish mechanisms for regular evaluation and assessment of gun control
     policies. This includes reviewing the effectiveness of existing laws, analysing
     trends in gun-related incidents, and making necessary adjustments.

11. Community Engagement:

   ○ Involve communities in the development and implementation of gun con-
     trol measures. Engaging with stakeholders, including law enforcement,
     mental health professionals, and community leaders, can foster a collabo-
     rative approach.

12. International Cooperation:

   ○ Collaborate internationally on efforts to control the illicit trade of firearms.
     Sharing information and coordinating policies can help prevent the
     cross-border flow of illegal weapons.

13. Public Awareness Campaigns:

   ○ Conduct public awareness campaigns to educate the general population
     about the risks associated with firearms and the importance of responsible
     gun ownership.

It is important to recognize that the effectiveness of gun control policies may vary based
on the specific socio-political context of each country or region. Therefore, a thoughtful
and context-specific approach is essential for crafting and implementing successful gun
control measures.

These criteria can be represented in a tabular manner, as shown in Table 2, with a rating system. This arrangement allows of a comparison of "effectiveness" of various gun control policies.

Table 2: Rating System for Effective Gun Control Policies.

Gun Control Policy Effectiveness	
Criteria	**Rating Guidelines**
Comprehensive Background Checks	1 - Minimal background checks; 5 - Thorough checks on criminal history, mental health, and relevant factors.
Licensing and Registration	1 - No licensing; 5 - Strict licensing involving application, good reason verification, and periodic renewals.
Restrictions on Firearm Types	1 - No restrictions; 5 - Stringent restrictions on high-capacity or rapid-fire firearms.
Waiting Periods	1 - No waiting periods; 5 - Mandatory waiting periods for additional background checks.
Safe Storage Requirements	1 - No specific storage requirements; 5 - Strict guidelines on secure storage using lockboxes or gun safes.
Education and Training	1 - No mandatory training; 5 - Mandatory training programs promoting responsible gun ownership, safety, and storage.
Red Flag Laws	1 - No red flag laws; 5 - Robust red flag laws allowing temporary firearm removal based on mental health or risk assessments.
Limits on Ammunition Sales	1 - No restrictions; 5 - Strict limits on high-capacity magazines and specific types of ammunition.
Universal Background Checks for All Sales	1 - Loopholes in background checks; 5 - Thorough background checks for all firearm sales, including private sales and gun shows.
Regular Policy Evaluation	1 - No regular evaluation; 5 - Establishes mechanisms for ongoing assessment and adjustments to gun control policies.
Community Engagement	1 - No community involvement; 5 - Actively involves communities and stakeholders in policy development and implementation.
International Cooperation	1 - No international collaboration; 5 - Actively collaborates internationally to control the illicit trade of firearms.
Public Awareness Campaigns	1 - No awareness campaigns; 5 - Conducts effective public awareness campaigns on firearm risks and responsible ownership.

On this basis, the lowest rating possible is 13 (with an allocation of one rating point for each criteria) and the highest rating is 65 (with a rating of 5 for each criteria). As such, the greater overall rating the more effective gun control policy is based on the criteria.

Applying this basic rating system to the gun control policies applied in the United States of America, noting that the assessment of the USA's gun control policy is subjective and can vary based on different perspectives, we get an outcome as noted in Table 3. The rating provided here is a general evaluation based on available information, and opinions on the effectiveness of gun control policies may differ.

Table 3: Effectiveness ratings for USA gun control policies.

Gun Control Policy Effectiveness - USA			
Criteria	Rating (1-5)	Rating Guidelines	Comments or Additional Considerations
Comprehensive Background Checks	[3]	Background checks exist but may have limitations, such as loopholes in private sales.	Efforts have been made, but gaps in coverage may impact effectiveness.
Licensing and Registration	[2]	Licensing requirements vary by state, and some states have minimal regulations.	Lack of uniformity and strict standards may hinder overall effectiveness.
Restrictions on Firearm Types	[2]	Limited restrictions on certain firearm types; high-capacity and rapid-fire weapons are often accessible.	Varied regulations across states may contribute to challenges.
Waiting Periods	[3]	Waiting periods exist in some states, but they are not uniform nationwide.	Inconsistencies may affect the ability to prevent impulsive acts.
Safe Storage Requirements	[2]	Safe storage guidelines are not universally enforced, leading to potential risks.	Lack of strict enforcement may impact overall safety.
Education and Training	[2]	Training programs exist, but they are not universally mandatory.	Inconsistent training requirements may affect responsible gun use.
Red Flag Laws	[3]	Some states have red flag laws, but not all, creating variations in preventive measures.	Adoption across all states could enhance effectiveness.
Limits on Ammunition Sales	[2]	Limited restrictions on ammunition sales; high-capacity magazines are available.	Stricter limitations on ammunition may contribute to enhanced safety.
Universal Background Checks for All Sales	[3]	Background checks exist for licensed dealers but may not cover all sales, such as private transactions.	Closing loopholes in private sales could improve effectiveness.
Regular Policy Evaluation	[2]	Evaluation mechanisms vary, and there may be gaps in assessing policy effectiveness.	Establishing consistent evaluation practices could enhance policymaking.
Community Engagement	[2]	Limited involvement of communities in policy development and implementation.	Increased community engagement may foster a more collaborative approach.
International Cooperation	[2]	Limited international collaboration in controlling the illicit trade of firearms.	Strengthening global partnerships could enhance efforts.
Public Awareness Campaigns	[3]	Awareness campaigns exist but may not be uniformly effective or widespread.	Increased outreach and consistency may improve public awareness.

Total Rating: 31

Comments or Additional Considerations: The ratings are based on a general evaluation, and perceptions of effectiveness may vary. The effectiveness of gun control policies
in the USA is influenced by a complex interplay of federal and state regulations, contributing to variations in implementation and impact. Additionally, ongoing debates and
discussions surrounding gun control further contribute to the dynamic nature of this
assessment.

Similarly, applying the approach to the United Kingdom, the outcome is as shown in
Table 4 and for Canada in Table 5.

Table 4: Effectiveness ratings for UK gun control policies.

Criteria	Rating (1-5)	Rating Guidelines	Comments or Additional Considerations
Comprehensive Background Checks	[5]	Thorough background checks, including criminal history, mental health, and relevant factors, are mandatory for all individuals seeking to purchase firearms.	Rigorous checks contribute to enhanced public safety.
Licensing and Registration	[5]	Strict licensing requirements involve a comprehensive application process, verification of good reason, and periodic renewals. Firearm registration is mandatory.	Robust regulations contribute to tracking and accountability.
Restrictions on Firearm Types	[5]	Stringent restrictions are imposed, especially on high-capacity or rapid-fire firearms, ensuring limited civilian access.	Focus on limiting firepower helps prevent mass shootings.
Waiting Periods	[5]	Mandatory waiting periods are instituted for additional background checks, contributing to the prevention of impulsive acts of violence.	Additional time enhances the effectiveness of background checks.
Safe Storage Requirements	[5]	Strict guidelines on secure storage using lockboxes or gun safes are enforced, minimizing accidents, theft, and unauthorized access.	Emphasis on responsible storage enhances overall safety.
Education and Training	[5]	Mandatory training programs promoting responsible gun ownership, safety, and storage are in place, fostering a culture of responsible gun use.	Training contributes to informed and responsible firearm ownership.
Red Flag Laws	[5]	Robust red flag laws allow temporary firearm removal based on mental health or risk assessments, providing preventive measures.	Swift action is taken to address potential risks to public safety.
Limits on Ammunition Sales	[5]	Strict limits are imposed on high-capacity magazines and specific types of ammunition, reducing the severity of potential incidents.	Restricting firepower contributes to overall safety.
Universal Background Checks for All Sales	[5]	Thorough background checks for all firearm sales, including private sales and gun shows, are mandatory, closing loopholes in the system.	Comprehensive checks for all sales contribute to effectiveness.
Regular Policy Evaluation	[5]	Mechanisms for ongoing assessment and adjustments to gun control policies are established, ensuring continuous improvement and adaptation.	Regular evaluations contribute to the effectiveness of policies.
Community Engagement	[5]	Actively involves communities and stakeholders in policy development and implementation, fostering a collaborative approach.	Community input enhances the relevance and acceptance of policies.
International Cooperation	[5]	Actively collaborates internationally to control the illicit trade of firearms, contributing to global efforts to prevent cross-border flow.	International collaboration strengthens control measures.
Public Awareness Campaigns	[5]	Conducts effective public awareness campaigns on firearm risks and responsible ownership, promoting informed decision-making.	Public awareness is actively addressed to ensure responsible ownership.

Comments or Additional Considerations: The ratings reflect a comprehensive and stringent gun control policy in the UK, emphasizing thorough background checks, strict licensing, and proactive measures to prevent firearm-related risks. The multifaceted approach, including community engagement and international collaboration, contributes to a robust framework for public safety and responsible firearm ownership. The effectiveness of these policies is influenced by their consistent enforcement and adaptation based on ongoing evaluations.

Total Rating: 65

Table 5: Effectiveness ratings for Canadian gun control policies.

Gun Control Policy Effectiveness - Canada			
Criteria	Rating (1-5)	Rating Guidelines	Comments or Additional Considerations
Comprehensive Background Checks	[5]	Thorough background checks, including criminal history, mental health, and relevant factors, are mandatory for all individuals seeking to purchase firearms.	Rigorous checks contribute to enhanced public safety.
Licensing and Registration	[4]	Strict licensing requirements involve a comprehensive application process, verification of good reason, and periodic renewals. Firearm registration is mandatory.	Strong licensing, but not as strict as some other countries.
Restrictions on Firearm Types	[4]	Stringent restrictions are imposed, especially on high-capacity or rapid-fire firearms, ensuring limited civilian access.	Restrictions contribute to reducing the potential for mass shootings.
Waiting Periods	[4]	Mandatory waiting periods are instituted for additional background checks, contributing to the prevention of impulsive acts of violence.	Additional time enhances the effectiveness of background checks.
Safe Storage Requirements	[4]	Strict guidelines on secure storage using lockboxes or gun safes are enforced, minimizing accidents, theft, and unauthorized access.	Emphasis on responsible storage enhances overall safety.
Education and Training	[4]	Mandatory training programs promoting responsible gun ownership, safety, and storage are in place, fostering a culture of responsible gun use.	Training contributes to informed and responsible firearm ownership.
Red Flag Laws	[4]	Robust red flag laws allow temporary firearm removal based on mental health or risk assessments, providing preventive measures.	Swift action is taken to address potential risks to public safety.
Limits on Ammunition Sales	[4]	Strict limits are imposed on high-capacity magazines and specific types of ammunition, reducing the severity of potential incidents.	Restrictions contribute to overall safety.
Universal Background Checks for All Sales	[3]	Thorough background checks for all firearm sales, including private sales and gun shows, are mandatory, closing loopholes in the system.	Background checks are comprehensive but may have some gaps.
Regular Policy Evaluation	[4]	Mechanisms for ongoing assessment and adjustments to gun control policies are established, ensuring continuous improvement and adaptation.	Regular evaluations contribute to the effectiveness of policies.
Community Engagement	[3]	Actively involves communities and stakeholders in policy development and implementation, fostering a collaborative approach.	Community input is considered, but there may be room for improvement.
International Cooperation	[4]	Actively collaborates internationally to control the illicit trade of firearms, contributing to global efforts to prevent cross-border flow.	International collaboration strengthens control measures.
Public Awareness Campaigns	[3]	Conducts effective public awareness campaigns on firearm risks and responsible ownership, promoting informed decision-making.	Public awareness is addressed but may not be as comprehensive.

Comments or Additional Considerations: Canada's gun control policies are generally robust, with a strong emphasis on background checks, licensing, and restrictions on firearm types. While the country actively collaborates internationally and has mechanisms for policy evaluation, there may be some room for improvement in community engagement and public awareness campaigns. The ratings reflect a balanced approach to gun control, with several effective measures in place to enhance public safety and responsible firearm ownership.

Total Rating: 50

The Australian approach to gun control is rated within Table 6.

Table 6: Effectiveness ratings for Australian gun control policies.

Gun Control Policy Effectiveness - Australia			
Criteria	**Rating (1-5)**	**Rating Guidelines**	**Comments or Additional Considerations**
Comprehensive Background Checks	[5]	Thorough background checks, including criminal history, mental health, and relevant factors, are mandatory for all individuals seeking to purchase firearms.	Rigorous checks contribute to enhanced public safety.
Licensing and Registration	[5]	Strict licensing requirements involve a comprehensive application process, verification of good reason, and periodic renewals. Firearm registration is mandatory.	Strong licensing measures contribute to overall control.
Restrictions on Firearm Types	[5]	Stringent restrictions are imposed, especially on high-capacity or rapid-fire firearms, ensuring limited civilian access.	Focus on restricting high-capacity and rapid-fire firearms.
Waiting Periods	[5]	Mandatory waiting periods are instituted for additional background checks, contributing to the prevention of impulsive acts of violence.	Waiting periods enhance the effectiveness of background checks.
Safe Storage Requirements	[5]	Strict guidelines on secure storage using lockboxes or gun safes are enforced, minimizing accidents, theft, and unauthorized access.	Emphasis on responsible storage enhances overall safety.
Education and Training	[5]	Mandatory training programs promoting responsible gun ownership, safety, and storage are in place, fostering a culture of responsible gun use.	Training contributes to informed and responsible firearm ownership.
Red Flag Laws	[5]	Robust red flag laws allow temporary firearm removal based on mental health or risk assessments, providing preventive measures.	Strong measures for addressing potential risks to public safety.
Limits on Ammunition Sales	[5]	Strict limits are imposed on high-capacity magazines and specific types of ammunition, reducing the severity of potential incidents.	Restrictions contribute to overall safety.
Universal Background Checks for All Sales	[5]	Thorough background checks for all firearm sales, including private sales and gun shows, are mandatory, closing loopholes in the system.	Comprehensive background checks for all sales.
Regular Policy Evaluation	[5]	Mechanisms for ongoing assessment and adjustments to gun control policies are established, ensuring continuous improvement and adaptation.	Regular evaluations contribute to the effectiveness of policies.
Community Engagement	[4]	Actively involves communities and stakeholders in policy development and implementation, fostering a collaborative approach.	Strong involvement, but there may be room for improvement.
International Cooperation	[5]	Actively collaborates internationally to control the illicit trade of firearms, contributing to global efforts to prevent cross-border flow.	International collaboration strengthens control measures.
Public Awareness Campaigns	[4]	Conducts effective public awareness campaigns on firearm risks and responsible ownership, promoting informed decision-making.	Public awareness is addressed but may have some room for improvement.

Comments or Additional Considerations: Australia's gun control policies receive high ratings across the board, reflecting a comprehensive and strict approach. The country has implemented robust measures, including thorough background checks, stringent licensing, and restrictions on firearm types. Additionally, the active collaboration internationally and ongoing policy evaluation contribute to the effectiveness of Australia's gun control policies. Community engagement is strong, but there may be opportunities for further improvement. Overall, Australia's approach demonstrates a commitment to public safety and responsible firearm ownership.

Total Rating: 63

Table 7 shows the ratings for Germany, ratings for Switzerland are outlined in Table 8, Japan is represented in Table 9, Brazil in Table 10, South Africa in Table 11 and finally, Russia is shown as Table 12.

Table 7: Effectiveness ratings for German gun control policies.

Gun Control Policy Effectiveness - Canada			
Criteria	**Rating (1-5)**	**Rating Guidelines**	**Comments or Additional Considerations**
Comprehensive Background Checks	[5]	Thorough background checks, including criminal history, mental health, and relevant factors, are mandatory for all individuals seeking to purchase firearms.	Germany emphasizes comprehensive background checks.
Licensing and Registration	[5]	Strict licensing requirements involve a comprehensive application process, verification of good reason, and periodic renewals. Firearm registration is mandatory.	Germany has robust licensing and registration procedures.
Restrictions on Firearm Types	[5]	Stringent restrictions are imposed, especially on high-capacity or rapid-fire firearms, ensuring limited civilian access.	The focus on restricting high-capacity and rapid-fire firearms is evident.
Waiting Periods	[5]	Mandatory waiting periods are instituted for additional background checks, contributing to the prevention of impulsive acts of violence.	Germany implements waiting periods to enhance background checks.
Safe Storage Requirements	[5]	Strict guidelines on secure storage using lockboxes or gun safes are enforced, minimizing accidents, theft, and unauthorized access.	Germany places emphasis on responsible storage.
Education and Training	[5]	Mandatory training programs promoting responsible gun ownership, safety, and storage are in place, fostering a culture of responsible gun use.	Germany prioritizes education and training for firearm owners.
Red Flag Laws	[5]	Robust red flag laws allow temporary firearm removal based on mental health or risk assessments, providing preventive measures.	Strong measures for addressing potential risks to public safety.
Limits on Ammunition Sales	[5]	Strict limits are imposed on high-capacity magazines and specific types of ammunition, reducing the severity of potential incidents.	Germany enforces restrictions on ammunition sales.
Universal Background Checks for All Sales	[5]	Thorough background checks for all firearm sales, including private sales and gun shows, are mandatory, closing loopholes in the system.	Comprehensive background checks for all sales.
Regular Policy Evaluation	[5]	Mechanisms for ongoing assessment and adjustments to gun control policies are established, ensuring continuous improvement and adaptation.	Germany emphasizes regular evaluation and policy adjustments.
Community Engagement	[4]	Actively involves communities and stakeholders in policy development and implementation, fostering a collaborative approach.	Strong involvement, but there may be room for improvement.
International Cooperation	[5]	Actively collaborates internationally to control the illicit trade of firearms, contributing to global efforts to prevent cross-border flow.	International collaboration strengthens control measures.
Public Awareness Campaigns	[4]	Conducts effective public awareness campaigns on firearm risks and responsible ownership, promoting informed decision-making.	Public awareness is addressed but may have some room for improvement.

Comments or Additional Considerations: Germany's gun control policies receive high ratings across the board, reflecting a comprehensive and strict approach. The country has implemented robust measures, including thorough background checks, stringent licensing, and restrictions on firearm types. Additionally, Germany actively collaborates internationally and conducts ongoing policy evaluations. Community engagement is strong, but there may be opportunities for further improvement. Public awareness campaigns are addressed, but there may be room for enhancement. Overall, Germany's approach demonstrates a commitment to public safety and responsible firearm ownership.

Total Rating: 63

Table 8: Effectiveness ratings for Swiss gun control policies.

Gun Control Policy Effectiveness - Switzerland			
Criteria	Rating (1-5)	Rating Guidelines	Comments or Additional Considerations
Comprehensive Background Checks	[4]	Switzerland conducts thorough background checks, including criminal history, mental health, and relevant factors, but may have some room for enhancement.	Background checks are comprehensive but may have room for improvement.
Licensing and Registration	[3]	Switzerland has a system of licensing involving application, good reason verification, and periodic renewals, but it may not be as strict as in some other countries.	Licensing system exists but may be considered less stringent.
Restrictions on Firearm Types	[2]	Switzerland has limited restrictions on high-capacity or rapid-fire firearms, allowing relatively broad civilian access.	Limited restrictions on firearm types compared to some other countries.
Waiting Periods	[3]	Switzerland has some waiting periods for additional background checks, but they may not be as mandatory or extensive as in other countries.	Waiting periods exist but may not be as mandatory or extensive.
Safe Storage Requirements	[4]	Switzerland enforces strict guidelines on secure storage, using lockboxes or gun safes, contributing to responsible storage practices.	Emphasis on secure storage helps prevent accidents and unauthorized access.
Education and Training	[3]	Switzerland does not have mandatory training but may offer training programs promoting responsible gun ownership, safety, and storage.	Lack of mandatory training, but there may be optional programs available.
Red Flag Laws	[3]	Switzerland does not have robust red flag laws, and temporary firearm removal based on mental health or risk assessments may not be as prevalent.	Limited measures for addressing potential risks based on mental health.
Limits on Ammunition Sales	[3]	Switzerland has some limits on high-capacity magazines and specific types of ammunition but may not be as strict as in other countries.	Limits exist but may not be considered as strict compared to some countries.
Universal Background Checks for All Sales	[4]	Switzerland conducts thorough background checks for all firearm sales, including private sales and gun shows, contributing to comprehensive checks.	Comprehensive background checks for all sales, including private transactions.
Regular Policy Evaluation	[3]	Switzerland has mechanisms for ongoing assessment, but the frequency and extent of regular policy evaluations may be less than in some other countries.	Some mechanisms for evaluation, but frequency and extent may vary.
Community Engagement	[3]	Switzerland has limited community involvement in policy development and implementation compared to some other countries.	Less emphasis on community involvement compared to some countries.
International Cooperation	[3]	Switzerland collaborates internationally to some extent but may not be as actively involved in controlling the illicit trade of firearms.	Limited involvement in international efforts to control illicit firearm trade.
Public Awareness Campaigns	[3]	Switzerland conducts awareness campaigns on firearm risks and responsible ownership but may not be as extensive or effective as in some other countries.	Public awareness efforts may have room for improvement.

Comments or Additional Considerations: Switzerland's gun control policies receive mixed ratings, reflecting a unique approach that allows relatively broad civilian access to firearms. While background checks are comprehensive, there are areas for improvement in licensing stringency, restrictions on firearm types, and waiting periods. Switzerland places strong emphasis on secure storage, but lacks mandatory training, robust red flag laws, and strict limits on ammunition sales. The country conducts thorough background checks for all sales and engages in some policy evaluation but has limited community involvement and international collaboration. Public awareness campaigns exist but may benefit from further development. Overall, Switzerland's approach reflects a balance between individual gun ownership and public safety considerations.

Total Rating: 41

Table 9: Effectiveness ratings for Japanese gun control policies.

Gun Control Policy Effectiveness - Japan			
Criteria	Rating (1-5)	Rating Guidelines	Comments or Additional Considerations
Comprehensive Background Checks	[5]	Japan conducts thorough background checks, including criminal history, mental health, and relevant factors, ensuring a high level of scrutiny.	Comprehensive background checks contribute to a thorough evaluation.
Licensing and Registration	[5]	Japan has strict licensing involving application, good reason verification, and periodic renewals, ensuring a robust process for firearm ownership.	Stringent licensing requirements contribute to a controlled environment.
Restrictions on Firearm Types	[5]	Japan imposes stringent restrictions on high-capacity or rapid-fire firearms, resulting in limited civilian access to such weapons.	Strict restrictions contribute to a controlled environment.
Waiting Periods	[5]	Japan enforces mandatory waiting periods for additional background checks, adding an extra layer of scrutiny before firearm acquisition.	Waiting periods contribute to a thorough evaluation process.
Safe Storage Requirements	[5]	Japan has strict guidelines on secure storage using lockboxes or gun safes, emphasizing responsible storage practices to prevent accidents and unauthorized access.	Emphasis on secure storage contributes to safety and prevention measures.
Education and Training	[5]	Japan mandates mandatory training programs promoting responsible gun ownership, safety, and storage, ensuring a culture of responsible gun use.	Mandatory training contributes to a culture of responsible gun ownership.
Red Flag Laws	[5]	Japan has robust red flag laws allowing temporary firearm removal based on mental health or risk assessments, contributing to preventative measures.	Robust red flag laws contribute to proactive risk management.
Limits on Ammunition Sales	[5]	Japan imposes strict limits on high-capacity magazines and specific types of ammunition, reducing the potential severity of incidents.	Strict limits contribute to reducing firepower available to individuals.
Universal Background Checks for All Sales	[5]	Japan conducts thorough background checks for all firearm sales, including private sales and gun shows, ensuring comprehensive evaluations.	Comprehensive background checks for all sales contribute to control.
Regular Policy Evaluation	[5]	Japan establishes mechanisms for ongoing assessment, ensuring regular evaluations and adjustments to gun control policies.	Regular policy evaluation contributes to adapting to changing circumstances.
Community Engagement	[5]	Japan actively involves communities and stakeholders in policy development and implementation, fostering a collaborative approach.	Strong community involvement contributes to policy development and acceptance.
International Cooperation	[5]	Japan actively collaborates internationally to control the illicit trade of firearms, contributing to global efforts to prevent illegal weapon flow.	Actively collaborating internationally contributes to global gun control efforts.
Public Awareness Campaigns	[5]	Japan conducts effective public awareness campaigns on firearm risks and responsible ownership, contributing to informed public attitudes.	Effective awareness campaigns contribute to public understanding and responsibility.

Comments or Additional Considerations: Japan's gun control policies receive the highest ratings across all criteria, reflecting a comprehensive and stringent approach. Thorough background checks, strict licensing, and restrictions on firearm types contribute to a controlled environment. Mandatory waiting periods, secure storage requirements, and education/training programs promote responsible gun ownership. Robust red flag laws and strict limits on ammunition sales contribute to proactive risk management. Japan's commitment to universal background checks, regular policy evaluation, community engagement, international collaboration, and public awareness campaigns underscores a holistic and effective approach to gun control.

Total Rating: 65

Table 10: Effectiveness ratings for Brazilian gun control policies.

Gun Control Policy Effectiveness - Brazil			
Criteria	Rating (1-5)	Rating Guidelines	Comments or Additional Considerations
Comprehensive Background Checks	[2]	Brazil conducts minimal background checks, with limited scrutiny on criminal history, mental health, and relevant factors.	Limited background checks may pose challenges to public safety.
Licensing and Registration	[2]	Brazil has minimal licensing, lacking a strict application process, good reason verification, and periodic renewals.	Minimal licensing may contribute to challenges in tracking firearm ownership.
Restrictions on Firearm Types	[3]	Brazil has some restrictions on firearm types, but they may not be as stringent, allowing certain high-capacity or rapid-fire firearms.	Partial restrictions may impact the potential for mass shootings.
Waiting Periods	[3]	Brazil has some waiting periods, but they may not be mandatory for additional background checks, potentially impacting the evaluation process.	Limited waiting periods may pose challenges to thorough evaluations.
Safe Storage Requirements	[2]	Brazil has minimal guidelines on secure storage, lacking strict requirements for lockboxes or gun safes.	Limited storage requirements may pose risks of accidents or unauthorized access.
Education and Training	[2]	Brazil lacks mandatory training programs for responsible gun ownership, safety, and storage, potentially hindering a culture of responsibility.	Lack of mandatory training may impact responsible gun use.
Red Flag Laws	[2]	Brazil lacks robust red flag laws allowing temporary firearm removal based on mental health or risk assessments.	Absence of robust red flag laws may pose challenges in proactive risk management.
Limits on Ammunition Sales	[3]	Brazil has some limits on ammunition sales, but they may not be as strict, allowing certain high-capacity magazines and ammunition types.	Partial limits may impact the severity of potential incidents.
Universal Background Checks for All Sales	[2]	Brazil has loopholes in background checks, potentially exempting certain firearm sales, including private sales and gun shows.	Loopholes may pose challenges to controlling the overall access to firearms.
Regular Policy Evaluation	[2]	Brazil lacks regular mechanisms for ongoing assessment, potentially hindering the ability to make timely adjustments to gun control policies.	Absence of regular evaluation may impact policy effectiveness.
Community Engagement	[2]	Brazil has minimal community involvement, lacking active engagement with communities and stakeholders in policy development.	Limited community involvement may impact policy acceptance.
International Cooperation	[2]	Brazil lacks active international collaboration to control the illicit trade of firearms, potentially contributing to challenges in preventing illegal weapon flow.	Limited international collaboration may impact global gun control efforts.
Public Awareness Campaigns	[2]	Brazil conducts minimal public awareness campaigns on firearm risks and responsible ownership, potentially impacting public understanding.	Limited awareness campaigns may hinder public knowledge on responsible ownership.

Comments or Additional Considerations: Brazil's gun control policies receive relatively low ratings across multiple criteria, indicating potential challenges in ensuring public safety and responsible firearm ownership. Minimal background checks, licensing, and limited restrictions on firearm types may contribute to difficulties in tracking and controlling access to firearms. The absence of robust red flag laws and limited waiting periods may pose challenges in proactive risk management. The lack of strict storage requirements and mandatory training programs may increase the risks of accidents or unauthorized access. Loopholes in background checks and the absence of regular policy evaluation may hinder the overall effectiveness of gun control measures. Limited community engagement and international collaboration may impact the acceptance and success of gun control efforts.

Total Rating: 29

Table 11: Effectiveness ratings for South African gun control policies.

Gun Control Policy Effectiveness – South Africa			
Criteria	Rating (1-5)	Rating Guidelines	Comments or Additional Considerations
Comprehensive Background Checks	[3]	South Africa conducts moderate background checks, with some scrutiny on criminal history, mental health, and relevant factors.	Moderate background checks may contribute to public safety to a certain extent.
Licensing and Registration	[3]	South Africa has moderate licensing, involving an application process and periodic renewals, but may have some gaps in good reason verification.	Moderate licensing may help track firearm ownership but may benefit from additional verification measures.
Restrictions on Firearm Types	[3]	South Africa has some restrictions on firearm types, but they may not be as stringent, allowing certain high-capacity or rapid-fire firearms.	Partial restrictions may impact the potential for mass shootings.
Waiting Periods	[3]	South Africa has some waiting periods, but they may not be mandatory for additional background checks, potentially impacting the evaluation process.	Limited waiting periods may pose challenges to thorough evaluations.
Safe Storage Requirements	[3]	South Africa has moderate guidelines on secure storage, encouraging secure storage using lockboxes or gun safes to a certain extent.	Moderate storage requirements may contribute to preventing accidents or unauthorized access.
Education and Training	[3]	South Africa has some mandatory training programs for responsible gun ownership, safety, and storage, promoting a culture of responsibility to a certain extent.	Mandatory training programs may enhance responsible gun use.
Red Flag Laws	[3]	South Africa has some red flag laws allowing temporary firearm removal based on mental health or risk assessments, but they may not be as robust.	Partial red flag laws may contribute to proactive risk management to a certain extent.
Limits on Ammunition Sales	[3]	South Africa has some limits on ammunition sales, but they may not be as strict, allowing certain high-capacity magazines and ammunition types.	Partial limits may impact the severity of potential incidents.
Universal Background Checks for All Sales	[3]	South Africa has some loopholes in background checks, potentially exempting certain firearm sales, including private sales and gun shows.	Loopholes may pose challenges to controlling the overall access to firearms.
Regular Policy Evaluation	[3]	South Africa has some mechanisms for ongoing assessment, but they may not be as regular, potentially impacting the timely adjustments to gun control policies.	Regular evaluation may enhance the effectiveness of gun control measures.
Community Engagement	[3]	South Africa has some community involvement, encouraging active engagement with communities and stakeholders in policy development.	Partial community involvement may contribute to policy acceptance.
International Cooperation	[3]	South Africa has some international collaboration to control the illicit trade of firearms, contributing to efforts in preventing illegal weapon flow.	Partial international collaboration may impact global gun control efforts.
Public Awareness Campaigns	[3]	South Africa conducts some public awareness campaigns on firearm risks and responsible ownership, contributing to public understanding to a certain extent.	Some awareness campaigns may enhance public knowledge on responsible ownership.

Comments or Additional Considerations: South Africa's gun control policies receive moderate ratings across multiple criteria, indicating efforts to balance public safety and individual rights. Moderate background checks, licensing, and restrictions on firearm types contribute to certain aspects of public safety. Some waiting periods and storage requirements aim to enhance evaluations and prevent accidents or unauthorized access. Mandatory training programs and partial red flag laws promote responsible gun use and proactive risk management to a certain extent. Limits on ammunition sales and partial universal background checks address certain concerns. Mechanisms for ongoing assessment and community involvement contribute to policy acceptance. International collaboration and some public awareness campaigns enhance global efforts and public understanding.

Total Rating: 39

Table 12: Effectiveness ratings for Russian gun control policies.

Gun Control Policy Effectiveness – Russia			
Criteria	Rating (1-5)	Rating Guidelines	Comments or Additional Considerations
Comprehensive Background Checks	[3]	Russia conducts moderate background checks, with some scrutiny on criminal history, mental health, and relevant factors.	Moderate background checks may contribute to public safety to a certain extent.
Licensing and Registration	[3]	Russia has moderate licensing, involving an application process and periodic renewals, but may have some gaps in good reason verification.	Moderate licensing may help track firearm ownership but may benefit from additional verification measures.
Restrictions on Firearm Types	[3]	Russia has some restrictions on firearm types, but they may not be as stringent, allowing certain high-capacity or rapid-fire firearms.	Partial restrictions may impact the potential for mass shootings.
Waiting Periods	[3]	Russia has some waiting periods, but they may not be mandatory for additional background checks, potentially impacting the evaluation process.	Limited waiting periods may pose challenges to thorough evaluations.
Safe Storage Requirements	[3]	Russia has moderate guidelines on secure storage, encouraging secure storage using lockboxes or gun safes to a certain extent.	Moderate storage requirements may contribute to preventing accidents or unauthorized access.
Education and Training	[3]	Russia has some mandatory training programs for responsible gun ownership, safety, and storage, promoting a culture of responsibility to a certain extent.	Mandatory training programs may enhance responsible gun use.
Red Flag Laws	[3]	Russia has some red flag laws allowing temporary firearm removal based on mental health or risk assessments, but they may not be as robust.	Partial red flag laws may contribute to proactive risk management to a certain extent.
Limits on Ammunition Sales	[3]	Russia has some limits on ammunition sales, but they may not be as strict, allowing certain high-capacity magazines and ammunition types.	Partial limits may impact the severity of potential incidents.
Universal Background Checks for All Sales	[3]	Russia has some loopholes in background checks, potentially exempting certain firearm sales, including private sales and gun shows.	Loopholes may pose challenges to controlling the overall access to firearms.
Regular Policy Evaluation	[3]	Russia has some mechanisms for ongoing assessment, but they may not be as regular, potentially impacting the timely adjustments to gun control policies.	Regular evaluation may enhance the effectiveness of gun control measures.
Community Engagement	[3]	Russia has some community involvement, encouraging active engagement with communities and stakeholders in policy development.	Partial community involvement may contribute to policy acceptance.
International Cooperation	[3]	Russia has some international collaboration to control the illicit trade of firearms, contributing to efforts in preventing illegal weapon flow.	Partial international collaboration may impact global gun control efforts.
Public Awareness Campaigns	[3]	Russia conducts some public awareness campaigns on firearm risks and responsible ownership, contributing to public understanding to a certain extent.	Some awareness campaigns may enhance public knowledge on responsible ownership.

Comments or Additional Considerations: Russia's gun control policies receive moderate ratings across multiple criteria, indicating efforts to balance public safety and individual rights. Moderate background checks, licensing, and restrictions on firearm types contribute to certain aspects of public safety. Some waiting periods and storage requirements aim to enhance evaluations and prevent accidents or unauthorized access. Mandatory training programs and partial red flag laws promote responsible gun use and proactive risk management to a certain extent. Limits on ammunition sales and partial universal background checks address certain concerns. Mechanisms for ongoing assessment and community involvement contribute to policy acceptance. International collaboration and some public awareness campaigns enhance global efforts and public understanding.

Total Rating: 39

For further comparison and to increase the data set, additional countries were ranked, including China, Poland, Mexico and the Philippines. These are shown as Table 13, Table 14, Table 15 and Table 16.

Table 13: Effectiveness ratings for Chinese gun control policies.

Gun Control Policy Effectiveness – China			
Criteria	**Rating (1-5)**	**Rating Guidelines**	**Comments or Additional Considerations**
Comprehensive Background Checks	[5]	China conducts thorough background checks, with a focus on criminal history, mental health, and relevant factors.	Thorough background checks contribute significantly to public safety.
Licensing and Registration	[5]	China has strict licensing involving an application process, good reason verification, and periodic renewals.	Strict licensing enhances tracking of firearm ownership and responsible use.
Restrictions on Firearm Types	[5]	China has stringent restrictions on high-capacity or rapid-fire firearms, contributing to the reduction of potential mass shootings.	Stringent restrictions enhance public safety by limiting access to certain firearms.
Waiting Periods	[5]	China imposes mandatory waiting periods for additional background checks, enhancing the evaluation process.	Mandatory waiting periods contribute to thorough evaluations and prevention of impulsive acts.
Safe Storage Requirements	[5]	China has strict guidelines on secure storage, promoting the use of lockboxes or gun safes.	Strict storage requirements help prevent accidents, theft, and unauthorized access.
Education and Training	[5]	China has mandatory training programs promoting responsible gun ownership, safety, and storage, fostering a culture of responsibility.	Mandatory training enhances responsible gun use and safety awareness.
Red Flag Laws	[5]	China has robust red flag laws allowing temporary firearm removal based on mental health or risk assessments.	Robust red flag laws contribute significantly to proactive risk management.
Limits on Ammunition Sales	[5]	China has strict limits on high-capacity magazines and specific types of ammunition, reducing the firepower available to individuals.	Strict limits contribute to reducing the severity of potential incidents.
Universal Background Checks for All Sales	[5]	China ensures thorough background checks for all firearm sales, including private sales and gun shows, closing loopholes.	Thorough background checks for all sales contribute to comprehensive control.
Regular Policy Evaluation	[5]	China establishes mechanisms for ongoing assessment and adjustments to gun control policies, ensuring regular evaluations.	Regular evaluation enhances the adaptability and effectiveness of policies.
Community Engagement	[4]	China involves communities and stakeholders in policy development, but there may be some limitations on active engagement.	Community involvement contributes to policy acceptance but may benefit from increased engagement.
International Cooperation	[3]	China has some international collaboration to control the illicit trade of firearms, but the level of collaboration may be limited.	Partial international collaboration impacts global efforts in controlling illegal weapon flow.
Public Awareness Campaigns	[4]	China conducts some public awareness campaigns on firearm risks and responsible ownership, contributing to public understanding.	Public awareness campaigns enhance knowledge on responsible ownership but may benefit from increased outreach.

Comments or Additional Considerations: China's gun control policies receive high ratings across multiple criteria, indicating a strong emphasis on public safety and responsible gun ownership. Thorough background checks, strict licensing, and stringent restrictions on firearm types contribute significantly to reducing potential risks. Mandatory waiting periods and strict storage requirements enhance evaluations and prevent accidents or unauthorized access. Mandatory training programs and robust red flag laws foster a culture of responsibility and proactive risk management. Strict limits on ammunition sales contribute to reducing the severity of potential incidents. Thorough background checks for all sales and regular policy evaluation ensure comprehensive control and adaptability. Community involvement and public awareness campaigns contribute to policy acceptance and public understanding, although there may be some room for improvement in active engagement and international collaboration.

Total Rating: 61

Table 14: Effectiveness ratings for Polish gun control policies.

Gun Control Policy Effectiveness – Poland			
Criteria	Rating (1-5)	Rating Guidelines	Comments or Additional Considerations
Comprehensive Background Checks	[4]	Poland conducts thorough background checks, focusing on criminal history, mental health, and relevant factors.	Thorough background checks contribute significantly to public safety.
Licensing and Registration	[4]	Poland has strict licensing involving an application process, good reason verification, and periodic renewals.	Strict licensing enhances tracking of firearm ownership and responsible use.
Restrictions on Firearm Types	[3]	Poland has some restrictions on high-capacity or rapid-fire firearms, contributing to risk reduction but not as stringent as in some other countries.	Stringent restrictions enhance public safety by limiting access to certain firearms, but there may be room for improvement.
Waiting Periods	[4]	Poland imposes mandatory waiting periods for additional background checks, enhancing the evaluation process.	Mandatory waiting periods contribute to thorough evaluations and prevention of impulsive acts.
Safe Storage Requirements	[3]	Poland has guidelines on secure storage, but the level of strictness may vary, potentially benefiting from more specific requirements.	Strict storage requirements help prevent accidents, theft, and unauthorized access; further specificity may enhance effectiveness.
Education and Training	[3]	Poland has some mandatory training programs promoting responsible gun ownership, safety, and storage, but there may be room for improvement.	Mandatory training enhances responsible gun use and safety awareness; additional efforts can further promote a culture of responsibility.
Red Flag Laws	[3]	Poland has some red flag laws allowing temporary firearm removal based on mental health or risk assessments, but the system may benefit from further development.	Robust red flag laws contribute significantly to proactive risk management; continued development could enhance effectiveness.
Limits on Ammunition Sales	[3]	Poland has some limits on high-capacity magazines and specific types of ammunition, but the restrictions may be subject to improvement.	Strict limits contribute to reducing the severity of potential incidents; periodic reviews can enhance effectiveness.
Universal Background Checks for All Sales	[4]	Poland ensures thorough background checks for all firearm sales, including private sales and gun shows, closing loopholes effectively.	Thorough background checks for all sales contribute to comprehensive control.
Regular Policy Evaluation	[4]	Poland establishes mechanisms for ongoing assessment and adjustments to gun control policies, ensuring regular evaluations.	Regular evaluation enhances the adaptability and effectiveness of policies.
Community Engagement	[3]	Poland involves communities and stakeholders in policy development, but there may be room for improvement in active engagement.	Community involvement contributes to policy acceptance but may benefit from increased engagement.
International Cooperation	[3]	Poland has some international collaboration to control the illicit trade of firearms, but the level of collaboration may be limited.	Partial international collaboration impacts global efforts in controlling illegal weapon flow.
Public Awareness Campaigns	[3]	Poland conducts some public awareness campaigns on firearm risks and responsible ownership, contributing to public understanding.	Public awareness campaigns enhance knowledge on responsible ownership but may benefit from increased outreach.

Comments or Additional Considerations: Poland's gun control policies demonstrate a commitment to public safety, with notable strengths in thorough background checks, licensing, waiting periods, and universal background checks. While there are restrictions on high-capacity firearms and some limits on ammunition sales, there may be room for improvement in the level of stringency. Safe storage requirements and education/training programs are in place, but additional specificity and efforts could further enhance responsible gun ownership. The red flag laws have been initiated but may benefit from further development. Community engagement and public awareness campaigns contribute positively, but there is potential for improvement, especially in international collaboration. Overall, Poland's gun control policies are effective, with opportunities for refinement in specific areas.

Total Rating: 44

Table 15: Effectiveness ratings for Mexican gun control policies.

Gun Control Policy Effectiveness – Mexico			
Criteria	Rating (1-5)	Rating Guidelines	Comments or Additional Considerations
Comprehensive Background Checks	[3]	Mexico conducts background checks on criminal history, mental health, and relevant factors, but the process may not be as thorough as in some other countries.	Improved thoroughness in background checks could enhance effectiveness.
Licensing and Registration	[3]	Mexico has licensing requirements involving an application process, good reason verification, and periodic renewals, but the system may need strengthening.	Strengthening licensing measures could improve tracking and responsible use.
Restrictions on Firearm Types	[2]	Mexico has some restrictions on high-capacity or rapid-fire firearms, but the limitations may not be as stringent as in some other countries.	Strengthening restrictions on certain firearms could enhance public safety.
Waiting Periods	[3]	Mexico imposes mandatory waiting periods for additional background checks, contributing to the evaluation process.	Mandatory waiting periods contribute to thorough evaluations and prevention of impulsive acts.
Safe Storage Requirements	[2]	Mexico has guidelines on secure storage, but the level of strictness may vary, potentially benefiting from more specific requirements.	Strict storage requirements help prevent accidents, theft, and unauthorized access; further specificity may enhance effectiveness.
Education and Training	[2]	Mexico has some mandatory training programs promoting responsible gun ownership, safety, and storage, but there may be room for improvement.	Mandatory training enhances responsible gun use and safety awareness; additional efforts can further promote a culture of responsibility.
Red Flag Laws	[2]	Mexico has initiated red flag laws allowing temporary firearm removal based on mental health or risk assessments, but the system may benefit from further development.	Robust red flag laws contribute significantly to proactive risk management; continued development could enhance effectiveness.
Limits on Ammunition Sales	[3]	Mexico has some limits on high-capacity magazines and specific types of ammunition, contributing to risk reduction.	Strict limits contribute to reducing the severity of potential incidents; periodic reviews can enhance effectiveness.
Universal Background Checks for All Sales	[3]	Mexico ensures thorough background checks for all firearm sales, including private sales and gun shows, closing loopholes effectively.	Thorough background checks for all sales contribute to comprehensive control.
Regular Policy Evaluation	[3]	Mexico establishes mechanisms for ongoing assessment and adjustments to gun control policies, ensuring regular evaluations.	Regular evaluation enhances the adaptability and effectiveness of policies.
Community Engagement	[2]	Mexico involves communities and stakeholders in policy development, but there may be room for improvement in active engagement.	Community involvement contributes to policy acceptance but may benefit from increased engagement.
International Cooperation	[2]	Mexico has some international collaboration to control the illicit trade of firearms, but the level of collaboration may be limited.	Partial international collaboration impacts global efforts in controlling illegal weapon flow.
Public Awareness Campaigns	[2]	Mexico conducts some public awareness campaigns on firearm risks and responsible ownership, contributing to public understanding.	Public awareness campaigns enhance knowledge on responsible ownership but may benefit from increased outreach.

Comments or Additional Considerations: Mexico's gun control policies show efforts toward public safety, but there is room for improvement. Thorough background checks, licensing, and waiting periods contribute positively, but these measures could benefit from increased stringency. Strengthening restrictions on certain firearms and increasing the strictness of storage requirements could enhance public safety. While there are training programs, further efforts can promote a stronger culture of responsibility. Red flag laws are initiated but may need further development. Community engagement and international collaboration could be improved for more effective policy development and implementation. Public awareness campaigns are conducted but may benefit from increased outreach for better results. Overall, Mexico has implemented measures, but enhancements in various areas could lead to more robust gun control policies.

Total Rating: 32

Table 16: Effectiveness ratings for Philippine gun control policies.

Gun Control Policy Effectiveness – Philippines			
Criteria	Rating (1-5)	Rating Guidelines	Comments or Additional Considerations
Comprehensive Background Checks	[3]	The Philippines conducts background checks on criminal history, mental health, and relevant factors, but there may be areas for improvement.	Strengthening the thoroughness of background checks could enhance public safety.
Licensing and Registration	[3]	The Philippines has licensing requirements involving an application process, good reason verification, and periodic renewals, but there may be room for improvement.	Strengthening licensing measures could improve tracking and responsible use.
Restrictions on Firearm Types	[2]	The Philippines has some restrictions on high-capacity or rapid-fire firearms, but the limitations may not be as stringent as in some other countries.	Strengthening restrictions on certain firearms could enhance public safety.
Waiting Periods	[3]	The Philippines imposes mandatory waiting periods for additional background checks, contributing to the evaluation process.	Mandatory waiting periods contribute to thorough evaluations and prevention of impulsive acts.
Safe Storage Requirements	[2]	The Philippines has guidelines on secure storage, but the level of strictness may vary, potentially benefiting from more specific requirements.	Strict storage requirements help prevent accidents, theft, and unauthorized access; further specificity may enhance effectiveness.
Education and Training	[2]	The Philippines has some mandatory training programs promoting responsible gun ownership, safety, and storage, but there may be room for improvement.	Mandatory training enhances responsible gun use and safety awareness; additional efforts can further promote a culture of responsibility.
Red Flag Laws	[2]	The Philippines has initiated red flag laws allowing temporary firearm removal based on mental health or risk assessments, but the system may benefit from further development.	Robust red flag laws contribute significantly to proactive risk management; continued development could enhance effectiveness.
Limits on Ammunition Sales	[3]	The Philippines has some limits on high-capacity magazines and specific types of ammunition, contributing to risk reduction.	Strict limits contribute to reducing the severity of potential incidents; periodic reviews can enhance effectiveness.
Universal Background Checks for All Sales	[3]	The Philippines ensures thorough background checks for all firearm sales, including private sales and gun shows, closing loopholes effectively.	Thorough background checks for all sales contribute to comprehensive control.
Regular Policy Evaluation	[3]	The Philippines establishes mechanisms for ongoing assessment and adjustments to gun control policies, ensuring regular evaluations.	Regular evaluation enhances the adaptability and effectiveness of policies.
Community Engagement	[2]	The Philippines involves communities and stakeholders in policy development, but there may be room for improvement in active engagement.	Community involvement contributes to policy acceptance but may benefit from increased engagement.
International Cooperation	[2]	The Philippines has some international collaboration to control the illicit trade of firearms, but the level of collaboration may be limited.	Partial international collaboration impacts global efforts in controlling illegal weapon flow.
Public Awareness Campaigns	[3]	The Philippines conducts some public awareness campaigns on firearm risks and responsible ownership, contributing to public understanding.	Public awareness campaigns enhance knowledge on responsible ownership but may benefit from increased outreach.

Comments or Additional Considerations: The Philippines has implemented measures to regulate firearms, with efforts in background checks, licensing, waiting periods, and awareness campaigns. However, there is room for improvement in certain areas. Strengthening background checks and licensing measures, as well as enhancing restrictions on certain firearms, could contribute to more robust gun control policies. Specific and strict storage requirements can further prevent accidents and unauthorized access. Increased efforts in mandatory training programs and community engagement could promote a stronger culture of responsible gun ownership. Further development of red flag laws and increased international collaboration can contribute to a more comprehensive approach. Overall, the Philippines has taken steps, but additional measures and improvements could enhance the effectiveness of gun control policies.

Total Rating: 33

In the People's Republic of China, the general public's access to firearms is governed by some of the most stringent control measures globally. Civilian firearm ownership is largely limited to non-individual entities, with exceptions for individuals holding hunting permits and certain ethnic minorities. Law enforcement, military, paramilitary, and security personnel have the authority to use firearms. Police are mandated to use issued pistols solely for the purpose of preventing serious or dangerous crimes. The use of airsoft guns is practically prohibited in China due to muzzle energy limits categorizing them as real firearms.

Polish gun control laws allow civilian ownership of modern firearms on a shall-issue basis, subject to police-issued permits for individuals providing a valid reason. Common reasons include hunting, sport shooting, and collection, requiring membership in relevant organizations. Self-defence permits are exceptions, involving a may-issue permit. Antique gunpowder firearms and most air guns are accessible without a permit. Mental health and domestic violence laws, akin to U.S. red flag laws, apply to firearm owners.

Poland's regulation of civilian firearms ownership is outlined in the Weapons and Munitions Act of 1999, which imposes strict conditions, administrative procedures, and penalties (Krzywicka, 2023). This legislation has contributed to Poland ranking 166th globally in civilian firearms per 100 people, with less than 0.8% of citizens holding valid firearm permits (Krzywicka, 2023). The Act also allows for the indefinite issuance of permits, but they can be revoked based on specific conditions (Krzywicka, 2023).

The application process involves demonstrating an "important reason," passing medical and psychological evaluations, and paying administrative fees. Permit holders must own a certified gun safe, and firearm transactions require certifications and registration with the Police. Firearms permits also specify the types and quantity allowed, determined by the Police.

Gun handling permits allow temporary possession and use, mainly for private security guards or individuals with sport permits. Institutional permits apply to specific organizations for various purposes. Deactivated guns and some air guns require registration, and a European Firearms Pass is available upon request for legal firearm owners.

The law restricts fully automatic firearms, sound suppressors, ammunition types, and magazine capacities. Essential firearm parts are regulated similarly to functional firearms. Storage requirements mandate certified gun safes, and carrying firearms is restricted, emphasizing concealed carry. Carrying firearms during public events, in certain locations, or under the influence of alcohol is prohibited.

Unrestricted weapons include pre-1885 black powder firearms, their replicas, and certain other categories. Other weapons like brass knuckles or crossbows require permits. Some uses, such as sport shooting or museum collections, do not require permits. The law also outlines restrictions on specific weapons, such as incapacitating gas dispensers or certain melee weapons.

Poland's gun control laws are detailed, covering various aspects from permit issuance to usage restrictions and technical specifications. The system combines shall-issue and may-issue principles, balancing individual rights with public safety considerations.

In Poland, shooting ranges are regulated facilities, and it's illegal to use firearms and other weapons outside officially recognized shooting ranges. The regulations cover environmental, safety, and general laws, including building codes. Specific regulations are outlined in the Weapons and Munitions Act. Outdoor shooting ranges must adhere to environmental rules, and noise limits must be observed. Indoor ranges follow safety rules set by the Minister of Internal Affairs.

Self-defence permits are limited, allowing possession of specific weapons and requiring periodic evaluations. The number of active self-defence permits is decreasing, possibly due to administrative decisions or permit holders losing interest. Private security businesses have a separate licensing system.

Penalties for firearm-related offenses include fines, jail time, and potential forfeiture of weapons. Misdemeanours include unlicensed sale, possession, and various violations, while felonies involve intentional abandonment of firearms or ammunition. The Penal Code outlines penalties for using weapons during crimes and unlicensed possession, manufacture, or sale of firearms.

As of December 2022, Poland had 760,218 registered firearms and 286,751 active permits (Policja, 2022). The purposes include self-defence, hunting, sport shooting, historical re-enactments, collection, memorial, training, and others.

In Mexico, firearms regulation is governed by legislation that dictates the acquisition, ownership, possession, and carrying of firearms by armed forces, law enforcement, and private citizens. Gun possession is heavily restricted, with only two authorized stores in the country, and legal acquisition involves extensive paperwork.

While Mexico has strict gun laws, it's a misconception that firearms are entirely illegal. Constitutional rights allow Mexican citizens and legal residents to acquire and own certain firearms, subject to fulfillment of legal requirements (Burke et al., 2018). The right to keep and bear arms was initially recognized in the 1857 Constitution but underwent modifications in 1917, restricting carrying arms outside the home.

The Federal Law of Firearms and Explosives is the primary legal framework overseeing firearms, covering import, manufacture, sale, purchase, ownership, and possession. The regulation specifies the right to keep arms within the home, requiring registration with the Secretariat of National Defense. Citizens are generally limited to 10 registered firearms per household.

Carrying firearms outside the home requires a license, which is typically granted to specific groups, including military, police, private security personnel, and individuals in rural areas or potentially targeted by crime. The types and calibres of permitted firearms are detailed in the law, and citizens are generally restricted to semi-automatic handguns, revolvers, rifles up to .22 calibre, and shotguns up to 12 gauge.

Transportation of firearms outside the home requires a permit from the Secretariat of National Defense, with additional restrictions for those belonging to hunting or shooting clubs. Bringing firearms into Mexico or exporting them requires specific permits, and strict penalties exist for unauthorized possession.

Private ownership of firearms is limited to the home, and only Mexican citizens and legal residents can purchase and keep firearms. The Directorate of Commercialization of Arms and Munitions (DCAM) is the authorized outlet for firearm sales. Legal procedures for acquiring firearms involve obtaining a firearm acquisition permit, submitting required documents, and following a detailed process.

Overall, private citizens in Mexico can lawfully own firearms for purposes such as home defence, hunting, target practice, shooting sport competition, and collection, with each purpose requiring specific authorization and compliance with legal regulations.

Ratings were also completed for India resulting in a total rating of 33. India has implemented measures to regulate firearms, with efforts in background checks, licensing, waiting periods, and awareness campaigns. However, there is room for improvement in certain areas. Strengthening background checks and licensing measures, as well as enhancing restrictions on certain firearms, could contribute to more robust gun control policies. Specific and strict storage requirements can further prevent accidents and unauthorized access. Increased efforts in mandatory training programs and community engagement could promote a stronger culture of responsible gun ownership. Further development of red flag laws and increased international collaboration can contribute to a more comprehensive approach. Overall, India has taken steps, but additional measures and improvements could enhance the effectiveness of gun control policies.

Pakistan is rated with an overall rating of 26. Pakistan has implemented measures to regulate firearms, with efforts in background checks, licensing, waiting periods, and awareness campaigns. However, there is room for improvement in certain areas. Strengthening background checks and licensing measures, as well as enhancing restrictions on certain firearms, could contribute to more robust gun control policies. Specific and strict storage requirements can further prevent accidents and unauthorized access. Increased efforts in mandatory training programs and community engagement could promote a stronger culture of responsible gun ownership. Further development of red flag laws and increased international collaboration can contribute to a more comprehensive approach. Overall, Pakistan has taken steps, but additional measures and improvements could enhance the effectiveness of gun control policies.

The Czech Republic has implemented robust measures to regulate firearms, with strong emphasis on background checks, safe storage, and regular policy evaluations. While licensing requirements exist, there is room for strengthening the process, and further development of red flag laws could enhance risk management. The country demonstrates a commitment to international collaboration, which can contribute to global efforts against illegal firearms trade. Continued efforts in community engagement and public awareness campaigns can strengthen a culture of responsible gun ownership. Overall, the Czech Republic has a solid foundation in gun control policies with potential areas for improvement. The effectiveness of the Czech Republic was given an overall rating of 42.

Thailand has an overall rating of 40. Thailand has implemented a range of measures in gun control policies, with effective background checks, licensing, and restrictions on certain firearm types. While existing policies contribute to public safety, further development and periodic reviews can enhance their effectiveness. Continued efforts in education and training, community engagement, and public awareness campaigns can strengthen a culture of responsible gun ownership. The commitment to regular policy evaluation and international cooperation contributes to adaptability and global efforts against the illicit trade of firearms. Overall, Thailand has a foundation in gun control policies with potential areas for improvement.

All of the above-mentioned overall ratings are tabulated into Table 17 and graphically as Figure 21.

Table 17: Country Gun Control Measure Overall Ratings.

Country/Region	Effectiveness of Gun Control Measures Rating
USA	31
UK	65
Canada	50
Australia	63
Germany	63
Switzerland	41
Japan	65
Brazil	29
South Africa	39
Russia	39
China	61
Poland	44
Mexico	32
Philippines	33
India	33
Pakistan	26
Czech Republic	42

Effectiveness of Gun Control Measures Rating

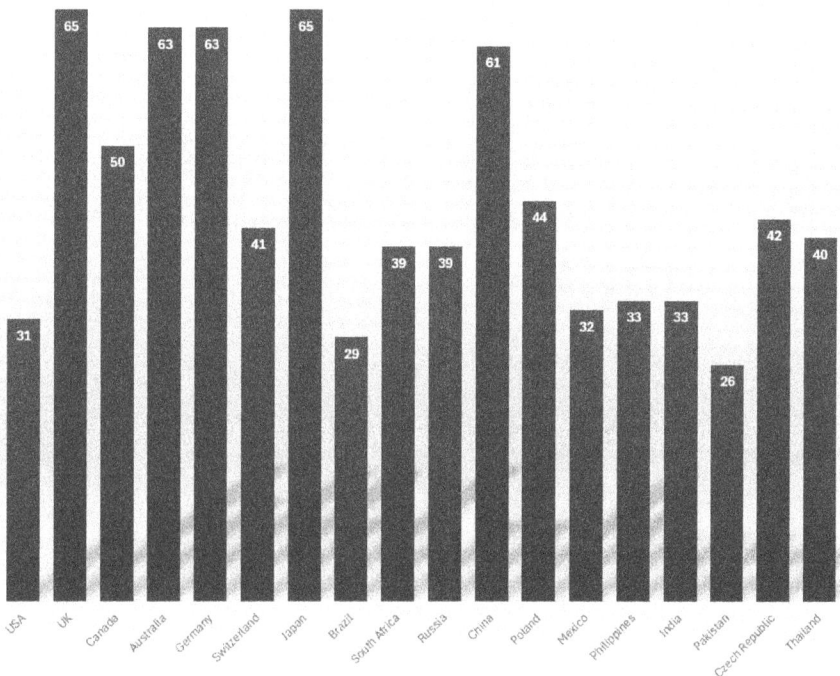

Figure 21: Graphic representation of allocated gun control policy ratings by country.

The calculated statistics offer insights into the distribution and central tendency of effectiveness ratings for gun control measures across the listed countries or regions. The mean effectiveness rating is approximately 44.44, indicating that, on average, the perceived effectiveness of gun control measures falls around this value.

The median effectiveness rating is 47, and its proximity to the mean suggests a relatively symmetric distribution of ratings. The range of effectiveness ratings is 39, signifying the spread or variability in ratings. This range illustrates the difference between the highest and lowest effectiveness scores. Additionally, the standard deviation, approximately 13.7 6, suggests a moderate amount of variability or spread in the effectiveness ratings from the mean. A higher standard deviation implies greater variability in opinions across countries.

In summary, these statistics provide an overview of the diversity in opinions regarding the effectiveness of gun control measures. The relatively high standard deviation indicates variability in how countries perceive and implement gun control, with a wide range of effectiveness ratings. The absence of a mode suggests a lack of consensus on a specific effectiveness rating dominating the dataset.

To apply percentiles to the given dataset, we need to sort the effectiveness ratings in ascending order first:

Sorted Ratings: 26, 29, 31, 32, 33, 39, 39, 40, 41, 42, 44, 50, 61, 63, 63, 65, 65

Now, let's calculate some percentiles:

1. 25th Percentile (Q1):

- Q1 is the value below which 25% of the data falls.

- In this case, Q1Q1 falls between the 4th and 5th observations (32 and 33).

- Q1=(32+33)/2=32.5

2. 50th Percentile (Median or Q2):

- Q2 is the median and is the value below which 50% of the data falls.

- It is the average of the 8th and 9th observations (39 and 39).

- Q2=(39+39)/2=39

3. 75th Percentile (Q3):

- Q3 is the value below which 75% of the data falls.

- It falls between the 13th and 14th observations (63 and 63).

- Q3=(63+63)/2=63

These percentiles provide insights into the distribution of effectiveness ratings:

- 25% of countries have an effectiveness rating of 32.5 or lower.

- 50% of countries have an effectiveness rating of 39 or lower (median).

- 75% of countries have an effectiveness rating of 63 or lower.

This information helps understand the spread and central tendency of the dataset, indicating that only 25% of the countries considered had a rating above 63.

Global Firearm Policy Spectrum

The ratings from the Rating System for Effective Gun Control Policies can be used to classify the gun control measures around the world into a 'Global Firearm Policy Spectrum" as follows:

- Score 13-26: Highly Permissive Gun Control Policies

  ○ Countries falling within this range are characterized by highly permissive gun control policies. They generally have minimal restrictions, with lower scores indicating a more lenient approach to firearm regulation.

- Score 27-39: Moderately Permissive Gun Control Policies

  ○ This category signifies countries with moderately permissive gun control policies. While they may have some restrictions in place, the overall approach is more lenient compared to nations with higher scores.

- Score 40-52: Balanced Gun Control Policies

  ○ Falling into this range indicates a balanced approach to gun control policies. These countries strike a middle ground between permissive and restrictive measures, ensuring a reasonable level of regulation.

- Score 53-65: Highly Restrictive Gun Control Policies

  ○ Countries with scores in this range have highly restrictive gun control policies. They generally enforce stringent regulations, with higher scores indicating a more comprehensive and restrictive approach to firearm control.

The spectrum is displayed graphically as *Figure 22*.

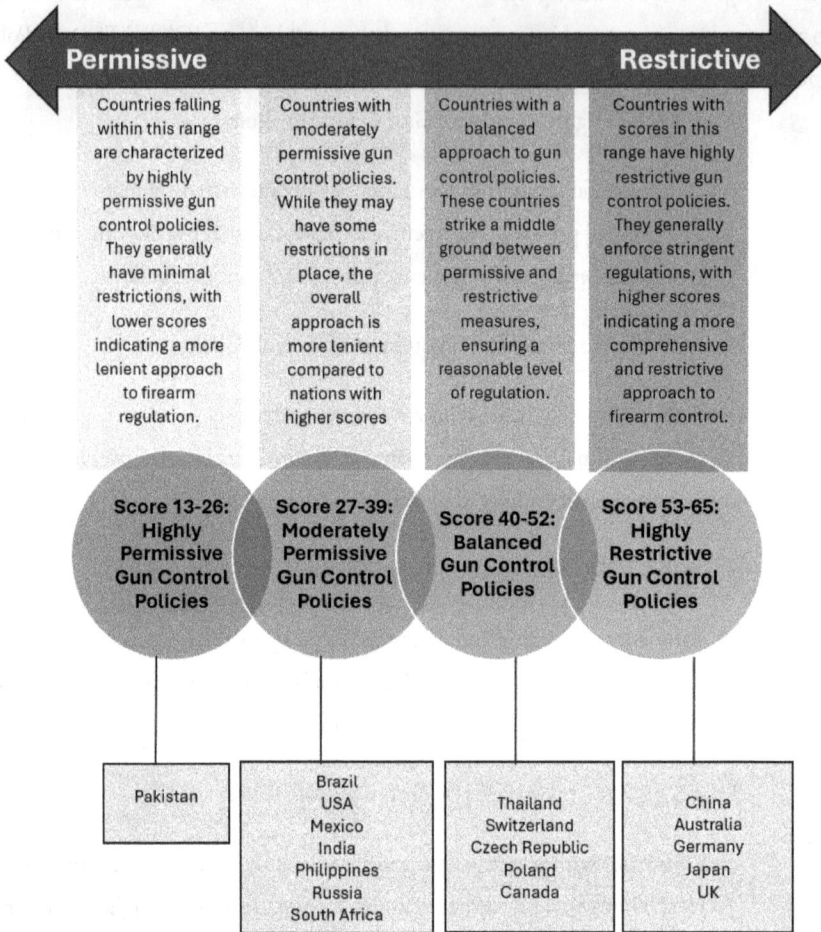

Figure 22: Global Firearm Policy Spectrum.

Figure 22: Global Firearm Policy Spectrum.

The Rating System for Effective Gun Control Policies, combined with the classification into a Global Firearm Policy Spectrum, holds significant utility for diverse stakeholders, ranging from policymakers and researchers to advocacy groups and the general public. This system offers a multifaceted approach to understanding and assessing gun control policies globally.

Policymakers can employ the rating system to scrutinize the effectiveness of their nations' existing gun control measures. The comparative nature of the system enables them to juxtapose their policies against those of other countries, facilitating the identification of areas requiring improvement or adjustment.

For countries, the system provides a tool for international benchmarking. By aligning their gun control policies with those in similar score ranges, nations can engage in a comparative analysis, drawing lessons from one another's experiences and adopting best practices in regulating firearms.

Advocacy groups focused on gun control can leverage the ratings to raise awareness about the global landscape of firearm regulation. The categorization into different policy effectiveness levels simplifies the communication of the relative permissiveness or restrictiveness of various countries' gun control measures.

Researchers investigating the impact of gun control on societal factors can utilize the rating system to categorize countries based on the stringency of their policies. This categorization forms the basis for more in-depth analyses and academic studies on the intricate relationship between gun control and societal outcomes.

The classification into a spectrum serves as a simplified framework for public understanding. It aids individuals in comprehending whether their country's gun control policies are relatively permissive, balanced, or restrictive compared to those of other nations.

International organizations and experts can draw upon the ratings to formulate evidence-based policy recommendations. Analysing the experiences of countries with similar scores enables them to propose effective strategies for enhancing gun control measures on a global scale.

Citizens and civil society can hold governments accountable by referencing the rating system. Serving as a standardized tool, it allows for the assessment of whether a country's gun control policies align with the desired level of permissiveness or restrictiveness.

Policymakers engaged in reforming gun control legislation can utilize the classification to gauge their country's current standing in terms of policy effectiveness. This information serves as a guide for the development of new legislation or amendments to existing laws.

The spectrum not only categorizes countries but also encourages dialogue and collaboration between nations with similar policy approaches. It facilitates the exchange of ideas and strategies for addressing common challenges related to gun control.

In summary, the Global Firearm Policy Spectrum, derived from the rating system, emerges as a practical and versatile tool. It empowers stakeholders across various levels to make informed decisions, collaborate effectively, and contribute to ongoing efforts aimed at striking a balance between individual rights and public safety.

The most ideal gun control approach would depend on various factors, including the cultural, social, and political context of a particular country. However, a balanced approach to gun control policies (Score 40-52 on the Rating System for Effective Gun Control Policies or Balanced Gun Control Policies on the Global Firearm Policy Spectrum) seems to offer a middle ground that aims to strike a balance between permissiveness and restrictiveness. This approach suggests that the country is implementing reasonable regulations without being excessively permissive or overly restrictive.

A balanced approach typically takes into account the need for public safety while respecting the rights of law-abiding citizens to own firearms. It may involve measures such as background checks, waiting periods, and restrictions on certain types of firearms, aiming to prevent gun violence without unduly infringing on individual rights.

It's essential to note that the effectiveness of gun control policies also depends on how well they are enforced, the level of public support, and other contextual factors. The specific details of the policies within the balanced range would need to be carefully crafted and continually evaluated to ensure they meet the evolving needs of society.

SOCIOLOGICAL ASPECTS OF SPORTS SHOOTING

Historical Development of Sports Shooting

Sports shooting has a rich historical development that spans centuries, evolving from practical skills necessary for survival to organized and competitive events. Initially, shooting was primarily associated with military training and hunting, reflecting the importance of marksmanship in warfare and subsistence (Martin, 2011). As societies transitioned from agrarian to more urbanized settings, shooting became a recreational activity, contributing to the emergence of organized competitions (Martin, 2011). The development of shooting sports has been influenced by various factors, including the transformation of lowland game shooting, the impact of environmental stress on cognitive performance, and the prevention of noise-induced hearing loss from recreational firearms (Martin, 2011; Martin et al., 2019; Meinke et al., 2017). Furthermore, the popularization of shooting sports has been recognized as a means of introducing young people to a healthy lifestyle and involving them in sports that they may not have succeeded in otherwise (Meinke et al., 2017).

Shooting, defined as the sport involving the firing of rifles, handguns (pistols and revolvers), and shotguns at various targets to test marksmanship, has a rich history that dates back to the early days of archery, around 1300, before the advent of firearms (The Editors of Encyclopaedia Britannica, 2023). The use of firearms in warfare eventually extended to sport shooting, including hunting. However, the precise origins of target shooting remain unclear due to the shadowy history of firearms.

The earliest recorded shooting match occurred in Eichstät, Bavaria, in 1477, where participants, likely using matchlocks, competed at a distance of 200 meters. A Swiss painting from 1504 depicted a rifle shooting setup that resembled modern practices, with enclosed shooting booths and concealed target markers (The Editors of Encyclopaedia Britannica, 2023). Target shooting with rifled arms gained popularity in 16th-century Europe, especially in Germanic countries, evidenced by elaborately decorated wheel locks with rifled bores.

The sport further evolved, with Empress Anna establishing a target-shooting range in Russia in 1737, focusing on live birds as targets. In 1806, the Society of Shooting Amateurs in St. Petersburg emphasized handgun shooting with flintlock pistols (The Editors of Encyclopaedia Britannica, 2023). By 1834, the first shooting range or club for rifles and handguns was founded in St. Petersburg, marking the beginning of public shooting grounds. The interest in shooting grew, leading to the formation of various shooting societies and championships in the late 19th and early 20th centuries (The Editors of Encyclopaedia Britannica, 2023).

The 19th century marked a pivotal period for the formalization of sports shooting. Shooting clubs and organizations were established, and rules for various shooting disciplines were codified. The rise of firearms technology played a crucial role, with advancements in accuracy and efficiency contributing to the popularity of shooting as a sport. The first international shooting competitions, such as the Wimbledon Cup, were organized during this time, fostering a sense of camaraderie among shooting enthusiasts.

The 20th century saw further standardization and specialization in shooting sports. Different disciplines, such as rifle, pistol, and shotgun shooting, emerged, each with its own set of rules and competitions. The inclusion of shooting in the Olympic Games beginning in the late 19th century elevated the sport's status and globalized its appeal.

In North America, rifle shooting played a significant role on the frontier and in farming settlements during the colonial period. The flintlock Kentucky rifle, produced from around 1750, became a popular choice for protection, hunting, and target shooting (The Editors of Encyclopaedia Britannica, 2023). Shooting matches, attracting numerous marksmen, were common in villages and settlements.

Target rifle shooting was already a popular sport in Great Britain before 1800, and Queen Victoria herself participated in the first prize meeting of the National Rifle Association in 1860 (The Editors of Encyclopaedia Britannica, 2023). Long-range shooting gained prominence, leading to international competitions that included teams from Australia and New Zealand (The Editors of Encyclopaedia Britannica, 2023).

Schuetzen shooting, of Germanic-Swiss origin, was a centuries-old practice prevalent in central Europe. Although it declined after World War I, interest in target rifle shooting grew in the early 20th century, particularly in small-bore (.22-calibre rimfire) shooting (The Editors of Encyclopaedia Britannica, 2023).

Handguns were included in the Olympic Games from 1896, and pistol shooting became a part of the National Rifle Association championships in the late 19th century. Similarly, shotguns' target shooting originated as practice for shooting game, evolving from live pigeons to glass balls and ultimately clay pigeons (The Editors of Encyclopaedia Britannica, 2023).

Shooting has been part of the Olympic Games since 1896, featuring events for rifles, pistols, shotguns, and various target shooting disciplines (The Editors of Encyclopaedia Britannica, 2023). The International Shooting Union (ISU), later rebranded as the International Shooting Sport Federation (ISSF) in 1998, oversees world championships in different shooting categories.

Cultural and Social Factors in the Emergence and Evolution of Shooting Sports

Cultural and social factors have indeed played a significant role in shaping the landscape of shooting sports. Firearms have been deeply intertwined with historical traditions in many cultures, symbolizing power and the ability to provide sustenance (Boine et al., 2020). As societies evolved, the transition from viewing firearms as tools for survival to instruments of leisure and competition contributed to the establishment of shooting as a sport. This transition is influenced by various factors such as balance ability, psychological aspects, physical fitness, and sociocultural norms (Chen & Yue, 2023; Hrysomallis, 2011; Ihalainen et al., 2015; Mon-López et al., 2019; Peljha et al., 2018; Silva et al., 2021). The importance of balance to activities such as rifle shooting and its relationship to performance in many sports and motor skills hasn't been fully elucidated (Hrysomallis, 2011). Postural balance is an important factor determining shooting performance (Ihalainen et al., 2015). The ability to stabilize the gun is affected by movements of the centre of pressure that reach the gun through the kinetic chains of the body and the movements caused by muscular tremor (Mon-López et al., 2019). Psychological aspects like anxiety, injuries' effects, professional psychological support, psychological training, and athlete-coach relationships could influence shooters' performance (Silva et al., 2021). Physical fitness is a critical factor for the sport's skill level, and functional training can effectively improve the shooter's technical level, ensuring greater athlete stability (Chen & Yue, 2023).

Moreover, the sociocultural aspects of shooting sports are evident in the demographics of firearm owners, where sociocultural factors such as conformity to masculine role norms and political ideology play a significant role (McDermott et al., 2021). The symbolic connections between guns and masculinity hint toward masculinity insecurity or fragility, contributing to the precarious masculinity of firearm ownership (Borgogna et al., 2022). Gun culture is not monolithic and varies substantially between states, with the recreational gun subculture falling in prominence over time, while the self-defence subculture has been rising (Boine et al., 2020). The sociocultural explanation for why most firearm owners are male, White, and politically conservative further emphasizes the influence of cultural and social factors on shooting sports (McDermott et al., 2021).

In addition, the political processes concerning sports are influenced by cultural factors, as demonstrated in the political mobilization of sports issues (Seippel et al., 2018). The absence of social science and sociological attention on country sports, such as game shooting, has been noted, indicating a lack of sociological contribution to the debate on shooting sports (Hillyard & Burridge, 2012).

Furthermore, the transition from viewing firearms as tools for survival to instruments of leisure and competition is also influenced by the broader social and macro-determinant factors, including control of and access to firearms (Souto et al., 2017). The popularization of shooting sports is recognized as a factor of the national security of the state, emphasizing the broader societal implications of shooting sports (Moiseeva et al., 2021). The discussions about lead ammunition extend beyond shooting, encompassing organizations advancing wildlife conservation, public health, and animal welfare, indicating the broader societal and environmental impact of shooting sports (Newth et al., 2019).

The role of shooting clubs and associations in the social context of sports shooting is crucial for understanding the standardization of rules, organization of competitions, and the mitigation of concerns about the misuse of firearms. Shooting clubs and associations provide a platform for enthusiasts to gather, facilitate the standardization of rules, and organize competitions (McElroy & Coley, 2020). These organizations play a significant role in the acceptance of shooting sports within broader society by providing a disciplined and regulated environment for the sport, thus addressing concerns about the misuse of firearms (Hemenway et al., 2018).

Shooting sports organizations at colleges and universities have political implications and are not merely leisure activities. They are significant in promoting social movements and can help explain the presence of shooting sports organizations at educational institutions (McElroy & Coley, 2020). Furthermore, the sense of civic responsibility among shooting sports club members is a key facilitator in preventing firearm injury, emphasizing the positive impact of these organizations on society (Trinka et al., 2023).

The establishment of shooting as a disciplined and regulated sport has contributed to the acceptance of shooting sports within broader society. This is in line with the EU Work Plan for Sport, which claims that sport plays a critical role in influencing wider society by promoting social cohesion, especially for young people from diverse ethnic backgrounds (Dagkas, 2016). Additionally, the theories of justice and social processes play a key role in today's sport clubs, emphasizing the broader societal impact of sports organizations (Zimányi & Géczi, 2018).

The cultural perception of firearms and marksmanship is a complex and multifaceted issue that varies significantly across different regions and societies. This variation is influenced by a multitude of factors including social norms, political climates, and historical contexts. The influence of these factors on the perception and acceptance of shooting sports is evident in the literature.

In some cultures, shooting sports are deeply ingrained in national identity, reflecting historical connections to marksmanship (Youngson et al., 2021). This historical connection has contributed to the popularity and acceptance of shooting sports in these regions. On the other hand, in cultures where there are different attitudes towards firearms, the popularity and acceptance of shooting sports are influenced accordingly (Youngson et al., 2021). The presence of guns and gun culture in rural communities has been noted in the literature, indicating the influence of geographical and social factors on the perception of firearms and shooting sports (Youngson et al., 2021).

Moreover, the influence of cultural values on sport attitudes and team identification has been studied, highlighting the role of cultural norms in shaping individuals' attitudes towards sports (Gau & Kim, 2011). This suggests that cultural values play a significant role in shaping the perception of shooting sports in different societies.

The influence of social norms on participation intention in sports has also been explored, with significant influences of attitude and subjective norms found in both men and women (Kim & Kim, 2021). This indicates that social norms play a crucial role in shaping individuals' intentions to participate in shooting sports, reflecting the broader cultural perception of firearms and marksmanship.

Furthermore, the spatial organization of sport and recreation has been implicated as a source of marginalization, with culturally diverse women highlighting the role of access-enhancing initiatives in promoting social inclusion through sport (Cortis, 2009). This underscores the broader societal impact of shooting sports and the cultural significance of promoting inclusivity in sports participation.

In addition, the emergence of gun culture has been documented, indicating the evolving nature of societal attitudes towards firearms and marksmanship (Yamane et al., 2020). This highlights the dynamic nature of cultural perceptions and the need to consider historical and contemporary influences on the acceptance of shooting sports.

Overall, the emergence and evolution of shooting sports reflect a dynamic interplay between historical developments, technological advancements, and shifting cultural and social attitudes towards firearms and marksmanship. Understanding this historical context is essential for comprehending the multifaceted nature of sports shooting as a recreational and competitive activity.

Socialization into the Culture of Sports Shooting

The process of socialization into the culture of sports shooting is a multifaceted journey where individuals acquire the knowledge, values, and behaviours associated with this distinct community. Socialization plays a pivotal role in shaping how individuals perceive and engage with shooting sports, influencing their identity within the larger shooting community. Several key factors contribute to the socialization of individuals into the culture of sports shooting.

The family plays a crucial role in the socialization of individuals into shooting sports. It serves as a primary agent for introducing individuals to firearms and shooting activities, creating a generational link to the sport. Informal gatherings such as family trips to shooting ranges and hunting outings contribute to early exposure and positive reinforcement of shooting practices. Additionally, peer groups, particularly among younger individuals, also play a significant role in influencing newcomers to join the shooting sports community, fostering a sense of camaraderie and shared interests (Greendorfer & Lewko, 1978; Hayoz et al., 2017; Kay, 2000).

Sociologists and social psychologists have emphasized the family's role as a socializing agent and a source of emotional support, highlighting the practical resources contributed by families and their central role in facilitating young people's entry into sports (Kay, 2000). Furthermore, research has focused on the intergenerational transfer of a sports-related lifestyle within the family, emphasizing the family as an agent of socialization, particularly in the context of sports participation during childhood (Hayoz et al., 2017).

The influence of family members on the sport socialization of children has been a subject of scholarly interest, emphasizing the role of family in shaping children's attitudes and participation in sports (Greendorfer & Lewko, 1978). This underscores the significance of family in introducing and shaping individuals' involvement in shooting sports from a young age.

In addition to the family, peer groups also play a significant role in influencing individuals to join the shooting sports community, particularly among younger individuals. Friends who participate in shooting sports can influence newcomers to join the community, creating a sense of camaraderie and shared interests (Kay, 2000).

Formal socialization occurs within shooting clubs and organizations. These groups provide structured environments where novices can learn from experienced shooters, participate in training sessions, and engage in competitions. To appreciate the role of formal socialization within shooting clubs and organizations, it is essential to explore the structured environments that these groups provide for novices to learn from experienced shooters, participate in training sessions, and engage in competitions. Additionally, these clubs serve as hubs for knowledge exchange, skill development, and the reinforcement of cultural norms within the shooting community. Mentoring relationships within these organizations foster a sense of belonging and shared identity, where newcomers not only learn the technical aspects of shooting but also the values and traditions associated with the community.

The concept of formal socialization within shooting clubs and organizations is supported by several relevant references. Lower-Hoppe et al. (2020) found that formal socialization enhances club members' feelings of attachment, emphasizing the role of structured socialization processes in fostering a sense of belonging and shared identity within clubs. Furthermore, (Rosso & McGrath, 2012) highlighted the significance of social capital in the transition of young players from recreational/informal settings to formal clubs, indicating that formal club environments play a crucial role in shaping individuals' social networks and identities. These findings underscore the importance of formal socialization in facilitating the integration of newcomers into the shooting community and transmitting cultural values and traditions.

A study by Emrich et al. (2012) emphasized the role of social incentives and mutual recognition in reinforcing voluntary engagement within smaller groups like sports clubs, indicating that formal socialization processes contribute to the development of a shared identity and a sense of belonging among club members. This aligns with the notion that formal socialization within shooting clubs and organizations not only imparts technical skills but also shapes individuals' social identities and fosters a collective sense of purpose and belonging.

Formal training and education programs play a significant role in the socialization process by imparting essential knowledge and skills related to firearm safety, marksmanship, and ethical aspects of shooting sports. These programs, often conducted by certified instructors, reinforce responsible and safe gun handling and instil a sense of sportsmanship, fair play, and respect for fellow participants (Berrigan et al., 2019). Exposure to standardized training contributes to the development of a culture of safety and responsibility among individuals who own or handle firearms (Azrael et al., 2018).

Figure 23: Firearms training at indoor firing range using M16 rifle. NIOSH, Public domain, via Wikimedia Commons.

The importance of formal training in promoting responsible firearm handling is underscored by the findings of a national survey on formal firearm training among adults in the USA. The study by revealed that formal firearm training is crucial for enhancing safety and responsible firearm use among both firearm owners and non-owners (Rowhani-Rahbar et al., 2017). This emphasizes the broader societal impact of formal training programs in promoting a culture of safety and responsibility in firearm handling.

Participating in shooting competitions and cultural events can play a significant role in the socialization process, providing individuals with opportunities for skill enhancement, personal growth, and community interaction. Competing alongside experienced shooters exposes individuals to the competitive nature of the sport, contributing to their skill development and personal growth (Ihalainen et al., 2017). Additionally, cultural events such as gun shows and exhibitions create spaces for enthusiasts to interact, share experiences, and reinforce their shared identity as members of the sports shooting community (Moiseeva et al., 2021). These events contribute significantly to the socialization process by fostering a sense of community and shared identity among participants.

The influence of media, including magazines, online forums, and social media platforms, on shaping perceptions and providing information about shooting sports is significant. Thorpe (2016) highlights that new media technologies are contributing to new relationships between corporations, action sport bodies, and communities, indicating the evolving role of media in the shooting sports community. Additionally, (Thompson et al., 2016) emphasize that fans perceive the usage of social media by professional sports events to be about interaction, insight, and brand anthropomorphism, underscoring the impact of social media on the perception of shooting sports.

Arif et al. (2022) discuss the positive role of mass media in promoting sports and disseminating information about the value of sports participation, which aligns with the idea that media acts as a supplementary agent of socialization, contributing to the formation and reinforcement of the shooting community's culture. Furthermore, (Moiseeva et al., 2021) delve into the popularization of shooting sports as a means of introducing young people to a healthy lifestyle, indicating the influence of media in shaping perceptions and promoting the sport.

Socialization into the culture of sports shooting is a dynamic process involving a combination of familial, peer, organizational, educational, and cultural influences. This journey imparts practical knowledge and instils a sense of identity, shared values, and belonging within the broader community of shooting enthusiasts.

Community and Belonging in Sports Shooting

Sports shooting can indeed serve as a powerful catalyst in fostering community and forging social bonds among individuals who share a passion for firearms and marksmanship. This sense of community is particularly pronounced within shooting clubs and organizations, where enthusiasts come together to engage in their shared interest. Understanding the dynamics of how sports shooting contributes to community and belonging involves exploring both the broader impact of the activity and the specific roles played by clubs and organizations.

The role of sports in fostering social capital and community bonds has been widely studied. Tonts (2005) highlights that sports, including shooting sports, can be used to foster new friendships and social connectivity, often across class, religious, and ethnic boundaries. Similarly, McElroy and Coley (2020) emphasize that shooting sports, like other sports, can serve as a platform for activism and contribute to political debates, indicating the broader impact of sports shooting beyond the individual level.

Furthermore, the specific role of shooting clubs and organizations in fostering community and social bonds is evident in the study by Nichols et al. (2012), which aims to re-evaluate the nature of bonding and bridging social capital in sports clubs. This study provides insights into how sports clubs, including shooting clubs, contribute to both bonding within the group and bridging with external networks, thereby enhancing social capital and community cohesion.

In addition, the study by Trinka et al. (2023) on bystander intervention to prevent firearm injury among 4-H shooting sports participants sheds light on the importance of understanding the broader impact of sports shooting, including addressing firearm-related risks and promoting safety within the community. This underscores the need for sports shooting organizations to not only foster community bonds but also address potential risks associated with firearms.

Role of Sports Shooting in Fostering Community and Social Bonds

Sports shooting can indeed foster a unique community where individuals bond over a shared interest in firearms and marksmanship, transcending demographic differences and bringing together people from diverse backgrounds (Trinka et al., 2023). The camaraderie and mutual understanding established through participating in shooting activities, whether at a range or during competitions, create a sense of unity among participants (Tamir, 2018). This sense of community is further reinforced by the role of sports shooting in identity construction, with athletes serving as prominent representatives of the community (Tamir, 2018).

The shooting community's concerns about the political climate and the perceived threat to shooting activities reflect the larger social and political issues surrounding shooting, which may be overlooked or unaddressed (Hillyard, 2007). Additionally, the memorialization of shooting incidents within the context of commercial sport may lead to the neglect of underlying social and political issues (Burroughs et al., 2019).

The cooperative nature of shooting sports, especially in team-based competitions, encourages teamwork, communication, and mutual support. Participants form bonds through shared challenges and achievements, fostering a sense of belonging to a larger community with a shared purpose. Whether engaging in recreational shooting or competitive events, individuals often find that the pursuit of excellence in marksmanship creates strong social ties.

Figure 24: 10 metre air rifle range in Thailand. B20180, CC BY-SA 3.0 <https://creative commons.org/licenses/by-sa/3.0>, via Wikimedia Commons.

The inclusivity of shooting sports is also evident in the 4-H program, where shooting sports are offered as part of the curriculum in states like Florida, emphasizing the widespread reach of shooting activities across different regions and communities (Benge et al., 2019).

The 4-H program, a youth development organization dedicated to young people aged 5 to 18, focuses on fostering personal growth and development in four key areas: head, heart, hands, and health. Renowned for its "learning by doing" approach, the program reaches youth through a network of local clubs, camps, and various educational initiatives.

Shooting sports constitute one of the diverse project areas within the 4-H program, aiming to instruct young individuals on firearm safety, marksmanship, and the responsible use of firearms in both recreational and competitive settings. This program creates a safe and structured environment where youth can learn and refine their skills under the guidance of certified instructors.

In states such as Florida, the 4-H shooting sports program offers a spectrum of disciplines, including archery, rifle, shotgun, and pistol. Each discipline follows a curriculum covering safety protocols, proper firearm handling, marksmanship fundamentals, and the ethical use of firearms for recreational purposes.

Key features of the 4-H shooting sports program in states like Florida encompass certified instructors who undergo specialized training to teach youth about shooting sports, ensuring proper guidance and supervision. Safety is a paramount focus, with participants learning the importance of adhering to safety procedures, using protective gear, and practicing responsible behaviour around firearms.

Emphasizing skill development across various shooting disciplines, the program allows participants to progress from basic techniques to advanced skills based on their interests and commitment. While introducing youth to the competitive aspects of shooting sports, the program equally underscores the recreational and lifelong aspects. Participants can opt for personal enjoyment or pursue competitive opportunities based on their preferences.

Beyond marksmanship, the 4-H shooting sports program seeks to instil essential life skills such as responsibility, discipline, teamwork, and sportsmanship, contributing to holistic participant development. The program values inclusivity, creating an environment where youth from diverse backgrounds can engage in shooting sports, accommodating different skill levels and abilities.

Participation in the shooting sports program is typically voluntary, requiring parental consent. The program operates with a steadfast commitment to safety, education, and positive youth development. Participants often have opportunities to showcase their skills at local, regional, and national competitions organized by 4-H.

In states like Florida, the 4-H shooting sports program aligns with the broader mission of the organization—to empower youth with the skills and knowledge needed to become confident, responsible, and engaged citizens.

Contribution of Shooting Clubs and Organizations to a Sense of Belonging

Shooting clubs and organizations play a crucial role in fostering a sense of community and camaraderie within the sports shooting community. These entities provide a structured environment for enthusiasts to come together, share experiences, and learn from one another, ultimately contributing to the development of lasting friendships and social interactions. emphasize that sports clubs serve as a hub for social integration, where both individual and organizational factors contribute to fostering a sense of belonging and community (Elmose-Østerlund et al., 2019). Furthermore, the study by highlights that participation in sport clubs is associated with a sense of attachment to the community, indicating the social significance of these clubs (Lower-Hoppe et al., 2020).

The historical origins of shooting societies can be traced back to medieval and early modern times, where these groups initially organized into civic militias to undertake policing and defence functions in German and European villages and towns. This historical context underscores the deep-rooted tradition of community defence and sociability within shooting associations, further emphasizing their role in fostering a sense of belonging and shared purpose among members.

Within shooting clubs, individuals are not only exposed to the technical aspects of shooting but also to the cultural and ethical dimensions of the community. Clubs often organize regular meetings, training sessions, and social events, fostering a supportive environment where members feel valued and understood. The mentorship relationships that often emerge within these organizations contribute significantly to newcomers' sense of belonging, as experienced shooters guide and integrate them into the community.

Shooting organizations often promote a sense of identity among their members, reinforcing shared values and traditions. This shared identity contributes to a collective sense of pride and camaraderie, fostering a deep connection among individuals who share a passion for sports shooting. Clubs and organizations, through their activities and outreach efforts, contribute to creating a space where individuals feel they belong, fostering a strong sense of community within the broader shooting culture.

Sports shooting serves as a powerful catalyst for community building, bringing individuals together through a shared passion for firearms and marksmanship. The role of shooting clubs and organizations in this process is instrumental, providing structured environments, fostering mentorship, and promoting a shared identity that contributes to a strong sense of belonging within the sports shooting community. Moreover, Månsson et al. (2017) conducted a controlled study on the influence of participation in target-shooting sport for children with inattentive, hyperactive, and impulsive symptoms, indicating the positive impact of sports shooting on children's development and well-being. This supports the idea that sports shooting can provide a structured environment and foster mentorship, contributing to a strong sense of belonging within the community.

Inclusivity

Shooting stands out as a sport that can foster unity without regard to gender, physique, age, or physical condition. It exemplifies inclusivity, extending a welcoming environment for diverse participants to engage in various competitions, thereby enriching the sport and challenging societal boundaries (Benčina, 2022). Nevertheless, the gender dynamics within sports shooting represent a complex interplay of societal expectations, historical influences, and evolving perspectives on gender roles. Traditionally perceived as a male-dominated activity, sports shooting has been influenced by historical associations between firearms and masculinity (Khan et al., 2022). This historical association has led to the alignment of gender roles within the community with stereotypical expectations, positioning men as more naturally inclined towards firearms proficiency (Khan et al., 2022). These stereotypes manifest in assumptions about women lacking interest in shooting and expectations that men should excel in marksmanship (Khan et al., 2022). Societal norms regarding femininity and masculinity may also influence the types of firearms and shooting disciplines individuals are encouraged to pursue, creating potential barriers for those who do not conform to traditional expectations (Jeanes et al., 2020).

Figure 25: Gender inclusive – Woman at shooting range with Instructor. Photo by Remy Gieling on https://unsplash.com/photos/two-women-are-aiming-a-gun-at-a-target-AHK7 uOwb4Aw, Unsplash.

Gender influences individuals' involvement in sports shooting through various channels. Societal expectations and stereotypes may discourage women from entering the sport, contributing to a gender gap in participation (Jeanes et al., 2020). Additionally, access to firearms and shooting ranges, influenced by cultural attitudes towards gender, economic factors, and legal regulations, can impact women's participation rates (Khan et al., 2022). The underrepresentation of men and women within the sports shooting community is noticeable in competitive shooting events, leadership positions within shooting organizations, and visibility in media coverage (Jeanes et al., 2020). This lack of representation reinforces stereotypes and may deter women from considering sports shooting as a viable and inclusive pursuit (Jeanes et al., 2020).

Individual experiences within the sports shooting community are shaped by gender dynamics. Women who participate may encounter challenges such as bias, stereotypes, or microaggressions (Marshall et al., 2022). The availability of female-focused training programs, mentorship opportunities, and supportive networks significantly impact women's experiences in sports shooting, fostering a more inclusive and empowering environment (Marshall et al., 2022).

Efforts to address gender dynamics within sports shooting involve challenging stereotypes, promoting inclusivity, and advocating for equal opportunities (Jeanes et al., 2020). Creating awareness about diverse experiences and accomplishments within the shooting community contributes to a more inclusive culture that welcomes participants regardless of gender (Jeanes et al., 2020). Initiatives focused on breaking down gender-related barriers, improving representation, and fostering supportive networks can contribute to a more equitable and diverse sports shooting community (Marshall et al., 2022).

Gender Equality is a distinctive feature of shooting, with a historical commitment to fostering gender parity. Despite being traditionally considered male-dominated, the sport has evolved significantly. Catherine Woodring marked a milestone in 1937 by becoming the first woman to participate in an open world championship, contributing to the USA's gold win in the 50 m rifle prone team event (Benčina, 2022). The International Shooting Sport Federation (ISSF) recognized its events as 'mixed' in 1966, allowing women to participate alongside men. In 1980, the ISSF Women's Committee was established, leading to the addition of three women's events in the Olympic Games Programme in 1984. Achieving gender balance, the ISSF World Cup now features six men's events, six women's events, and three mixed team events (Benčina, 2022).

Shooting demonstrates an unusual equality in which the results of men and women are directly comparable. A recent comparison from the Cairo 2022 World Cup illustrates this parity, with both genders achieving similar scores in events such as the 50 m 3 positions (Benčina, 2022).

Inclusion of Persons with Disabilities is a prominent aspect of shooting para sport, featured in the Paralympic Games since 1976 (Benčina, 2022). With 13 Paralympic events, seven are open to both women and men, three exclusively to women, and three to men. Adaptations in the rulebook accommodate athletes with varying disabilities, categorized into three groups: shooting without support, shooting with support, and visually impaired shooting. Modifications to equipment, such as the use of a spring-tension stand for those unable to support the rifle independently, facilitate inclusivity (Benčina, 2022).

Figure 26: Athletes compete in the kneeling phase of the 3-Position rifle match at the 2023 Welsh 50 Metre Championship. Para athletes are visible in the foreground, shooting from wheelchairs. Hemmers, CC BY-SA 4.0 <https://creativecommons.org/licenses/by-sa/4.0> , via Wikimedia Commons.

A Sport to Enjoy in All Ages, shooting contrasts with sports like gymnastics, as it accommodates participants of all ages, even at the highest competition levels (Benčina, 2022). The absence of sport-related injuries, coupled with the ability to mitigate age-related challenges through equipment adjustments, makes shooting accessible to individuals of varying ages. Furthermore, the sport places a premium on experience, making it a pursuit where participants can find a discipline to enjoy, whether recreationally or competitively (Benčina, 2022).

The exploration of race and ethnicity within the sports shooting community reveals a multifaceted interplay of cultural influences, historical contexts, and contemporary challenges. To comprehend racial and ethnic dynamics, it is crucial to delve into the existing landscape of diversity, representation, and inclusivity within the realm of sports shooting.

Within the sports shooting community, there is a diverse range of participants from various racial and ethnic backgrounds, akin to many other recreational and competitive pursuits. Historical and cultural factors have contributed to nuanced dynamics, where associations between firearms and specific communities may influence participation trends. The cultural significance of shooting sports in certain regions or communities adds layers to the varied representation within the sports shooting landscape.

Despite the presence of individuals from diverse racial and ethnic backgrounds engaging in sports shooting, challenges related to inclusivity and representation persist. Factors such as access to resources, cultural perceptions of firearms, and historical associations with marksmanship may impact the extent to which different racial and ethnic groups participate. Addressing these dynamics requires a comprehensive understanding of existing barriers and a commitment to fostering a welcoming and inclusive environment for all participants.

Issues related to diversity, representation, and inclusivity within sports shooting manifest in various ways. Diversity concerns often arise from historical associations, perpetuated stereotypes, and differing levels of access to resources among participants. Initiatives to enhance diversity focus on promoting access to training, facilities, and education about sports shooting across different communities, aiming to break down barriers and encourage participation from individuals of all racial and ethnic backgrounds.

The representation of diverse racial and ethnic groups within sports shooting may vary, leading to disparities in visibility and opportunities. This underrepresentation can contribute to the perpetuation of stereotypes and hinder the growth of a more inclusive community. Initiatives aimed at improving representation involve highlighting the accomplishments and contributions of individuals from diverse backgrounds, showcasing the breadth of talent within the sports shooting community.

Inclusivity in sports shooting necessitates creating an environment where individuals from all racial and ethnic backgrounds feel welcome and valued. Addressing potential biases, fostering cultural awareness, and providing equal opportunities for participation are integral to achieving inclusivity. Inclusive practices encompass outreach programs, cultural competency training, and mentorship initiatives actively working to break down barriers and ensure that individuals from diverse backgrounds can fully engage in sports shooting without facing discrimination or exclusion.

Economic Factors

Exploring the economic aspects of sports shooting involves a comprehensive analysis of the financial considerations associated with equipment, training, and participation. These factors play a crucial role in shaping the accessibility and inclusivity of shooting sports, making it essential to understand how economic considerations may impact individuals' ability to engage in this recreational and competitive activity.

Sports shooting often requires specialized equipment, including firearms, ammunition, safety gear, and accessories. The cost of this equipment can vary significantly based on factors such as the type of firearm, its specifications, and the quality of accessories. For example, competitive shooters may invest in precision rifles, high-quality optics, and specialized ammunition, contributing to higher overall costs. Understanding the economic implications of acquiring and maintaining this equipment is vital for individuals considering participation in sports shooting.

Figure 27: Trap shooting at Kokkovuori shooting range, Finland. Elina Eskola, CC BY 3.0 <https://creativecommons.org/licenses/by/3.0>, via Wikimedia Commons.

The average cost of a gun around the world can vary significantly, taking into account factors such as the type of firearm, its intended purpose, brand, and adherence to local regulations. These cost variations apply broadly, and it's important to recognize that the following figures are rough estimates in US Dollars using US pricing, subject to change over time.

When it comes to handguns, including pistols and revolvers, the pricing spectrum reflects different tiers. Entry-level handguns are typically priced in the range of $200 to $500, while mid-tier options may extend from $500 to $1,000. Premium or specialized handguns, characterized by advanced features or brand reputation, can command prices starting at $1,000 and above.

For rifles, the cost differentiation follows a similar pattern. Basic rifles, suitable for general purposes, often initiate the pricing at approximately $300 to $500. Mid-tier rifles, designed for versatility and wider applications, can fall within the $500 to $1,500 range. Specialized or high-performance rifles, exceeding the $1,500 threshold, cater to specific needs and may extend to several thousand dollars.

Shotguns, including entry-level models, generally range between $200 and $500. Mid-tier shotguns, offering enhanced features or build quality, often come with price tags spanning from $500 to $1,500. High-quality or specialized shotguns, characterized by advanced craftsmanship or unique functionalities, can surpass the $1,500 mark.

In the category of assault rifles and tactical firearms, prices can exhibit considerable variability. Military-style firearms, including civilian versions of military rifles, can be priced at over $1,000, depending on factors like brand recognition and specific features.

It is essential to note that these estimations are general and subject to influence from diverse factors such as the prevailing gun laws in a country, import/export regulations, and the local demand for firearms. Additional costs related to firearm accessories, ammunition, and licensing fees contribute to the overall expense of gun ownership. Moreover, the dynamic nature of the firearms market, coupled with political developments and regulatory changes, can introduce fluctuations in prices. Individuals seeking accurate and up-to-date pricing information are advised to consult with local gun dealers, manufacturers, or authorized sellers in their specific region.

The worldwide average cost of firearms can vary significantly, influenced by factors such as firearm type, purpose, brand, and local regulations (Buck, 2022). Generally, handguns, including pistols and revolvers, span a range from $200 to $800. Concealed carry pistols, a subset of handguns, typically fall around the $500 mark. Hunting rifles, among the most popular, tend to cost around $700, with high-selling shotguns averaging approximately $600. AR-15 rifles, a distinct category, are commonly sold for about $750 (Buck, 2022).

For hunting rifles, various models are available at different price points. Options like the Savage Axis and TC Compass start at around $350, offering functional performance, although with potential variations in quality (Buck, 2022). Moving up the scale, rifles like the Ruger American at $425 provide better accuracy and triggers. Higher-end choices like the Springfield 2020 Waypoint at $2100 offer top-tier features such as a carbon stock and barrel (Buck, 2022).

Recommendations for hunting rifles within specific price ranges are outlined by Buck (2022). Under $500, the Ruger American Predator is suggested for its reliability and decent features. The CVA Cascade, priced under $600, is considered an upgrade with a cerakoted barrel and improved stock. The Bergara B-14 Ridge, under $800, hits a sweet spot with durability, reliability, and accuracy, surpassing some pricier alternatives (Buck, 2022).

AR-15 rifles, categorized by various models, range in price from $550 for the Anderson AM-15, known for its affordability and functionality, to $2500 for advanced options like the Desert Tec MDR, offering high accuracy and a compact design (Buck, 2022). The cost analysis suggests that between $500 and $750, one can acquire a basic AR, while the $1000 range introduces more durable, reliable options with enhanced features.

Shotguns, ranging from $240 for the Mossberg Maverik 88 to $2000 for the high-end Beretta M4, display variations in design and functionality (Buck, 2022). The average cost for shotguns among hunters is $500, with $700 to $1000 being a common price range. Sport shooters may opt for more aesthetically pleasing shotguns, while hunters prioritize ruggedness (Buck, 2022).

Handguns, including models like the Hi Point C9 at $180 and the Colt Python at $2000, cater to various budgets and preferences. Recommendations are offered based on price ranges, such as the Ruger American at under $200 for dependability and the Sig Cross at under $1600 for a revolutionary platform with a folding stock (Buck, 2022).

In the realm of 22 Rimfire firearms, prices range from $170 for the Heritage Rough Rider revolver to $460 for the Ruger Precision Rimfire bolt-action rifle (Buck, 2022). Generally, most 22lr guns cost under $350, with the popular Ruger 10/22 and Marlin 60 being cost-effective choices. High-end competition rifles may reach $1000 to $2000, but the majority of 22lr guns are available for under $400 (Buck, 2022).

Key considerations for buyers include knowing their budget, intended use, and seeking recommendations for reliable brands (Buck, 2022).

The cost of ammunition is subject to significant variation based on several factors, including the calibre, type (e.g., handgun, rifle, shotgun), and brand. Moreover, market conditions, availability, and regional influences can exert considerable impact on prices. While the following examples offer a general overview, again based on US pricing, it is important to bear in mind that prices are subject to fluctuation.

Handgun Ammunition: The 9mm Luger (9x19mm) represents a common and widely used calibre, with prices typically ranging from $0.20 to $0.40 per round. In contrast, the .45 ACP, a larger calibre often employed in handguns, generally commands prices between $0.30 and $0.50 per round. The .380 ACP, a smaller calibre commonly utilized in compact handguns, exhibits price variations from $0.25 to $0.45 per round.

Rifle Ammunition: The .223 Remington/5.56mm NATO, which serves as the standard for many AR-15 rifles, may be priced between $0.25 and $0.50 per round. On the other hand, the .308 Winchester/7.62mm NATO, commonly used in larger rifles, can exhibit price fluctuations from $0.40 to $1.00 per round.

Shotgun Ammunition: The 12 Gauge, a widely used shotgun shell, typically ranges from $0.20 to $0.50 per shell. In comparison, the 20 Gauge, which is smaller than the 12 gauge, generally commands prices between $0.25 and $0.60 per shell.

Rimfire Ammunition: The .22 LR (Long Rifle), popular for plinking and target shooting, may be priced between $0.05 and $0.15 per round.

Specialized or Premium Ammunition: Hollow Point (HP) or Self-Defence Rounds, which feature design elements tailored for self-defence, often command higher prices than standard ammunition, with costs ranging from $0.50 to $2.00 per round.

Access to proper training is important for safe and effective participation in sports shooting. Training programs, led by certified instructors, may incur additional expenses. Training costs can encompass fees for courses, range time, and the use of facilities. Individuals seeking advanced training or specialized coaching may face higher expenses. The economic considerations associated with training highlight the financial commitment required to develop the skills necessary for sports shooting.

Beyond equipment and training, there are costs associated with participating in shooting events and competitions. Entry fees, travel expenses, accommodation, and additional costs related to competition-specific requirements contribute to the overall cost of participation. Competitive sports shooting, in particular, may demand a significant financial investment, influencing individuals' decisions to engage in this aspect of the sport.

Socio-economic factors play a crucial role in shaping access to and participation in shooting sports. These factors encompass a wide range of economic and social variables that can either facilitate or hinder individuals' involvement in sports shooting. Research has shown that socio-economic status, gender, age, motivational factors, availability of sports infrastructure, and government support are significant determinants of sports participation (Downward et al., 2014; Hallmann & Breuer, 2012; Scheerder et al., 2005). Additionally, the level of education or income has been identified as one of the strongest correlates of different energy balance-related behaviours, including sports participation (Jensen et al., 2012). Furthermore, the relationship between sports participation and socio-economic factors has been highlighted as an area needing further examination, particularly concerning minority and majority youth (Strandbu et al., 2017). Moreover, the effects of socio-economic background have been confirmed to influence social integration in sports clubs (Elmose-Østerlund et al., 2019).

In the context of shooting sports, the cost of participation and access to resources such as firearms and shooting facilities are influenced by socio-economic factors. For instance, the cost of measuring the performance of Olympic sport shooters using various technologies, including electronic targets and mobile phone applications, varies based on economic considerations (Mon-López & Tejero-González, 2019). Furthermore, the presence of shooting sports organizations at educational institutions has been linked to political implications, indicating that shooting sports are not solely leisure activities but also have significant socio-political dimensions (McElroy & Coley, 2020).

In the context of firearms ownership and usage, socio-economic factors have been found to be influential. Firearms suicides have been linked to rural living and ownership profiles, where a significant proportion of guns are owned by individuals involved in game and sport shooting (Sarma & Kola, 2010). Additionally, tragic events related to firearms usage have prompted evaluations of youth access to and usage of firearms, reflecting the broader socio-economic and safety considerations associated with shooting sports (White & Smith, 2014).

Economic considerations directly impact the affordability of sports shooting for individuals from different socio-economic backgrounds. High costs associated with equipment, training, and participation may limit access for those with limited financial resources. Affordability becomes a critical factor in determining the inclusivity of sports shooting within diverse communities.

Socio-economic status often correlates with educational and employment opportunities. Individuals with higher socio-economic status may have greater access to resources, including the financial means to pursue sports shooting as a recreational or competitive activity. Conversely, economic disparities may limit opportunities for those with lower socio-economic status, impacting their ability to engage in the sport.

Socio-economic factors also influence geographic accessibility to shooting ranges and facilities. Individuals in economically disadvantaged areas may face challenges in accessing suitable training grounds or ranges, limiting their exposure and participation in sports shooting. This geographic disparity adds another layer to the socio-economic dynamics of the sport.

Cultural perceptions related to socio-economic factors can influence how sports shooting is perceived within different communities. In some cases, there may be cultural attitudes that either promote or discourage participation based on socio-economic considerations. Understanding and addressing these perceptions are essential for fostering a more inclusive and diverse sports shooting community.

Economic factors are integral to understanding the dynamics of sports shooting. The cost of equipment, training, and participation, coupled with socio-economic considerations, significantly shapes the accessibility and inclusivity of the sport. Addressing these economic factors is crucial for creating a more equitable and diverse environment within the sports shooting community.

Politics and Legislation in Sports Shooting

The intricate connection between sports shooting and the political landscape is characterized by lobbying efforts, legislative influences, and the profound impact of gun control policies and regulations (McElroy & Coley, 2020). This examination of the political dimensions of sports shooting reveals a complex interplay between the rights of firearm enthusiasts, considerations for public safety, and the broader socio-political context.

Within the political dimensions, advocacy, representation, and lobbying efforts by groups and organizations shape policies impacting sports shooting. Pro-gun advocacy groups, exemplified by entities like the National Rifle Association (NRA) in the United States, actively participate in influencing lawmakers, ensuring that the interests of sports shooters are considered in legislative decisions.

Lobbying efforts in the domain of sports shooting are strategically aimed at influencing legislation in favour of gun rights and the interests of sports shooting enthusiasts. Organizations engaged in lobbying articulate the perspectives of their members, emphasizing the recreational and competitive aspects of sports shooting while advocating for policies that protect individuals' rights to own and use firearms responsibly.

Legislative decisions regarding firearms and sports shooting undergo ongoing debate and negotiation. Lawmakers grapple with the challenge of balancing the interests of sports shooters with broader concerns related to public safety and gun violence prevention. The influence of lobbying efforts and the alignment of legislators with pro-gun or gun control ideologies significantly impact the development of legislation that regulates sports shooting activities.

The direct and consequential impact of gun control policies and regulations on sports shooting is undeniable. These policies, ranging from background checks to restrictions on firearm types and capacities, shape the operational parameters for sports shooters. The stringency of gun control measures varies globally, with different countries implementing diverse approaches to balance individual rights with public safety concerns.

The impact of gun control policies and regulations on sports shooting is a complex and multifaceted issue that varies globally. Hemenway et al. (2018) found a strong association between household gun ownership and fatal shootings of civilians armed with guns, indicating that firearm availability influences fatal shootings. Additionally, (Rogowski & Tucker, 2018) examined the effect of major events, such as mass shootings, on support for public policies and found that events like the Sandy Hook Elementary School shooting can significantly impact public attitudes towards gun control. Furthermore, (Kantack & Paschall, 2019) highlighted that mass shootings increase the salience of the issue of gun violence, providing an opportunity for entrepreneurs in the gun control policy stream to pursue their policy goals.

Luca et al. (2019) presented three main findings about the impact of mass shootings on gun policy, emphasizing the direct influence of such events on shaping gun policies. This is further supported by Hurka and Nebel (2013), who analysed discourse networks following shooting rampages in different countries and found that these events led to varying levels of change in gun policies, indicating a direct impact on policy change.

The three main findings about the impact of mass shootings on gun policy, as presented by Luca et al. (2019), are significant in understanding the direct influence of such events on shaping gun policies. Firstly, Luca et al. (2019) highlighted that mass shootings lead to increased public support for gun control measures. This finding is supported by the work of (Rogowski & Tucker, 2018), who emphasized that critical events, such as mass shootings, can significantly impact public attitudes towards gun control. Secondly, Luca et al. (2019) indicated that mass shootings result in changes in gun policies. This is further corroborated by Kantack and Paschall (2019), who found that mass shootings increase the salience of the issue of gun violence, providing an opportunity for entrepreneurs in the gun control policy stream to pursue their policy goals. Lastly, Luca et al. (2019) suggested that the intensity of mass shootings influences the stringency of gun control measures. This aligns with the study by , which demonstrated a strong association between household gun ownership and fatal shootings of civilians armed with guns, indicating that firearm availability influences fatal shootings. Therefore, these findings collectively underscore the direct impact of mass shootings on shaping gun policies, including increased public support for gun control, changes in gun policies, and the influence of the intensity of mass shootings on the stringency of gun control measures.

The implementation of gun control policies can yield both positive and negative effects on sports shooting. While regulations prioritizing safety measures and responsible firearm ownership contribute to a safer environment for participants and the broader community, overly restrictive measures may limit access to certain firearms or impose onerous requirements, impacting the ability of sports shooters to engage in their chosen activities.

The political dimensions of sports shooting vary significantly on a global scale. Countries with a strong tradition of firearm ownership and sports shooting may adopt more permissive regulations, while others with stricter gun control policies may place additional restrictions on sports shooting activities. Understanding these global perspectives provides insights into the diverse ways in which politics and legislation intersect with sports shooting.

Politics and legislation surrounding sports shooting are undeniably influenced by public opinion and perception. Shifts in societal attitudes towards firearms and sports shooting can drive changes in legislation. Public debates, media coverage, and high-profile incidents involving firearms can sway public opinion, prompting lawmakers to revisit and revise existing gun control policies.

Deviance and Controversies in Sports Shooting

Controversies and instances of deviance within the sports shooting community present challenges that test the norms and ethical standards of the participants. These issues can span from minor disputes overrule interpretations during competitions to more serious matters like illegal practices, cheating, or unethical conduct by individuals. Such instances of deviance create tension within the community, sparking debates on topics such as fair play, sportsmanship, and the overall integrity of the sport.

Ethical considerations form a cornerstone in the realm of sports shooting, influencing the conduct of participants and contributing to the overall culture of the community. These ethical dimensions include values such as fair competition, respect for opponents, adherence to rules and regulations, and responsible firearm use. Practices perceived as deviant, like doping or exploiting regulatory loopholes, are scrutinized as challenges to the ethical foundations of sports shooting (Hillyard & Burridge, 2012).

The impact of controversies and deviance resonates deeply within the sociology of sports shooting. These events shape the community's identity, influencing the perceptions participants hold of themselves and their peers. Ethical breaches often lead to the establishment or reinforcement of norms within the community. Moreover, the community's response to these challenges can significantly impact its reputation, shaping public perception and the level of support it receives.

Public opinion becomes a pivotal factor in shaping the perception of controversies within sports shooting. Instances of ethical lapses or controversies that garner widespread attention can influence the public's perception of the entire sports shooting community. Negative publicity may lead to increased scrutiny, calls for stricter regulations, or shifts in societal attitudes towards firearms and shooting sports. Conversely, positive responses can enhance the community's image and contribute to its broader acceptance.

The societal impact of controversies within sports shooting extends beyond the community itself. These events can influence public discourse on topics such as gun ownership, firearm regulations, and the role of shooting sports in society (Hillyard & Burridge, 2012). Societal debates may emerge regarding the delicate balance between individual freedoms, public safety, and the responsibilities of sports shooting enthusiasts. Such discussions contribute to the evolving landscape of firearms-related policies and societal attitudes.

Controversies often trigger a re-evaluation of existing regulations and governance structures within the sports shooting community. Instances of deviance may lead to calls for stricter rule enforcement, improved oversight, or changes in competition formats to prevent future ethical breaches. The community's response to controversies becomes instrumental in shaping internal governance mechanisms, reinforcing its commitment to maintaining ethical standards.

The cultural impact of controversies within sports shooting is substantial, influencing how shooting sports are perceived within the broader culture. Instances of deviance may contribute to the formation of stereotypes or reinforce existing biases about firearms enthusiasts. Positive responses to controversies, such as transparent investigations and decisive actions against unethical behaviour, play a role in contributing to the positive cultural representation of the sports shooting community (Hillyard & Burridge, 2012).

Deviance and controversies within the sports shooting community are integral aspects that deeply influence its sociology. Ethical considerations, controversies, and public opinion collectively shape the community's identity, impact its relationship with society, and contribute to ongoing discussions about the role of sports shooting in contemporary culture. Addressing these challenges requires a nuanced understanding of the ethical dimensions involved and a commitment to maintaining the integrity of the sport.

Health and Well-being in Sports Shooting

Sports shooting involves physical activities that contribute to various aspects of physical health. The precision and control required for accurate shooting enhance hand-eye coordination, fine motor skills, and overall body awareness. Maintaining a stable shooting stance and controlling breathing during shooting can contribute to improved muscular strength and endurance. Regular participation may be seen as a form of low-impact physical exercise engaging various muscle groups.

Mental aspects in sports shooting are crucial, requiring concentration, focus, and mental discipline for success. Athletes must manage stress, control anxiety during competitions, and maintain composure. The meditative nature of precision shooting can contribute to stress reduction and mental well-being, although the pressure of competition may pose challenges for some participants.

Participation in shooting sports can positively contribute to overall well-being. Engaging in a sport that combines physical and mental skills provides a sense of accomplishment and satisfaction. The camaraderie within shooting communities fosters social connections, contributing to emotional well-being. The structured nature of sports shooting, including training routines and goal-setting, can bring purpose and routine to participants' lives.

Despite potential benefits, there are associated risks in sports shooting. The use of firearms introduces safety considerations, and accidents can lead to severe injuries. Noise from shooting may impact hearing, necessitating protection. The intense focus on precision and performance may contribute to stress, anxiety, or performance-related mental health challenges.

Figure 28: A shooter in the indoor firearm lanes at H&H Shooting Sports Complex wearing eye and ear protection. Shoop73, CC BY 3.0 <https://creativecommons.org/licenses/by/3.0>, via Wikimedia Commons.

Sports shooting accommodates various fitness levels, requiring specific physical skills like stability, strength, and flexibility. Its inclusivity allows individuals of different ages and fitness levels to participate, promoting a diverse and welcoming community.

Engaging in sports shooting develops skills such as marksmanship, gun handling, and adherence to safety protocols. These contribute to cognitive benefits, including enhanced focus, attention to detail, and decision-making. The mental discipline required in sports shooting can positively transfer to other aspects of life.

The focused and repetitive nature of shooting sports can serve as a form of mindfulness, promoting stress reduction and relaxation. However, the competitive nature introduces stressors, requiring recognition.

Ensuring the health and well-being of sports shooting participants emphasizes proper training and safety measures. Adequate training in firearm handling, adherence to safety protocols, and the use of protective gear are crucial elements in mitigating potential risks.

Individual differences play a significant role in how sports shooting affects health and well-being. Factors like age, physical condition, mental health history, and individual preferences should be considered. Tailoring training routines and ensuring a supportive community environment contribute to a holistic approach.

Sports shooting has multifaceted effects on participants' health and well-being. While offering physical and mental health benefits, there are potential risks that require careful consideration. Balancing positive aspects with safety measures, proper training, and individual considerations contributes to a comprehensive understanding of the sport's impact on health and well-being.

Balancing the Sociological Benefits of Sports Shooting and Hunting and the need for self-defence with Gun Control Policies

The intersection of sociological benefits derived from sports shooting and hunting with the need for effective gun control policies presents a complex challenge, as outlined throughout this book. As a basis, comprehensive education and training programs are essential for individuals interested in sports shooting and hunting. Emphasizing mandatory courses on firearm safety, responsible gun ownership, and ethical hunting practices can contribute to a more informed and responsible community. By ensuring that individuals possess the necessary knowledge and skills, the risk of accidents and misuse can be mitigated, thereby promoting a culture of safety and responsibility.

Strengthening and enforcing background checks is important to ensuring that individuals with a history of violence, mental health issues, or criminal activity are restricted from owning firearms. This measure enhances public safety by preventing potentially dangerous individuals from accessing weapons. By implementing rigorous background checks, the likelihood of firearms falling into the wrong hands is significantly reduced, thereby contributing to a safer society.

Implementing a licensing system that requires individuals to demonstrate their knowledge of firearm safety and usage before obtaining a license can contribute to responsible gun ownership. Additionally, promoting the registration of firearms ensures traceability and accountability. By requiring individuals to undergo a formal process to obtain a license and register their firearms, the authorities can better monitor and regulate the ownership and usage of firearms, thereby enhancing overall safety and accountability.

Enforcing laws that mandate safe storage practices is essential to prevent unauthorized access to firearms, particularly in households with children or individuals with mental health issues. This measure aims to reduce the risk of accidents and misuse. By promoting safe storage practices, the potential for unauthorized access to firearms is minimized, thereby contributing to a safer environment, especially in settings where there is a heightened risk of misuse.

Fostering a sense of community responsibility is important in promoting responsible firearm use. Encouraging sports shooting and hunting organizations to actively participate in their communities and establishing mentorship programs can contribute to a culture of safety and ethics. By engaging the community and promoting mentorship programs, a supportive environment can be created, where responsible firearm use is encouraged and upheld, thereby contributing to a culture of safety and ethical practices. Likewise, increasing public awareness about the positive aspects of sports shooting and hunting is crucial. Highlighting their cultural, recreational, and economic contributions can help dispel misconceptions and stereotypes surrounding firearm enthusiasts. By raising public awareness about the positive aspects of sports shooting and hunting, misconceptions and stereotypes can be addressed, leading to a more informed and balanced understanding of these activities within the broader society.

Implementing measures to regulate and monitor the sale of ammunition, ensuring accessibility only to individuals with valid licenses, is an important step. Consideration of limits on the quantity of ammunition that can be purchased within a specified time period adds an extra layer of control. By regulating the sale of ammunition and imposing limits on its quantity, the potential for misuse and unauthorized access to ammunition can be minimized, thereby contributing to enhanced overall safety.

Exploring the integration of technology, such as smart gun technology, can enhance firearm safety and reduce the risk of unauthorized use. Technological advancements may offer additional safeguards in preventing accidents and misuse. By embracing technological advancements, such as smart gun technology, the potential for enhancing firearm safety and reducing the risk of unauthorized use can be realized, thereby contributing to a safer environment for firearm ownership and usage.

Engaging in open dialogues with sports shooting and hunting communities, as well as gun control advocacy groups, is essential. Finding common ground and developing policies that address concerns from all perspectives promotes inclusivity and effective regulation. By fostering open dialogues and collaboration with diverse stakeholders, policies can be developed that take into account a wide range of perspectives, thereby promoting inclusivity and effective regulation that addresses the needs and concerns of various stakeholders.

Establishing policies that can adapt to evolving societal needs and advancements in technology is imperative. Regularly evaluating the effectiveness of gun control policies and making adjustments based on their impact on public safety and the sociological benefits of sports shooting and hunting ensures ongoing improvement and relevance. By ensuring that policies are adaptable and subject to regular evaluation, the potential for addressing evolving societal needs and technological advancements can be realized, thereby ensuring ongoing improvement and relevance in the context of gun control policies.

The issue of balancing the need for firearm ownership for self-defence with gun control policies is a complex and contentious one. Crafting regulations that ensure public safety while respecting individual rights requires a nuanced and multi-faceted approach. This book explored various considerations in achieving this balance, including background checks and screening, training and education, licensing and registration, safe storage requirements, red flag laws, limitations on firearm types, community policing and engagement, strict enforcement of existing laws, mental health support, public awareness campaigns, and research and data analysis.

One of the key considerations in balancing firearm ownership for self-defence with gun control policies is the implementation of thorough background checks to screen for individuals with a history of violence, domestic abuse, or mental health issues. Research has shown that individuals with a history of violence or domestic abuse are at a higher risk of using firearms for harmful purposes. Additionally, establishing a waiting period to allow for a comprehensive review of applicants before they can obtain a firearm can minimize the risk of impulsive decisions, thereby contributing to public safety.

Mandating comprehensive training programs on firearm safety and self-defence for individuals seeking to own a firearm is another important aspect of balancing firearm ownership with gun control policies. Research has indicated that proper training in firearm safety can reduce the risk of accidental shootings and misuse of firearms. Emphasizing ongoing education to ensure gun owners are well-informed about the responsible use and storage of firearms can further contribute to enhancing public safety.

Requiring a license for firearm ownership, which could involve a demonstration of proficiency in firearm use and understanding of self-defence laws, is an important regulatory measure. Additionally, implementing a registration system to track firearm ownership can aid law enforcement in monitoring and regulating the distribution of firearms, thereby contributing to public safety.

Enforcing laws that mandate secure storage practices for firearms to prevent unauthorized access, especially in households with children or individuals with mental health concerns, is essential for minimizing the risk of firearm-related incidents. Promoting the use of gun safes and lockboxes can enhance security and prevent unauthorized use of firearms.

Implementing "red flag" laws that allow temporary firearm restrictions for individuals deemed a risk to themselves or others based on credible evidence is a proactive measure in balancing firearm ownership with public safety. Ensuring a fair and transparent process for individuals to challenge and appeal such restrictions is crucial for safeguarding individual rights while addressing potential risks associated with firearm ownership.

Considering restrictions on certain types of firearms that are deemed unnecessary for self-defence purposes is a contentious but important consideration. Evaluating and regulating high-capacity magazines and accessories that may contribute to the escalation of violence can be a crucial aspect of gun control policies aimed at enhancing public safety.

Encouraging community policing strategies to build trust between law enforcement and the community is an important aspect of gun control policies. Foster open communication to address concerns related to self-defence and work collaboratively to enhance public safety can contribute to a balanced approach that respects individual rights while prioritizing public safety. Further, strengthening the enforcement of existing gun control laws to ensure that individuals who pose a threat to public safety are promptly identified and addressed is crucial for maintaining public safety. This includes measures to prevent illegal firearm trafficking and possession.

Investing in mental health resources and support services to address the root causes of violence and promote overall community well-being is an important aspect of a comprehensive approach to balancing firearm ownership with public safety.

Conducting public awareness campaigns to educate firearm owners about responsible self-defence practices and the legal consequences of misuse can contribute to a culture of responsible firearm ownership and use.

Investing in research to analyse the impact of firearm ownership on self-defence and public safety is crucial for informing evidence-based policy decisions. Using data-driven insights to inform policy decisions and adjust regulations as needed is essential for maintaining an effective and balanced regulatory framework.

The complex challenge of reconciling sociological benefits from sports shooting and hunting with effective gun control policies prompts for an approach with emphasis on cultivating a culture of safety and responsibility through education, training, and stringent measures such as background checks, licensing systems, and safe storage requirements. Fostering community responsibility and increasing public awareness are also considered crucial to dispel misconceptions and stereotypes surrounding firearm enthusiasts. The integration of technology, exploration of smart gun technology, and open dialogues with stakeholders contribute to an adaptable regulatory framework that evolves with societal needs and technological advancements.

In the broader context of gun control policies, a balanced approach, scoring 40-52 on the Global Firearm Policy Spectrum, emerges as an ideal solution, acknowledging the cultural, social, and political context of a country. This approach seeks to strike a middle ground between permissiveness and restrictiveness, emphasizing reasonable regulations that prioritize public safety while respecting the rights of law-abiding citizens to own firearms. Background checks, waiting periods, and restrictions on certain firearms are integral components, and the effectiveness of these policies depends on robust enforcement, public support, and ongoing evaluation to align with the evolving needs of society. The concepts presented advocate for a comprehensive and adaptable approach to address the multifaceted aspects of gun control.

REFERENCES

Abelow, H., Crifasi, C. K., & Webster, D. (2020). The Legal and Empirical Case for Firearm Purchaser Licensing. *The Journal of Law Medicine & Ethics*.

Ajdacic-Gross, V., Killias, M., Hepp, U., Gadola, E., Bopp, M., Lauber, C., Schnyder, U., Gutzwiller, F., & Rössler, W. (2006). Changing Times: A Longitudinal Analysis of International Firearm Suicide Data. *American Journal of Public Health*.

Ak, S., & Fidelia, F. (2018). The International Cooperation to Eradicate Illicit Firearms Trafficking in Southeast Asian Region. *Sriwijaya Law Review*.

Aksoy, Y., Çankaya, S., & Taşmektepligil, M. Y. (2017). The Effects of Participating in Recreational Activities on Quality of Life and Job Satisfaction. *Universal Journal of Educational Research*.

Alleman, M. (2000). The Japanese Firearm and Sword Possession Control Law: Translator's Introduction. *9 Pac. Rim L & Pol'y J., 165*.

Allen, G., & Burton, M. (2022). *Firearm Crime Statistics: England & Wales*. H. o. C. Library.

Alpers, P., Pavesi, I., & Lovell, M. (2022). *Switzerland — Gun Facts, Figures and the Law*. School of Public Health, The University of Sydney. Retrieved 16/1/2024 from

Amnesty International. (2024). *Gun Violence*. Retrieved 9/1/2024 from

Andrés, A. R., & Hempstead, K. (2011). Gun Control and Suicide: The Impact of State Firearm Regulations in the United States, 1995–2004. *Health Policy*.

Andrés, A. R., & Hempstead, K. (2011). Gun control and suicide: The impact of state firearm regulations in the United States, 1995–2004. *Health Policy, 101*(1), 95-103.

Aneja, A., Donohue III, J. J., & Zhang, A. (2011). The impact of right-to-carry laws and the NRC report: lessons for the empirical evaluation of law and policy. *American Law and Economics Review*, *13*(2), 565-631.

Anestis, M. D., & Anestis, J. C. (2015). Suicide rates and state laws regulating access and exposure to handguns. *American Journal of Public Health*, *105*(10), 2049-2058.

Anestis, M. D., & Capron, D. W. (2017). Deadly Experience: The Association Between Firing a Gun and Various Aspects of Suicide Risk. *Suicide and Life-Threatening Behavior*.

Anestis, M. D., & Houtsma, C. (2017). The Association Between Gun Ownership and Statewide Overall Suicide Rates. *Suicide and Life-Threatening Behavior*.

Anguilano, N. (2018). Gun culture in Russia: How does it compare to the U.S.? *Russia Beyond, June, 2018*.

Anon. (2024, 17/1/2024). Gun politics in Russia (Right to Bear Arms). *Right to Bear Arms.*)

Arif, T., Roman, S., Saba, M., & Ali, I. (2022). Managing Sports: Exploring Innovative Strategies and Future Advancements. *Journal of Entrepreneurship Management and Innovation*.

Aronow, P. M., & Miller, B. (2016). Policy Misperceptions and Support for Gun Control Legislation. *The Lancet*.

Ashworth, T. R., & Kozinetz, C. A. (2021). The Mitigating Effect of Low Firearm Background Check Requirements on Firearm Homicides in Border States. *Journal of Injury and Violence Research*.

Ausman, J. I., & Faria, M. A. (2019). Is Gun Control Really About People Control? *Surgical Neurology International*.

Austin, K., & Lane, M. (2018). The Prevention of Firearm Injuries in Canadian Youth. *Paediatrics & Child Health*.

Austin, R. (2018). Civilians own 85% of world's 1bn firearms, survey reveals. *The Guardian*

Azad, H., Monuteaux, M. C., Rees, C. A., Siegel, M., Mannix, R., Lee, L. K., Sheehan, K., & Fleegler, E. W. (2020). Child Access Prevention Firearm Laws and Firearm Fatalities Among Children Aged 0 to 14 Years, 1991-2016. *Jama Pediatrics*.

Azrael, D., Cohen, J. S., Salhi, C., & Miller, M. (2018). Firearm Storage in Gun-Owning Households With Children: Results of a 2015 National Survey. *Journal of Urban Health*.

Azrael, D., Miller, M., & Hemenway, D. (2000). Are Household Firearms Stored Safely? It Depends on Whom You Ask. *Pediatrics*.

Bachmann, H. (2012, 20/12/2012). The Swiss Difference: A Gun Culture That Works. *Time*.

Bailey, H. M., Zuo, Y., Li, F., Min, J., Vaddiparti, K., Prosperi, M., Fagan, J., Galea, S., & Kalesan, B. (2019). Changes in Patterns of Mortality Rates and Years of Life Lost Due to Firearms in the United States, 1999 to 2016: A Joinpoint Analysis. *Plos One*.

Balakrishna, M., & Wilbur, K. C. (2021). How the Massachusetts Assault Weapons Ban Enforcement Notice Changed Firearm Sales. *SSRN Electronic Journal*.

Bandel, S. L., Bond, A., & Anestis, M. D. (2023). Interactions at the Point of Firearm Purchase and Subsequent Use of Locking Devices. *Injury epidemiology*.

Bankston, W. B., Thompson, C. Y., Jenkins, Q. A. L., & Forsyth, C. J. (1990). The Influence of Fear of Crime, Gender, and Southern Culture on Carrying Firearms for Protection. *Sociological Quarterly*.

Banwari, M. (2017). Twenty-Three Years (1993–2015) of Homicide Trends in the Transkei Region of South Africa. *Medicine Science and the Law*.

Barcellos, C., & Zaluar, A. (2014). Homicídios E Disputas Territoriais Nas Favelas Do Rio De Janeiro. *Revista De Saúde Pública*.

Barnard, L. M., McCarthy, M., Knoepke, C. E., Kaplan, S. H., Engeln, J., & Betz, M. E. (2021). Colorado's First Year of Extreme Risk Protection Orders. *Injury epidemiology*.

Barney, D. J., & Schaffner, B. F. (2019). Reexamining the Effect of Mass Shootings on Public Support for Gun Control. *British Journal of Political Science*.

Barnhorst, A., Gonzales, H., & Asif-Sattar, R. (2021). Suicide Prevention Efforts in the United States and Their Effectiveness. *Current Opinion in Psychiatry*.

BBC. (2021, 13/1/2024). Plymouth shooting: Who can own a firearm or shotgun in the UK? *BBC News*.

Beautrais, A. L., Fergusson, D. M., & Horwood, L. J. (2006). Firearms Legislation and Reductions in Firearm-Related Suicide Deaths in New Zealand. *Australian & New Zealand Journal of Psychiatry*.

Beidas, R. S., Rivara, F. P., & Rowhani-Rahbar, A. (2020). Safe Firearm Storage: A Call for Research Informed by Firearm Stakeholders. *Pediatrics*.

Bellesiles, M. A. (1998). Gun Laws in Early America: The Regulation of Firearms Ownership, 1607–1794. *Law and History Review*.

Benčina, S. (2022). *Inclusivity in Shooting Sport*. Retrieved 17/1/2024 from

Benge, M., Mendoza, G., & Israel, G. D. (2019). Assessing Risk Management Knowledge of Florida 4-H Professionals Relating to Shooting Sports. *Journal of Youth Development*.

Bennett, N., Karkada, M., Erdogan, M., & Green, R. S. (2022). The effect of legislation on firearm-related deaths in Canada: a systematic review. *Canadian Medical Association Open Access Journal, 10*(2), E500-E507.

Bennett, N., Karkada, M., Erdoğan, M., & Green, R. S. (2022). The Effect of Legislation on Firearm-Related Deaths in Canada: A Systematic Review. *Cmaj Open*.

Berlow, A. (2023). The Myth of the Responsible Gun Owner: An American Nightmare (Part II) *Washington Monthly*.

Berrigan, J., Azrael, D., Hemenway, D., & Miller, M. (2019). Firearms Training and Storage Practices Among US Gun Owners: A Nationally Representative Study. *Injury prevention*.

Berrigan, J., Azrael, D., & Miller, M. J. (2022). The Number and Type of Private Firearms in the United States. *The Annals of the American Academy of Political and Social Science*.

Black, J. (2022, 15/1/2024). Australia already has a national gun database – so why has a police shooting prompted calls for a new one?

Blau, B. M., Gorry, D., & Wade, C. (2016). Guns, Laws and Public Shootings in the United States. *Applied Economics*.

Blocher, J., Charles, J. D., & Miller, D. A. H. (2023). Firearms Law and History in a New Doctrinal Era.

Boaz, J. (2022). *Research suggests it is easier than ever for criminals to get guns illegally in Australia*. A. News.

Boine, C., Siegel, M., & Maiga, A. A. (2022). The Effectiveness of Value-Based Messages to Engage Gun Owners on Firearm Policies: A Three-Stage Nested Study. *Injury epidemiology*.

Boine, C., Siegel, M., Ross, C. S., Fleegler, E. W., & Alcorn, T. (2020). What Is Gun Culture? Cultural Variations and Trends Across the United States. *Humanities and Social Sciences Communications*.

Bonomi, A. E., Zeoli, A. M., Shanahan, S., & Martin, D. S. (2021). Saving Lives: Working Across Agencies and Individuals to Reduce Intimate Homicide Among Those at Greatest Risk. *Journal of Family Violence*.

Borba, A., & Gomes, A. d. O. (2021). The Attitude of Brazilian Federal Police Officers Towards Firearms. *Revista De Administração Pública*.

Borgogna, N. C., McDermott, R. C., & Brasil, K. M. (2022). The Precarious Masculinity of Firearm Ownership. *Psychology of Men & Masculinity*.

Brady United. (2024). *Key Statistics*. Retrieved 9/1/2028 from

Braga, A. A., & Pierce, G. L. (2005). Disrupting Illegal Firearms Markets in Boston: The Effects of Operation Ceasefire on the Supply of New Handguns to Criminals*. *Criminology & Public Policy*.

Branas, C. C., Han, S., & Wiebe, D. J. (2016). Alcohol Use and Firearm Violence. *Epidemiologic Reviews*.

Branas, C. C., Reeping, P. M., & Rudolph, K. E. (2021). Beyond Gun Laws—Innovative Interventions to Reduce Gun Violence in the United States. *Jama Psychiatry*.

Branas, C. C., Richmond, T. S., Culhane, D. P., Have, T. R. T., & Wiebe, D. J. (2009). Investigating the Link Between Gun Possession and Gun Assault. *American Journal of Public Health*.

Bräuer, J., Montolio, D., & Trujillo-Baute, E. (2016). How Do US State Firearms Laws Affect Firearms Manufacturing Location? An Empirical Investigation, 1986–2010. *Journal of Economic Geography*.

Bridi, C. (2023). Brazil's Lula places new restrictions on gun ownership, reversing predecessor's pro-gun policy. *AP News*.

Brown, P. (2016). Impact of Gun Law Reforms on Rates of Homicide, Suicide and Mass Shootings in Australia. *Evidence-Based Mental Health*.

Browne, B. (2019). *Hunters and collectors-Gun use and ownership in Australia*.

Brownlee, C. (2022). Gun Violence in 2022, By the Numbers. *The Trace, December, 2022*.

Brownstein, J. S., Nahari, A. D., & Reis, B. Y. (2020). Internet Search Patterns Reveal Firearm Sales, Policies, and Deaths. *NPJ Digital Medicine*.

Brueck, H. (2023). Switzerland has a stunningly high rate of gun ownership — here's why it doesn't have mass shootings. *Business Insider*.

Buck, J. (2022, 17/1/2024). How Much Do Typical Guns Cost? (Rifle, handgun, shotgun).

Burke, M., González, F., Baylis, P., Heft-Neal, S., Baysan, C., Basu, S., & Hsiang, S. (2018). Higher Temperatures Increase Suicide Rates in the United States and Mexico. *Nature Climate Change*.

Burroughs, B., Rugg, A., Becker, D. K., & Edgmon, M. (2019). #VegasStrong: Sport, Public Memorialization, and the Golden Knights. *Communication & Sport*.

Burrows, S., Auger, N., Gamache, P., & Hamel, D. (2013). Leading Causes of Unintentional Injury and Suicide Mortality in Canadian Adults Across the Urban-Rural Continuum. *Public Health Reports*.

Burton, A. L., Logan, M. W., Pickett, J. T., Cullen, F. T., Jonson, C. L., & Burton, V. S. (2021). Gun Owners and Gun Control: Shared Status, Divergent Opinions. *Sociological Inquiry*.

Bushman, B. J., Newman, K. S., Calvert, S. L., Downey, G., Dredze, M., Gottfredson, M. R., Jablonski, N. G., Masten, A. S., Morrill, C., Neill, D. B., Römer, D., & Webster, D. (2016). Youth Violence: What We Know and What We Need to Know. *American psychologist*.

Butts, J. A., Roman, C. G., Bostwick, L., & Porter, J. R. (2015). Cure Violence: A Public Health Model to Reduce Gun Violence. *Annual Review of Public Health*.

Caddick, A., & Porter, L. (2011). Exploring a Model of Professionalism in Multiple Perpetrator Violent Gun Crime in the UK. *Criminology & Criminal Justice*.

Callcut, R. A., Robles, A. J., Kornblith, L. Z., Plevin, R., & Mell, M. W. (2019). Effect of Mass Shootings on Gun Sales—A 20-Year Perspective. *Journal of Trauma and Acute Care Surgery*.

Cantor, C., & Slater, P. J. B. (1995). The Impact of Firearm Control Legislation on Suicide in Queensland: Preliminary Findings. *The Medical Journal of Australia*.

Caputi, T. L., Ayers, J. W., Dredze, M., Suplina, N., & Burd-Sharps, S. (2020). Collateral Crises of Gun Preparation and the COVID-19 Pandemic: Infodemiology Study. *Jmir Public Health and Surveillance*.

Carlsen, A., & Chinoy, S. (2019, 6 August, 2019). How to Buy a Gun in 16 Countries. *The New York Times*.

Carlson, J. (2013). States, Subjects and Sovereign Power: Lessons From Global Gun Cultures. *Theoretical Criminology*.

Carter, J., & Binder, M. (2016). Firearm Violence and Effects on Concealed Gun Carrying: Large Debate and Small Effects. *Journal of Interpersonal Violence*.

Castillo-Carniglia, Á., Kagawa, R. M. C., Webster, D., Vernick, J. S., Cerdá, M., & Wintemute, G. J. (2017). Comprehensive Background Check Policy and Firearm Background Checks in Three US States. *Injury prevention*.

Castillo, L. (2023). *Gun Violence In Europe Statistics [Fresh Research]*. Gitnux.

Celinska, K. (2007). Individualism and Collectivism in America: The Case of Gun Ownership and Attitudes Toward Gun Control. *Sociological Perspectives*.

Ceylan, H. H., McGowan, A., & Stringer, M. D. (2002). Air Weapon Injuries: A Serious and Persistent Problem. *Archives of Disease in Childhood*.

Chapman, S., Alpers, P., Agho, K., & Jones, M. (2015). Australia's 1996 Gun Law Reforms: Faster Falls in Firearm Deaths, Firearm Suicides, and a Decade Without Mass Shootings. *Injury prevention*.

Charbonneau, A. (2023a). *Effects of Background Checks on Violent Crime*. R. Corporation.

Charbonneau, A. (2023b). *Effects of Child-Access Prevention Laws on Violent Crime*. R. Corporation.

Charles, P. J. (2024). gun control. In *Encyclopedia Britannica*.

Cheema, R. (2023). Guns per Capita by Country Vs Crime Rate: Top 20 Countries. *Yahoo! Finance, July, 2023*.

Chen, T., & Yue, J. (2023). Reflections of Functional Training on Shooters' Grip Stability. *Revista Brasileira De Medicina Do Esporte*.

Cheng, C., & Hoekstra, M. (2013). Does strengthening self-defense law deter crime or escalate violence?: Evidence from expansions to castle doctrine. *Journal of Human Resources*, 48(3), 821-854.

Cheung, A., & Dewa, C. S. (2005). Current Trends in Youth Suicide and Firearms Regulations. *Can J Public Health*.

Cloud, L. K., Prood, N., & Ibrahim, J. (2022). Disarming Intimate Partner Violence Offenders: An in-Depth Descriptive Analysis of Federal and State Firearm Prohibitor Laws in the United States, 1991–2016. *Journal of Interpersonal Violence*.

Collins, T., Greenberg, R., Siegel, M., Xuan, Z., Rothman, E. F., Cronin, S., & Hemenway, D. (2018). State Firearm Laws and Interstate Transfer of Guns in the USA, 2006–2016. *Journal of Urban Health*.

Cook, P. J., & Ludwig, J. (2004). Does Gun Prevalence Affect Teen Gun Carrying After All?*. *Criminology*.

Cook, P. J., & Ludwig, J. (2006). The Social Costs of Gun Ownership. *Journal of Public Economics*.

Cook, P. J., & Ludwig, J. (2013). The limited impact of the Brady Act. *REDUCING GUN VIOLENCE*, 21.

Copelyn, J. (2022). *These gun laws saved 30 lives a month in two big cities. Here's what it could mean for SA.* B. C. f. H. Journalism.

Cortis, N. (2009). Social Inclusion and Sport: Culturally Diverse Women's Perspectives. *Australian Journal of Social Issues.*

Crifasi, C. K., Merrill-Francis, M., McCourt, A., Vernick, J. S., Wintemute, G. J., & Webster, D. W. (2018). Association between firearm laws and homicide in urban counties. *Journal of Urban Health, 95,* 383-390.

Crifasi, C. K., Meyers, J. S., Vernick, J. S., & Webster, D. W. (2015). Effects of changes in permit-to-purchase handgun laws in Connecticut and Missouri on suicide rates. *Preventive Medicine, 79,* 43-49.

Curcuruto, J. (2021, 12/1/2024). Target Shooting: A Range of Possibilities.

Dagkas, S. (2016). Problematizing Social Justice in Health Pedagogy and Youth Sport: Intersectionality of Race, Ethnicity, and Class. *Research Quarterly for Exercise and Sport.*

Dare, A., Holcroft, C., & Ahmed, N. (2023). Canada Risks Following the Path of the U.S. on Gun Violence. *Time.*

Dawson, J. (2019). Shall Not Be Infringed: How the NRA Used Religious Language to Transform the Meaning of the Second Amendment. *Palgrave Communications.*

DeGrazia, D. (2014). The Case for Moderate Gun Control. *Kennedy Institute of Ethics Journal.*

DeKeseredy, W. S. (2019). Intimate Violence Against Rural Women: The Current State of Sociological Knowledge. *International Journal of Rural Criminology.*

Dempsey, C. L., Benedek, D. M., Zuromski, K. L., Riggs-Donovan, C. A., Ng, T. H. H., Nock, M. K., Kessler, R. C., & Ursano, R. J. (2019). Association of Firearm Ownership, Use, Accessibility, and Storage Practices With Suicide Risk Among US Army Soldiers. *Jama Network Open.*

Diekert, F., Richter, A., Rivrud, I. M., & Mysterud, A. (2016). How Constraints Affect the Hunter's Decision to Shoot a Deer. *Proceedings of the National Academy of Sciences.*

Díez, C., Kurland, R. P., Rothman, E. F., Bair-Merritt, M., Fleegler, E., Xuan, Z., Galea, S., Ross, C. S., Kalesan, B., & Goss, K. A. (2017). State intimate partner violence–related firearm laws and intimate partner homicide rates in the United States, 1991 to 2015. *Annals of Internal Medicine, 167*(8), 536-543.

Dijk, J. v., Kesteren, J. v., & Smit, P. (2007). Criminal victimisation in international perspective.

Domagała, A. (2018). For and Against: Analysing the Determinants of Humanitarian Intervention. Libya (2011) and Syria (2011–2013) Compared. *Polish Political Science Review.*

Donohue III, J. J., & Levitt, S. D. (2001). The impact of legalized abortion on crime. *The Quarterly Journal of Economics, 116*(2), 379-420.

Donohue, J. J. (2022). The Effect of Permissive Gun Laws on Crime. *The Annals of the American Academy of Political and Social Science.*

Donohue, J. J., Aneja, A., & Weber, K. D. (2019). Right-to-carry laws and violent crime: A comprehensive assessment using panel data and a state-level synthetic control analysis. *Journal of Empirical Legal Studies, 16*(2), 198-247.

Doucette, M. L., Crifasi, C. K., & Frattaroli, S. (2019). Right-to-carry laws and firearm workplace homicides: a longitudinal analysis (1992–2017). *American Journal of Public Health, 109*(12), 1747-1753.

Downward, P., Lera-López, F., & Rasciute, S. (2014). The Correlates of Sports Participation in Europe. *European Journal of Sport Science.*

Durlauf, S. N., Navarro, S., & Rivers, D. A. (2016). Model uncertainty and the effect of shall-issue right-to-carry laws on crime. *European Economic Review, 81*, 32-67.

Edward, S. (2021). The Australian Gun-Control Narrative Just Isn't True. *NRA America's 1st Freedom.*

Edwards, G., Nesson, E., Robinson, J. J., & Vars, F. (2018). Looking down the barrel of a loaded gun: The effect of mandatory handgun purchase delays on homicide and suicide. *The Economic Journal, 128*(616), 3117-3140.

Edwards, S., & Koshan, J. (2023). Women Who Kill Abusive Men: The Limitations of Loss of Control, Provocation and Self-Defence in England and Wales and Canada. *The Journal of Criminal Law.*

Elmose-Østerlund, K., Seippel, Ø., Goig, R. L., Roest, J. W. v. d., Zwahlen, J. A., & Nagel, S. (2019). Social Integration in Sports Clubs: Individual and Organisational Factors in a European Context. *European Journal for Sport and Society.*

Emrich, E., Pitsch, W., Flatau, J., & Pierdzioch, C. (2012). Voluntary Engagement in Sports Clubs: A Behavioral Model and Some Empirical Evidence. *International Review for the Sociology of Sport.*

Engelbrecht, C., Blumenthal, R., Morris, N., & Saayman, G. (2017). Suicide in Pretoria: A Retrospective Review, 2007 - 2010. *South African Medical Journal*.

Etzersdorfer, E., Kapusta, N. D., & Sonneck, G. (2006). Suicide by Shooting Is Correlated to Rate of Gun Licenses in Austrian Counties. *Wiener Klinische Wochenschrift*.

Everytown Research & Policy. (2024). *Gun Safety Policies Save Lives: Which states have the ideal laws to prevent gun violence?*. Retrieved 10/1/2024 from

Faria, M. A. (2012). America, Guns and Freedom: Part II - An International Perspective. *Surgical Neurology International*.

Ferrazares, T., Sabia, J. J., & Anderson, D. M. (2021). Have U.S. Gun Buyback Programs Misfired?

Filindra, A. (2020). The Toughest Gun Control Law in the Nation: The Unfulfilled Promise of New York's SAFE Act. *Political Science Quarterly*.

Filindra, A., & Kaplan, N. (2017). Testing Theories of Gun Policy Preferences Among Blacks, Latinos, and Whites in America[*]. *Social Science Quarterly*.

Firearms (Amendment) Act 1997. (2013).

Fleegler, E. W., Lee, L. K., Monuteaux, M. C., Hemenway, D., & Mannix, R. (2013). Firearm Legislation and Firearm-Related Fatalities in the United States. *Jama Internal Medicine*.

Fleming, A. K., McLean, D. S., & Tatalovich, R. (2018). Debating Gun Control in Canada and the United States: <i>Divergent Policy Frames and Political Cultures</I>. *World Affairs*.

Fontanarosa, P. B., & Bibbins-Domingo, K. (2022). The Unrelenting Epidemic of Firearm Violence. *Jama*.

Foshee, V. A., Bauman, K. E., & Linder, G. F. (1999). Family Violence and the Perpetration of Adolescent Dating Violence: Examining Social Learning and Social Control Processes. *Journal of Marriage and Family*.

Fowler, K. A., Dahlberg, L. L., Haileyesus, T., & Annest, J. L. (2015). Firearm Injuries in the United States. *Preventive Medicine*.

Fraser, A., & Atkinson, C. (2014). Making Up Gangs: Looping, Labelling and the New Politics of Intelligence-Led Policing. *Youth Justice*.

Frattaroli, S., & Vernick, J. S. (2006). Separating Batterers and Guns. *Evaluation Review*.

Frew, E., & White, L. (2015). Commemorative Events and National Identity: Commemorating Death and Disaster in Australia. *Event Management*.

Frey, A., & Kirk, D. S. (2021). The Impact of Mass Shootings on Attitudes Toward Gun Restrictions. *Socius Sociological Research for a Dynamic World*.

Funari, G. (2021). 'Family, God, <scp>Brazil</Scp>, Guns...': The State of Criminal Governance in Contemporary <scp>Brazil</Scp>. *Bulletin of Latin American Research*.

Gagné, M., Robitaille, Y., Hamel, D., & St-Laurent, D. (2010). Firearms Regulation and Declining Rates of Male Suicide in Quebec. *Injury prevention*.

Galea, S., & Abdalla, S. M. (2022). State Firearm Laws and Firearm-Related Mortality and Morbidity. *Jama*.

Garverich, S., Carvalho, K., Ross, C. S., Baglivo, A., Farmer, J., Gully, M., Bass, B., Pierce, D., Strong, G., Zimmerman, J., & Lincoln, A. K. (2023). "I'm Not Going to Tell Him What I Tell You": A Community-Based Participatory Research Approach to Understand Firearm Owner Perspectives on Suicide Prevention. *Journal of Participatory Research Methods*.

Gau, L.-S., & Kim, J.-C. (2011). The Influence of Cultural Values on Spectators' Sport Attitudes and Team Identification: An East-West Perspective. *Social Behavior and Personality an International Journal*.

Gilmour, S., Wattanakamolkul, K., & Sugai, M. K. (2018). The Effect of the Australian National Firearms Agreement on Suicide and Homicide Mortality, 1978–2015. *American Journal of Public Health*.

Gius, M. (2014). An examination of the effects of concealed weapons laws and assault weapons bans on state-level murder rates. *Applied Economics Letters*, *21*(4), 265-267.

Gius, M. (2015). The impact of minimum age and child access prevention laws on firearm-related youth suicides and unintentional deaths. *The Social Science Journal*, *52*(2), 168-175.

Gius, M. (2016). The relationship between stand-your-ground laws and crime: a state-level analysis. *The Social Science Journal*, *53*(3), 329-338.

Gjertsen, F., Leenaars, A. A., & Vollrath, M. E. (2013). Mixed Impact of Firearms Restrictions on Fatal Firearm Injuries in Males: A National Observational Study. *International journal of environmental research and public health*.

Glasser, N. J., Pollack, H. A., Ranney, M. L., & Betz, M. E. (2022). Economics and Public Health: Two Perspectives on Firearm Injury Prevention. *The Annals of the American Academy of Political and Social Science*.

Gopal, A., & Greenwood, B. N. (2017). Traders, Guns, and Money: The Effects of Mass Shootings on Stock Prices of Firearm Manufacturers in the U.S. *Plos One*.

Greendorfer, S. L., & Lewko, J. H. (1978). Role of Family Members in Sport Socialization of Children. *Research Quarterly American Alliance for Health Physical Education and Recreation*.

Grene, K. L., Dharani, A. S., & Siegel, M. (2023). Gun Owners' Assessment of Gun Safety Policy: Their Underlying Principles and Detailed Opinions. *Injury epidemiology*.

Gun Free South Africa. (2024). *Gun violence and prevention in South Africa*

GunPolicy.org. (2023). *Australia — Gun Facts, Figures and the Law*. Retrieved 28/7/2023 from

Haider, M., & Frank, J. H. (2014). Firearms: Ownership, Laws &Amp; And the Case for Community Mobilization. *International Journal of Public Health Science (Ijphs)*.

Hallmann, K., & Breuer, C. (2012). The Influence of Socio-Demographic Indicators Economic Determinants and Social Recognition on Sport Participation in Germany. *European Journal of Sport Science*.

Harrison, C., Zissis, C., Gacs, D., & Glickhouse, R. (2023). *Explainer: Gun Laws in Latin America's Largest Economies*. AS/COA. Retrieved 16/1/2024 from

Haw, C., Sutton, L., Simkin, S., Gunnell, D., Kapur, N., Nowers, M., & Hawton, K. (2004). Suicide by Gunshot in the United Kingdom: A Review of the Literature. *Medicine Science and the Law*.

Hayoz, C. V., Klostermann, C., Schmid, J., Schlesinger, T., & Nagel, S. (2017). Inter-generational Transfer of a Sports-Related Lifestyle Within the Family. *International Review for the Sociology of Sport*.

Hays, G., & Jenzen-Jones, N. (2018). Small arms survey. *Small Arms Survey, Graduate Institute of International and Development Studies*.

Hemenway, D., Azrael, D., Conner, A., & Miller, M. (2018). Variation in Rates of Fatal Police Shootings Across US States: The Role of Firearm Availability. *Journal of Urban Health*.

Hemenway, D., & Miller, M. (2013). Public Health Approach to the Prevention of Gun Violence. *New England Journal of Medicine*.

Hepburn, L., Miller, M., Azrael, D., & Hemenway, D. (2004). The effect of nondiscre-tionary concealed weapon carrying laws on homicide. *Journal of Trauma and Acute Care Surgery*, 56(3), 676-681.

Hepburn, L., Miller, M., Azrael, D., & Hemenway, D. (2007). The US Gun Stock: Results From the 2004 National Firearms Survey. *Injury prevention*.

Hillyard, S. (2007). 'As Relevant as Banning Polo in Greenland': The Absence of Ethnographic Insight Into Country Sports in the UK. *Qualitative Research*.

Hillyard, S., & Burridge, J. (2012). Shotguns and Firearms in the UK: A Call for a Distinctively Sociological Contribution to the Debate. *Sociology*.

Hobson, Z., Yesberg, J. A., & Bradford, B. (2022). Fear Appeals in Anti-Knife Carrying Campaigns: Successful or Counter-Productive? *Journal of Interpersonal Violence*.

Hoffman, A. M., & Jengelley, D. (2020). Does Bottom-Line Pressure Make Terrorism Coverage More Negative? Evidence From a Twenty-Newspaper Panel Study. *Media War & Conflict*.

Hrysomallis, C. (2011). Balance Ability and Athletic Performance. *Sports Medicine*.

Hu, C., & Tkebuchava, T. (2022). Health in All Laws: A Better Strategy for Global Health. *Journal of Evidence-Based Medicine*.

Huang, K., Liu, J., Zhao, R., Guo-ling, Z., & Friday, P. C. (2010). Chinese Narcotics Trafficking. *International Journal of Offender Therapy and Comparative Criminology*.

Humphreys, D. K., Gasparrini, A., & Wiebe, D. J. (2017). Association Between Enactment of a "Stand Your Ground" Self-Defense Law and Unlawful Homicides in Florida. *Jama Internal Medicine*.

Hureau, D. M., & Braga, A. A. (2018). The Trade in Tools: The Market for Illicit Guns in High-risk Networks. *Criminology*.

Hurka, S., & Nebel, K. (2013). Framing and Policy Change After Shooting Rampages: A Comparative Analysis of Discourse Networks. *Journal of European Public Policy*.

Ihalainen, S., Kuitunen, S., Mononen, K., & Linnamo, V. (2015). Determinants of Elite-level Air Rifle Shooting Performance. *Scandinavian Journal of Medicine and Science in Sports*.

Ihalainen, S., Mononen, K., Linnamo, V., & Kuitunen, S. (2017). Which Technical Factors Explain Competition Performance in Air Rifle Shooting? *International Journal of Sports Science & Coaching*.

Ingraham, C. (2016). New evidence confirms what gun rights advocates have said for a long time about crime. *The Washington Post*.

Irvin, N., Rhodes, K. V., Cheney, R., & Wiebe, D. J. (2014). Evaluating the Effect of State Regulation of Federally Licensed Firearm Dealers on Firearm Homicide. *American Journal of Public Health*.

James, N., & Menzies, M. (2022). Dual-Domain Analysis of Gun Violence Incidents in the United States.

Jeanes, R., Spaaij, R., Farquharson, K., McGrath, G., Magee, J., Lusher, D., & Gorman, S. (2020). Gender Relations, Gender Equity, and Community Sports Spaces. *Journal of Sport and Social Issues.*

Jennissen, C. A., King, R., Wetjen, K., Denning, G. M., Wymore, C., Stange, N., Hoogerwerf, P., Liao, J., & Wood, K. E. (2021). Rural Youth's Exposure to Firearm Violence and Their Attitudes Regarding Firearm Safety Measures. *Injury epidemiology.*

Jensen, J. D., Bere, E., Bourdeaudhuij, I. D., Jan, N., Maes, L., Manios, Y., Martens, M., Molnár, D., Moreno, L. A., Singh, A. S., Velde, S. t., & Brug, J. (2012). Micro-Level Economic Factors and Incentives in Children's Energy Balance Related Behaviours - Findings From the ENERGY European Cross-Section Questionnaire Survey. *International Journal of Behavioral Nutrition and Physical Activity.*

Joslyn, M. R., & Haider-Markel, D. P. (2017). Gun Ownership and Self-Serving Attributions for Mass Shooting Tragedies*. *Social Science Quarterly.*

Joslyn, M. R., & Haider-Markel, D. P. (2018). The Direct and Moderating Effects of Mass Shooting Anxiety on Political and Policy Attitudes. *Research & Politics.*

Joslyn, M. R., Haider-Markel, D. P., Baggs, M., & Bilbo, A. (2017). Emerging Political Identities? Gun Ownership and Voting in Presidential Elections[*]. *Social Science Quarterly.*

Jussila, J., & Normia, P. (2004). International Law and Law Enforcement Firearms. *Medicine Conflict & Survival.*

Kafonek, K., Gray, A. C., & Parker, K. F. (2021). Understanding Escalation Through Intimate Partner Homicide Narratives. *Violence Against Women.*

Kalesan, B., Mobily, M., Keiser, O., Fagan, J., & Galea, S. (2016). Firearm Legislation and Firearm Mortality in the USA: A Cross-Sectional, State-Level Study. *The Lancet.*

Kantack, B. R., & Paschall, C. E. (2019). Does "Politicizing" Gun Violence Increase Support for Gun Control? Experimental Evidence From the Las Vegas Shooting. *Social Science Quarterly.*

Kappelman, J., & Fording, R. C. (2021). The effect of state gun laws on youth suicide by firearm: 1981–2017. *Suicide and Life-Threatening Behavior, 51*(2), 368-377.

Kapusta, N. D., Etzersdorfer, E., Krall, C., & Sonneck, G. (2007). Firearm Legislation Reform in the European Union: Impact on Firearm Availability, Firearm Suicide and Homicide Rates in Austria. *The British Journal of Psychiatry.*

Kay, T. (2000). Sporting Excellence: A Family Affair? *European Physical Education Review.*

Kendall, T. D., & Tamura, R. (2010). Unmarried fertility, crime, and social stigma. *The Journal of Law and Economics, 53*(1), 185-221.

Kennedy, A., Cerel, J., Kheibari, A., Leske, S., & Watts, J. H. (2021). A Comparison of Farming- and Non-farming-related Suicides From the United States' National Violent Deaths Reporting System, 2003–2016. *Suicide and Life-Threatening Behavior.*

Khan, A., Ahmed, K. R., Hidajat, T., & Edwards, E. J. (2022). Examining the Association Between Sports Participation and Mental Health of Adolescents. *International journal of environmental research and public health.*

Khorram-Manesh, A., Plegas, P., Högstedt, Å., Peyravi, M., & Carlström, E. (2019). Immediate Response to Major Incidents: Defining an Immediate Responder! *European Journal of Trauma and Emergency Surgery.*

Khubchandani, J., & Price, J. H. (2020). Public Perspectives on Firearm Sales in the United States During the COVID-19 Pandemic. *Journal of the American College of Emergency Physicians Open.*

Kiely, E. (2017). *Gun Control in Australia, Updated.* FactCheck.org. Retrieved 28/7/2023 from

Kim, Y.-J., & Kim, E. S. (2021). Analysis of Korean Fencing Club Members' Participation Intention Using the TPB Model. *International journal of environmental research and public health.*

King, A., Bennett, E., Simeona, C., Stanek, L., Roxby, A. C., & Rowhani-Rahbar, A. (2020). Firearm Storage Practices in Households With Children: A Survey of Community-Based Firearm Safety Event Participants. *Preventive Medicine.*

Klarevas, L., Conner, A., & Hemenway, D. (2019). The effect of large-capacity magazine bans on high-fatality mass shootings, 1990–2017. *American Journal of Public Health, 109*(12), 1754-1761.

Kleck, G., Kovandzic, T. V., & Bellows, J. (2016). Does Gun Control Reduce Violent Crime? *Criminal Justice Review.*

Klein, C. (2019). "They Didn't Even Realize Canada Was a Different Country". *Labour / Le Travail.*

Knight, B. (2022). *Gun control and firearms possession in Germany.* Retrieved 15/1/2024 from

Knopov, A., Siegel, M., Xuan, Z., Rothman, E. F., Cronin, S. W., & Hemenway, D. (2019). The impact of state firearm laws on homicide rates among black and white populations in the United States, 1991–2016. *Health & Social Work*, *44*(4), 232-240.

König, D., Swoboda, P., Cramer, R. J., Krall, C., Poštuvan, V., & Kapusta, N. D. (2018). Austrian Firearm Legislation and Its Effects on Suicide and Homicide Mortality: A Natural Quasi-Experiment Amidst the Global Economic Crisis. *European Psychiatry*.

Koo, Y. W., Kõlves, K., & Leo, D. D. (2017). Suicide in Older Adults: Differences Between the Young-Old, Middle-Old, and Oldest Old. *International Psychogeriatrics*.

Kopel, D. (1990). Gun Control and People Control in Japan: Is Japan's Effective Gun Control System a Candidate for Export?

Kopel, D. (1992). Japanese Gun Control Laws Are Oppressive (From Gun Control, P 252-259, 1992, Charles P Cozic, ed.--See NCJ-160164).

Kopel, D. (1993). Japanese Gun Control. *2 Asia Pac. L. Rev.* , 26-52.

Koper, C. S., Johnson, W. F., Nichols, J., Ayers, A. F., & Mullins, N. (2017). Criminal Use of Assault Weapons and High-Capacity Semiautomatic Firearms: An Updated Examination of Local and National Sources. *Journal of Urban Health*.

Kovandzic, T. V., & Marvell, T. B. (2003). Right-to-carry Concealed Handguns and Violent Crime: Crime Control Through Gun Decontrol?*. *Criminology & Public Policy*.

Kovandzic, T. V., Marvell, T. B., & Vieraitis, L. M. (2005). The Impact of "Shall-Issue" Concealed Handgun Laws on Violent Crime Rates. *Homicide Studies*.

Kovandzic, T. V., Marvell, T. B., & Vieraitis, L. M. (2005). The impact of "shall-issue" concealed handgun laws on violent crime rates: evidence from panel data for large urban cities. *Homicide Studies*, *9*(4), 292-323.

Kruis, N. E., Wentling, R. L., Frye, T. S., & Rowland, N. J. (2021). Firearm Ownership, Defensive Gun Usage, and Support for Gun Control: Does Knowledge Matter? *American journal of criminal justice*.

Krüsselmann, K., Aarten, P., & Liem, M. (2021). Firearms and Violence in Europe–A Systematic Review. *Plos One*.

Krzywicka, K. (2023). The Perspective of Firearms Licensing Under Polish and Czech Law. Study of Postulated Changes in 2022. *Studia Administracji I Bezpieczeństwa*.

Kuhn, E. M., Nie, C., O'Brien, M., Withers, R. L., Wintemute, G. J., & Hargarten, S. W. (2002). Missing the Target: A Comparison of Buyback and Fatality Related Guns. *Injury prevention*.

Kupfer, A. (2015). *Power and Education*.

Kwon, I. W. G., & Baack, D. (2005). The Effectiveness of Legislation Controlling Gun Usage. *American Journal of Economics and Sociology*.

La Valle, J. M. (2013). "Gun Control" vs." Self-Protection": A Case against the Ideological Divide. *Justice Policy Journal*, *10*(1).

La Valle, J. M., & Glover, T. C. (2012). Revisiting licensed handgun carrying: personal protection or interpersonal liability? *American journal of criminal justice*, *37*, 580-601.

Lacombe, M. J., Howat, A. J., & Rothschild, J. E. (2019). Gun Ownership as a Social Identity: Estimating Behavioral and Attitudinal Relationships. *Social Science Quarterly*.

Lakomaa, E. (2014). Safe Storage and Thefts of Firearms in Sweden: An Empirical Study. *European Journal of Criminology*.

Lang, B. J., & Lang, M. (2021). Pandemics, Protests, and Firearms. *American Journal of Health Economics*.

Lang, M. (2016). State Firearm Sales and Criminal Activity: Evidence From Firearm Background Checks. *Southern Economic Journal*.

Langmann, C. (2012). Canadian Firearms Legislation and Effects on Homicide 1974 to 2008. *Journal of Interpersonal Violence*.

Langmann, C. (2022). Mass Homicide by Firearm in Canada: Effects of Legislation.

LaPlant, J. T., Morris, J. C., & Shields, T. (2021). Introduction to the Symposium: A Reexamination of Southern Distinctiveness Through the Lens of Firearm Policy. *Social Science Quarterly*.

LaPlant, K. M., Lee, K. E., & LaPlant, J. T. (2020). Christmas Trees, Presidents, and Mass Shootings: Explaining Gun Purchases in the South and Non-South. *Social Science Quarterly*.

Lee, L. K., Fleegler, E. W., Farrell, C. A., Avakame, E., Srinivasan, S., Hemenway, D., & Monuteaux, M. C. (2017). Firearm Laws and Firearm Homicides. *Jama Internal Medicine*.

Lee, W. S., & Suardi, S. (2010). The Australian Firearms Buyback and Its Effect on Gun Deaths. *Contemporary Economic Policy*.

Leenaars, A. A., & Lester, D. (1994). Effects of Gun Control on Homicide in Canada. *Psychological Reports*.

Leigh, A., & Neill, C. (2010). Do Gun Buybacks Save Lives? Evidence From Panel Data. *SSRN Electronic Journal*.

Levine, P. B., & McKnight, R. (2017). Firearms and Accidental Deaths: Evidence From the Aftermath of the Sandy Hook School Shooting. *Science*.

Li, J., & Zeng, Z. (2021). A Controversial Right: Study on the Ambiguity of the Second Amendment to the Constitution of the United States.

Library of Congress. (2017). *Firearms-Control Legislation and Policy: Japan*.

Liu, G., & Wiebe, D. J. (2019). A Time-Series Analysis of Firearm Purchasing After Mass Shooting Events in the United States. *Jama Network Open*.

Liu, Y., Siegel, M., & Sen, B. (2022). Association of State-Level Firearm-Related Deaths With Firearm Laws in Neighboring States. *Jama Network Open*.

Liu, Z. (2019). Criminal State: Understanding Narcotics Trafficking Networks in North Korea. *Journal of Financial Crime*.

Loftin, C., McDowall, D., Wiersema, B., & Cottey, T. J. (1991). Effects of Restrictive Licensing of Handguns on Homicide and Suicide in the District of Columbia. *New England Journal of Medicine*.

Lott, J., John R, & Mustard, D. B. (1997). Crime, deterrence, and right-to-carry concealed handguns. *The Journal of Legal Studies*, *26*(1), 1-68.

Lott Jr, J. R., & Whitley, J. (2007). Abortion and Crime: Unwanted Children and Out-of-Wedlock Births. *Economic Inquiry*, *45*(2), 304-324.

Lower-Hoppe, L. M., Beattie, M., Wray, D. E., Bailey, R., Newman, T. J., & Farrell, A. (2020). The Relationships Between Sport Club Activities and University and Member Attachment. *Recreational Sports Journal*.

Luca, M., Malhotra, D., & Poliquin, C. (2017). Handgun waiting periods reduce gun deaths. *Proceedings of the National Academy of Sciences*, *114*(46), 12162-12165.

Luca, M., Malhotra, D., & Poliquin, C. (2019). The Impact of Mass Shootings on Gun Policy.

Ludwig, J., & Cook, P. J. (2000). Homicide and suicide rates associated with implementation of the Brady Handgun Violence Prevention Act. *Jama*, *284*(5), 585-591.

Lynch, K. R., Boots, D. P., Jackson, D. B., & Renzetti, C. M. (2021). Firearm-Related Abuse and Protective Order Requests Among Intimate Partner Violence Victims. *Journal of Interpersonal Violence*.

Magome, M., & Mosamo, S. (2022). South Africa's many illegal guns a factor in bar shootings. *News 10*.

Maia, A. B. P., Assis, S. G. d., & Minayo, M. C. d. S. (2022). Repercussions on Work, Health and Family Relationships of Police Officers Wounded by Gunshot to the Face. *Ciência & Saúde Coletiva*.

Malta, D. C., Filho, A. M. S., Pinto, I. V., Minayo, M. C. l. d. S., Lima, C. R. d. O., Machado, Í. E., Teixeira, R. A., Neto, O. L. M., Ladeira, R. M., Merchán-Hamann, E., Marinho, F., Vasconcelos, C. H., Vidotti, C. C. F., Cousin, E., Glenn, S., Bisignano, C., Chew, A., Ribeiro, A. L. P., & Naghavi, M. (2020). Association Between Firearms and Mortality in Brazil, 1990 to 2017: A Global Burden of Disease Brazil Study. *Population Health Metrics*.

Mann, J. J., & Michel, C. A. (2016). Prevention of Firearm Suicide in the United States: What Works and What Is Possible. *American Journal of Psychiatry*.

Manski, C. F., & Pepper, J. V. (2018). How do right-to-carry laws affect crime rates? Coping with ambiguity using bounded-variation assumptions. *Review of Economics and Statistics*, *100*(2), 232-244.

Månsson, A. G., Elmose, M., Dalsgaard, S., & Roessler, K. K. (2017). The Influence of Participation in Target-Shooting Sport for Children With Inattentive, Hyperactive and Impulsive Symptoms – A Controlled Study of Best Practice. *BMC Psychiatry*.

Marshall, S., McNeil, N., Seal, E., & Nicholson, M. (2022). The "Boys' Club", Sexual Harassment, and Discriminatory Resourcing: An Exploration of the Barriers Faced by Women Sport Officials in Australian Basketball. *International Review for the Sociology of Sport*.

Martin, C. (2012). Desperate Mobilities: Logistics, Security and the Extra-Logistical Knowledge of 'Appropriation'. *Geopolitics*.

Martin, J. (2011). The Transformation of Lowland Game Shooting in England and Wales Since the Second World War: The Supply Side Revolution. *Rural History*.

Martin Jr, R. A., & Legault, R. L. (2005). Systematic measurement error with state-level crime data: evidence from the "more guns, less crime" debate. *Journal of research in crime and delinquency*, *42*(2), 187-210.

Martin, K., McLeod, E. M., Périard, J. D., Rattray, B., Keegan, R., & Pyne, D. B. (2019). The Impact of Environmental Stress on Cognitive Performance: A Systematic Review. *Human Factors the Journal of the Human Factors and Ergonomics Society*.

Marvell, T. B. (2001). The impact of banning juvenile gun possession. *The Journal of Law and Economics*, *44*(S2), 691-713.

Masters, J. (2022). *U.S. Gun Policy: Global Comparisons*.

Mathews, S., Abrahams, N., Martin, L. J., Lombard, C., & Jewkes, R. (2019). Homicide Pattern Among Adolescents: A National Epidemiological Study of Child Homicide in South Africa. *Plos One*.

Matzopoulos, R., Groenewald, P., Abrahams, N., & Bradshaw, D. (2016). Where Have All the Gun Deaths Gone? *South African Medical Journal*.

McClellan, C., & Tekin, E. (2016). Stand Your Ground Laws, Homicides, and Injuries. *The Journal of Human Resources*.

McClellan, C., & Tekin, E. (2017). Stand your ground laws, homicides, and injuries. *Journal of Human Resources, 52*(3), 621-653.

McCourt, A. D., Crifasi, C. K., Stuart, E. A., Vernick, J. S., Kagawa, R. M., Wintemute, G. J., & Webster, D. W. (2020). Purchaser licensing, point-of-sale background check laws, and firearm homicide and suicide in 4 US states, 1985–2017. *American Journal of Public Health, 110*(10), 1546-1552.

McCourt, A. D., Crifasi, C. K., Stuart, E. A., Vernick, J. S., Kagawa, R. M. C., Wintemute, G. J., & Webster, D. (2020). Purchaser Licensing, Point-of-Sale Background Check Laws, and Firearm Homicide and Suicide in 4 US States, 1985–2017. *American Journal of Public Health*.

McDermott, R. C., Brasil, K. M., Barinas, J., & Borgogna, N. C. (2021). Associations Between Men's and Women's Conformity to Masculine Role Norms and Firearm Ownership: Contributions Beyond, Race, Gender, and Political Ideology. *Psychology of Men & Masculinity*.

McElroy, J. R., & Coley, J. S. (2020). Gun-free Zones? Political Opportunities, Resource Mobilization, and Shooting Sports Organizations at U.S. Colleges and Universities. *Sociological Inquiry*.

McLeod, R. S., Moore, E. E., Crozier, J., Civil, I., Ahmed, N., Bulger, E. M., & Stewart, R. M. (2021). A Public Health Approach to Prevent Firearm Related Injuries and Deaths. *Annals of Surgery Open*.

McPhedran, S. (2017). An Evaluation of the Impacts of Changing Firearms Legislation on Australian Female Firearm Homicide Victimization Rates. *Violence Against Women*.

Meel, B. L. (2018). Twenty-Three-Year Trend in Firearm Deaths in the Transkei Subregion of South Africa (1993–2015). *Medicine Science and the Law*.

Meinke, D. K., Finan, D. S., Flamme, G. A., Murphy, W. J., Stewart, M. G., Lankford, J. E., & Tasko, S. M. (2017). Prevention of Noise-Induced Hearing Loss From Recreational Firearms. *Seminars in Hearing*.

Meitl, M. B., Wellman, A., & Kinkaid, P. (2021). Texas Sheriffs' Perceptions on Firearm Regulations and Mass Shootings. *International Journal of Police Science & Management*.

Merry, M. K. (2015). Constructing Policy Narratives in 140 Characters or Less: The Case of Gun Policy Organizations. *Policy Studies Journal*.

Merry, M. K. (2017). Angels Versus Devils: The Portrayal of Characters in the Gun Policy Debate. *Policy Studies Journal*.

Metzl, J. M., & MacLeish, K. (2015). Mental Illness, Mass Shootings, and the Politics of American Firearms. *American Journal of Public Health*.

Miller, S. V. (2018). What Americans Think About Gun Control: Evidence From the General Social Survey, 1972–2016. *Social Science Quarterly*.

Moczek, A. P., & Nijhout, H. F. (2004). Trade-offs During the Development of Primary and Secondary Sexual Traits in a Horned Beetle. *The American Naturalist*.

Moiseeva, O. A., Filippova, O., & Moiseev, E. (2021). Popularization of Shooting Sports as a Means of Introducing Young People to a Healthy Lifestyle. *E3s Web of Conferences*.

Mokdad, A. H., Ballestros, K., Echko, M., Glenn, S., Olsen, H. E., Mullany, E. C., Lee, A., Khan, A. R., Ahmadi, A., Ferrari, A. J., Kasaeian, A., Werdecker, A., Carter, A., Zipkin, B., Sartorius, B., Serdar, B., Sykes, B. L., Troeger, C., Fitzmaurice, C., . . . Murray, C. J. L. (2018). The State of US Health, 1990-2016. *Jama*.

Mon-López, D., & Tejero-González, C. M. (2019). Validity and Reliability of the TargetScan ISSF Pistol &Amp; Rifle Application for Measuring Shooting Performance. *Scandinavian Journal of Medicine and Science in Sports*.

Mon-López, D., Zakynthinaki, M. S., Cordente, C. A., & García-González, J. (2019). The Relationship Between Pistol Olympic Shooting Performance, Handgrip and Shoulder Abduction Strength. *Journal of Human Kinetics*.

Moody, C. E. (2001). Testing for the effects of concealed weapons laws: specification errors and robustness. *The Journal of Law and Economics*, *44*(S2), 799-813.

Moore, M. D. (2017). Firearm Prevalence and Homicide. *Criminal Justice Review*.

Moraes, C. L., Santos, É. B. d., Reichenheim, M. E., Taquette, S. R., Stochero, L., & Marques, E. S. (2021). Perceived Experiences of Community Violence Among

Adolescents: A School Survey From Rio De Janeiro, Brazil. *Journal of Interpersonal Violence.*

Morral, A. R. (2023a). *Effects of Licensing and Permitting Requirements on Suicide.* R. Corporation.

Morral, A. R. (2023b). *Effects of Prohibitions Associated with Mental Illness on Violent Crime.* R. Corporation.

Morral, A. R. (2023c). *Effects of Stand-Your-Ground Laws on Violent Crime.* R. Corporation.

Morral, A. R. (2023d). *Effects of Waiting Periods on Violent Crime.* R. Corporation.

Munslow, S. (2017, 15/1/2024). How Many Firearms Can A Shooter Own – The Loose Cannon. *Sporting Shooter.*

Mustard, D. B. (2001). The impact of gun laws on police deaths. *The Journal of Law and Economics, 44*(S2), 635-657.

Nascimento, S. G. d., Silva, R. S. d., Cavalcante, L. d. M., Carvalho, A. P. R. d., & Bonfim, C. V. d. (2018). Causas Externas De Mortalidade Em Mulheres Grávidas E Puérperas. *Acta Paulista De Enfermagem.*

National Rifle Association. (2020). *Surrender of MARS and Lever Release rifles under.* National Rifle Association. Retrieved 13/1/2024 from

National Rifle Association of America. (2024). *Why Gun Control Doesn't Work.* Retrieved 10/1/2024 from

Nawrotek, J. (2020). Small Arms of Russian Federation Armed Forces. *Problemy Techniki Uzbrojenia.*

Newman, B. J., & Hartman, T. K. (2017). Mass Shootings and Public Support for Gun Control. *British Journal of Political Science.*

Newth, J. L., Lawrence, A. J., Cromie, R., Swift, J. A., Rees, E. C., Wood, K. A., Strong, E., Reeves, J., & McDonald, R. A. (2019). Perspectives of Ammunition Users on the Use of Lead Ammunition and Its Potential Impacts on Wildlife and Humans. *People and Nature.*

Nichols, G., Tacon, R., & Muir, A. (2012). Sports Clubs' Volunteers: Bonding in or Bridging Out? *Sociology.*

Norman, R. (2007). The High Burden of Injuries in South Africa. *Bulletin of the World Health Organization.*

Oliveira, C. A. d., & Neto, G. B. (2015). The Deterrence Effects of Gun Laws in Games With Asymmetric Skills and Information. *Review of Law & Economics.*

Otieno, G., Marinda, E., Bärnighausen, T., & Tanser, F. (2015). High Rates of Homicide in a Rural South African Population (2000–2008): Findings From a Population-Based Cohort Study. *Population Health Metrics*.

Ozanne-Smith, J., Ashby, K. M., Newstead, S., Stathakis, V., & Clapperton, A. (2004). Firearm Related Deaths: The Impact of Regulatory Reform. *Injury prevention*.

Pallin, R., & Barnhorst, A. (2021). Clinical Strategies for Reducing Firearm Suicide. *Injury epidemiology*.

Parker, K., Horowitz, J. M., Igielnik, R., Oliphant, J. B., & Brown, A. (2017). *The demographics of gun ownership*. Pew Research Center.

Parsons, C., Vargas, E. W., & Bhatia, R. (2020). *The Gun Industry in America: The Overlooked Player in a National Crisis*. C. f. A. P. A. Fun.

Peljha, Z., Michaelides, M., & Collins, D. (2018). The Relative Importance of Selected Physical Fitness Parameters in Olympic Clay Target Shooting. *Journal of Human Sport and Exercise*.

Phillips, S. W. (2020). A Historical Examination of Police Firearms. *The Police Journal Theory Practice and Principles*.

Phillips, S. W., Kim, D.-Y., & Sobol, J. J. (2013). An Evaluation of a Multiyear Gun Buy-Back Programme: Re-Examining the Impact on Violent Crimes. *International Journal of Police Science & Management*.

Pirelli, G., & Witt, P. H. (2017). Firearms and Cultural Competence: Considerations for Mental Health Professionals. *Journal of Aggression Conflict and Peace Research*.

Policja. (2022). *Liczba osób, którym wydano pozwolenie na broń*. Retrieved from

Price, M., & Norris, D. M. (2010). Firearm Laws: A Primer for Psychiatrists. *Harvard Review of Psychiatry*.

Prickett, K. C., Martin-Storey, A., & Crosnoe, R. (2014). State Firearm Laws, Firearm Ownership, and Safety Practices Among Families of Preschool-Aged Children. *American Journal of Public Health*.

Proctor, E. (2023a). Gun laws in Germany. *I Am Expat*.

Proctor, E. (2023b). Gun laws in Switzerland. *I Am Expat*.

Public Safety Canada. (2024). *Firearms*. Retrieved 12/1/2024 from

Quenzer, F., Givner, A., Dirks, R., Coyne, C. J., Ercoli, F., & Townsend, R. N. (2021). Self-Inflicted Gun Shot Wounds: A Retrospective, Observational Study of U.S. Trauma Centers. *Western Journal of Emergency Medicine*.

Raifman, J., Larson, E., Barry, C. L., Siegel, M., Ulrich, M., Knopov, A., & Galea, S. (2020). State handgun purchase age minimums in the US and adolescent suicide rates: regression discontinuity and difference-in-differences analyses. *Bmj, 370.*

Raissian, K. M. (2015). Hold Your Fire: Did the 1996 Federal Gun Control Act Expansion Reduce Domestic Homicides? *Journal of Policy Analysis and Management.*

Raissian, K. M. (2016). Hold your fire: Did the 1996 Federal Gun Control Act expansion reduce domestic homicides? *Journal of Policy Analysis and Management, 35*(1), 67-93.

RAND Corporation. (2023). *How Gun Policies Affect Hunting and Recreation.* Retrieved 12/1/2024 from

Ranney, M. L., Zeoli, A. M., & Beidas, R. S. (2020). Evidence-Based Solutions to Pediatric Firearm Deaths—The Need for Out-of-the-Box Answers. *Jama Pediatrics.*

Reeping, P. M., Cerdá, M., Kalesan, B., Wiebe, D. J., Galea, S., & Branas, C. C. (2019). State Gun Laws, Gun Ownership, and Mass Shootings in the US: Cross Sectional Time Series. *Bmj.*

Richards, R. (2017). The Role of Interest Groups and Group Interests on Gun Legislation in the U.S. House*. *Social Science Quarterly.*

Richardson, E. T., & Hemenway, D. (2011). Homicide, Suicide, and Unintentional Firearm Fatality: Comparing the United States With Other High-Income Countries, 2003. *Journal of Trauma and Acute Care Surgery.*

Rivara, F. P., Grossman, D. C., & Cummings, P. (1997). Injury Prevention. *New England Journal of Medicine.*

Roberts, D. W. (2009). Intimate partner homicide: Relationships to alcohol and firearms. *Journal of contemporary criminal justice, 25*(1), 67-88.

Rodrigues, N. C. P., Lino, V. T. S., Bastos, L. S., O'Dwyer, G., Monteiro, D. L. M., Reis, I. N. C., Frossard, V. C., & Andrade, M. K. N. (2021). Temporal Evolution of Homicide Mortality in Brazilian Capitals From 2005 to 2019. *Journal of Aggression Conflict and Peace Research.*

Rodway, C., Flynn, S., Swinson, N., Roscoe, A., Hunt, I. M., Windfuhr, K., Kapur, N., Appleby, L., & Shaw, J. (2009). Methods of Homicide in England and Wales: A Comparison by Diagnostic Group. *Journal of Forensic Psychiatry and Psychology.*

Rogowski, J. C., & Tucker, P. D. (2018). Critical Events and Attitude Change: Support for Gun Control After Mass Shootings. *Political Science Research and Methods.*

Rose, V. (1994). *Gun Control Legislation in Canada.* T. C. G. Assembly.

Rosenbaum, J. E. (2011). Gun Utopias? Firearm Access and Ownership in Israel and Switzerland. *Journal of Public Health Policy*.

Rosengart, M., Cummings, P., Nathens, A., Heagerty, P., Maier, R., & Rivara, F. (2005). An evaluation of state firearm regulations and homicide and suicide death rates. *Injury prevention*, *11*(2), 77.

Rosengart, M. R. (2005). An Evaluation of State Firearm Regulations and Homicide and Suicide Death Rates. *Injury prevention*.

Rosso, E., & McGrath, R. (2012). Beyond Recreation: Personal Social Networks and Social Capital in the Transition of Young Players From Recreational Football to Formal Football Clubs. *International Review for the Sociology of Sport*.

Rowhani-Rahbar, A., Lyons, V. H., Azrael, D., & Miller, M. J. (2017). Formal Firearm Training Among Adults in the USA: Results of a National Survey. *Injury prevention*.

Royal Canadian Mounted Police. (2019). *2019 Commissioner of Firearms Report*.

Royal Canadian Mounted Police. (2024). *Safety courses*. Retrieved 12/1/2024 from

Roza, D. (2024). *What Is a Gun? A primer*. Guns of New York. Retrieved 11/1/2024 from

Rozel, J. S., & Mulvey, E. P. (2017). The Link Between Mental Illness and Firearm Violence: Implications for Social Policy and Clinical Practice. *Annual Review of Clinical Psychology*.

Ruby, E., & Sher, L. (2013). Prevention of suicidal behavior in adolescents with post-traumatic stress disorder. *International journal of adolescent medicine and health*, *25*(3), 283-293.

Sabbath, E. L., Hawkins, S. S., & Baum, C. F. (2020). State-level changes in firearm laws and workplace homicide rates: United States, 2011 to 2017. *American Journal of Public Health*, *110*(2), 230-236.

Sanjurjo, D. (2021). Why Are Brazilians So Interested in Gun Control? Putting the Multiple Streams Framework to the Test. *Opinião Pública*.

Sarchiapone, M., Mandelli, L., Iosue, M., Andrisano, C., & Roy, A. (2011). Controlling Access to Suicide Means. *International journal of environmental research and public health*.

Sarma, K., & Kola, S. (2010). Firearm Suicide Decedents in the Republic of Ireland, 1980–2005. *Public Health*.

Sato, Y., & Haselswerdt, J. (2022). Protest and State Policy Agendas: Marches and Gun Policy After Parkland. *Policy Studies Journal*.

Saunders, N., Lee, H., Macpherson, A., Guan, J., & Guttmann, A. (2017). Risk of Firearm Injuries Among Children and Youth of Immigrant Families. *Canadian Medical Association Journal*.

Saunders, N., Pratt, M., & Hepburn, C. (2022). Dangerous "Toys": The Burden of Non-Powdered Firearm Injuries in Canadian Children and Youth. *Healthcare Quarterly*.

Schaeffer, K. (2023). *Key facts about Americans and guns*. Pew Research Center.

Scheerder, J., Vanreusel, B., & Taks, M. (2005). Stratification Patterns of Active Sport Involvement Among Adults. *International Review for the Sociology of Sport*.

Schell, T. L. (2023). *Effects of Child-Access Prevention Laws on Unintentional Injuries and Deaths*. R. Corporation.

Schell, T. L., Cefalu, M., Griffin, B. A., Smart, R., & Morral, A. R. (2020). Changes in Firearm Mortality Following the Implementation of State Laws Regulating Firearm Access and Use. *Proceedings of the National Academy of Sciences*.

Schenck, C., Wilson, M., Tiyyagura, G., & Bechtel, K. (2022). Parental Attitudes, Beliefs, and Practices Related to Firearm Storage: A Qualitative Study. *Injury epidemiology*.

Schildkraut, J., & Geller, L. (2022). Mass Shootings in the United States: Prevalence, Policy, and a Way Forward. *The Annals of the American Academy of Political and Social Science*.

Schwartz, N. S. (2022). Aiming for Success. *World Affairs*.

Seippel, Ø., Dalen, H. B., Sandvik, M., & Solstad, G. M. (2018). From Political Sports to Sports Politics: On Political Mobilization of Sports Issues. *International Journal of Sport Policy and Politics*.

Semenza, D. C., Stansfield, R., Steidley, T., & Mancik, A. M. (2021). Firearm Availability, Homicide, and the Context of Structural Disadvantage. *Homicide Studies*.

Sen, B., & Panjamapirom, A. (2012a). State Background Checks for Gun Purchase and Firearm Deaths: An Exploratory Study. *Preventive Medicine*, 55(4), 346-350.

Sen, B., & Panjamapirom, A. (2012b). State Background Checks for Gun Purchase and Firearm Deaths: An Exploratory Study. *Preventive Medicine*.

Shalhope, R. E. (1982). The Ideological Origins of the Second Amendment. *Journal of American History*.

Shapira, H., Chen, L., & Lin, K.-H. (2021). How Attitudes About Guns Develop Over Time. *Sociological Perspectives*.

Sharkey, P., Schwartz, A. E., Ellen, I. G., & Lacoe, J. (2014). High Stakes in the Classroom, High Stakes on the Street: The Effects of Community Violence on Student's Standardized Test Performance. *Sociological Science*.

Sheptycki, J. (2009). Guns, Crime and Social Order. *Criminology & Criminal Justice*.

Shi, W., & Lee, L.-f. (2018). The effects of gun control on crimes: a spatial interactive fixed effects approach. *Empirical economics*, 55(1), 233-263.

Siegel, M., Pahn, M., Xuan, Z., Fleegler, E., & Hemenway, D. (2019). The impact of state firearm laws on homicide and suicide deaths in the USA, 1991–2016: a panel study. *Journal of general internal medicine*, 34, 2021-2028.

Siegel, M., Solomon, B., Knopov, A., Rothman, E. F., Cronin, S., Xuan, Z., & Hemenway, D. (2019). The Impact of State Firearm Laws on Homicide Rates in Suburban and Rural Areas Compared to Large Cities in the United States, 1991-2016. *The Journal of Rural Health*.

Siegel, M., Solomon, B., Knopov, A., Rothman, E. F., Cronin, S. W., Xuan, Z., & Hemenway, D. (2020). The impact of state firearm laws on homicide rates in suburban and rural areas compared to large cities in the United States, 1991-2016. *The Journal of Rural Health*, 36(2), 255-265.

Silva, F. M. d., Sousa, P., Pinheiro, V., López-Torres, O., Refoyo, I., & Mon-López, D. (2021). Which Are the Most Determinant Psychological Factors in Olympic Shooting Performance? A Self-Perspective From Elite Shooters. *International journal of environmental research and public health*.

Silver, A. (2020). Donkey Work: Congressional Democrats in Conservative America, 1974-1994. *Political Science Quarterly*.

Silver, J., Fisher, W. H., & Horgan, J. (2018). Public Mass Murderers and Federal Mental Health Background Checks. *Law & Policy*.

Simpson, K. R., & Rohan, A. (2023). Gun Violence and Risk to Children and Youth in the United States. *MCN the American Journal of Maternal/Child Nursing*.

Skiba, R. (2020). Conflict de-escalation: Workplace training.

Small Arms Survey. (2018). *Global Firearms Holdings*. Small Arms Survey. Retrieved 8/1/2024 from

Smart, R. (2023a). *Effects of Assault Weapon and High-Capacity Magazine Bans on Mass Shootings*. R. Corporation.

Smart, R. (2023b). *Effects of Child-Access Prevention Laws on Suicide*. R. Corporation.

Smart, R. (2023c). *Effects of Concealed-Carry Laws on Violent Crime*. R. Corporation.

Smart, R. (2023d). *Effects of Minimum Age Requirements on Suicide*. R. Corporation.

Smart, R. (2023e). *Effects of Waiting Periods on Suicide*. R. Corporation.

Smart, R., Schell, T. L., Cefalu, M., & Morral, A. R. (2020). Impact on Non-firearm Deaths of Firearm Laws Affecting Firearm Deaths: A Systematic Review and Meta-Analysis. *American Journal of Public Health*.

Smith, M. R., & Petrocelli, M. (2018). The Effect of Concealed Handgun Carry Deregulation in Arizona on Crime in Tucson. *Criminal Justice Policy Review*.

Smith, M. R., & Petrocelli, M. (2019). The effect of concealed handgun carry deregulation in Arizona on crime in Tucson. *Criminal Justice Policy Review, 30*(8), 1186-1203.

Smucker, S. (2023a). *Effects of Prohibitions Associated with Domestic Violence on Violent Crime*. R. Corporation.

Smucker, S. (2023b). *Effects of Surrender of Firearms by Prohibited Possessors on Violent Crime*. R. Corporation.

Snider, C., Ovens, H., Drummond, A., & Kapur, A. (2009). CAEP Position Statement on Gun Control. *Canadian Journal of Emergency Medicine*.

Solmi, F., Dykxhoorn, J., & Kirkbride, J. (2017). Urban-Rural Differences in Major Mental Health Conditions.

Souto, R. M. C. V., Barufaldi, L. A., Nico, L. S., & Freitas, M. G. d. (2017). Perfil Epidemiológico Do Atendimento Por Violência Nos Serviços Públicos De Urgência E Emergência Em Capitais Brasileiras, Viva 2014. *Ciência & Saúde Coletiva*.

Stanko, E. A. (2006). Theorizing About Violence. *Violence Against Women*.

Statista. (2023a). *Development of cases involving the use of firearms in Germany from 2017 to 2022*. S. R. Department.

Statista. (2023b). *Monthly number of shootings in Rio de Janeiro from 2021 to 2023*. S. R. Department.

Statista. (2023c). *Number of crimes involving the use of firearms, gas weapons, ammunition, explosives, and explosive devices in Russia from 2015 to 2021* S. R. Department.

Statista. (2023d). *Number of firearm offences (excluding air weapons) in London from 2015/16 to 2022/23 (in 1,000s)* S. R. Department.

Steidley, T. (2019). Sharing the Monopoly on Violence? Shall-Issue Concealed Handgun License Laws and Responsibilization. *Sociological Perspectives*.

Steidley, T., & Yamane, D. (2021). Special Issue Editors' Introduction: A Sociology of Firearms for the Twenty-First Century. *Sociological Perspectives*.

Stetsenko, V., Bellman, V., Agha, S., Dellenbaugh, A., Guryeva, V., Namdev, V., & Wise, S. A. (2022). School Shootings in Russia vs. The United States: New Reality, Key Similarities and Differences. *Global Psychiatry Archives*.

Strandbu, Å., Bakken, A., & Sletten, M. A. (2017). Exploring the Minority–majority Gap in Sport Participation: Different Patterns for Boys and Girls? *Sport in Society*.

Strnad, J. (2007). Should legal empiricists go Bayesian? *American Law and Economics Review*, *9*(1), 195-303.

Stroebe, W., Kreienkamp, J., Leander, N. P., & Agostini, M. (2021). Do Canadian and U .S. American Handgun Owners Differ? *Canadian Journal of Behavioural Science/Revue Canadienne Des Sciences Du Comportement*.

Stroebe, W., Leander, N. P., & Kruglanski, A. W. (2017). The Impact of the Orlando Mass Shooting on Fear of Victimization and Gun-Purchasing Intentions: Not What One Might Expect. *Plos One*.

Stucky, T. D., Miller, G. M., & Murphy, L. (2008). Gender, Guns, and Legislating: An Analysis of State Legislative Policy Preferences. *Journal of Women Politics & Policy*.

Susmann, M. W., Dixon, G., Bushman, B. J., & Garrett, R. K. (2022). Correcting Misperceptions of Gun Policy Support Can Foster Intergroup Cooperation Between Gun Owners and Non-Gun Owners. *Plos One*.

Swanson, J. W., McGinty, E. E., Fazel, S., & Mays, V. M. (2015). Mental Illness and Reduction of Gun Violence and Suicide: Bringing Epidemiologic Research to Policy. *Annals of Epidemiology*.

Swanson, J. W., Robertson, A. G., Frisman, L. K., Norko, M. A., Lin, H.-J., Swartz, M. S., & Cook, P. J. (2013). Preventing gun violence involving people with serious mental illness. *Reducing gun violence in America: Informing policy with evidence and analysis*, 33-52.

Swart, L.-A., Seedat, M., & Nel, J. A. (2015). The Situational Context of Adolescent Homicide Victimization in Johannesburg, South Africa. *Journal of Interpersonal Violence*.

Swedler, D. I., Simmons, M. M., Dominici, F., & Hemenway, D. (2015). Firearm Prevalence and Homicides of Law Enforcement Officers in the United States. *American Journal of Public Health*.

Sycafoose, A. (2014). Police officers talking about gun control: A case study of a rural sheriff's department.

Talapins, S., & Agafonovs, E. (2020). Theoretical and Practical Aspects of Use of Electroshock Weapon. *Border Security and Management*.

Tamir, I. (2018). Digital Video Recorder Dodgers – Sport-Viewing Habits in the Face of Changing Media Reality. *Time & Society*.

Taylor, B. J., & Li, J. (2015). Do Fewer Guns Lead to Less Crime? Evidence From Australia. *International Review of Law and Economics*.

Taylor, P. L. (2019). Dispatch Priming and the Police Decision to Use Deadly Force. *Police Quarterly*.

Teitelbaum, J. B., & Spector, E. (2009). <i>District of Columbia v. Heller</I>: Implications for Public Health Policy and Practice. *Public Health Reports*.

Temeña, A. A. R., Medina, M. S. P., Angco, B. A. C., Binaoro, H. T., Manatad, S. L. B., Santos, S. H. I., & Monzon-Po, S. (2022). Study on the Tourism Activities of Retirees: Basis for Development of Proposed Recreational Plan in Antipolo, Rizal. *International Journal of Research Studies in Management*.

The Editors of Encyclopaedia Britannica. (2023). shooting. In *Encyclopedia Britannica*.

Thompson, A. J., Martin, A. J., Gee, S., & Geurin, A. N. (2016). Fans' Perceptions of Professional Tennis Events' Social Media Presence. *Communication & Sport*.

Thompson, J. A., & Stidham, R. (2010). Packing Heat in the Tar Heel State: A County-Level Assessment of Concealed Carry Permits. *Criminal Justice Review*.

Thorpe, H. (2016). Action Sports, Social Media, and New Technologies. *Communication & Sport*.

Timsina, L., Qiao, N., Mongalo, A. C., Vetor, A., Carroll, A. E., & Bell, T. M. (2020). National Instant Criminal Background Check and Youth Gun Carrying. *Pediatrics*.

Toigo, S., Pollock, N. J., Liu, L., Contreras, G., McFaull, S. R., & Thompson, W. (2023). Fatal and Non-Fatal Firearm-Related Injuries in Canada, 2016–2020: A Population-Based Study Using Three Administrative Databases. *Injury epidemiology*.

Tonts, M. (2005). Competitive Sport and Social Capital in Rural Australia. *Journal of Rural Studies*.

Trinka, T., Oesterle, D. W., Silverman, A. C., Vriniotis, M. G., Orchowski, L. M., Beidas, R. S., Betz, M. E., Hudson, C., Kesner, T., & Ranney, M. L. (2023). Bystander Intervention to Prevent Firearm Injury: A Qualitative Study of 4-H Shooting Sports Participants. *Journal of Community Psychology*.

Tsvetkov, S. (2021). Production of and Supply of the Army With Small Arms on the Eve of the Russo-Turkish War (1877–1878). A Brief Overview of the Russian Military Industry. *Epohi*.

Turuban, P., & Stegmüller, C. (2024). *How Switzerland combines a passion for guns with safety*. swissinfo.ch.

Ulrich, M. R. (2019). A Public Health Approach to Gun Violence, Legally Speaking. *The Journal of Law Medicine & Ethics*.

Ulrich, M. R. (2022). Balancing Rights and Responsibilities: The Role of Government and Citizens in Combatting Gun Violence. *The Annals of the American Academy of Political and Social Science*.

Vargas, L. G., Guiora, A. N., & Minutolo, M. C. (2021). Report on an Analytic Network Process (ANP) Model to Estimate the Benefits, Opportunities, Costs, and Risks (BOCR) That Gun Policies and Violence Prevention Interventions Have on Legal Users of Firearms. *International Journal of the Analytic Hierarchy Process*.

Vernick, J. S., Alcorn, T., & Horwitz, J. (2017). Background Checks for All Gun Buyers and Gun Violence Restraining Orders: State Efforts to Keep Guns From High-Risk Persons. *The Journal of Law Medicine & Ethics*.

Vernick, J. S., Hodge, J. G., & Webster, D. (2007). The Ethics of Restrictive Licensing for Handguns: Comparing the United States and Canadian Approaches to Handgun Regulation. *The Journal of Law Medicine & Ethics*.

Vigdor, E. R., & Mercy, J. A. (2006). Do Laws Restricting Access to Firearms by Domestic Violence Offenders Prevent Intimate Partner Homicide? *Evaluation Review*.

Vigdor, E. R., & Mercy, J. A. (2006). Do laws restricting access to firearms by domestic violence offenders prevent intimate partner homicide? *Evaluation Review*, *30*(3), 313-346.

Violence Policy Center. (2022). *States with Weak Gun Laws and Higher Gun Ownership Lead Nation in Gun Deaths, New Data for 2020 Confirms*. Violence Policy Center. Retrieved 8/1/2024 from

Vu, A. V., Wilson, L., Chua, Y. T., Shumailov, I., & Anderson, R. (2021). ExtremeBB: Enabling Large-Scale Research Into Extremism, the Manosphere and Their Correlation by Online Forum Data.

Vuorio, A., Laukkala, T., Navathe, P., Budowle, B., Eyre, A., & Sajantila, A. (2015). On Doctors' Accountability and Flight Deck Safety. *Croatian Medical Journal*.

Walker, H., Collingwood, L., & Bunyasi, T. L. (2020). White Response to Black Death. *Du Bois Review Social Science Research on Race*.

Wallin, M., & Durfee, A. (2020). Firearm Removal, Judicial Decision-Making, and Domestic Violence Protection Orders. *Violence and Gender*.

Wallin, M., Holliday, C. N., & Zeoli, A. M. (2021). The Association of Federal and State-Level Firearm Restriction Policies With Intimate Partner Homicide: A Re-Analysis by Race of the Victim. *Journal of Interpersonal Violence*.

Walters, R. (2000). Serious Firearm Offending in New Zealand — Issues for Gun Controls and Public Safety. *Australian & New Zealand Journal of Criminology*.

Wang, J. (2021). Re-Thinking the Mediating Role of Emotional Valence and Arousal Between Personal Factors and Occupational Safety Attention Levels. *International journal of environmental research and public health*.

Wanzinack, C., Signorelli, M. C., & Reis, C. (2018). Homicides and Socio-Environmental Determinants of Health in Brazil: A Systematic Literature Review. *Cadernos De Saúde Pública*.

Warner, T. D., & Ratcliff, S. (2021). What Guns Mean: Who Sees Guns as Important, Essential, and Empowering (And Why)? *Sociological Inquiry*.

Webster, D. (2016). Lessons From Australia's National Firearms Agreement. *Jama*.

Webster, D., McCourt, A. D., Crifasi, C. K., Booty, M. D., & Stuart, E. A. (2020). Evidence Concerning the Regulation of Firearms Design, Sale, and Carrying on Fatal Mass Shootings in the United States. *Criminology & Public Policy*.

Webster, D., Vernick, J. S., & Bulzacchelli, M. T. (2009). Effects of State-Level Firearm Seller Accountability Policies on Firearm Trafficking. *Journal of Urban Health*.

Webster, D., & Wintemute, G. J. (2015). Effects of Policies Designed to Keep Firearms From High-Risk Individuals. *Annual Review of Public Health*.

Webster, D. W., McCourt, A. D., Crifasi, C. K., Booty, M. D., & Stuart, E. A. (2020). Evidence concerning the regulation of firearms design, sale, and carrying on fatal mass shootings in the United States. *Criminology & Public Policy*, *19*(1), 171-212.

Webster, D. W., Vernick, J. S., Zeoli, A. M., & Manganello, J. A. (2004). Association between youth-focused firearm laws and youth suicides. *Jama*, *292*(5), 594-601.

Weisbord, N. (2020). Who's Afraid of the Lucky MOOSE? Canada's Dangerous Self-Defence Innovation. *McGill Law Journal*.

White, D. J., & Smith, J. D. (2014). Acquisition, Custody, and Storage of Firearms Used in 4-H Shooting Sports Programs. *Journal of extension*.

Wightman, G., Cochrane, R., Gray, R. A., & Linton, M. (2013). A Contribution to the Discussion on the Safety of Air Weapons. *Science & Justice*.

Williams, N. (2022, 12/1/2024). Explainer: Are guns illegal in Canada? Key questions answered.

Wilson, O. W. A., Whatman, C., Walters, S., Keung, S., Enari, D., Rogers, A. M., Millar, S.-K., Ferkins, L., Hinckson, E., Hapeta, J., Sam, M., & Richards, J. (2022). The Value of Sport: Wellbeing Benefits of Sport Participation During Adolescence. *International journal of environmental research and public health*.

Wintemute, G. J. (2012). Characteristics of Federally Licensed Firearms Retailers and Retail Establishments in the United States: Initial Findings From the Firearms Licensee Survey. *Journal of Urban Health*.

Wintemute, G. J. (2013). Support for a Comprehensive Background Check Requirement and Expanded Denial Criteria for Firearm Transfers: Findings From the Firearms Licensee Survey. *Journal of Urban Health*.

Wisevoter. (2024). *Gun Ownership by Country*. Retrieved 12/1/2024 from

World Population Review. (2024). *Countries with Gun Control 2024*.

Wozniak, K. H. (2016). Public Opinion About Gun Control Post–Sandy Hook. *Criminal Justice Policy Review*.

Wright, G. (2023, 22 July 2023). Brazil: Lula tightens gun control amid surge in ownership. *BBC News*.

Wyant, B. R., & Taylor, R. B. (2007). Size of Household Firearm Collections: Implications for Subcultures and Gender*. *Criminology*.

Xin, Q., Page, A., & Tong, S. (2014). Dynamic Pattern of Suicide in Australia, 1986-2005: A Descriptive-Analytic Study. *BMJ Open*.

Xue, J., Chen, J., Hu, R., Chen, C., Zheng, C., Su, Y., & Zhu, T. (2020). Twitter Discussions and Emotions About the COVID-19 Pandemic: Machine Learning Approach. *Journal of Medical Internet Research*.

Yakubovich, A. R., Esposti, M. D., Lange, B. C. L., Melendez-Torres, G. J., Parmar, A., Wiebe, D. J., & Humphreys, D. K. (2021). Effects of Laws Expanding Civilian Rights to Use Deadly Force in Self-Defense on Violence and Crime: A Systematic Review. *American Journal of Public Health*.

Yamane, D. (2017). The Sociology of U.S. Gun Culture. *Sociology Compass*.

Yamane, D., Yamane, P., & Ivory, S. L. (2020). Targeted Advertising: Documenting the Emergence of Gun Culture 2.0 in Guns Magazine, 1955–2019. *Palgrave Communications*.

Youngson, N., Saxton, M., Jaffe, P. G., Chiodo, D., Dawson, M., & Straatman, A. L. (2021). Challenges in Risk Assessment With Rural Domestic Violence Victims: Implications for Practice. *Journal of Family Violence*.

Zeoli, A. M., Malinski, R., & Brenner, H. (2017). The Intersection of Firearms and Intimate Partner Homicide in 15 Nations. *Trauma Violence & Abuse*.

Zeoli, A. M., McCourt, A. D., & Paruk, J. (2022). Effectiveness of Firearm Restriction, Background Checks, and Licensing Laws in Reducing Gun Violence. *The Annals of the American Academy of Political and Social Science*.

Zeoli, A. M., & Webster, D. W. (2010). Effects of domestic violence policies, alcohol taxes and police staffing levels on intimate partner homicide in large US cities. *Injury Prevention: Journal of the International Society for Child and Adolescent Injury Prevention*, *16*(2), 90.

Zhang, L., Wang, K., Pan, G., & Wang, D. S. Y. (2023). A Review on Life Prediction Methods of Gun Barrel. *Journal of Physics Conference Series*.

Zimányi, R. G., & Géczi, G. (2018). Justice at Sport Clubs According to the Theory of Utilitarianism and Libertarianism. *Physical Culture and Sport Studies and Research*.

Zimmerman, P. R. (2014). The deterrence of crime through private security efforts: theory and evidence. *International Review of Law and Economics*, *37*, 66-75.

Баурина, С., Savchenko, E. O., Nazarova, E. V., & Golubev, A. (2019). Ensuring the Quality of Defense Industry Products of Russia in the Conditions of Import Substituition.

INDEX

J
Jagdschein, 174

K
Kleiner Waffenschein, 175,
180

L
large-scale violence, 17, 138
Law Enforcement Officers
Safety Act, 66
Legislative measures, 154,
156
Long guns, 79–94, 102,
135–136, 145, 186, 188

M
M16, 290
Mass shootings, 13, 20–21,
64–65, 76, 101–102, 106,
109, 111, 124–126, 131,
137, 141, 145–146,
148–150, 187, 190, 197,
200, 210, 307–308
Mental health, 13, 15, 18–21,
68, 96–97, 109, 112–113,
130, 136–138, 146, 153,
158, 161, 193, 206, 214,
223–225, 234–236, 311,
313–314
military launching devices,
186, 194, 196
Modern sporting rifles, 96–97

N
National Firearms Act, 64–65,
81, 86–87
National Firearms Agreement,
155–171
national security, 14, 24–25,
286

O
Omnibus Crime Control and
Safe Streets Act of 1968,
65
Open carry, 77–78, 81–83,
85–86, 88–90, 92, 94–95,
97–98

P
permitless carry, 83–84,
89–90, 92–94, 110
political context, 9
Possession and Acquisition
License, 127–131, 137
preventing crime and violence,
13, 18
Protection of Lawful
Commerce in Arms Act, 66
Public opinion, 41, 118, 142,
223, 230–231, 300–302
public order, 14, 26–27
public safety, 13–14, 17,
19–21, 27, 96–98, 101,
205, 210–212, 228–229
pump guns, 194